W9-CNI-993
USM BOOKSTORE
$10.95

Interdisciplinary perspectives on modern history

Editors
Robert Fogel and Stephan Thernstrom

Eight hours for what we will

SUE BLACK
Bondogarden, R. F. D. 1
Bridgton, Maine 04009

Other books in this series

Eric H. Monkkonen: *Police in urban America, 1860–1920*
Mary P. Ryan: *Cradle of the middle class: the family in Oneida County, New York, 1790–1865*
Ann Kussmaul: *Servants in husbandry in early modern England*
Tamara K. Hareven: *Family time and industrial time*
David Rosner: *A once charitable enterprise*
Arnold R. Hirsch: *Making the second ghetto*

Eight hours for what we will

Workers and leisure in an industrial city, 1870–1920

ROY ROSENZWEIG

The right of the University of Cambridge to print and sell all manner of books was granted by Henry VIII in 1534. The University has printed and published continuously since 1584.

CAMBRIDGE UNIVERSITY PRESS
Cambridge
London New York New Rochelle
Melbourne Sydney

Published by the Press Syndicate of the University of Cambridge
The Pitt Building, Trumpington Street, Cambridge CB2 1RP
32 East 57th Street, New York, NY 10022, USA
10 Stamford Road, Oakleigh, Melbourne 3166, Australia

© Cambridge University Press 1983

First published 1983
First paperback edition 1985

Printed in the United States of America

Library of Congress Cataloging in Publication Data

Rosenzweig, Roy.

Eight hours for what we will.

(Interdisciplinary perspectives on modern history)

Includes bibliographical references and index.

1. Labor and laboring classes – Massachusetts – Worcester – Recreation – History. 2. Worcester (Mass.) – Social conditions. I. Title. II. Series.
HD7395.R4R67 1983 306'.48'097443 82-25256
ISBN 0 521 23916 8 hard covers
ISBN 0 521 31397 X paperback

To my parents

Contents

Acknowledgments

Over the past several years, during which I have studied, worked, and lived in Worcester, I have developed great affection for the city. In that period many people have helped me to understand Worcester and its complex history. Timothy J. Meagher has been extraordinarily generous in sharing ideas and data from his important work on the Worcester Irish as well as in commenting upon my work. Some of my debt to him should be evident from even a quick glance at the notes to this book. The organizers of the Community Studies Program of Assumption College – Kenneth J. Moynihan, Charles Estus, Kevin Hickey, and John McClymer – made available to me a large amount of fascinating and valuable primary source material. Their generosity and openness is a model of what cooperative scholarship should be. My friends at the Worcester Historical Museum – especially the director, Bill Wallace, and the indefatigable librarian, Dorothy Gleason – always welcomed me and facilitated my research. At a crucial early stage in my research, historian and City Councilman John Anderson went out of his way to ease my access to city records. With his help – and that of Francis McGrath, Thomas W. Taylor, and Thomas Donoghue – I was able to examine the records of the Parks and Recreation Commission and the Board of Aldermen. Finally, I would like to thank the thirty or so longtime Worcester residents who shared with me their recollections of growing up, working, and playing in Worcester, as well as Paul C. Faler, Charles Blinderman, and Vincent E. Powers, who helped me locate these repositories of living history.

Among the many librarians and archivists who have assisted my research I would like to thank particularly the staffs of the American Antiquarian Society and the Worcester Public Library as well as Steve Lebergott of Wesleyan University's Olin Library. Several talented research assistants – especially Carl Rosen, Laurie Kaszas, Shelia Gaffney, Paul Gordon, and Dora Fisher – helped me with a variety of important tasks. Greg Lopiccolo provided invaluable help in translating Swedish newspapers. The manuscript would never have been completed without the efforts of Pat Camden, who typed sections of the manuscript, and especially Jean Berry, who patiently entered several drafts into George Mason University's word processor. Ann Ivins copyedited the manuscript with great care and precision. And Frank Smith, my editor at Cambridge University Press, expertly supervised the editing and production of the book.

None of my research or writing would have been possible without the financial support of several institutions. In its early stages my work was supported by travel grants from the Charles Warren Center for Studies in American History, by an Arthur Lehman Fellowship from Harvard University, and by a Samuel Stouffer Fellowship from the Joint Center for Urban Studies of Harvard and the Massachusetts Institute of Technology. The manuscript was first written in the cheerful environs of the Joint Center and was later rewritten in the equally cheerful setting of the Center for the Humanities at Wesleyan University, where I was supported by an Andrew Mellon Post-Doctoral Fellowship. At the Joint Center I was the "token" humanist and at the Center for the Humanities I was the "token" social scientist, but colleagues and staff members at both institutions stimulated my thinking as well as tolerated my sometimes eccentric work habits. After I had migrated from New England, George Mason University generously provided typing and copying services as well as travel funds for some last-minute research.

The most important support for this project has come from a large number of friends and colleagues. Their assistance has strengthened my conviction that history does not have to be an isolated, individualistic, and competitive enterprise, that the most creative and critical scholarship will grow out of an environment of mutual support and the collective sharing of ideas. I would like to take this opportunity to thank some of the many people who assisted me on this project – and fostered this cooperative atmosphere – while also absolving them of responsibility for the defects that remain. I hope that the many friends who have contributed their ideas so generously will forgive the necessity of just listing them by name rather than singling out their specific contributions as I would prefer to do.

I would like to thank first Stephan Thernstrom, who advised the doctoral dissertation from which this book eventually grew. He urged me to proceed with an unconventional topic and he has continued to support this project with insight and generosity. For thoughtful comments on portions of this manuscript circulated in draft or presented in various forms, I am grateful to Eric Foner, Michael Frisch, Maurine Greenwald, Gary Kornblith, Harry Gene Levine, David Montgomery, Richard Ohmann, Jon A. Peterson, Chris Rosen, Ron Schatz, Eric Schneider, and Sean Wilentz. A number of people took time from busy schedules to read the entire manuscript. For their sharp, perceptive, and supportive comments and suggestions I would like to thank Jeremy Brecher, Milton Cantor, Paul Faler, Steve Fraser, Herbert Gutman, Daniel Horowitz, David Jaffee, Bruce Laurie, Barry Leiwant, and Frank Smith. Jean-Christophe Agnew, Alan Brinkley, Jack Censer, Gary Gerstle, Carol Lasser, and Warren Leon not only provided extremely helpful (almost page-by-page) criticisms of this book but enriched my work with their friendship. At almost every stage of the writing and rewriting I turned to my close friends Betsy Blackmar and Nick Salvatore for advice; their painstaking and provocative comments on successive drafts have immensely improved the final product. The encouragement and insights of all these people have nourished this project and all my experiences over the past several years. Finally, Deborah Kaplan has lived with the burdens of this book for the past few years and has scrutinized its pages more than once. I thank her for taking time from her own work to provide good-humored intellectual and moral support for mine.

Introduction

On December 2, 1889, hundreds of trade unionists paraded through the streets of Worcester in a show of strength and determination. "Eight Hours for Work, Eight Hours for Rest, Eight Hours for What We Will" declared a banner held high by local carpenters. The banner drew upon the chorus line of "Eight Hours," the official song of the eight-hour movement and probably the most popular labor song of that period. Twenty-three years later Worcester's labor newspaper still used the first two stanzas of "Eight Hours" to express the goals of the city's machinists:

> We mean to make things over;
>   We're tired of toil for naught;
> We may have enough to live on,
>   But never an hour for thought.
>
> We want to feel the sunshine,
>   We want to smell the flowers;
> We are sure that God has willed it,
>   And we mean to have eight hours.[1]

Like the words to "Eight Hours," the actual quest for "eight hours for what we will" reverberated through the labor struggles of the late nineteenth and early twentieth centuries. As a compositor told the U.S. Senate Committee on Relations Between Labor and Capital in 1883: "A workingman wants something besides food and clothes in this country . . . He wants recreation. Why should not a workingman have it as well as other people?"[2] And in industrial communities across America workers fought not only for the right to time and space for leisure but also for control over the time and space in which that leisure was to be enjoyed. This study examines how workers struggled to maintain "eight hours for what we will" and what that "eight hours" meant to them.

Despite the importance that working people attached to a sphere of life free from the constraints imposed by their employers, the subject of leisure has attracted little attention from American labor historians. In part, this may reflect a general scholarly reluctance to take up seemingly "nonserious" subjects like play. "Many people are uncomfortable when discussing leisure," observes a sociologist of his colleagues; "as with sex, they want to make a joke of it." But for labor historians, the neglect of leisure stems from a more general inhibition than notions of academic propriety. It reveals the narrowness of their field as it has been traditionally conceived. Until recently most labor history, as one scholar notes, has been little more than "a category of political economy, a problem of industrial relations, a canon of saintly working-class leaders, a chronicle of militant strike actions." This institutional and economic perspective is largely the legacy of John R. Commons and his students at the University of Wisconsin, who in the early twentieth century wrote the first systematic history of American labor. However, as the bedrock of all later work in labor history, the solid and often brilliant foundation laid by the Commons school threatened to undermine the field that subsequently tried to build upon it. In its neglect of the social and cultural dimensions of working-class experience, the Commons approach severely restricted the range of questions that labor historians asked and, correspondingly, the types of answers they found.[3]

Fortunately, in the 1960s such scholars as David Brody, Herbert Gutman, David Montgomery, and Stephan Thernstrom began to remedy the deficiencies of the old Commons school. Their work – and that of a generation of younger historians – has moved beyond the history of trade unionism and has initiated the transformation of labor history into working-class history.[4] Still, many crucial aspects of American working-class life have yet to be considered. Much of the new scholarship has concentrated on the workplace – the possibility of occupational mobility, the changing job structures, the formal and informal resistance to new forms of work discipline. Despite the increasingly important place of recreation in the lives of workers in the late nineteenth and early twentieth centuries, we still know relatively little about their lives outside the factory.

But why should labor historians – or indeed, any historians – concern themselves with the history of leisure? In fact, the study of popular recreation helps to explain some of the distinctive features of American working-class development: the absence of a mass-based labor or socialist party, the weakness of working-class consciousness and solidarity, and the late emergence of industrial unions. The failures of the socialist movement cannot be understood merely by studying the internal workings of the Socialist party. Nor can the weakness of unionism among steelworkers before the 1930s be explained simply by reference to the institutional history of the

Amalgamated Association of Iron, Steel, and Tin Workers. Only, as one historian urges, when workers are "studied in a totality that includes their cultural backgrounds and social relations, as well as their institutional memberships and economic and political behaviour" can we begin to address these issues adequately.[5] Thus, this study of working-class recreational patterns in Worcester, Massachusetts, from 1870 to 1920 attempts to contribute to a more comprehensive history of the American working class in its broadest social, economic, and political context. To do this, it seeks not simply to describe the pastimes and amusements of Worcester workers but to shed light on three central questions about American labor and social history. First, what have been the central values, beliefs, and traditions of the American working class, and how have they shaped workers' views of themselves and the society at large? Second, what are the interclass bonds and conflicts within America's industrial communities? Third, how did both working-class culture and class relations change in the transition from the nineteenth to the twentieth century?

In exploring such questions of culture, class, and change, labor historians face more than the usual problems of studying a group that has left few written records; they also confront the vexing difficulties of examining that group's private behavior. One solution to this research problem would be to write a national study, drawing on fragments of information from a large number of scattered sources. Unfortunately, such national studies cannot always critically control all the material they gather. They face the danger of distorting or misinterpreting discrete local and ethnic patterns. This problem would be less disturbing had not the nineteenth century American working-class experience been an intensely local experience.[6] Granting this, a community study – such as that of Worcester – offers the best opportunity for capturing workers' lives in all their complexity.

But why look at Worcester in particular? Authors of community studies have often advanced exaggerated claims that "their" community embodies an "ideal-typical expression" of American society.[7] Of course, there is no such thing as an "ideal-typical" American community – not Newburyport, Massachusetts, not Muncie, Indiana, and certainly not Worcester. "The notion," writes anthropologist Clifford Geertz, "that one can find the essence of national societies, civilizations, great religions, or whatever summed up and simplified in so-called 'typical' small towns and villages is palpable nonsense. What one finds in small towns and villages is (alas) small-town or village life."[8] The same holds for medium-sized industrial cities like Worcester. Admitting the limitations of a single community study should not, however, lead us to conclude that a study of Worcester tells us only about that one city. In Worcester we can test analytical categories – class, ethnicity, and religion, for example – and social processes – class conflict and cultural change, for instance – which may prove useful in examining other American communities, large and small. The study of working-class recreation in Worcester provides a building block for more general theorizing about the nature of working-class life in America. To understand how the Worcester working-class experience fits into this broader perspective, however, we must initially consider the peculiarities of the city itself.

The first chapter (Part I) therefore describes some distinguishing features of Worcester: the power of the city's industrialists, the weakness of working-class political parties and trade unions, and the importance and cohesiveness of ethnic communities and organizations. Beginning with this context, Part II (Chapters 2 and 3) pursues the cultural dimensions of the late nineteenth century Worcester working-class experience. Chapter 2 examines how workers developed the saloon as a distinctive ethnic working-class leisure institution – a separate and largely autonomous cultural sphere. It then considers the saloon as an expression of a value system that rejected, but did not actively challenge, the moral order of Worcester's upper and middle classes.

The "alternative culture" visible in the late nineteenth century working-class saloon did not provide, however, the basis for class-wide solidarity or consciousness. In Worcester, at least, this culture remained rooted in distinctive, insular, and often antagonistic ethnic communities. Chapter 3 explores how Worcester's immigrant workers used July Fourth celebrations to affirm and mark out their cultural distance not only from the city's elite and native middle class but also from fellow immigrants.[9]

Despite its insularity and its divisions, the alternative culture of Worcester's ethnic working class did not go unchallenged by the dominant forces in Worcester society. Part III (Chapters 4, 5, and 6) looks at struggles – covering the years 1870 to 1920 – over working-class leisure to understand better the vertical dimensions of working-class life in Worcester – the interrelationships of workers and the middle and upper classes. In particular, these chapters consider the temperance, parks, playground, and Safe and Sane July Fourth movements as concerted campaigns to thwart working-class efforts at carving out and maintaining distinctive and autonomous spheres of leisure time and space. Yet these class struggles over recreation also reveal the ambiguities and complexities of Worcester's class structure – both the internal divisions within the city's working class (often along ethnic or religious lines) and the collaborative ties across class boundaries.[10]

In the end, this study argues, Worcester workers successfully protected their leisure time and space from outside encroachment. Although they exercised very limited control over their work time, workers effectively managed to preserve their nonwork hours as a relatively autonomous sphere of existence. Nevertheless, the late nineteenth century world of the saloon and the holiday picnic as well as the cultural attitudes embedded in these institutions could not remain static and unchanged in the early twentieth century. Part IV (Chapters 7 and 8) describes the gradual and uneven transformation of the working-class world described in Chapters 2 and 3. Chapter 7 looks specifically at the rise of a leisure market as seen at the amusement park as well as at the impact of commercialization on both the celebration of the Fourth and the saloon. It points out, however, strong indications of continuity amid the obvious signs of change. Indeed, even when workers went to the movies – the subject of Chapter 8 – they shaped the moviegoing experience according to the dictates of preexisting recreational patterns and longstanding cultural inclinations. Still, working-class life in America was changing. By 1920 the movie theater had begun to express a working-class culture very different from that found in the late nineteenth century saloon – a culture that brought workers closer to the mainstream of American society without ever giving them real power within that society.

PART I

Context

1 *Workers in an industrial city, 1870–1920*

In spring 1892, Emma Goldman, Alexander Berkman (Sasha), and Modiste Aronstamm (Feyda) opened an ice-cream parlor and lunchroom in the Jewish section of Worcester's immigrant working-class East Side. Yearning to return to their native Russia to join the anarchist movement, they hoped that the ice-cream parlor's profits would pay for the trip. "We secured a store," Goldman recalls in her autobiography, "and within a couple of weeks Sasha's skill with hammer and saw, Feyda's with his paint and brush, and my own good German housekeeping training succeeded in turning the neglected ramshackle place into an attractive lunch room." Their coffee, sandwiches, pancakes, and ice cream found an eager clientele. And this American capitalist success seemed to promise foreign revolutionary activity: "We felt," Goldman writes, "we were on the way to the realization of our long-cherished dream."[1]

American events soon altered their plans. That summer the Carnegie Steel Company locked out the workers at its Homestead (Pennsylvania) Works. "Far away from the scene of the struggle, in our little ice-cream parlour in the city of Worcester," writes Goldman, "we eagerly followed developments. To us it sounded the awakening of the American worker, the long-awaited day of his resurrection. The native toiler had risen." The eviction of strikers from company houses convinced Goldman that the heart of the international class struggle was no longer Russia, but Homestead. Berkman agreed. " 'We must go tonight,' he said; 'the great moment has come at last!' Being internationalists, he added, it mattered not . . . where the blow was struck by the workers; we must be with them." The next morning Goldman and Berkman left Worcester and their ice-cream parlor in a journey that would culminate in Berkman's unsuccessful attempt to assassinate Henry Clay Frick, the chairman of the Carnegie Steel Company.[2]

Despite their wholehearted dedication to the cause of Homestead workers, Goldman and Berkman's understanding of the American proletariat remained limited. Berkman, his Worcester dentist recalled, "talked occasionally of labor troubles, but always referred to those in Russia." Goldman's own account of their sojourn in

Worcester is remarkable for the absence of any references to workers, bosses, factories, strikes, radicals, unions, or conflict in that industrial city. From her description, one might easily conclude that they had opened an ice-cream parlor in a rural village rather than in the twenty-fifth leading manufacturing city in the United States with almost 1,000 industrial establishments and about 20,000 industrial workers. Goldman and Berkman's own customers probably included employees of the nearby Washburn and Moen Wire Manufacturing Company, which employed almost as many workers as the Homestead plant, and which would soon merge with the Carnegie company and other major steel companies to form the giant U.S. Steel Corporation.[3]

Despite Goldman's implicit dismissal, Worcester, like Homestead, *was* a major industrial center with a large working class. But, unlike Homestead, Worcester failed to capture the imagination of radicals like Goldman, because dramatic strikes, working-class political parties, and powerful unions were largely, although not entirely, absent. Even such moderate working-class voices as craft unions and urban political machines were generally muted, if not silent. By these conventional standards, Goldman was right: The class struggle was in Homestead, not Worcester.

Trade unions and political parties are not, however, the only forms of working-class organization. Ethnic communities and institutions – churches, clubs, saloons, groceries, schools – have often provided an alternative organizational focus for the lives of America's immigrant working class. Indeed, it was through the lens of their tightly organized ethnic working-class communities that Worcester workers intensely scrutinized Emma Goldman even while she ignored them.

Playwright S. N. Behrman, who grew up in the poor Jewish Providence Street community where Goldman briefly dished out ice cream, recalls her local notoriety: "The epithet applied to her during my childhood by my elders was so lethal, so searing, that it seemed to me impossible then that anyone could survive it." But "the rumors and horrid allegations" about the proprietor of the new ice-cream parlor had nothing to do with her politics. To the working-class Jews of Providence Street, Goldman was an "*apikorista,*" a Yiddish word that in Behrman's community "connoted the ultimate in human depravity." An apikorista, he explains, "was a renegade from the Jewish religion, but the word had the even deeper and more sinister connotation of treachery not merely to the Jewish religion but to God himself." Even after her departure Goldman remained a vivid presence for Behrman and other Worcester Jews: "The Providence Street parents cited her to us constantly, using her name somewhat as English parents used Napoleon's in the first decades of the nineteenth century, to frighten and admonish."[4]

Goldman's rejection of Jewish religious and marital traditions concerned Worcester Jews more than her attacks on capitalism and the state, because it was the cultural values and institutions of the ethnic community that provided the moral and social principles around which they organized their lives. In some industrial cities and towns, workers oriented themselves around trade unions or political parties, but in Worcester most workers fastened on the cultural world of their ethnic communities. Within these self-enclosed immigrant settlements Worcester's workers both resisted and accommodated themselves to the rule of the city's industrial elite – the men that Behrman's parents called "Yankees."[5] Workers used the physical and psychological space afforded by their ethnic communities to carry out their lives as they chose. But to understand the importance of those ethnic communities – as well as to set the stage for more detailed analyses of working-class recreation – requires that we first briefly survey industry, politics, and labor in Worcester in the late nineteenth and early twentieth centuries.

Industry and industralists

Worcester is an unlikely industrial city. Lacking the usual prerequisites of antebellum industrial and urban development – a navigable body of water, waterpower, and raw materials – it nevertheless developed into a major industrial center, the twenty-eighth largest city in the United States by 1880.[6] Jonas Rice established a permanent settlement in Worcester in 1713, but it still had fewer than 3,000 residents more than a century later. In the next thirty years, however, this sleepy town was transformed into a burgeoning industrial city. The opening of the Blackstone Canal in 1828 and, more important, the development of extensive railroad connections between 1835 and 1847 made new markets accessible to Worcester products. At the same time, the adoption of steampower around 1840 freed Worcester from reliance on its limited waterpower. Industry and population boomed. Between 1820 and 1850 population multiplied almost five times; between 1837 and 1855 the value of the city's manufactured product leapt from $1 million to $5.5 million. By 1870 population had doubled again, reaching more than 41,000 and making Worcester the second largest city in Massachusetts. It had also become a major manufacturing center, with several hundred manufacturing establishments employing more than 10,000 workers.[7]

In the next half century the basic structure of Worcester industry changed remarkably little: Factory products remained diverse; factory owners remained native-born, locally rooted, unified, and paternalistic; factory workers remained ethnic and divided. Yet, as Worcester moved into the twentieth century, the precise makeup of that overall structure shifted: Factories turned to new products; factory owners consolidated; immigrant workers were replaced by new generations and newer immigrants.

Diversity best characterized Worcester industry. "Probably no city in the country has so great a variety of manufactures in proportion to its size" boasted a local author in 1884. The claim was certainly justified as far as the state of Massachusetts was concerned. In 1880, for example, whereas almost 83 percent of Fall River workers toiled in cotton mills and more than 82 percent of Lynn workers found jobs in boot and shoe shops, Worcester's three largest industries *combined* employed only 41 percent of the factory work force. Throughout the late nineteenth and early twentieth centuries, no Worcester industry ever engaged more than one-quarter of the city's wage earners. In the U.S. Census of Manufactures, the category "other" perennially led the list of Worcester's industries.[8]

Although the promotional slogan City of Diversified Industries remained appropriate throughout the late nineteenth and early twentieth centuries, the actual output of Worcester's factories changed in important ways during these years. In the 1870s the boot and shoe industry was the city's largest with more than one-fifth of its industrial workers. During the next ten years, however, two heterogeneous groups of industries, "metals and metallic goods" and "machines and machinery," both of which actually preceded the boot and shoe industry in importance, overtook that locally declining industry. And in subsequent years they continued to be the most dynamic sector of the Worcester economy. Metal trades and machinery usually accounted for about 40 percent of the city's industrial output by the late nineteenth and early twentieth centuries. Moreover, they made Worcester a nationally known center of the metal and machine trades. According to one 1914 account: "More machine tool builders, machinists, and metal trades people are to be found in Worcester and suburbs than any other county on the American continent."[9]

Preeminent among the city's metal industries was wire manufacturing, particularly the Washburn and Moen Wire Manufacturing

Company, which merged into the American Steel and Wire Company in 1899 and the U.S. Steel Corporation two years later. Established in 1831 with thirteen employees, Washburn and Moen boomed in the late nineteenth century as western settlers demanded its barbed wire. In 1875 it had 700 employees, but it tripled in size in the next five years; by 1899 it was by far the city's largest employer with more than 3,000 workers on the payroll at three large plants scattered over the city; by 1919 more than 6,000 workers labored in its wire factories. Whereas the city's metal industry centered on wire production, no single product dominated the machine and machine tool industry, which included the manufacture of wrenches, lathes, paper machines, paper box machines, looms, plows, twisting machines, and woodworking machinery.[10]

A miscellany of other industries filled out the city's manufacturing sector. Textiles, although declining in Worcester during the late nineteenth century, remained a major employer. As late as 1919 almost 2,000 Worcester workers produced cotton, woolen, and worsted goods. Clothing increased in absolute and relative importance over these years with close to 1,800 workers by 1895. Corsets, under the leadership of the Royal Worcester Corset Company, developed into a major local industry; more than 1,200 workers, mostly women, found work in this trade in 1919. Other important Worcester industries included envelopes (U.S. Envelope), leather belting (Graton and Knight), carpets (Whittall Carpet), and abrasives (Norton).[11]

Stereotypically, the founders of Worcester's industries were poor boys of mechanical ability who migrated to Worcester from the New England countryside and set up shop in one of the factory buildings owned by Stephen Salisbury II or William T. Merrifield. The legends about these inventive Yankee mechanics have sometimes exaggerated their abilities and accomplishments, but the careers of such men as wire manufacturer Ichabod Washburn, loom builder Lucius J. Knowles, wrench makers Loring and A. G. Coes, and railroad-car builder Osgood Bradley lend some credence to this version of Worcester's industrial history. Not only did these men found the city's major industries in the early nineteenth century, but they (or their families) continued to control those industries in the late nineteenth century. An 1884 account, for example, noted that "private capital" dominated Worcester manufacturing to an unusual degree and added that "all these enterprises, large and small, with scarcely an exception are owned by residents of Worcester."[12]

Of course, Worcester was not immune from the trends toward

incorporation and concentration of economic power that marked late nineteenth century American industry. Between 1880 and 1919 the average number of wage earners per firm grew two and a half times and the average capitalization of each firm jumped almost seventeen times. As in the rest of the nation, the wave of consolidations surged in the aftermath of the depression of the 1890s. Between 1898 and 1903 five of the city's eight largest companies participated in mergers. Two Worcester companies – Washburn and Moen and Logan, Swift, and Brigham – joined national trusts (U.S. Steel and U.S. Envelope).[13]

These outside take-overs proved exceptional; Worcester generally retained its distinctive pattern of local ownership. More commonly, Worcester mergers involved two or more local companies such as the consolidations of Crompton and Knowles and of Reed and Prince. When four local machine-tool companies consolidated into the Reed-Prentice Company in 1912, the new corporation brought together not only these four firms but also capital and capitalists from two other major local metal trades concerns, Crompton and Knowles and Wyman and Gordon. Worcester industry in the early twentieth century was reorganizing and consolidating, but it was not ceding control to outside corporations. Even a study done in the 1960s found most Worcester industries still under local ownership and management.[14]

In part, the mergers of the early twentieth century formalized a complex web of informal connections that had knit together the city's industrial elite throughout the late nineteenth century. Business ties were one powerful bond uniting different parts of industrial Worcester. Wyman and Gordon, for example, initially found its major customers within Worcester – forging parts for Crompton and Knowles looms and producing copper rail bonds for Washburn and Moen. Supporting and reinforcing these business connections as well as a network of interlocking corporate and bank directorates were extensive social and cultural ties. Worcester industrialists worshipped at the same Protestant churches, belonged to the same clubs, attended the same schools, lived in the same West Side neighborhoods, vacationed at the same resorts, and married into each other's families. To cite just one example: Harry Worcester Smith, the son of a cotton manufacturer, grew up next door to the wire manufacturing Washburn family, studied at Worcester Polytechnic Institute (endowed by the city's leading industrialists), married the daughter of loom manufacturer George Crompton, organized the elite-dominated Grafton Country Club, and arranged the merger of Reed-Prentice Company.[15]

Despite this intricate web of business and social connections, Worcester's industrial leadership was not a closed or fixed elite. The growing size of individual firms required large corps of managers, lawyers, engineers, and sales people; technological change and the quest for profits led to the organization of new enterprises. Yet the patterns of recruitment for newer industrial leaders tended to ensure a continuing high degree of homogeneity in background and outlook, particularly in the metal trades. "The Washburn and Moen Manufacturing Company," writes the grandnephew of the founder, "was controlled from the broad aisle of Union Church. Hence there were always plenty of candidates to teach in the Sunday School which was looked upon as a transition to a job on Grove Street." Worcester Polytechnic Institute (WPI) provided a more formal route to leadership in the metal trades and the machine shops. A 1914 survey counted seventy-two WPI graduates in ownership or top executive positions in Worcester metal trades shops. In 1924 a Clark University graduate student reported "the conviction on the part of some that the presence in Worcester of an appreciable percentage of metal trades executives who are graduates of the local Polytechnic Institute, as well as of numerous minor executives who come from the Boys Trade School tends to make the city one in which a feeling of solidarity as opposed to labor may be, and is, easily fostered."[16]

In the nineteenth century this "solidarity as opposed to labor" was rooted largely in informal social and business networks. In the 1890s and especially the early 1900s, businessmen and manufacturers mobilized against labor by creating such local trade groups as the Builders Exchange, the Granite Dealers Association, the Electrical Contractors Association, the Machine Tool Builders Association, the Employers Association of Worcester County, and most important, the Worcester branch of the National Metal Trades Association (NMTA). Under the energetic leadership of its secretary, Donald Tulloch, the NMTA effectively rallied employers and the general public against unionization and maintained a citywide blacklist to drive out potential organizers. But its influence apparently went well beyond the metal trades shops. In the early 1920s, for example, Clark University professor Harry Elmer Barnes angrily complained to novelist Upton Sinclair of the NMTA's censorship of public school teaching on unions or economics. The *Labor News* was even more sweeping in its condemnation. "Through interlocking directorates" in manufacturing, banking, insurance, and real estate, it charged in 1916, the NMTA has "for years held sway over principally everything that spells business and finance in Worcester."[17]

The NMTA's blacklists and propaganda supplemented a more subtle, paternalistic labor and civic policy on the part of its leading members. Worcester industrialists did not rule as unenlightened despots; they worked hard to persuade the city's middle and working classes that they had the best interests of all Worcesterites at heart. Their civic generosity endowed Worcester with large numbers of churches, parks, colleges, hospitals, and monuments. For their own employees they provided clubhouses, outings, and Christmas turkeys. In the twentieth century these paternalistic gestures tended to give way to more formal and even more extensive welfare capitalist policies. The *Norton Spirit,* published beginning in 1914 by the city's largest employer, reported regularly on the Norton Company's sponsorship of an Athletic Association, a Camera Club, garden plots, a boathouse, a Mutual Benefit Association, and English classes, as well as its disapproval of "Bolsheviks" and the Industrial Workers of the World (IWW). Most highly touted of its programs was Indian Hill, a housing development that Norton hoped would foster "industrial ownership, permanency and contentment in employment, and resultant general efficiency."[18]

In the fifty years between 1870 and 1920, then, Worcester industry consolidated; its leadership shifted from inventors and entrepreneurs to professional managers and engineers; it formalized its internal ties through trade associations; and its employee relations policies changed from paternalism to welfare capitalism. What remained constant was the unity, class consciousness, and power of the city's industrialists. These men did not agree on all major issues, nor did they rule every aspect of life in Worcester, but their overwhelming economic power, their close business and social ties, their civic generosity and corporate paternalism made them the preeminent force in late nineteenth and early twentieth century Worcester.

Workers, politics, and unions

But how far down did this hegemony extend? What organizational structures – political, economic, and cultural – did workers create to combat the power of the city's industrialists? Before we can answer these questions, we need first to survey the composition of Worcester's work force. Although such a quick once-over must inevitably distort complex and changing patterns, two basic characteristics of

Worcester's working class stand out: its ethnic diversity and its constantly changing composition.

In 1887 clergyman Samuel Lane Loomis observed that "not every foreigner is a workingman, but in the cities, at least, it may almost be said that every workingman is a foreigner." If Loomis meant to include the children of immigrants in the term "foreigner," then Worcester statistics support his observation. In 1900 first- and second-generation immigrants made up more than 70 percent of every major blue-collar job category. In the least skilled jobs, the dominance was overwhelming: Foreign-stock Worcesterites made up 83 percent of the city's iron- and steelworkers, 89 percent of its domestic servants, and 92 percent of its wireworkers and manual laborers.[19]

This immigrant dominance of Worcester's blue-collar work force only emerged in the second half of the nineteenth century. By 1850 Worcester's newly arrived Irish immigrants already held most of the city's laboring jobs, but its native-born, or Yankee, workingmen and -women still occupied four-fifths of the positions in the boot and shoe factories and nine-tenths of those in the machine shops. The next thirty years saw dramatic changes: The Irish increased their dominance of "pick and shovel" jobs and at the same time – along with smaller numbers of French Canadians (who also were prominent among local carpenters) – displaced the Yankees from the boot and shoe factories, reducing them to less than a third of all workers in that industry. Native-stock Americans remained the largest group among machinists, but their reduced numbers and higher ages indicated their continuing decline in that skilled category.[20]

The 1880s and 1890s saw another remaking of the Worcester working class. Large numbers of Swedes came to work in the city's booming wire mills and in the Norton Company's plant. By 1900 almost half of all male Scandinavians worked in some aspect of the metal trades.[21] The arrival of the Protestant Swedes revived Catholic–Protestant religious divisions in the work force, which had been fading with the gradual disappearance of the Yankee workers.

The entry into Worcester of large numbers of "new immigrants" from southern and eastern Europe in the years after 1890 crosscut the working class with further ethnic, religious, and linguistic divisions. At the wire mills, for example, Swedes tended to fill the more skilled jobs in the steel rolling mills and the more specialized aspects of wire making, whereas the Irish and the more recently arrived Lithuanians, Poles, Finns, and Armenians took the unskilled positions. Italians also found themselves in unskilled work but less often within factories. In 1875, 88 percent of Worcester Italians were manual laborers, and their share never dropped below 40 percent in the next fifty years. Jews, although predominantly working class, followed a slightly deviant pattern with disproportionate numbers opening small businesses.[22]

Gender as well as religion and ethnicity divided the Worcester working class. Work opportunities for women were more limited in Worcester than in other Massachusetts cities, particularly those with large textile factories. The metal trades and machine shops were largely closed to women workers. Not only wireworkers but also wool spinners and carpet weavers struck to keep their jobs as male prerogatives. Nevertheless, Worcester women – particularly immigrant and single women – did work for wages. Irish and Swedish women took the bulk of the city's domestic service positions, French-Canadian women spun and wove in the textile mills, and Jewish women ran sewing machines in the small clothing shops.[23]

Even this cursory summary of industrial and working-class Worcester reveals some of the major obstacles to working-class organization. On the one hand, Worcester manufacturers were well organized, united, and vigorously anti-union. In addition, their local residence, civic responsibility, and paternalistic policies rendered them less vulnerable to attack than were outside, corporate capitalists. On the other hand, Worcester workers (unlike their counterparts in, say, Lynn or Fall River) were segmented into dissimilar occupations and trades, making it difficult for them to perceive common working-class – rather than occupational – economic and political interests. Ethnic and especially religious differences further fragmented the labor force, inhibiting communication and the development of shared goals. Faced with these formidable barriers, Worcester workers did not develop the sort of radical political parties, urban political machines, trade unions, or militant strikes that historians have usually seen as evidence of working-class vitality. But the relative weakness of political and economic organizations, which we will discuss in this section, did not inhibit vigorous self-organization along cultural or ethnic lines, which we will examine in the next section.

Local politics in Worcester generally reinforced the power of the industrial elite. In late nineteenth century Lynn, men of working-class backgrounds dominated political office, whereas factory owners "hardly showed their faces."[24] The opposite was true in Worcester. Between 1871 and 1920 factory owners or top officials of manufacturing concerns held the mayor's seat for a total of twenty-two years. During the other years, bankers, lawyers, merchants, and doctors – many of them with close ties to the industrialists – controlled the mayoralty. Blue-collar workers made only slightly greater inroads in the Board of Aldermen and the Common Council. In 1885, 1890, and 1895 workers composed only one-twelfth of the Board of Aldermen and less than one-eighth of the Common Council. Worcester city officials, the *Labor News* repeatedly and bitterly complained, were "corporation owned [and] monopoly bound," "subservient to [the] big business machine," and "extremely antagonistic and positively indifferent" to workers.[25]

In part, the absence of worker-politicians reflects the failure of explicitly pro-labor political movements in Worcester. Although the Knights of Labor in other New England towns and cities captured local governments in the mid-1880s, their Worcester counterparts could claim no local victories.[26] Similarly, during the same years that Brockton and Haverhill shoe workers elected Socialist city administrations, Worcester Socialists never garnered more than 9 percent of the votes. In the first two decades of the twentieth century the combined vote for all Socialist mayoral candidates exceeded 2 percent in only one election.[27] Even the mainstream of the labor movement had only very limited electoral success. The Wage Earners Club, organized in 1906 by the Central Labor Union, commanded some prestige and influence around 1910, but three years later it was moribund.[28]

If radical or union-based political movements found few adherents in Worcester, the Republican and Democratic parties did not present themselves as alternative avenues for working-class political mobilization. Unlike Boston, where the Democratic political machine aggressively pursued the interest of Irish working-class constituents, neither of Worcester's two mainstream political parties consistently championed working-class candidates or causes. The Republican party was closely aligned with the city's industrialists and received their financial support and backed their programs. Given these elite ties in a blue-collar city, the Republicans were remarkably successful, losing only seven of thirty-five mayoral contests between 1885 and 1919. Their electoral dominance rested largely on ethnic divisions within the city's working class – especially the Irish-Catholic/Yankee-Protestant conflict – as well as internal divisions within the Democratic party, subjects treated in greater detail in subsequent chapters.[29]

Whereas the local Swedish newspaper promoted the Republican party as "responsive to and concerned for the needs of workers," the Irish and French-Canadian press argued the opposite. *Le Travailleur,* for example, charged "exclusive control by monopolizers" of the Republican party and attributed its 1880 victory to "the oppression of workers' consciences by manufacturers."[30] The Irish and French-Canadian newspapers could probably present more evidence for advertising the local Democratic party as the "workingman's party" than their Swedish Republican counterparts could for their party. Even so, in the late nineteenth century, many Democratic leaders felt, according to one Worcester newspaper, that they "must have blood at the head of their ticket" and usually nominated standard-bearers from the "aristocratic element" of their party. In the 1890s and later Democratic candidates for mayor increasingly had Gaelic rather than Yankee names, but these ethnic politicians usually came from the emerging Irish middle class rather than the working class and the labor movement. Nevertheless, the growing identification of the Democratic party with a burgeoning immigrant population seems to have strengthened it politically: In 1911, for the first time, it achieved a narrow majority on the Board of Aldermen. Yet the Democrats still lacked the strength to elect explicitly prolabor candidates. In 1915, for example, John Reardon, a former leader of the Street Railway Union, ran as the Democratic candidate for mayor with vigorous support from the labor movement in the midst of the largest strike in the city's history. The overwhelming victory of George M. Wright, a wire manufacturer with little sympathy for the strikers, symbolized the continuing limits on not only working-class political action but also working-class trade union activity.[31]

Such limits were evident even during the "best showing ever of united labor in Worcester." In December 1889, 1,400 union members affiliated with the Central Labor Union (CLU) – among them painters, carpenters, tailors, building-trades workers, horseshoers, and printers – paraded through the streets to impress Worcesterites with labor's strength. But all the fanfare did not hide the fundamental weakness of the city's labor movement. Even the keynote speaker at the subsequent mass meeting in Mechanics Hall – P. J. McGuire, the founder of the Carpenters' Union and a prominent leader of the American Federation of Labor – could not resist a pointed reference to the city's reputation: "Worcester," he declared to an agreeing crowd, "has been known for years as one of the scab holes of the state."[32]

Such blunt assessments of the dismal position of trade unionism in Worcester were not confined to out-of-town visitors. Worcester labor leaders themselves repeatedly lamented their lack of influence. In 1888 when local labor leaders sought to create the CLU as a coordinating body for the city's unions, their Call to Workingmen admitted: "The present organized condition of the wage earners of this city is a discredit to the intelligence and manhood of our community." The organization of the CLU responded, in part, to past failures. During the 1880s, the pro-labor *Worcester Daily Times* repeatedly criticized workers for "their lack of a labor organization worthy of the name" and labeled Worcester unions "signal failures." Even after the Worcester Knights of Labor had established five local assemblies in the mid-1880s, the *Times* pointed out that "in every city in New England this order is far in advance of the organization in this city, although there are not so many workmen comparatively."[33]

These grim self-assessments of the state of Worcester unionism continued in subsequent decades. The machine and metal trades, the city's largest industries, remained a particularly weak spot. The national membership of the International Association of Machinists grew eightfold between 1895 and 1911, but its Worcester branch languished. "Worcester Machinists," the *Labor News* editorialized in 1910, "have been made to realize that they are twenty years behind the times."[34] The Moulders' Union, the one well-organized union in the metal trades, gradually lost power and influence during the early twentieth century, because of the decline of local foundries. Even the building trades unions, the bulwark of the labor movement in most cities before the 1930s, never gained full control over construction in Worcester. Several major local construction companies that maintained an "open shop" routinely won contracts for important public buildings. Between 1911 and 1914 nonunion labor built six Catholic churches or schools, even though many unionized building-trades workers belonged to parishes responsible for the construction.[35]

Statistical comparisons further emphasize the relative weakness of the Worcester labor movement. In 1885 the shoe town of Lynn had about six times as many Knights of Labor assemblies as Worcester and more than ten times as many members, despite a smaller population.[36] In the twentieth century Worcester continued to lag behind most other Massachusetts cities. In 1910 it ranked eighth among the state's twelve largest cities in the percentage of its labor force unionized. Almost all the major industrial centers of the state had significantly stronger labor movements (see Table 1). Worces-

Table 1. *Proportion of work force unionized in Massachusetts cities with over 25,000 population, 1910*

City	Percentage of work force in unions
Brockton[a]	59.71
Lynn[a]	25.52
Haverhill	23.64
Quincy	22.83
Boston[a]	21.18
Salem	18.32
Springfield[a]	17.88
New Bedford[a]	16.68
Fall River[a]	14.17
Fitchburg	14.08
Chelsea	13.70
Lawrence[a]	11.20
Worcester[a]	10.71
Taunton	10.65
Holyoke[a]	10.43
Pittsfield	9.47
Lowell[a]	7.83
Chicopee	5.90
Newton	4.96
Waltham	3.98
Somerville[a]	3.65
Malden	2.19
Cambridge[a]	1.59

Note: Brookline and Everett are not included, because there is no data on union membership in those cities.
[a]Over 50,000 in population.
Source: Massachusetts Bureau of Statistics of Labor, *Third Annual Report on Labor Organizations, 1910* (Boston, 1911), 37. Population data from U.S. Bureau of the Census, *Thirteenth Census, 1910* (Washington, D.C., 1914), 4: 152–291.

ter's unionization rate of 11 percent was actually about average for the state and nation, but for residents of a northeastern manufacturing city, Worcester workers proved relatively slow to unionize.[37]

Even more remarkable than Worcester's low level of unionization was its still lower incidence of labor unrest. Between 1902 and 1911 Worcester workers struck only eighty times. On a per capita basis, of the twelve largest Massachusetts cities Worcester ranked ninth in frequency of strikes (see Table 2). Moreover, most Worcester strikes

Table 2. *Strikes (1902–11) and working days lost due to strikes (1906–10) in Massachusetts cities over 50,000 in population*

City	Strikes 1902–11	Strikes per 1,000 people[a]	Days lost due to strikes, 1906–10	Days lost per capita[b]
Lynn	200	2.53	292,826	3.28
Brockton	57	1.15	50,232	0.85
Holyoke	55	1.06	33,530	0.58
Fall River	115	1.03	55,887	0.47
Springfield	63	0.83	11,725	0.13
Lowell	73	0.75	52,978	0.50
New Bedford	52	0.65	47,120	0.49
Lawrence	47	0.63	28,222	0.33
Worcester	80	0.61	11,592	0.08
Boston	372	0.60	327,890	0.49
Cambridge	21	0.21	10,685	0.10
Somerville	8	0.12	6,086	0.08

[a]Based on average of 1900 and 1910 population.
[b]Based on 1910 population.
Source: Massachusetts Bureau of Statistics of Labor, *Strikes and Lockouts in Massachusetts, Seventh to Twelfth Annual Reports, 1906–1911* (Boston, 1907–12).

were relatively short. From 1906 to 1910 Worcester lost fewer working days as a result of strikes than did almost any other large Massachusetts city (see Table 2). On a per capita basis, most other Massachusetts cities lost about six times as many days from strikes, and volatile Lynn lost forty-one times as many.

What explains the weakness of the Worcester labor movement and the city's extraordinary record of labor tranquility? In part, as noted earlier, the strength and power of the city's industrialists inhibited organized working-class resistance. Manufacturers manipulated not only the carrot of paternalism but also the stick of repression to prevent unionization and strikes. Throughout the late nineteenth century Worcester manufacturers of such diverse products as shoes, wire, and pants routinely fired workers suspected of union activity.[38] By the early twentieth century the employers' associations had systematized this procedure through citywide blacklists. The Metal Trades Association maintained a central card file based on reports from employers and their company spies. A typical notation might read: "Joined union, a disturber." "Thru the system of spying and blacklisting in vogue by the employers' association," the *Labor*

News commented in 1915, "even the thought of belonging to a union made a man in danger of losing his job."[39]

Public officials generally cooperated with employers in suppressing strikes and unions. In 1902 striking machinists were not only prevented from holding open-air meetings on the Common but also prohibited from picketing by a court injunction. Outside labor organizers faced particularly severe harassment. When the IWW threatened to organize wireworkers in 1912, Police Chief David Matthews made it known that he would not tolerate these "disturbers." "They must not come here and kick our dog around," he told reporters. Similarly, when Emma Goldman returned to Worcester seventeen years after the closing of her ice-cream parlor, the Worcester police chief refused to let her speak "under any conditions." Even moderate and home-grown organizers ran afoul of the law. In 1918, for example, Worcester police arrested four officials of the Machinists' Union for distributing copies of the *Labor News* to Norton Company employees. The arresting officer advised them: "You'd better let up; that firm's got too much cash for labor to battle with."[40]

The power of the city's industrialists and the atmosphere of repressive anti-unionism help explain the failure of the Worcester labor movement. But Worcester trade unionists confronted not only a powerful and united ruling class but also a working class deeply divided along ethnic and, particularly, religious lines. Worcester boosters even advertised ethnic conflicts as an attraction to employers eager to escape unionization. An article in the Board of Trade's *Worcester Magazine* enumerating the "Advantages of Worcester as a Manufacturing Center" prominently cited the large "number of different nationalities," since "these nationalities do not affiliate, [and] concerted efforts for promoting strikes, labor unions, and similar movements among the working class become impossible." *Worcester Magazine* depicted manufacturers as passive beneficiaries of preexisting ethnic tensions, but industrialists actually actively manipulated these divisions to their own ends, particularly through their use of scabs. In October 1870, when Irish workers struck at the Quinsigamond Wire Works, the company quickly filled their places with native Americans, Germans, and French Canadians. The immediate result was a melee between strikers and scabs. The same pattern reoccurred in subsequent decades, although the nationalities of strikers and scabs changed over time. In a city with a constantly shifting population, employers could readily defuse unionizing efforts by playing off one ethnic group against another.[41]

The Worcester labor movement did little to combat these ethnic tensions. Labor organizers rarely spoke the language of the newest immigrant workers. And unions even sometimes undermined the economic position of recent arrivals. In 1893 the Central Labor Union led a successful fight to win preferential hiring for citizens on the Worcester Consolidated Street Railway. Subsequent strikes by stonecutters and leather workers also aimed at preventing the employment of "foreigners."[42]

Naturally, the ethnic ties that inhibited class-wide mobilization could also provide a basis for both unions and strikes. For example, French-Canadian and Swedish carpenters and Jewish bakers organized locals on the basis of their ethnic and linguistic affinities. The 1870 strike of Worcester boot and shoe workers, led by the Knights of St. Crispin, appears to have been rooted in the emergence of militant Irish workers, who were then flooding into this trade. Ten years later it was English carpet weavers, living in the relatively isolated and English-dominated mill village of South Worcester, who drew on ethnic ties and traditions in a strike against the Worcester Carpet Company. Every evening about one hundred strikers and friends would gather outside the factory and form processions to serenade and escort the female scabs from nearby Clinton with brass drums, tin horns, and "other acoustic instruments." Four decades later, Polish, Lithuanian, and Italian immigrant workers at the Graton and Knight leather factory, most of them employed in the tan yards and leather vats, refused to accept the strike settlement agreed to by other leather workers. With strong support from their ethnic communities, they staged mass demonstrations, which often culminated in violent clashes with city police.[43]

Yet for all this militancy, most ethnically based strikes ended in defeat. Indeed, the living memory of these and numerous other unsuccessful walkouts probably inhibited a more regular use of the strike weapon. Labor leaders routinely recalled failed strikes of ten, twenty, or even forty-five years past as a caution against precipitous action in the present.[44] Given this legacy of defeat as well as the obvious barriers to labor success, the evidence of local struggles is perhaps as remarkable as the overall record of quiescence. A brief look at the largest strike in Worcester during this period recalls both the existence of these periodic struggles as well as the reasons they so rarely succeeded.

In the fall of 1915 more than 3,000 machinists employed by Reed-Prentice, Crompton and Knowles, Whitcomb-Blaisdell, Leland-Gifford, and Norton struck for the eight-hour day, higher wages, and union recognition. Behind these concrete demands, however, lay deeper discontent fostered by changes in the work process brought about by scientific management. The job of the highly skilled, all-around machinist was increasingly being broken up into such less complex positions as lathe hand, driller, grinder, and assembler. Moreover, efficiency experts had introduced piecework schemes, which increased the pace of work to intolerable levels. "The dissatisfaction in the shops," explained one striker, "is caused by the way they drive men – driving to get a man to do twice the amount of work."[45]

The struggle between machinists and manufacturers over traditional craft prerogatives and control of the work process produced the most spectacular and prolonged conflict in Worcester labor history. Yet the machinists proved unable to overcome the same set of problems that had dogged the labor movement for the past forty-five years. The well-organized and well-financed Metal Trades Association kept up a steady barrage of propaganda against the strikers. And the threat of its efficient blacklist inhibited many from active or visible participation in the strike. At the same time, some manufacturers tried a more gentle approach, promising bonuses and Christmas turkeys to those who remained at work or broke the strike. The city government energetically cooperated with the manufacturers. The mayor's notion of an "impartial" arbitration panel included bankers, manufacturers, insurance executives, merchants, and professors but no workers. When police arrested the union's chief organizer for attempting to speak in front of a Gold Street factory, the *Labor News* complained of "the influence of local employers over authorities."[46]

Lacking community support and adequate funds, the machinists also failed to transcend their ethnic divisions. Although the union did initially attract immigrant workers to the strike, it was unable to build effective support within the ethnic communities. "All during the strike," notes a contemporary observer, "not one address or speech of any kind was made to the Finns, French Canadians, Swedes, Armenians, and so on, in their native tongue by any union organizer. This shows a defect in the organization for the men who have filled the shops since the strike have been largely local workmen of those nationalities." As scabs replaced strikers (many of whom simply took jobs in other cities), the strike was gradually broken.[47] Thus, the most visible outbreak of labor militancy in Worcester between 1870 and 1920 also pointed up the weakness of organized labor and the power of organized capital.

Ethnic communities

The failure of Worcester trade unions and the virtual absence of radical or working-class political parties did not give the city's industrialists an unchallenged hegemony over all aspects of working-class life. Instead, Worcester workers created tight ethnic communities with elaborate organizational infrastructures – churches, clubs, kinship networks, saloons – which served as alternatives to trade unions and political parties. These ethnic communities offered Worcester workers a sphere in which they could carry out a mode of life and express values, beliefs, and traditions significantly different from those prescribed by the dominant industrial elite. Although Worcester industrialists dominated within City Hall and the factory gates, their employees managed to retain a significant amount of control over their lives outside the job and within their ethnic communities.

As the city's first major non-English or non-native immigrant group, the Irish were also the first to develop a separate and distinct ethnic community. The first Irish, who came to Worcester in the 1820s, were overwhelmed by the massive influx of poorer Irish following the 1845 famine. By 1885 more than one-third of the city's total population was of Irish heritage. In this period the Worcester Irish created a vibrant social and cultural world centered in four neighborhoods, all but one of them located in the southeastern section of the city and within walking distance of the downtown shops and factories. In these East Side neighborhoods, notes Worcester Irish historian Vincent E. Powers, "the major institution remained the neighborhood church." Parochial schools, temperance societies, saloons, nationalist groups, militia companies, and numerous women's, social, athletic, and charitable organizations provided the basis – along with the churches – for the development and preservation of a distinctive way of life and set of values. "Before the [twentieth] century," concludes Powers, "it was possible to live an ethnically enclosed life on the Irish 'East Side.'"[48]

Prior to 1880 the French Canadians were the only other Worcester immigrant group of major importance. They began arriving even before the Civil War to work in the city's shoe factories and textile mills. By 1875 more than 2,000 French Canadians lived in Worcester, composing about 4.5 percent of the total city population and 17 percent of the foreign-born population. Thirty-five years later there were more than 14,000 Worcesterites of French-Canadian background, composing about 10 percent of the city's population. The

French Canadians joined the Irish on the East Side, seeking out homes convenient to the factories in which they worked and the churches in which they worshipped. The French-Catholic churches and their associated schools and organizations played an even more vital role in the life of the French-Canadian communities than they had for the Irish. These institutions served as bulwarks of an anti-assimilationist strategy of *survivance,* a belief brought by immigrants from Quebec that French Canadians had a "divine mission to preserve their national 'race' and religion against Anglo-Saxon inroads, by insuring the survival and transmission of their native language and customs."[49]

In the years after 1880 ethnic Worcester changed in two major ways. First, specific ethnic communities – especially the one created by the Irish – gradually lost some of their old insularity as a new American-born generation matured and increasing numbers of immigrants and their children gained a tenuous hold in the middle class. By 1885 the second-generation Irish outnumbered the first. And by 1900 about one-quarter of those Irish Americans had obtained white-collar positions. Just twenty years earlier only 5 percent of their parents' generation could claim this mark of middle-class status. Many of the more successful Irish used their increased incomes to move from their old neighborhoods to the new "lace curtain" districts like Vernon Hill and Union Hill. The second major change affecting ethnic Worcester was the arrival of thousands and thousands of additional immigrants from Europe, Canada, and the Near East. Although the Irish remained the largest single ethnic group in the city, the terms "Irish" and "foreigner" were no longer synonymous in Worcester. By 1920 the first- and second-generation Irish made up only 17 percent of the city's population. Moreover, the old Irish East Side neighborhoods were gradually taken over by new migrants. In 1880 the Irish held a firm majority in all these settlement areas; twenty years later they composed one-third or less of the population.[50]

The massive influx of Swedes in the last quarter of the nineteenth century was the most important force in the transformation of Worcester into a multiethnic city. In 1875 only about 166 Swedes resided in Worcester, but within ten years their numbers had increased almost thirteen times to 2,112, and in ten more years tripled again. By the turn of the century, Swedish-stock residents made up about 10 percent of the total population of 118,421. Swedish communities were separatist not only in outlook but also in location. The

Irish and French Canadians mingled on the East Side, but the two largest Swedish neighborhoods remained relatively isolated from both other immigrant groups and the city itself. Quinsigamond Village, located about two and a half miles south of downtown, centered on the South Works of Washburn and Moen, and Greendale, about three and a half miles north of downtown, grew up around the plant of the city's second major employer of Swedes, Norton Company. A mixture of Swedes, Swede-Finns (Swedish-speaking immigrants from Finland), and Finns, who worked in the Washburn and Moen North Works, populated Belmont Hill, the third Swedish settlement in Worcester and the only one in the vicinity of downtown. As with the French Canadians and Irish, the church dominated the lives of Worcester Swedes. The crucial difference was that whereas the Catholic church provided at least a tenuous link between the Irish and the French Canadians, the Protestantism of the Swedes created an almost unbridgeable gap between them and their immigrant predecessors.[51]

The diversification of Worcester's ethnic landscape begun by the Swedes in the 1880s and 1890s was accelerated in the next thirty years as large numbers of Jews, Italians, Poles, and Lithuanians, and smaller numbers of Albanians, Armenians, Syrians, Greeks, and Finns entered the city. By 1920 almost 72 percent of Worcester's residents were of foreign birth or parentage. These "newcomers" of the late nineteenth century and the early twentieth shared with previous immigrants an affinity for close-knit ethnic neighborhoods. The Italians, the largest contingent among the new immigrants with more than 12,000 residents (first and second generation) in Worcester by 1930, developed along the formerly Irish Shrewsbury Street, a community of stores, churches, and clubs that was, in the words of an ethnic geographer, "virtually a self-contained unit."[52]

The Poles and Lithuanians – with about 10,000 first- and second-generation residents each in 1930 – also settled on the East Side, particularly along Millbury Street and in the southeastern triangle known as the "Island," where they also gradually displaced the former Irish residents. Although the Poles and Lithuanians initially shared a church and continued to inhabit the same neighborhood, their communities remained quite distinct. "The Worcester Lithuanian," writes a student of that community, "sought survival through near universal isolation from the WASP society and the polyglot society in which they found themselves." Among Poles, another local observer adds, "there was a strong tendency . . . to carry on a Polish society in Worcester in which social life revolved around the Polish-speech church, the parochial school, and the national fraternal clubs."[53]

Russian-Jewish immigrants initially settled near, but not among, the Poles and Lithuanians on the working-class East Side. "For many years," writes one contemporary sociologist, the boundaries of this "voluntary ghetto . . . were so precise that any well-informed Worcesterite could name them almost to the house number." Other smaller immigrant groups took up correspondingly smaller pieces of the East Side. The Syrians, for example, populated the western slope of Oak Hill near the Syrian Orthodox Church on Wall Street. The original Armenian colony was on Laurel Hill, where the Armenian National Apostolic Church was erected in 1890.[54]

The complex interweaving of church, neighborhood, fraternal lodge, and family provided a strong basis for organized immigrant working-class life in Worcester. Yankee industrialists may have dominated the factories and the civic life of the city, but immigrants retained control over their own churches, neighborhoods, clubs, and often schools. And immigrant working-class values, beliefs, and traditions – not those of the manufacturers – governed those areas of life. Still, this ethnic basis of working-class life created strains for the broader working-class community. Although the ethnic groups usually lived in harmony, the harmony was built mainly on lack of contact rather than on mutual respect. Moreover, internecine warfare periodically broke out, particularly between the younger residents of the ethnic neighborhoods. Longtime Lithuanian residents of Worcester similarly recall the disruption of their church services by Irish and French-Canadian youngsters from the surrounding neighborhood. Common workplaces as well as common "turf" also fostered interethnic conflict. In the shoe factories, French-Canadian "straw-bosses" reportedly discriminated against less skilled Italian workers.[55]

Yet despite the separateness, diversity, and even animosity that pervaded ethnic Worcester, these disparate immigrant working-class communities also shared similar structures of life, a common location, and a similar occupational structure. Although Worcester immigrants had little to do with each other, their daily lives often followed the same rhythms. The common experience of low pay, long hours, and unsafe work patterned immigrant lives in the most fundamental ways. The equivalence of the words "immigrant" and "blue-collar worker" in late nineteenth and early twentieth century

Worcester provided the most significant bond uniting Worcester's ethnic communities. In addition, the family and the extended kinship network formed the basic unit of social life for most immigrant groups. Similarly, churches and their associated women's groups, temperance societies, and mutual benefit associations provided the physical and spiritual center of the ethnic communities. In general, the same social institutions – churches, families, lodges, saloons, cafés – structured the experience of most Worcester immigrants.[56]

Not only did Worcester's immigrants share similar, but not always common, jobs and social institutions, they also shared similar neighborhoods and similar types of dwellings. In the late nineteenth and early twentieth centuries, any Worcester resident knew that "West Side" meant middle- or upper-class status, native-American background, and single family homes, whereas "East Side" meant working-class status, immigrant background, and triple-decker homes. Even as late as 1975 a sociological study found: "The split of Worcester between east and west was well understood by almost everyone to whom we spoke."[57] Of course, both designations included a variety of neighborhoods; some middle- and upper-class Worcesterites occupied the hilltops of East Side neighborhoods, and working-class Swedes lived in the northern reaches of the city in Greendale. But, overall, spatial divisions reinforced class lines.

Ethnicity and class, then, shaped the lives of Worcester workers in contradictory ways. On the one hand, ethnic divisions militated against class-wide mobilization of workers in trade unions or political parties. And these divisions fostered rivalries – and sometimes violent animosities – between people who shared many of the same problems. Consequently, the insularity and separatism of the immigrant communities limited immigrant working-class influence over economic or political issues. On the other hand, these ethnic enclaves not only gave workers a shared basis of experience – similar life-styles, housing, neighborhoods, and jobs – but, more important, provided a refuge and resource for those who confronted the unemployment, poverty, disease, and accidents that accompanied life and work in industrializing America.

How did the "freedom" offered by these ethnic communities and the constraints imposed by the industrial system shape working-class culture in late nineteenth century Worcester? What values and beliefs did workers develop in a community with a strong local ruling class, limited working-class political organization, a weak labor movement, and cohesive, but separate, ethnic communities? In search of an answer, the next section examines the ethnic working-class saloon and popular celebrations of July Fourth in late nineteenth century Worcester. As case studies, these chapters are intended to be illustrative and not exhaustive, to suggest the complex interplay of Worcester's particular social and economic structure and the particular values and traditions of its immigrant workers in the realm of leisure time.

PART II

Culture: the working-class world of the late nineteenth century

2 *The rise of the saloon*

In 1829 Ichabod Washburn, the co-owner of a small Worcester machine shop who was later to become the city's leading manufacturer, sought help in building his new house, specifying, however, that there be no provision of rum for the workers. The carpenter was skeptical, since a house-raising "without the stimulus of spirits . . . had not before been done for many years." Most of Washburn's own workmen refused to take part in the experiment. "The work, however," Washburn later recalled, "proceeded noiselessly and successfully to its completion without rum." The local newspaper celebrated the novel achievement under the caption "Progress of the Temperance Reform." Washburn's workmen, however, had a less approving reaction: They watched and, "by their jeers, ridiculed the undertaking, and did their best to make it a failure."[1]

While his workmen laughed, the sober and pious Washburn prospered. At his death in 1868 he presided over a million-dollar manufacturing concern that produced more than half the wire in the United States. The years that marked Washburn's rise from master of a shop with fewer than 30 craftsmen to president of a corporation with more than 700 employees also saw the triumph of his ideas about sobriety and order in the workplace. By the time of Washburn's death a series of seven factory whistles precisely dictated the daily comings and goings of his wireworkers, and detailed, written "Regulations" governed their movements within the factory gates. "There shall be *no change* of workmen from one department to another without *special permission* from the office: in which case *both Time-Keepers* will consult with the pay-roll Clerk regarding the keeping of the time," commanded a typical rule.[2]

The large factories of late nineteenth century Worcester would not tolerate the casual informality – the gambling, storytelling, singing, debating, and especially drinking – that had characterized its small workshops in the earlier years of the century or its farms in the previous century. Yet while the factory workers of the 1870s faced a more structured work regimen than the artisans of the 1820s, they also generally had more free time in which to pursue some of the socializing that had been removed from their workday. The drinking that manufacturers like Washburn repressed on the job now found a new temporal and physical locus in public, commercial leisure-time institutions known as saloons. Thus, it was in response to a complex set of social forces – tightened work discipline, shorter workdays, intensified regulation of public recreation, increased working-class incomes – that the saloon emerged as a center of working-class social life.[3] Although the saloon was a commercial enterprise, its ethnic working-class customers still decisively shaped its ritual and character. Somewhat paradoxically, they infused the saloon with a set of values that differed from those of the dominant industrial capitalist society that had given rise to the saloon in the first place.

Drink and work: the emergence of leisure time

As Washburn's house-raising experience indicates, workers in the eighteenth and early nineteenth centuries considered drinking an inextricable, and even mandatory, aspect of work. In the shoe shops of Lynn in the 1820s, a half pint of "white eye" was an expected part of the daily wage and the workers themselves financed further heavy drinking. In Rochester workshops of the same period "drinking was universal" and "was embedded in the pattern of irregular work and easy sociability."[4] This intermingling of work and socializing, of work and drink, marked manual as well as artisanal labor. Account books from the building of Worcester's town hall in the 1820s record payments for "labor and grog." Similarly, for the unskilled laborers – mostly Irish immigrants – who toiled from sunrise to sunset building the nation's canals and railroads, the four to six daily breaks for a "jigger" of whiskey provided the only relief from a brutal work regimen. In Worcester the contractors on the Blackstone Canal and the Boston and Worcester Railroad distributed whiskey to Irish immigrant laborers as part of their daily wage. "The rum barrel," writes Worcester Irish antiquarian Richard O'Flynn, "was always near the work – ready for distribution, by this means they kept the men hard at work all day."[5]

The pervasiveness of workplace drinking was hardly surprising in an era when it suffused all areas of life. "Americans between 1790 and 1830," a carefully documented recent study shows, "drank more alcoholic beverages than ever before or since." Even the church was not immune. Under the pulpit of Worcester's Old South Church was a large cupboard containing, "for the accommodation of the congregation, at noon time, a home manufactured beverage from the choicest products of the orchard."[6]

The antebellum temperance crusades, which began in the late 1820s, rapidly undermined the universality of these drinking habits, particularly among the native upper and middle classes. Between 1830 and 1850, according to one estimate, annual per capita consumption of absolute alcohol plummeted from 3.9 gallons to 1 gallon. Testifying before a Massachusetts legislative committee in 1867, Emory Washburn, a Worcester lawyer and a former governor, described the social impact of this new abstinence: "Before 1828 I do not know of any families that pretended to anything like hospitality who did not make a free use of liquor." But by 1867 Washburn noted of these same "respectable" circles that "it was as rare to see liquor offered in a man's house as it would be to see medicine offered."[7]

The early temperance movement appealed particularly to the middle- and upper-class men and women who dined with Emory Washburn. Industrialists and others tied to "the emerging industrial society" led Worcester's temperance movement in the 1830s, according to a recent historian of that movement. And by the 1840s "there was mounting evidence of the broadening appeal of prohibition among not only manufacturers and their allies, but also all respectable and propertied elements in the community." Although some working people – particularly those attracted to revivalist religion – did join the temperance crusades, larger numbers remained attached to their traditional drinking habits and customs. In the 1830s, at least, Worcester workers showed little interest in the city's temperance movement. Of twenty-six temperance activists engaged in manufacturing, at least two-thirds were employers of labor and only one was definitely an employee – and he was a foreman at Ichabod Washburn's new wire works.[8]

The prohibitory ordinances passed by local temperance forces were never fully effective, but new workplace bans on drinking had a more direct impact on popular customs. The Worcester Temperance Society reported in 1831 that twenty-six "mechanics shops" and six "manufactories," employing more than 200 workers in all had banned drinking during work hours and had stopped employing intemperate workmen. Beginning around 1830, then, rules against workplace and workday drinking spread at an uneven pace through innumerable trades and cities. By the late nineteenth century most employers tended to view workplace drinking as part of a bygone era. Oliver Ames, the head of Ames Plow Company, with factories in Worcester and Easton, Massachusetts, commented in 1867 that about thirty years earlier "the work would be frequently broken up by the intemperance of the men. Now we have no trouble of that kind." A New York carriage maker placed the change in his trade in the 1860s. "I can remember twenty or twenty-five years ago," he told a Senate committee in 1883, "when in our trade, even in our shop, there was a constant sending out for beer and spirits, and it was universally permitted." Now, he noted, bringing liquor into the shop "is a violation of rule which affords reason for discharge."[9]

Rules against alcohol consumption were the firmest in the most mechanized industries. Where traditional production methods or heavy manual labor prevailed, drinking was more likely to be tolerated. As late as 1898 the superintendent of Worcester's Sewer Department accepted his workers' consumption of "copious amounts of beer" during their noon break, because "the men had a right to drink when off duty if they chose to do so." Drinking, Dr. Samuel Hartwell told the Massachusetts Bureau of Statistics of Labor, was heaviest among those "who perform labor physically exhaustive, and those who are exposed to extremes of heat and cold." Moreover, when labor was short, even the strictest manufacturers tolerated drinking. "We have to put up with it [intemperance] when help is scarce," one textile manufacturer admitted in 1881. Even where employers successfully repressed on-the-job drinking, they could rarely confine it entirely to weekends and holidays. Excessive Sunday drinking often meant high Monday absenteeism or "blue Mondays."[10]

Despite the exceptions and evasions, numerous government reports demonstrate the growing repression of workplace drinking in the course of the nineteenth century. In 1881, for example, the Massachusetts Bureau of Statistics of Labor questioned workers and manufacturers about intemperance in the textile mills. Only one-sixth of the workers and one-quarter of the manufacturers reported substantial drinking. Sixteen years later a U.S. Department of Labor survey of 30,000 employers found that more than three-quarters considered an employee's drinking habits in hiring decisions.[11]

The gradual tightening of workplace discipline – as exemplified by the anti-drink regulations – was accompanied by a more favorable change for the working class: the gradual shortening of the workday. The precise connection between these two developments is difficult to specify, but they appear to have occurred in tandem. Agitation for the ten-hour day, for example, began in the mid-1820s at the same time that men like Washburn were challenging such basic forms of workplace sociability as drinking. Rochester carpenters – "unable," according to one historian, "to control their conditions of work or to mix work and leisure" – struck in 1834 and announced: "We will be faithful to our employers during the ten hours and no longer." Although such other motives as the desire to reduce pervasive unemployment influenced movements for the shorter workday, the growing articulation of a "right to leisure" played an important part. What workers wanted, the Knights of Labor explained, was "more of the leisure that rightfully belongs to them." The "division and specialization of labor" and the "intensity" of work dictated by "modern methods in industry" had reduced "the social opportunities of the masses," an American Federation of Labor pamphlet similarly argued; the only solution was "more leisure, more physical and mental repose, more and larger periods of relief, from the strain which the specialized industrial life imposes."[12]

As early as the 1840s the ten-hour movement had begun to have some impact, particularly in Massachusetts. In 1845, for example, workers at T. K. Earle's Machine Shop and Foundry in Worcester won a two-hour daily reduction to ten hours. Early the following year the Worcester Workingmen's Association invited "the employers of this village to meet us at our weekly meetings and show cause, if they have any, why *men* ought to work more than ten hours a day." And by the early 1850s the ten-hour day was "all but universal" among Worcester's skilled mechanics.[13]

Progress was, of course, uneven and varied enormously by industry. Massachusetts textile workers, for example, made some gains in the 1850s, but many continued to work eleven and a half to twelve hours until the 1874 law mandated ten hours for women and children. Even then, longer hours remained quite common. In 1879 a letter writer to the *Worcester Evening Star* wondered: "Why is Packachoag Mill, South Worcester, allowed to run 13 hours a day, or is the ten hour law of any use but to fill the Statute book?" In general, however, the political and economic struggles of the working class brought shorter workdays. In 1830 eleven hours per day or more was the standard at more than half the establishments surveyed in a U.S. Census Bureau study; by 1860 the figure had dropped to less than one-third. In Massachusetts, at least, ten hours was the "normal" workday in the 1870s and 1880s with 80 percent of 2,500 firms surveyed by the Bureau of Statistics of Labor in 1883 reporting the ten-hour day.[14]

Workers used their increased leisure time in a wide range of ways: gossiping with neighbors, lounging in pool halls, studying in night classes, visiting dance halls, mending worn clothing, organizing temperance societies, tending gardens, raising money for their churches, arguing over trade union strategy, and watching melodramas. But for many, drinking occupied an important portion of their growing, but still limited, leisure hours. Indeed, it is hardly surprising that a diversion like drinking, which had once played such a central role during work time, would also have a central place in leisure time. In a similar way, the songs that had once modulated the work rhythms of black manual laborers did not disappear with mechanization and urbanization; black music – in the form of the blues – found a new home in leisure time rather than work time.[15] In both cases, the diverse customs and traditions that once dominated the workplace continued to shape newly emerging leisure-time institutions. The saloon and similar working-class leisure institutions thus developed in the context of tightening work discipline and decreasing work hours. But just as the saloon owed its existence to the growing temporal separation of drinking and working, of socializing and working, it was also predicated on the growing spatial separation of male sociability from the home.

From shebeen *to saloon: the emergence of leisure space*

Formal drink places – taverns – existed in Worcester almost from its first founding in the late seventeenth century. By the 1730s Worcester had five well-regarded taverns with four of the proprietors holding town offices. By the time of the temperance crusades of the 1820s, however, the taverns had begun to lose their social respectability: None of the seventeen tavernkeepers in 1828 held an important town office. Their status declined further with the rise of temperance sentiment among the "respectable" citizens of Worcester and the passage of various prohibitory ordinances, beginning in 1835 and remaining in effect with only temporary breaks until 1875.[16]

These anti-drink measures had a limited impact on the drink trade. The city's small police force, which consisted of just one watchman before 1851, could not effectively enforce the law. When Mayor Henry Chapin attempted to suppress liquor traffic in 1850, pro-drink protesters responded by bombing his office. Even the use of special police and vigorous prosecutions "did not substantially suppress the sale of liquor," one Worcester mayor admitted. In the late 1850s, for example, with Worcester under a strict anti-drink ordinance, a socially prominent Worcesterite met an acquaintance of his from New Orleans on the street in Worcester. The New Orleans man suggested they go for a drink. The Worcesterite replied: "You cannot get anything to drink here, the places for the sale of liquor have all been closed up." But the New Orleans man (who had been in the city only two days) corrected him: "Why, yes you can; I have been to more than twenty places here in this city."[17]

At least a few of these illicit drink places – the Bay State House, for example – even catered to the city's more "respectable" citizens. But most working-class drinking went on in much less formal and elegant surroundings. As early as the 1830s the city's pioneer Irish laboring community had established a number of popular *shebeens* (unlicensed and home- or kitchen-based liquor sellers) of the type so common in nineteenth century Ireland. In the 1840s and 1850s on the immigrant and working-class East Side of the city, Worcester Irish historian Vincent E. Powers notes, "temperance laws had little effect and illegal shebeens and blind-pigs continued to operate. Irish freighters and railroad crews found an eager market for the liquor they easily smuggled into the city." Throughout Massachusetts those in contact with working-class neighborhoods observed the same close connection of drink selling and home life in the face of official prohibition statutes. A Boston Catholic priest observed that "among the poorer classes . . . in almost every house (and every tenement having a number of families in it) they have some liquor, and they sell it to those in the house."[18]

Although there is only limited descriptive evidence, it is unlikely that these kitchen barrooms were especially lavish or spacious since they shared the physical limitations of most working-class dwellings of this period. Even skilled workers in Worcester could not expect to house a family of five in anything larger than a five-room apartment. Unskilled laborers – often immigrants with larger families – lived in more crowded conditions. An investigator for the Bureau of Statistics of Labor in 1875 found a Worcester Irish laborer and his family of eight living in a four-room tenement, which provided only "two privies for about fifty people."[19] In such a setting a shebeen was likely to be little more than a table and a few chairs set up in the kitchen or bedroom of a tenement or three-decker apartment.

Massachusetts's passage of a comprehensive liquor license law in 1875, which finally allowed the legal operation of public drink places, did not immediately remove drink selling from its location in the kitchens and bedrooms of these working-class tenements. In the poorest sections of the city drinking continued to take place in the "amateur grog shops" and kitchen barrooms that had predominated during the prohibition era of the previous three decades. When City Marshal James Drennan raided the home of Bridget McCarthy in the Irish working-class district known as the Island, he found seven men and women sitting in the kitchen with a number of beer glasses on the table and two barrels of beer on draft in the front room. Leaving the apartment was a young woman carrying a pail of beer home to her family. On the same day Drennan also visited the house of John Mehan on nearby Ward Street and found four people sitting in the front room "with beer glasses frothing" and a table set with beer. "A man with a pail of beer was talking to Mehan outside the door [and] went off in a hurry as we entered," Drennan reported. Some raids turned up rather elaborate equipment and provisions. In the cellar of John Mehan's Ward Street neighbor John Daily police officers found fifty gallons of ale in two barrels, two gallons of whiskey in two jugs and three bottles, twenty-four bottles of lager beer, and smaller quantities of rum and gin. A pipe connected the barrels of ale to the kitchen faucet.[20]

Many of these Irish kitchen saloonkeepers did not bother to take out licenses under the 1875 law, particularly since they could not afford the $200 required for a first-class license or the $100 for a second-class license (beer and light wine only), given their marginal profits. Moreover, fines imposed on the few violators actually prosecuted were usually small ($10 and costs) and often could be avoided by appeal to sympathetic judges and juries. Of 245 people prosecuted for liquor violations during the first four years of the license law only 35 faced any immediate fine or imprisonment; most cases were simply lost in the drawn-out appeal process. The nature of search and seizure laws and the location of sales in private dwellings further hindered the process of obtaining liquor law convictions. City Marshal W. Ansel Washburn complained: "It is not hard to detect the places where the article is kept and sold, even though it be in the privacy of the kitchen or bedroom. Yet, as the law now stands, an officer, in attempting to enforce the same, would become a trespasser."[21]

The centrality of women as both sellers and consumers of liquor in the kitchen grog shops further emphasizes their close connection to immigrant home and family life. Arrest records give ample evidence of the prominence of Irish women drink sellers in Worcester. Whenever temperance-minded Worcester mayors of the 1850s and 1860s decided to crack down on illegal liquor selling, the most immediate impact was that "half a dozen Irish women [would] . . . be sent to the house of correction."[22]

Whereas Worcester officials viewed these female liquor dealers as disreputable and criminal, the Irish community apparently looked at them quite differently. In Ireland the keeping of a shebeen was a "recognized resource of widows," and they had a "privileged" status in the liquor trade. In Worcester Irish immigrants continued to insist on the propriety of this form of communal charity, despite the failure of American laws to recognize it. Almost invariably, a woman arrested for illegal liquor selling would plead, as did Honora Lyon, that "she was compelled to sell a little beer and whiskey in order to make a living. She was sick, destitute and unable to provide for herself and child without having recourse to liquor selling." Even Irish temperance supporters might also affirm the communal impulses behind the shebeen. On the same day that he denounced liquor dealers, James H. Mellen, editor of the *Worcester Daily Times*, complained of police raids on "hard working honest women and cripples," who were entitled to "sympathy."[23]

The practices, as well as the proprietorship, of the kitchen grog shops indicate their close connection to the home and the everyday patterns of Irish immigrant life. Often operating outside the established legal framework, these shops casually dispensed liquor at all hours to friends and neighbors, men and women alike, for both on- and off-premise consumption. Although more formal and more public drink places existed well before the 1870s, much drinking in that decade and even later remained rooted in the more informal and less visible kitchen grog shop. The saloon, as a spatially distinct public and commercialized leisure-time institution, had not yet entirely triumphed.

Gradually, however, the tighter regulations did have some impact, and Worcester saloons began to emerge from the back rooms and kitchens and take on a more standardized and regulated form. Initially, the Board of Aldermen did not discriminate very carefully in their selection of licensees, issuing an average of 235 licenses yearly over the first four years of licensing. In 1879, however, the Board of Aldermen decided to cut back sharply and so issued only 131 licenses.[24] Although the Board of Aldermen never articulated their motives in the license cutbacks, their targets – women, economically marginal operators, and saloons outside of downtown – reveal their goal of ending the kitchen grog shop and fostering the public working-class saloon.

Women – the group most commonly identified with the kitchen

trade – were the most visible victims of the license shake-up. Forty-one women, who comprised 22 percent of all saloonkeepers in 1878, lost their licenses during the next two years. Only two women managed to hang on in the drink trade by obtaining fourth-class grocer's licenses. R. G. Dun and Company credit ratings of Worcester saloonkeepers make clear the marginal financial status of those – both men and women – who lost their licenses after 1878. A rating of "worthless" in 1878 or 1879 invariably presaged the loss of one's liquor license within the next year or two. The saloonkeepers themselves were well aware of this economic discrimination in the award of licenses. "One Who Knows How the Thing Works" wrote to the *Worcester Evening Star* to complain of "the injustice shown vs. *small dealers* in liquor."[25] In addition to gender and economic status, location figured importantly in the 1878–80 license cutbacks. In those two years the Board of Aldermen eliminated more than 85 percent of the saloons in areas more than a half mile from City Hall. The Irish working-class Island district lost fifteen of its existing seventeen licensed drink places.

The effect of the license cutbacks was to eliminate the least public and visible, the hardest-to-regulate, and the least capitalized drink places. In so doing, the board, in effect, endorsed the creation of a more standardized and public institution – the late nineteenth century saloon – as a leisure place clearly separated from both work and home. This spatial segregation was given legal force in 1880 with the passage of a state law prohibiting liquor licenses for premises with "any interior connection or communication with any apartments occupied as a residence or for lodging purposes." The passage that same year of a "screen law," which prohibited obstructions of "a view of the interior" of the saloon as well as side and back doors, further removed drinking from the private, informal world of the home-based kitchen barroom and set it in a public, recreational institution.[26]

Naturally, the kitchen barrooms that seem to have been the predominant Irish drinking places in the 1850s and 1860s (and remained prominent in the 1870s) did not simply disappear with the decrees of the Board of Aldermen. "Certain it is," one local paper commented in 1879 of those who lost their licenses, "that some of them will continue to sell in the defiance of the law." The police records confirm this prediction. Almost 30 percent of those prosecuted for illegal liquor sales between May 1880 and May 1881 had been legal licensees before the 1878–80 purges. Typically, those prosecuted kitchen barroom proprietors lived in working-class neighborhoods and operated out of either their home or a small grocery store. In 1878, for example, Alice Dignan ran a saloon out of her home on 23 Nashua Street, near the Washburn and Moen North Works, where her husband, Peter, was a laborer. Although she lost her license in the 1879 shake-up, the Dignans appear to have retained their kitchen saloon for which they were prosecuted at least once in 1880 and twice in 1882. When police raided the Dignans in 1880, they found Alice serving four large glasses of beer in the kitchen and ample supplies of lager beer, ale, whiskey, and gin hidden in the bedroom and cellar.[27]

Although unlicensed and kitchen-based liquor selling continued well into the twentieth century, public, legal, and formal saloons dominated the drink trade in Worcester by the mid-1880s. According to the R. G. Dun credit records, unlicensed dealers appear to have stayed in business for only about a year and a half on the average after they lost their licenses. In part, the demise of the kitchen sellers reflected surveillance and prosecutions by an increasingly professional police force. Between 1869 and 1878 prosecutions for liquor violations averaged about thirty-two per year, but in the next ten-year period they quadrupled. A single liquor seizure could be enough to put a marginal dealer out of business. In addition, unlicensed liquor dealers could not easily obtain credit.[28] Finally, the kitchen barrooms simply could not compete with the better appointed and more spacious legal saloons. Working-class patrons, not just government regulators, ultimately preferred the public saloon over the kitchen grog shop.

The gradual emergence of the saloon as a leisure space clearly distinct from home thus gave workers a more comfortable and appealing place to spend their leisure time. But most working-class women did not share in this modest improvement in working-class life. For married women who did not engage in paid labor, recreation was an integral part of everyday life; in effect, they mixed work and play much in the manner of the early nineteenth century artisan. Thus, despite their home-centered responsibilities, women could have an important place in the kitchen barrooms as both proprietors and customers. However, when leisure was removed from the home or its immediate vicinity, it became predominantly a male privilege. While some women continued to patronize saloons, these public leisure spaces increasingly became male preserves. In this way, the male saloon became a mirror image of the male factory.

The liquor business: the emergence of leisure spending

The development of the saloon as a leisure institution temporally distinct from work and spatially distinct from home thus represented a contradictory series of gains and losses for Worcester workers: a decrease in control over work combined with an increase in free time; the demise of a traditional, home-centered, and sexually integrated gathering place along with the development of a more ample and comfortable public meeting spot. The economic context for the rise of the saloon had an equally mixed character: a growth in working-class incomes coupled with the extraction of a portion of those incomes by a commercial liquor business.

Although statistics on nineteenth century working-class incomes are unreliable and controversial, most historians agree that real wages rose in the second half of the century. Clarence Long, for example, argues that both daily and annual earnings increased about 50 percent between 1860 and 1890.[29] Discretionary expenditures for such items as amusement and alcohol probably increased with these growing – albeit still inadequate – real incomes.

Yet discretionary spending could not expand in a vacuum; it was also necessary that amusement and alcohol become purchasable commodities. In fact, both processes occurred together. In the late nineteenth century such commodities became both available and affordable to more and more working-class consumers. In comparing working-class family budgets from 1874 and 1901, historian John Modell finds more spending for virtually all nonessential items. For example, workers were more likely to rely on cash-bought and publicly consumed alcohol than on home-produced drink. In 1889 only 30 percent of the native-American families and 42 percent of the Irish-born families completing family budgets for the Bureau of Statistics of Labor listed any annual expenditures for alcoholic beverages. By 1901, however, these figures had jumped by about half.[30]

In this context, increased public consumption of alcohol might indicate the growing prosperity of the working class rather than its pathological degeneration, as it is sometimes depicted. According to an 1889 survey by the U.S. Department of Labor, the best paid workers were 50 percent more likely to purchase "indulgences" like alcohol and tobacco than those at the bottom of the income scale. "The workers who drank the most," historian Michael Marrus writes similarly of *Belle Epoque* France, "were not the most miserable, not those who were drowning their socioeconomic sorrows, but rather those with time and money to spend." What happened, Marrus argues, "was that as working conditions began to improve, and as wages slowly went up, workers naturally turned to drink during a transitional period because they were still adjusting to a more affluent state of affairs. What was new to them was the prospect of having any pleasure at all which was not furtively snatched from the grip of necessity." Indeed, beneath the persistent middle- and upper-class complaints about the "extravagance" and "thriftlessness" of working-class drinking habits lay a recognition and resentment of this nascent "prosperity." Speaking of skilled mechanics in 1883, the secretary of the New York Board of Health admitted that "they all do what I would like to do now, and what I do a good deal of myself – they smoke a great deal; they drink considerable, more or less, and I think their families are extravagant."[31]

Drinking and the saloon, then, offered recreational diversions well suited to growing, but still modest, working-class incomes. As a result, a liquor business developed, particularly from the middle to the late nineteenth century, to take advantage of this emerging market. In Worcester the growth of the drink trade, which was especially rapid in the 1870s and 1880s, can be charted in the careers of successful liquor dealers and saloonkeepers. In 1860s Worcester, liquor selling offered neither social respectability nor economic security. In 1863, for example, R. G. Dun and Company entered its first report on George F. Hewitt, who had started a liquor business in Worcester in 1860: He "is entirely unworthy of credit . . . no reliance can be placed on him in the matter of business." A few months later they cautioned creditors: "Public opinion . . . added to the liquor law is great inducement to repudiate." These warnings proved prescient, as Hewitt suffered both arrest and bankruptcy in the next twelve years. But Hewitt's remarkable success in the late 1870s and early 1880s suggests "boom" conditions in the Worcester drink business in that period. By 1882 the previously bankrupt and disreputable Hewitt had been a member of the Board of Aldermen, erected a block of stores and tenements, and was estimated to be worth $50,000.[32]

Even more dramatic was the success of John and Alexander Bowler, who entered the brewery business in Worcester in 1883. Within three years they had tripled their output and within six years their net worth had multiplied more than six times. The success of Hewitt and the Bowlers reflected the expansion of the Massachusetts liquor industry in these years. Between 1865 and 1885 the capitalization of the industry multiplied almost ten times, the number of employees three times, and the number of firms four times.[33]

Worcester saloonkeepers shared in this prosperity. In December 1885 the *Worcester Sunday Telegram* recalled that in the late 1870s Worcester "rumsellers had just emerged from the trials of the prohibition years" and "were as poor as the men they had sent to the almshouse." But "of late years their incomes have rapidly increased, and they have indulged in fast horses, elegant apparel, a self-contented swagger, and above all, have from year to year increased their political power." This new affluence was reflected in more lavish and more businesslike saloons. "The old homely and ungrateful beer saloons of the last generation have given way to comfortable and costly premises where liquor is now dispensed to the impatient consumer," the *Sunday Telegram* commented in 1886. As the *Telegram*'s language indicates, the saloon had become more of a commercial institution with drink as a commodity, the worker as a consumer, and the saloonkeeper as a businessman. Although Worcester's rum sellers were hardly considered "respectable" by the city's Yankee elite, they were becoming reasonably stable small-business men. To cite just one example of many recorded by Irish antiquarian Richard O'Flynn and the credit reporters from R. G. Dun: John McGrail was "not worth anything of any account" in 1875, but by 1884 he was doing "a good business" and was worth at least $2,000.[34]

But one should not exaggerate saloonkeeper affluence: Very few managed any substantial accumulations of wealth. "Doing a modest living," "doing well in a small way," or "gets a living" were the most often reported comments in the credit reports. Indeed, the insufficiently capitalist mentality of the saloonkeepers seems to have frustrated the more aggressive credit investigators. They implicitly chastise the saloonkeepers for living too extravagantly, for failing to "accumulate," and for not being very "progressive."[35] Apparently, many saloonkeepers were content to earn a modest working-class income from their businesses and had no larger aspirations.

Although saloonkeepers were not always aggressive entrepreneurs, by the late nineteenth century in Worcester (and perhaps earlier elsewhere) they presided over a clearly commercial leisure-time institution. Indeed, the very term "saloon" was a relatively new one, which suggested the spaciousness and luxury of a French salon or a large cabin on a passenger ship. The word was used as early as 1841, but it seems to have only come into common usage in Worcester after the Civil War and particularly in the 1870s. Richard O'Flynn, writing in 1880, refused to use the newer term: "I must be pardoned for the use of the word 'Rum Shop.' I cannot conscientiously give any other name no matter how magnificent the surroundings."[36]

Despite O'Flynn's resistance, the saloon had triumphed. Its emergence was rooted in long-term changes: the separation of work and play, the segregation of recreation from home life, and the commercialization of this leisure time and space. Although the changes were broad and general, their impact was class-specific. The emergence of the saloon depended upon and reflected improvements in working-class living standards: the achievement of growing amounts of leisure time free from the constraints of the workplace, the development of alternative spaces to spend that leisure time away from crowded homes and tenements, and the possession of sufficient disposable income to purchase more than the bare necessities of life. Yet the rise of the saloon equally grew out of the subordination of the working class: its lack of freedom at the workplace, its very limited free time and disposable income, and its inferior housing conditions. Thus, as Worcester's saloons formalized and grew in the late nineteenth century, they remained decisively shaped by the circumstances – both economic and cultural – of the city's large immigrant working class.

The ethnic working-class saloon: proprietors and patrons

In April 1885 three Irish-Catholic pastors startled local liquor dealers, as well as members of their congregations, with a bold attack on the drink trade. The Reverend John J. McCoy reportedly "denounced the saloons as hells, and their owners as murderers." What made this rebuke surprising was its source in the Irish-Catholic clergy, who ministered to most of the city's saloonkeepers. Seventeen of the nineteen applicants for liquor licenses in Sacred Heart parish belonged to that church, its pastor, the Reverend Thomas Conaty, ruefully admitted. And two-thirds of all Worcester liquor license applicants were Irish, whereas only one-third of the city's population was of Irish origin, the Reverend Thomas Griffin added.[37]

The 1880 U.S. Manuscript Census confirms these clerical estimates. Although only one-sixth of Worcester's people were born in Ireland, about half of the 1880 saloonkeepers who could be traced into the census were Irish natives, and another 10 percent were the children of Irish immigrants. Even more overrepresented in the drink trade, however, were the Germans, who made up less than 1 percent of the city's population but more than 15 percent of its saloonkeepers. A nativist rhyme popular in Worcester after the Civil War captured the ethnic flavor of its drink trade: "The Irish and the Dutch; they don't amount to much, / For the Micks have their whiskey and the Germans guzzle the beer, / And all we Americans wish they had never come here."[38]

Although nativists blamed the drink trade entirely on immigrants, at least one-fifth of the saloonkeepers in 1880 were identifiable as "American." A few of the native-stock saloonkeepers kept relatively respectable restaurants, which also dispensed beer and liquor, but the others were part of a "sporting crowd," which spurned the Protestant values of their fellow "Americans." "A little flashy . . . likes to live well and make a show," the R. G. Dun credit investigator wrote of one. "Rather fond of horseflesh," he observed of another. In 1875 when native-born Worcester machinist A. V. Newton wrote *The Saloon Keeper's Companion* and subtitled it *Sporting Manual*, he probably had these saloonkeepers in mind.[39]

As Worcester's other ethnic communities – French Canadian, English, and Swedish – grew in the late nineteenth century, they also developed their own drink centers. As early as the 1860s the Christopher brothers established the first French-Canadian saloon in Worcester, and there were four or five French-Canadian saloons throughout the 1870s and 1880s. Despite occasional rumblings of temperance sentiment among their clergy, French-Canadian liquor dealers generally received respect within their community. The local French newspapers, for example, proudly reported the number of French Canadians who had received liquor licenses each year. Revocation of one of these licenses could provoke community protests. In 1891, for example, the *Worcester Telegram* reported that "many of the Frenchmen are considerably annoyed because [Adrien] Girardin has been refused a license. His place is just below St. Jean Baptiste Hall, and was quite a rallying place for some of the French people when anything was going on in the hall."[40]

The smaller community of English carpet weavers in South Worcester also appears to have supported three or four saloons. Worcester's Swedes, as will be discussed in Chapter 4, were much less indulgent of the liquor trade. Nevertheless, Swedish saloons began to develop by the late 1880s despite the vociferous opposition of Swedish fundamentalists. The Swedish newspaper *Skandinavia* reflected the more indulgent view of at least one segment of the Swedish community when it asked: "Would it perhaps not be preferable to have our young men spend their time in a Scandinavian saloon as opposed to Irish, German, and American saloons, where they now spend their time?"[41]

Although Worcester saloons drew on ethnic communities and ethnically rooted drinking habits, they also operated in a specifically working-class context.[42] In 1891 a temperance-minded publication complained about the after-work pattern of the city's ethnically diverse work force: "Watch the 'dinner pail' brigade as it files down, at nightfall, from the shops north of Lincoln Square and see how many men and boys drop into the saloons along the north end of Main Street." Whatever the views of its founder and its management, a location near Washburn and Moen's North Works usually proved quite lucrative for the saloonkeeper. Patrick J. Welch's business picked up considerably when he moved his saloon to that area. Washburn and Moen's South Works provided an equally eager clientele. In May 1893 John Reynolds managed to obtain a license in the vicinity of that factory. On the first day of business wireworkers – presumably representing the different ethnic groups that toiled at the South Works – flooded into Reynolds's saloon on the first floor of a Millbury Street tenement and crowded around the bar three-deep.[43]

Drinking, of course, was not limited to the working class. But saloongoing was. Those in the middle and upper classes who did drink – and the numbers were probably considerably smaller than among the working class in the late nineteenth century – generally drank at home, private clubs, or expensive hotels. At the exclusive Worcester Club, members apparently formed a "yellow label club" through which they purchased liquor as a group. Similarly, the *Worcester Daily Times* noted that the "rich scions of nobility" who are "not seen at a public bar . . . have the good stuff at home."[44]

Working-class dominance of public drinking places produced a corresponding working-class predominance among those arrested for public drunkenness. The published Worcester police statistics do not break down drunkenness arrests by occupation, but they do report all arrests by occupation. From these figures it is possible at least to infer that unskilled laborers made up a disproportionate number of those arrested for excessive drinking. During years in which drunkenness arrests went up, arrests of laborers always increased at a much faster rate than those of other occupational groups.[45] The same pattern appears in other criminal and drunkenness statistics. In an 1881 Bureau of Statistics of Labor study of Massachusetts "criminals," laborers were three times as likely to be excessive drinkers as clerks and only one-third as likely to be total abstainers. Similarly, of those arrested for drunkenness in Worcester during June 1880, who could be located in that year's *Worcester Directory*, almost three-quarters held unskilled or semiskilled jobs.[46] In part, this occupational profile helps to explain the Irish dominance of those arrested for drunkenness. The Irish were particularly concentrated in jobs – especially manual, outdoor labor, and transport – that allowed and encouraged heavy drinking. Although heavy drinking and saloongoing were not necessarily equivalent, it seems likely that many of those arrested for public drunkenness were also regular saloon patrons.

Not only did the saloons draw a largely working-class clientele, they also possessed a "working-class" management. While saloonkeepers were by definition small-business people, they should not be automatically assigned to a "middle-class" category. In the late nineteenth century, at least, Worcester saloonkeepers seem to have shown strong ties to, and identification with, their working-class customers. The social origins of the saloonkeepers provide one clue. Of forty-seven saloonkeepers in 1900 who were traced back ten years in the *Worcester Directory*, thirteen were already saloonkeepers and four were bartenders. But of the thirty-one not in the drink trade in 1890, more than two-thirds held blue-collar positions. Saloonkeepers in 1880 and 1918 shared these humble origins. For example, Michael Murphy, an overweight, clean-shaven, and unmarried Green Street saloonkeeper known to his patrons as "Father Murphy," began his work life as a laborer. He entered the saloon business in 1874, but left in 1882 to visit Ireland. When he returned to Worcester, he worked in a boot and shoe shop for a few years before returning to the liquor trade.[47]

The occupational world of the saloonkeeper, then, was not particularly distinct from that of the blue-collar worker. And, according to the R. G. Dun and Company records, their economic standing was often only marginally better. Most important, many saloonkeepers demonstrated and preserved their working-class ties by living in the same neighborhood as their saloon. In 1880 half of the city's saloonkeepers lived in the same building as their saloon or next door; 90 percent lived within a half mile. In addition, those saloonkeepers who shared their dwelling with other families almost invariably lived alongside blue-collar workers and their families. The native-American saloonkeepers offered the only partial exception to this rule. However, the working-class links of the saloonkeepers began to wane very gradually with growing affluence. By 1900, for example, less than one-eighth lived at the same address or next door, but three-quarters lived within a half mile of their saloon.[48] Whether or not the late nineteenth century Worcester saloonkeeper was a member of the working class, he was part of a working-class community.

The workingman's club

What explains the strong ties between the working class and the saloon? Most simply, it effectively met the needs of workers. "The saloon, in relation to the wage-earning classes in America," noted Walter Wyckoff, who had studied it firsthand, "is an organ of high development, adapting itself with singular perfectness to its functions in catering in a hundred ways to the social and political needs of men." Public toilets, food, warmth, clean water, meeting space, check-cashing services, newspapers – often otherwise unavailable to workers in the late nineteenth century city – could be found free of charge in the saloon. Often the saloon served as a communications center, a place where workers picked up their mail, heard the local political gossip, or learned of openings in their trade.[49]

Different types of saloons emphasized different features and functions. The "occupational saloon," which drew on customers from a particular trade or factory, for example, promoted its free lunch and its check-cashing services. Ethnic saloons, which attracted more of an evening business, provided a center for such immigrant communal celebrations as weddings and holidays as well as a meeting place for fraternal orders and gangs. The neighborhood saloon might attract a local multiethnic working-class crowd and provide a constituency for small-time politicians.[50] Not all saloons fit neatly into these categories. Some Worcester saloons could be simultaneously "neighborhood," "occupational," and "ethnic." For example, Michael Taylor, a former English carpet weaver, located his saloon on Cambridge Street in the midst of fellow countrymen who worked in the nearby carpet mills.

The utilitarian services of these different types of saloons only partially explain the saloon's attraction to its working-class patrons. More fundamentally, the saloon flourished because of its social and recreational appeal. Social reformers and early sociologists who entered the saloon to "ascertain the secret of its hold" upon the workingman invariably found – often to their surprise – that it was "man's social nature" and his "craving for companionship," rather than a desire for strong drink, that led him to the saloon. Almost three-quarters of 540 people arrested for drunkenness in Boston around 1907 told an inquiring Columbia University graduate student that their "special reason for drinking" was "social." Only 8 percent attributed it to a "taste for drink." Without the benefit of graduate training, a seventy-year-old Irish Fall River worker similarly explained the social and recreational nature of the saloon: "In England, where I was reared, the habit was for a man, when he drew his pay every Saturday night, to go in and enjoy himself. He was not a drunkard; neither do I consider the people of Fall River drunkards. . . . They go in and get their glass of beer as they do in the old country."[51]

The saloonkeeper presided over and fostered this atmosphere of good-hearted, informal socializing. "As a rule," observed the author of the locally published *Saloon Keeper's Companion,* "the saloonkeeper is a jolly, easy going fellow, free with his money." Even Worcester temperance advocate Richard O'Flynn, with his hatred for the "vendors of the deadly cup," found the word "genial" the most appropriate to describe Worcester's rum sellers when he wrote profiles of them: Michael J. Leach was "a genial, generous man"; William Molloy, "a genial, warm hearted man, harmless in all save his calling"; and William H. Foley, "full of fun – always ready with a pleasant anecdote or story." Similarly, when *Light,* a Worcester society weekly, complained in 1890 of "loud and boisterous laughter, obscene pleasantries and curses," it also hinted at the cheerful sociability that prevailed in Worcester saloons.[52]

Upper- and middle-class hostility to the saloongoer's "boisterous laughter" is hardly surprising since these men and women were probably the butts of barroom humor. *The Saloon Keeper's Companion* provided Worcester bar owners with about fifty pages of jokes and stories with which to amuse their customers. The jokes most often ridicule hypocritical temperance advocates, dishonest police and politicians, unsophisticated and easily fooled clergy and churchgoers, and stupid or pompous judges.[53]

Singing, like joke- and storytelling, was an important part of the informal socializing that formed the core of saloon life. In other cities saloons offered more formal entertainment, but in Worcester the singing was usually informal and participatory. The Massachusetts Bureau of Statistics of Labor denounced the saloongoer's music as "the ribald song of fellow drunkards." But George Ade, a Chicago columnist who regularly frequented that city's saloons in the 1890s, discerned a more complex pattern. He thought songs about "dear old Mother" were most popular, followed by songs about "the poor girl who was tempted and who either fell or did not fall." Third most popular were songs about "the organized workingmen and their nobility of character as compared with millionaire employers."[54]

In Worcester saloons ethnic music probably accompanied the products of Tin Pan Alley. John C. Blos called his German saloon on Mechanic Street Orchestrion Hall, and his advertisements featured a picture of that elaborate musical device. Patrick Curran, the Irish proprietor of a saloon known as the Little House Round the Corner, was "fond of story and song," and "being a very good comic singer, he attracted many of the gay spirits to his place." No doubt the patrons at the Little House Round the Corner as well as Worcester's numerous other Irish bars drew on the rich Irish-American musical heritage. In the late nineteenth century, according to historian Michael Gordon, Irish Americans favored laments about "loved ones still in Ireland" and "specific rural scenes," as well as "evocative nationalist verses like Collins's 'Defiant Still.'" All these songs, Gordon points out, "were fundamentally political because they spoke of events and sentiments inseparable from a historical context shaped by English and Anglo-Saxon rule."[55]

The singing and storytelling of Worcester barrooms was undoubtedly punctuated by conversations about sports. *The Saloon Keeper's Companion* considered sports rules and the results of major sporting contests as essential knowledge for barkeepers. Patrick Ryan decorated his Mechanic Street saloon "with pictures of pugilists, sprinters, and clogdancers." Sometimes a popular local fighter, like Jack Gray, William H. Foley, or Robert Mahagan, might retire from the ring to become a saloonkeeper, placing his "well-worn boxing gloves" on "the shelf behind the bar" as a reminder of more glorious days. Other saloonkeepers, like Michael Kelley, gained some fame for their intimacy with sporting heroes like John L. Sullivan, whose picture adorned the walls of many, if not most, 1890s saloons.[56]

Prizefighting was illegal in nineteenth century Massachusetts, and, indeed, the saloon often championed the shadier or, at least, less socially approved side of sports. Gambling, whether on cards, billiards, horse races, or sports matches, enlivened many Worcester saloons. In the 1870s those arrested for gambling violations also often found themselves in trouble for illegal liquor sales. Even cockfighting, ostensibly eradicated much earlier in the nineteenth century, enjoyed the patronage of Worcester saloonkeepers and their customers. In 1886, for example, Washington Square saloonkeeper Tim Delaney reportedly led Worcester "sports" to Cherry Valley for cockfights each Sunday morning. The same secluded spot also furnished a locale for illicit prizefights.[57]

For all its importance as a social center, the saloon was not the only recreational outlet for workers in Worcester and other industrial cities. "In this town, as in all others," one worker told the Bureau of Statistics of Labor in 1870, "there is a great difference in the habits and tastes of the working classes." Even the small group who answered a bureau questionnaire on recreation that year amply demonstrated this diversity. Their pursuits included dancing, walking, gardening, skating, ball and billiard playing, bowling, attending minstrel shows and concerts, listening to lectures, and visiting lodge and union halls and reading rooms. Yet, despite this variety of pursuits, probably only the church and the home rivaled the saloon as working-class social centers. Both, however, had important limitations. Even those workers who owned homes usually lacked the space or furniture to accommodate large numbers of visitors. The homes of the unskilled and the immigrant lacked space not only for socializing but often for the needs of everyday life. Tenements in Fall River, complained a local union official in 1883, "have two bedrooms and a kitchen . . . and if a friend comes in they have got to meet him there. . . . There is no comfort at all. If a man had a little room where he could go and read his paper and be comfortable, I think he would be more likely to stay at home instead of going abroad to seek other kinds of enjoyment." A Worcester reformer reached the same conclusion some years later: "A large number of people, men and boys particularly, cannot possibly find or make this reasonable social life in the lodging house or in such a home as falls to their lot."[58]

Lodging-house life provided a particularly strong incentive to seek, as a Cambridge printer put it in 1883, "amusement in public places, in the billiard room, and in the saloon." "In the boarding house," he explained, "there is nothing to entertain or to cheer him; seldom any pictures, or books, or female companionship of the proper kind; and in order to gratify his social faculties he frequently seeks pleasure in the forms in which it is met with in the saloon." In late nineteenth century Worcester the majority of immigrant Irishmen in their early twenties were boarders.[59] And the city's boardinghouse district was within easy walking distance of its largest concentration of saloons.

Single workingmen and -women who lived at home rather than at a boardinghouse faced a different, but related, problem: socializing under the watchful gaze of their parents. This was particularly difficult for Worcester's second-generation Irish males, who did not marry until age thirty-one on the average. Drinking and the saloon seem to have had a central place in their "bachelor" subculture, as it did in Ireland. It is not surprising, then, that relatively young, single males were overrepresented among those arrested for drunkenness.[60]

As a social and cultural force the church undoubtedly had a greater importance than the saloon, particularly for women and fundamentalist Protestants. Nevertheless, many noted its failure to compete effectively with the saloon for the worker's recreational time. "The church doors," complained Worcester reformer U. Waldo Cutler, "are closed except an hour or two on one evening a week, when the 'social meeting' is in progress, and even if these people were to force their way in, the churches would not know how to adapt themselves to their needs." Such complaints, of course, reflect more on the native Protestant churches than on their immigrant, and usually Catholic, counterparts. One manufacturer explained to the Bureau of Statistics of Labor in 1870 that only the Catholics in his community attended services regularly: "The Catholic Church is democratic; the Protestant Church is too aristocratic for the clothes they (the working people) are able to wear." Even the immigrant churches did not reach all their potential parishioners. Only 46 to 66 percent of New York Catholics attended church on Sundays in the 1860s. Moreover, even regular churchgoers saw the saloon as filling recreational needs that were ignored at the church. Some saloongoers, columnist George Ade writes with an exaggeration born of nostalgia, found the church "about as cheerful as a mausoleum while the place on the corner reeked with the kind of unrestrained gayety which has been in partnership with original sin since the beginning of history."[61]

For these reasons, the saloon remained the axis of the recreational world for large numbers of working-class men. One Saturday night in December 1883, several temperance advocates canvassed fifteen saloons between 6 and 10 P.M. and counted 1,832 patrons, "mostly young men." Thus, even if the city's other ninety-three legal drinking places were only half as popular as these, more than 7,500 Worcesterites would have stopped at the saloon that night – a significant percentage of the city's 30,000 males and easily a majority of its young working-class males.[62]

The culture of the saloon

For many Worcester workers the saloon offered a variety of attractive activities from social services to informal socializing to singing and gambling. But did the late nineteenth century saloon hold any significance beyond its role as a social service and recreational center? Does the nature of the late nineteenth century saloon suggest anything about the central values and beliefs of Worcester workers? Such cultural analysis is inevitably difficult and speculative, particularly in the absence of the firsthand observations that are the stock-in-trade of the cultural anthropologist. Such problems are compounded here because of the diversity of types of saloons (ethnic, neighborhood, and occupational), the diversity of saloongoers (Irish, French Canadians, English, and Yankees; first- and second-generation immigrants; skilled and unskilled), and the changing nature of the saloon, which was undergoing a process of commercialization through which it distinguished itself from the kitchen groggeries that had preceded it. No single set of generalizations can do justice to the range of experiences, social styles, and cultural meanings embodied in the late nineteenth century saloon. Nevertheless, based on the limited available evidence, it does seem possible to argue that many Worcester saloons of the late nineteenth century reflected and reinforced a value system very much different from that which governed the dominant industrial, market, and social relations of that era.

Many observers trumpeted the saloon as "the rooster-crow of the spirit of democracy." It was, proclaimed the Reverend George L. McNutt, "the one democratic club in American life," the "great democratic social settlement." Of course, the saloon was much less open and democratic in fact than these commentators would have us believe. Most saloons at least informally barred members of the "wrong" sex, ethnic group, race, neighborhood, or occupation. Still, the commentators were partially right; the saloon was actually a "democracy" of sorts – an *internal* democracy where all who could safely enter received equal treatment and respect. An ethic of mutuality and reciprocity that differed from the market exchange mentality of the dominant society prevailed within the barroom.[63] Although collective and cooperative social relations were not the exclusive property of the immigrant working class, the saloon was one of the few late nineteenth century institutions that publicly and symbolically celebrated these alternative values.

Some understanding of the potential role of drink and the saloon in fostering this ethic of reciprocity and mutuality can be gained by looking at rural Ireland, the birthplace of many Worcester saloon patrons. "Drinking together," notes anthropologist Conrad Arensberg, "is the traditional reaffirmation of solidarity and equality among males" in Ireland. The most important drink custom for fostering such sentiments was "treating" – "a social law in Catholic Ireland enforced with all the vigour of a Coercion Act," according to one commentator. "If a man happens to be in an inn or public-house alone, and if any of his acquaintances come in, no matter how many, it is his duty to 'stand,' that is, to invite them to drink and pay for all they take. . . . It is a deadly insult to refuse to take a drink from a man, unless an elaborate explanation and apology be given and accepted."[64] Treating thus provided the nineteenth-century Irishman with a crucial means of declaring his solidarity and equality with his kin and neighbors.

These drink rituals were not an isolated sphere of Irish life; they were firmly embedded in a reciprocal life-style that governed at least some social relationships in the Irish countryside. Although the Irish rural economy was subject to external, exploitative, colonial rule, local social and economic relations were often based on a system of mutual rights and obligations rather than a rationalized market of monetary exchange. Helping a neighbor with a house-raising, for example, was often part of that local system of mutual obligation, which existed outside of the realm of direct cash exchange. The liberal provision of liquor at such an event offered a means of reciprocating, of symbolizing one's acceptance of the mutuality, friendliness, and communality on which it was based. A similar mentality lay behind the American work rituals of the eighteenth century and early nineteenth, such as the "chopping frolic," where it was "the practice to *treat* all who came to work." According to Robert Bales, when Irish farmers aided one another or the local gentry with harvesting, the only acceptable "payment" was the abundant provision of liquor, because "it had no utilitarian taint, but indicated good will and friendship, and because it was not in any exact sense 'payment in full,' but implied a continued state of mutual obligation."[65]

The precise connection between these reciprocal Irish drink customs and the rituals of Worcester saloons is difficult to demonstrate. Even less certain is how the prior background of other Worcester workers shaped their saloon behavior. What is striking, however, is the degree to which reciprocal modes – similar to those found in rural Ireland – seem to have operated within the new context of the ethnic working-class saloon. The most persuasive evidence of these modes is found in what the Massachusetts Bureau of Statistics of Labor called "the prevailing custom of treating." Observers as diverse as Upton Sinclair, Jack London, Thorstein

Veblen, and the Anti-Saloon League cited the centrality of treating in the saloon of the late nineteenth and early twentieth centuries. "Here in noisy carousal," commented an 1871 observer, "the 'treat' goes round, the poor vanity of the free-hearted meets its reward, the mean man is scorned."[66]

These treating rituals embodied a resistance of sorts to the transformation of social relationships into "commodities" – a means of preserving reciprocal modes of social interaction within a capitalist world. Jack London, for example, explained his realization of the non-economic mutuality behind treating: "I had achieved a concept. Money no longer counted. It was comradeship that counted." This ethic was probably strongest in the least commercialized saloons and drink places. Patronage of the shebeen, for example, rested on larger notions of communal obligation for the well-being of widows. Similarly, when Worcester City Marshal Drennan caught John Mehan illegally serving liquor on a Sunday in 1880, Mehan simply explained that "he was *treating* some friends and a greenhorn (girl) named Leonard." Bridget McCarthy offered precisely the same explanation for the illegal liquor trade going on in her house.[67] In a sense, these may not have been alibis: The system of treating was based on an ethic of mutuality that was simply not reducible to the sort of market exchange that the police sought as proof of illegal liquor sales.

Of course, this was only partially true. The saloon was an increasingly commercial institution and alcohol was a commodity to be bought and sold. Veblen even explained treating as a working-class variant of "conspicuous consumption." Temperance reformers complained that saloonkeepers manipulated "hospitality" and the "social instinct" to their own economic advantage. In an editorial calling "treating" the "curse of this age in the U.S." a Worcester Catholic temperance newspaper described what it saw as the saloonkeeper's manipulation: "If two men not previously acquainted . . . come into his bar-room together . . . he introduces them and sets the ball rolling. Two or three rounds of drink are not enough for him. He is getting the money. So he produces the dice box and proposes 'to shake' for the drinks. He never lets up as long as his customers can stand on their feet and there is any money in sight."[68]

Although few saloonkeepers so baldly "traded" on the "social instinct," saloongoers did increasingly enact their reciprocal treating rituals within the commercialized confines of the saloon. Despite the contradiction, the prevalence and persistence of the custom points to a continuing predilection for reciprocal forms of social interaction. Itself a product of a commercializing society, the saloon became a refuge for values implicitly hostile to such a society.

As "a norm of equality and solidarity," treating rituals implied resistance to individualism as well as acquisitiveness. Indeed, the whole saloongoing experience affirmed communal over individualistic and privatistic values. After 1800, historian W. J. Rorabaugh notes, "drinking in groups . . . became a symbol of egalitarianism. All men were equal before the bottle." Inebriation further encouraged the breaking down of social barriers.[69] For some, to be sure, saloongoing was a solitary experience, but for most it was a group activity. It was a way of carousing with friends, neighbors, and fellow workers whom one could not (or should not) bring into the home. And because such socializing took place outside the home, it was more of a public occasion, and therefore open to a much wider group than the kinfolk that one might normally bring into the home. More than just the size of the gathering, the nature of the event – the drinking, singing, talking, card playing, billiard shooting – brought workers together for a collective public sharing of their recreation. As such, the saloon rejected the developing individualistic, privatistic, and family-centered values of the dominant society.

The saloon clashed with the values of industrial America not just in its communality and mutuality but also in the unwillingness of some patrons to endorse fully the work ethic of that society. Critics of drinking frequently lumped together the very rich and the very poor as unproductive classes "most exposed to the temptation of intemperate drinking." Employers, beginning in Ichabod Washburn's day, depicted drinking as a major threat to steady work habits. Thus, the Washburn and Moen Wire Manufacturing Company petitioned against saloons in the vicinity of their North Works because "the opportunities for slipping into a dram shop either on the way to work or from work, make it so much easier for the men to squander their wages which means a lessening of their efficiency for us."[70]

Not only did drinking and the squandering of wages lead to a loss of work efficiency; it also made it difficult for workers to move ahead in socially approved ways. Temperance advocates repeatedly pointed out that the money spent on drink might instead go toward "a modest working class home." The Worcester Five Cents Savings Bank, "the poor man's bank," claimed a one-third increase in local deposits during one no-license year. "It cannot be emphasized too strongly," Stephan Thernstrom writes in his study of nineteenth-century social mobility, "that the real estate holdings and savings accounts of Newburyport laborers depended on underconsumption. . . . A recreational luxury like drinking, for example, was out of the question."[71] Moreover, it was the sober and thrifty worker who might win the approval of his employer or learn new skills and advance occupationally. It was perhaps no accident that unskilled workers predominated among those arrested for drunkenness. Drinking and saloongoing could represent a rejection – albeit not an articulated rejection – of the dominant social mobility ideology of nineteenth-century America.

The rejection of the success ideal was far from total. Ironically, saloonkeeping was the most accessible means of upward social mobility for immigrants. More than three-quarters of Worcester's Irish immigrants who had become small proprietors by 1900 were engaged in some aspect of the liquor trade. Still, even these exemplars of immigrant success were not always models of acquisitive individualism, as the R. G. Dun and Company reports demonstrate. Arguably, then, the saloon culture partook of a larger suspicion of materialism and ambition that was common among many immigrant groups, particularly the Irish. As Timothy J. Meagher points out in his study of the Worcester Irish, even Catholic clergy like the Reverend John J. McCoy and the Reverend Thomas Conaty, "who enthusiastically celebrated American opportunity before assemblies of Catholic young men, frequently blasted 'wild ambition' and praised resignation to low status in their Sunday pulpits." Material success was often depicted as a threat to the maintenance of more important ethnic, religious, and spiritual values.[72]

Not only did the saloongoers implicitly question and sometimes explicitly reject the goals and values of industrial society, such as homeownership, thrift, social mobility, and punctuality; they also often found themselves in direct legal conflict with the police authorities. Most commonly, this happened through public drunkenness, by far the most common late nineteenth century "crime" – an offense that accounted for approximately 60 percent of all arrests in Worcester in these years. Moreover, patrons sometimes joined with saloonkeepers in such illegal pursuits as gambling, prizefighting, and cockfighting. Nineteenth century saloon patrons thus found themselves part of a culture that operated outside of, if not against, the formal legal system.

Finally, and in a rather complex way, saloon culture increasingly clashed with the dominant culture because it segregated leisure by gender in a society in which family-centered recreation was becoming the middle-class norm. Women temperance advocates, argues a recent historian, sought "to curb the self-assertive, boisterous masculinity of the saloon, to support and protect the family, and to return the husband – the immigrant workingman in particular – to the home." "The purpose of prohibition," agrees another historian, "was to protect the values sheltered by the American nuclear family."[73]

This analysis should not imply that working-class women did not drink. As suggested previously, women were present in – and often ran – the kitchen dives that predominated earlier in the nineteenth century. Even after the emergence of the saloon as a spatially distinct and usually male institution, many immigrant working-class women continued to drink. One grim indicator of this pattern comes from the statistics on alcohol-related deaths. Among the Irish, at least, male and female rates in the late nineteenth century are remarkably close.[74] Most commonly, female drinking seems to have taken place at home. A study of Boston's South End in the 1890s notes that although "women . . . are forbidden by police regulation to patronize the bar-rooms," the "liquor habit . . . is practically universal among both men and women."[75]

Some women – German and English immigrants, for example – did drink in saloons, but these few exceptions emphasize the character of the saloon as "essentially a male refuge" pervaded by an "aura of freewheeling masculinity." As a historian of Denver saloons observes, "the obsession with virility, with potency, with body building, with sports that characterized turn-of-the-century America permeated the saloon." In this context, hard drinking was an expression of both "hospitality and manliness." Significantly, even where women entered the saloon, they seem to have been excluded from "treating," which according to one commentator served as a "ritual of masculine renewal."[76]

In its maleness and gender segregation, the saloon both challenged and affirmed the dominant culture. On the one hand, the saloon was a male institution in an era when the middle-class ideal was increasingly that of family-centered leisure. On the other hand, both the saloon and the bourgeois family mandated subservient roles for women. Thus, whereas saloongoers apparently departed from some of the basic values of industrial America, they nevertheless shared some of its deepest patriarchal assumptions.

In general, however, the saloon stood outside the dominant cultural values of the late nineteenth century, even if neither the saloon nor its patrons mounted an organized or disciplined challenge to those values. In Raymond Williams's terms, the culture of the saloon was "alternative," that of "someone who simply finds a different way to live and wishes to be left alone with it," rather than "oppositional," that of "someone who finds a different way to live and wants to change society in its light." Thus, Worcester saloongoers may have shared the "conservative and defensive culture" that John Bodnar finds among Slavic-American industrial workers. Such a culture, Bodnar argues, was a synthesis of earlier peasant values with the exigencies of survival in urban, industrial, capitalist America. Among the dimensions of this culture were limited occupational mobility, traditional family ties, retention of ethnic culture, antimaterialism, and collectivism. Unlike British workers, who responded to industrialization with class combativity, Bodnar's Slavic workers – and Worcester saloongoers – adopted a conservative, defensive posture as the best means of coping with the new economic order.[77]

The nineteenth-century ethnic working-class saloon, then, was a form of both accommodation and resistance to the capitalist order that workers faced. Unlike a trade union or a socialist party, the saloon did not openly confront or challenge the dominant society, though neither did it embrace the values and practices of that society. Instead, it offered a space in which immigrants could preserve an alternative, reciprocal value system. This was only partially an act of historical preservation, for the saloon was a new institution and, as such, was a creative response by immigrants to the trials of late nineteenth century urban life. The creation of such new, urban working-class styles, note two urban anthropologists, "is a living continuation, an active development and constant reworking of . . . traditions." Workers, they conclude, not only "survive and build the industrial economy, the cities, and transportation networks, but they also create distinctive cultures."[78] The nineteenth-century saloon was one of the central institutions of that distinctive culture.

3 *Immigrant workers and the Fourth of July*

On July 4, 1870, a Massachusetts shoemaker and his family of six celebrated the nation's birthday. It was evidently a welcome break, since the shoemaker normally spent ten hours per day (more than twelve until quite recently) six days a week at a "low stool . . . in the same posture," repeating "the same motions . . . every four or five minutes." Many of his co-workers, he noted, suffered "great pain" from constantly stooping forward and pressing on their stomachs. And of the five legal holidays celebrated in Massachusetts at that time, July Fourth was the only one that fell in the seven-month stretch between Fast Day in early April and Thanksgiving. As befit such an occasion, the shoe worker spent $8 on his family's celebration – his total recreational budget for the year.[1]

What the shoemaker did with his $8 on July 4, 1870, is unknown. But it is unlikely that his activities would have met the approval of the Fall River textile manufacturer who commented that same year about his workers: "I have boasted a good deal about them since our last Fourth of July celebration, when all were clean, well-dressed and orderly; when everything was quiet; when there was a smile on the face of everyone and no one was in liquor."[2] For this manufacturer, July Fourth offered an opportunity to extend the discipline of the workday to the holiday and to affirm the hierarchical arrangements that permitted him to think of his workers as children.

But workers – like the shoemaker – had their own priorities and values. And in Worcester in the last three decades of the nineteenth century, they were able to use the Fourth of July in ways that reflected, in part, their own needs and beliefs and not those of the city's manufacturers. Some engaged in boisterous, public celebrations, which contrasted sharply with the more exclusive and restrained gatherings of the city's middle and upper classes. Even those immigrant workers who pursued more respectable recreation at picnics sponsored by churches or temperance societies generally demonstrated their distinctiveness from their more affluent Yankee neighbors through their attachment to ethnic customs and communities and their collective modes of celebration. Both groups of celebrations suggested a version of the mutual, reciprocal, and collective alternative culture that could also be glimpsed in the saloons of that era. At the same time, however, the form that these celebrations took – usually segregated by ethnic group, religion, and cultural style – revealed deep cultural cleavages within the city's working class and, thus, some of the fundamental limitations of that alternative culture.

The genteel Fourth

In 1878 the *Worcester Evening Gazette* looked back nostalgically to a time when July Fourth "was generally devoted to keeping alive the sentiment of true patriotism." But it added with regret that "this style has gone out of fashion." Such complaints, which echo through Worcester newspaper editorials in the 1870s, imply a "golden age" of July Fourth celebrations, and like most golden ages the reality of this one never matched its later reputation. Nevertheless, early and middle nineteenth century celebrations of the Fourth were more likely to involve communitywide participation, patriotic reflection, and elite leadership than those of the 1870s and later decades. The return of a victorious Union Army from the battles of the Civil War in 1865 provides a particularly dramatic example of the earlier rituals of communal and national affirmation. On the morning of July 4, 1865, 5,000 schoolchildren paraded and showered the soldiers with bouquets of flowers. An afternoon procession of trades and societies represented virtually all segments of Worcester society: manufacturers and workers, natives and immigrants.[3]

Marching in the first division of the procession was Stephen Salisbury III, the thirty-year-old heir to one of the city's largest fortunes. Three years later Salisbury again joined in a civic commemoration of the Fourth, serving as an aide to Colonel A. B. R. Sprague, a local Civil War hero, in the military procession that highlighted the day. Gradually, such an active public role in the city's Independence Day ceremonies became less and less common for leaders of the city's elite like Salisbury. By the early 1870s Salisbury was passing the Fourth quietly with a small number of friends in the more isolated and rural surroundings of northern Worcester County. In 1871, for example, he joined William E. Rice, the treasurer of Washburn and Moen, the city's largest manufacturing concern, in a "dog cart" ride to Mount Wachusett, where he spent four days. "Very quiet, but an appropriate day," he noted in his diary on the Fourth: "Walked in morning and drove in afternoon."[4]

At first, only the wealthy like Salisbury could afford to retreat from the heat, noise, and immigrant masses of the city to what one newspaper called "the various high toned watering places." By the 1880s and 1890s, however, middle-class Worcesterites – aided by larger salaries and cheaper and more abundant transportation – were also leaving the city in growing numbers on the Fourth. The newspaper lists of those "At Summer Resorts" now included clerks, insurance agents, and small-business men as well as manufacturers and bank presidents. The retreat from the city and the avoidance of public celebration had become so acceptable that even the mayor spent July 4, 1887, at his farm in nearby Leicester, where he dispensed lemonade to visiting constituents.[5]

Those members of the middle and upper classes who remained within the city limits on the Fourth also sought out exclusivity, privacy, and refinement, rather than public commemoration. As early as July 4, 1870, the *Worcester Evening Gazette* noticed "among the quiet people . . . a growing disposition to utilize the day by picnics and social gatherings." On July 4, 1884, for example, James Draper invited two hundred friends and fellow members of the Massachusetts Grange to his fifteen-acre estate. After a morning spent at croquet, quoits, swings, baseball, tenpins, and target practice, the guests sat down for a formal meal in the storeroom of Draper's drainpipe works, which was "tastefully decorated" for the occasion. After lunch William H. Earle, a seed merchant, spoke on his two-month trip to Florida, and lawyer Silas A. Burgess discoursed on "Women's True Sphere."[6]

While some withdrew to the private picnic on the Fourth, others retired to the private club. Worcester's Sportsmen's Club, apparently a favorite of rich young men, held annual shooting matches and gatherings on the Fourth during the 1870s and 1880s. The number of such exclusive private clubs grew in the 1880s and 1890s as Worcester's wealthy, like the social elite of other cities, took on some characteristics of a "caste." On July 4, 1891, for example, members of the city's social elite might lunch at the Worcester Club and then play tennis at the Quinsigamond Boat Club. They might also drop by the Worcester Continentals' open house, a slightly more "democratic" affair than lunch at the Worcester Club, which limited its membership to the city's wealthiest families. Those signing the Continentals' guest book on the Fourth in the 1880s and 1890s included large numbers of clerks and small-business men as well as manufacturers, lawyers, and city officials – but very few blue-collar workers.[7]

The importance of organizations like the Worcester Continentals, whose members dressed in the uniforms of *officers* of the Continental Army of 1776, suggests that the wealthy and the middle class did not abandon their patriotism along with their public commemorations of the Fourth. To the contrary, the late nineteenth century saw a growth in patriotic, historical, and genealogical societies. But it was an exclusive patriotism to be pursued within the more restricted confines of the American Antiquarian Society or the local branches of the Sons and Daughters of the American Revolution.[8]

Not all middle- and upper-class Worcesterites avoided public, active, or ritualistic forms of celebration. Such special occasions as the Centennial in 1876 or the Columbian Year of 1892 might lead to a revival of more formal parades and commemorations with elite participation and sponsorship.[9] In addition, large sporting events – particularly trotting races and boating regattas – attracted a mixed crowd. But more affluent patrons maintained their distance from the rabble by watching the races from their carriages instead of sitting in the grandstand or standing on the edge of the lake. Overall, upper- and middle-class July Fourth celebrations acquired a predominantly private and exclusive character: The formal dinner party, the game of croquet or lawn tennis, the social visit, the private picnic, the lunch at the club, the piano recital, and the ramble in the country became the preferred ways to spend Independence Day.[10]

Working-class holidays and the industrial calendar

The withdrawal of Worcester's middle and upper classes from public commemorations of the Fourth reflected not simply the rupturing of older civic ties and obligations in a rapidly growing and increasingly divided immigrant industrial city and the availability of transportation to suburban resorts but also the declining significance of the Fourth as a middle-class summer holiday. By the late nineteenth century, summer vacations were becoming common for white-collar workers, and they offered more ample opportunities for summertime relaxing. For blue-collar workers, most of whom did not win summer vacations until the 1940s, July Fourth existed within a very different context and thus loomed much larger in summertime plans.[11]

An 1887 controversy over the newly established holiday of Labor Day revealed these differing class attitudes toward summer holidays. When the *Worcester Telegram* complained that Labor Day came at an inopportune time because most people were just returning from vacation, the pro-labor *Worcester Daily Times* retorted: "The freshness of this editor is amusing. The vast majority of workingmen and women of this community don't have summer vacations. They are not to be found at the seaside or the mountain retreat. The best most of them can do is to go on one of the cheap excursions for a day in mid-Summer. The men who have vacations are the professional people, the clerks, merchants, traders, and others who would frown if you ranked them as labor people." For workers, even a single day off for a summer excursion or picnic might require defiance of their employers. In July 1886, for example, the popularity of the Sacred Heart parish picnic forced South Worcester millowners to close unexpectedly for the day. Similarly, in June 1892 when foremen at the Royal Worcester Corset Company refused to let female workers leave their sewing machines to watch a circus parade, the women responded by sabotaging production for the rest of the day. As a result, one of the women reported triumphantly, the front office ordered the foremen "to let us out to see the parade next time we wanted."[12]

Probably more common than summer holidays won through disobedience or sabotage were those dispensed by employers as part of a paternalist labor policy. Company-sponsored summer outings could offer a break from factory discipline while also affirming the power relations that lay behind that discipline. In 1895 Matthew Whittall treated 800 employees of his carpet company to a summer picnic at Lake Quinsigamond so that they could celebrate his son's (and heir's) twenty-first birthday.[13]

Despite the combination of benevolence and disobedience, the number of holidays remained rather small. "It would be well to have more holidays," a Massachusetts machinist argued in 1871, "so that the laboring people could escape, by a change of air and scenery, the continual monotony of toil." This "continual monotony of toil" was probably felt most strongly by immigrant workers who often arrived in industrial Worcester directly from more rural societies in which an agricultural and religious calendar governed the work year. Their traditional holidays, fairs, and festivities often clashed directly with an American and industrial calendar. While French Canadians considered January First "the most joyous day in the year," it was not a legal holiday in Massachusetts until around 1920. As a result, in late nineteenth century Worcester "the French-speaking man thought it a crime to work on New Years when all his compatriots were celebrating," and many seem to have absented themselves from work to attend public and family parties.[14]

In general, however, traditional festivities could not be maintained unchanged in the face of new work rules and economic necessity. "Midsummer Day," the local Swedish newspaper, *Worcester Veckoblad*, reported on June 24, 1887, "will not be celebrated as it is at home, since everyone is forced to work." Similarly, in 1880 the local French-Canadian press pointed to the high cost of transportation and the abundance of work in Worcester to explain the reluctance of Worcester French Canadians to journey to Quebec for their national feast day, St. Jean Baptiste Day. Sometimes, traditional cultural authorities might even abet the process of change. In 1870, for example, the Reverend J. B. Primeau urged his French-Catholic parishioners to keep working on St. Jean Baptiste Day and contribute their wages to the building of a new church.[15]

Most immigrant groups in Worcester adapted their traditional holidays to an urban and industrial environment rather than entirely abandon them. Worcester's Irish community transformed the "fairs," which had figured so prominently in Irish rural and agricultural life, into church fund raisers. "Only a few sheaves of wheat on the walls or their titles," writes historian Timothy J. Meagher of such celebrations, as the St. Peter's Parish Harvest Fair of 1885 "perpetrated the fiction that these affairs had any links to agriculture." At the Norton Company with a predominantly Swedish work force and a partially Swedish management, Midsummer Day became the equivalent of the company picnic – a benefit dispensed by a paternalist management. Swedish workers from other plants took the expedient of joining their families at Midsummer Day gatherings in the early evening after they had finished work, and those who worked the night shift at the wire mills attended during the day.[16]

Attending a picnic after ten or twelve hours in a wire mill and no sleep was not exactly the same as the free-spirited and all-night revelry that marked Midsummer celebrations in Sweden. Thus, in the context of an exacting industrial and American work calendar, Worcester's immigrants attached particular importance to the few legal holidays provided to them – especially the single summer holiday of July Fourth. Indeed, as one New York City Irish political leader recognized, the recreational significance of the Fourth resulted from the broader transformation of work and leisure under the impact of industrial capitalism. "The gloomy, churlish, money-worshipping, all-pervading spirit of the age," Mike Walsh wrote at midcentury, "has swept all the poetry of life out of the poor man's sphere. . . . Ballad-singing, street dancing, tumbling, public games, all are either prohibited or discountenanced, so that Fourth of July and election sports alone remain."[17] If, as Walsh tells us, July Fourth celebrations were a form of working-class poetry, what did these poems express? The rest of this chapter takes up this question by describing the variety of working-class July Fourth festivities in late nineteenth century Worcester and by speculating on their cultural meanings.

Chasing the greased pig: the boisterous Fourth

In 1874 the *Worcester Daily Press* called July Fourth the "most abused as well as the most celebrated day of the year." Although it conceded that some devoted the day to what it termed "legitimate recreation," it decried the large number of presumably working-class Worcesterites who had "desecrated" Independence Day with the "sound of the fish-horn," the chasing of shaved and lubricated pigs, the climbing of greased poles, and various sack and wheelbarrow races. "Most disgraceful," according to the newspaper, was that "one of the most prominent features of an American holiday is the marked tendency of so many persons to get gloriously drunk."[18]

The newspapers provided only sketchy descriptions of these popular and unstructured celebrations, but they devoted a good deal of attention to what they saw as their inevitable outcome: fights and drunkenness. Almost ritualistically, the local press intoned against those who spent the Fourth partaking "recklessly of stimulants," filling up "with liquid disturbance," indulging in "brutish celebration," and joining in "rum rows."[19] Such comments reflect pro-temperance and anti-immigrant biases, but the newspapers' perceptions of the centrality of drinking to July Fourth celebrations do find objective confirmation in the court and police records.

Though Worcester police both made vigorous efforts to suppress illegal sales of what the newpapers called "liquid patriotism" and tended to treat Independence Day inebriates with leniency, drunkenness arrests invariably shot up on July Fourth. They ran about three times the daily average in the early 1870s and about two and a half times in the early 1880s. This heavy volume of July Fourth drinking and drunkenness suggests that workers who remained sober on most occasions may have seen the Fourth as an opportunity for extravagant and exuberant celebrating – a momentary release from the burdens of the workaday world. The social profile of those arrested on the Fourth supports this interpretation. Given the prevailing class and ethnic biases of the legal system, it is not surprising that virtually all those arrested held blue-collar jobs and that most were Irish along with a handful of French Canadians and native Americans and an even smaller number of Swedes. What is more revealing is to compare Fourth of July drunkenness arrests with those for other days. Skilled workers seem to have been almost twice as likely to be picked up for drunkenness on the Fourth as on other days. Moreover, those facing the district court judge on July fifth appear to have been more likely to be older and married than on other mornings of the year.[20]

The drunkenness data not only indicate that even stable, settled, and skilled workers joined in July Fourth revelry; they also hint at the location of this boisterous celebrating. A major reason why middle- and upper-class drinkers were unlikely to be arrested for drunkenness on the Fourth – and, interestingly, they appear to have been less vulnerable on that day than on others – was that their celebrations took place in private homes, clubs, or yards. Lacking access to enclosed and ample private spaces, working people, however, drank and celebrated on the streets and in empty lots and enclosed fields, where they were especially susceptible to arrest. Although newspaper accounts often imply that drunkenness and brawling were the entirety of working-class holiday celebrations, these activities probably represented only the excesses of a *public* and collective form of celebrating, which involved not only drinking and fighting but also active games, lively socializing, noisemaking and fireworks, singing and dancing, and even relaxed talking. It was the prevalence of such public socializing among the immigrant working class that provoked a local nativist newspaper to complain in 1892 of people "who herd together on doorsteps, street corners, [in] public parks or in saloons."[21]

The use of the public streets as a venue for Independence Day celebrating was particularly common on the night before the Fourth. Increasingly in the late nineteenth century, crowds gathered both downtown and in working-class neighborhoods for an all-night carnival of noisemaking and fireworks. Despite repeated efforts by the police to keep the city quiet until 4 A.M. on the Fourth, crowds assembled as early as 8 P.M. the previous night to bang drums, blow tin horns, shoot powder pistols, and set off cannon crackers and torpedoes.[22]

The drunkenness and rowdiness of July Fourth crowds can be interpreted as a rejection of, or release from, the discipline and orderliness that Worcester workers faced on the job, but it is often difficult to assign it a more precise meaning. However, the gaiety and abandon of at least some July Fourth crowds apparently reflected not just a holiday rejection of the hierarchy and discipline of everyday life but also a hostility toward the men who benefited most from that hierarchy and discipline. Throughout the 1880s and 1890s, residents of Worcester's more affluent neighborhoods, especially the South End and the West Side, were the victims of pranks and vandalism on the night before the Fourth: the unhinging of gates, shifting of signs, overturning of sheds, blocking of trolley tracks, and ringing of doorbells. These attacks on what one pro-labor newspaper called the "palatial mansions" of the "nabobs at the South End" sometimes singled out particularly prominent individuals. In 1885, for example, the *Worcester Daily Times* reported that pranksters had moved a "Tripe and Pigs' Feet" sign to the "piazza of a wealthy real estate dealer." The unnamed real estate dealer was probably R. C. Taylor, the city's largest landowner, its heaviest taxpayer, and the owner of a large colonial-style mansion in the South End of Worcester. Taylor had begun his business career in Worcester as the manager of his father's tripe factory, but by the 1880s he preferred "to forget" his more humble origins. Thus, the placement of the sign was, as the cop who removed it observed, "a suggestive as well as practical joke."[23]

There is, of course, no hard evidence on who placed the sign on Taylor's porch or who unhinged the gates of his neighbors. Newspaper accounts seem to hint that young working-class males in their teens and twenties – possibly members of gangs – were responsible, but it is also possible that some of the pranks may have been carried out by middle-class youths expressing generational rather than class antagonisms. Evidence from a firsthand account of a night-before-the-Fourth ritual (when combined with data from the U.S. Manuscript Census), however, indicates that a muted form of class hostility must have infused at least some Independence Day celebrations.

In the late 1870s several workers in the machine shop at the South Works of Washburn and Moen, the wire factory located in Quinsigamond Village, built a cannon out of the broken shaft of the waterwheel that had been used to run the shop's machinery. Each year before July Fourth, according to a reminiscence, the men took up "a collection to buy powder for the grand celebration in order to make the cannon talk." Any worker "too mean to chip in . . . was sure to be sent to Coventry, until the next year, when he had a chance to chip in again."[24]

On the night of July third the younger wireworkers as well as the children and younger relatives of the workers wheeled the cannon through Quinsigamond Village. Given their strong links to the wireworker community, the first stop of the multiethnic group of native-

American, Irish-American, and Swedish-American youths, ranging in ages from nine to twenty-five, is particularly meaningful. "There was always one place to discharge it [the cannon] first," one of the participants recalled for a newspaper reporter in 1916, "that was in front of Ben Booth's house. Ben was superintendent of the Washburn shops and we always gave him the first salute." After they had awakened the mill superintendent, the group, equipped with tin horns, twelve-inch firecrackers, shotguns, and powder pistols, marched off to fire the cannon, steal fruit, or remove carriage wheels from the property of lesser dignitaries. Although subsequent stops lacked the obvious significance of the first encounter, taken as a group, the victims of these pranks shared some revealing characteristics. Most were property owners in a community where few owned land or houses. Booth was the only wire mill employee. The others were merchants (particularly grocers), small farmers, self-employed artisans, and small-business men. In general, they were older, longtime residents of a community that was being rapidly settled by younger immigrants coming to work in the expanding wire mills.[25]

The cannon-firing escapade both reveals social tensions in Quinsigamond Village and recalls the general cultural conflict over how the Fourth should be celebrated. Not only was Superintendent Booth the first target of the cannon firing; unlike the pranksters, he chose to spend his own Independence Day mingling with the elite and middle-class crowd at the Worcester Continentals' sedate open house.[26] In their more boisterous and more active style of celebrating the Fourth, Worcester's workers demonstrated the differences of their social and cultural mores from those of the city's elite and sometimes their direct antagonism. Thus, the various informal celebrations of Independence Day – drinking, noisemaking, moving signs, firing cannons – were not always the mindless "orgies" denounced by the press. They demonstrated a distinctive style and set of values, characteristics that also infused the more organized July Fourth celebrations sponsored by Worcester's Irish organizations.

Rough and respectable: the Irish Fourth

The annual July Fourth picnics of the Ancient Order of Hibernians (AOH) in the 1880s offer the clearest example of the "rough" or boisterous celebratory style reflected by those who used Independence Day to get drunk, let off steam, or settle old scores. The 1885 picnic, for example, which attracted between 3,000 and 4,000 participants, started relatively quietly with dancing and a clambake provided by James H. Joyce, a local soda-water manufacturer who also seems to have dabbled in the illegal liquor business. Around 4 P.M. the sports of the day began with various track and field events, wrestling, and a tug-of-war. Contestants competed for cash prizes and spectators apparently bet on the outcomes. Both the organizers and the participants in the day's events came from clearly working-class backgrounds. Indeed, unlike some other Irish societies, even the officers of the AOH held blue-collar jobs.[27]

The "principal interest" of the day centered on the sparring matches. Boxing was illegal in Massachusetts, but sparring exhibitions provided a legal cover for a less violent form of this popular sport. The defeat of John F. Gray, a boilermaker at the Worcester gasworks, in the final bout of the day did not, however, end the fighting. "Fights were numerous and many of them were severe," the *Worcester Sunday Telegram* reported the next day. Although the *Telegram* liked to exaggerate the rowdiness of the city's Irish immigrants, even the Irish-controlled *Worcester Daily Times* observed "young men in different parts of the grove who were on the muscle." Heavy drinking seems to have nourished the fighting. Whether or not caterer Joyce sold liquor at the picnic itself, the *Telegram* reporter noticed that large numbers of "intoxicated persons . . . stepped off the [railway] cars from Worcester in this condition." Certainly, many saloonkeepers must have attended the picnic since, as one Irish temperance leader complained, "there was not . . . [a] rumseller however low, but was a member of the organization [the AOH]."[28]

Drunkenness and fighting also marked the 1887 AOH picnic. The sparring matches went well beyond the bounds of what was normally considered sparring; a dispute over the sculls race provoked a fight between friends of competing oarsmen; and at least the *Telegram* reported heavy drinking and "a 'scrap' every 15 minutes." Not all AOH picnics, however, ended in disorder. In 1883 at the largest of their picnics, "the very best of order prevailed," according to two different accounts.[29]

Even without the boxing, beer, and brawls, the AOH picnics had a distinctively unrestrained style, best seen by recalling contemporary middle-class gatherings. Typically, the 1893 picnic of the Loyal Women of American Liberty held at a private home featured a sit-down meal, a poetry reading, and formal speeches. But the contrast between this gathering and those of the AOH is best captured by their conclusions: The Loyal Women closed their picnic with thanks to their hostess and the singing of "God Be With You Until We Meet Again"; the AOH ended its 1886 picnic with the chasing of a greased pig.[30]

The high-spirited revelry of the AOH picnics had roots and resonances within Irish rural peasant religious and agricultural celebrations. "The excitement at 19th century fairs, races and patterns," Irish historian Patrick O'Donnell writes, "owed much to faction fighting, drinking, singing, and dancing." In rural Ireland such revelry was closely associated with the annual cycle of agricultural activity and may have served both to allay fears over the uncertainty of food supplies and to provide an acceptable place for courting activities.[31]

Although such customary festivities gradually faded in post-famine Ireland, their style and spirit apparently continued to influence Irish holiday celebrations in late nineteenth century America. Native Americans may have seen such behavior as a "desecration" of the Fourth, but some Irish Americans did not agree. Some Worcester Irish, as Timothy J. Meagher points out, contrasted the "romantic and playful" Irish with the "gloomy" Yankee whose world was dominated by work and "bereft of playfulness." The Reverend John McCoy, for example, complained that "all the wheels of the factories whirled as rapidly" on Christmas and Easter as on any other day.[32]

Such attitudes toward recreation and celebration shaped Irish views of the Fourth. "Even the *Irish News*," observes a recent study of the New York Irish, "which vilified poor-Irish rioters, called for the boisterous and exuberant celebration of Independence Day" as a justified break from more temperate and disciplined patterns. The Irish-owned *Worcester Daily Times* made a similar point in 1880 when it wrote that "in these days of few holidays" Independence Day was one of the few occasions when "all restraint is thrown off and noise and confusion reign supreme." On a later occasion, although the *Times* criticized July Fourth drunkenness, it also worried that more refined and restrained celebrations failed to give "the toadyism of our aristocracy . . . the censure it deserves." It added that "the manners, games, and ideas of Europe are adopted too freely by our rich people and are fast becoming a power to wean and lead away the people from the early moorings of the Republic." Such statements reflected the pervasive Irish-American fear that America might become "Anglo-Saxonized" – a fear that led them to propound their own Irish form of Republicanism.[33] Thus, the exuberance and excesses of the AOH picnic can be seen both as a preservation of Irish customs and as a defense of American freedoms.

There is, of course, no way of knowing whether those who got drunk at AOH picnics acted out of this rather complex vision. As we have seen, the boisterous behavior that pervaded celebrations of the Fourth – from drunkenness to vandalism to chasing greased pigs – probably filled a variety of functions and expressed a range of different values. On the simplest level, such behavior represented a release from, and an implicit rejection of, the discipline, order, hierarchy, and sobriety of the workday and workplace and provided a vision of a less structured, less demanding, less constrained world. At times, it could also serve as a vehicle for expressing the hostility felt toward social betters and bosses whose rules governed on other days of the year. Finally, these celebrations affirmed the solidarity of the ethnic community. That thousands chose to commemorate America's birthday under the auspices of an Irish nationalist society – and in a manner that recalled rural Ireland – reveals the importance that many placed on emphasizing the Irish portion of their Irish-American identity.

Whatever meanings celebrants may have attached to their boisterous behavior, many Irish leaders preferred that their fellow countrymen conduct themselves in a more sober and restrained manner. Painfully aware of the popular stereotype of the Irish as drunkards and brutes, they saw July Fourth as an occasion to project a more respectable image. One approach was to join enthusiastically in citywide celebrations of the Fourth. In the 1876 commemoration, for example, the Irish community mobilized to build the "most elaborate" national float in the Centennial parade and to turn out the largest delegation of marchers.[34] But a more widely used means of presenting an image of respectability was to organize formal gatherings under the aegis of the Irish-Catholic temperance societies and the church – two key institutional supports of those Irish committed to a more settled and respectable life-style.

During the 1880s the annual July Fourth picnics sponsored by Worcester's Irish temperance societies generally competed with those organized by the AOH. Although attendance varied, each picnic usually attracted crowds of about 3,000 to 5,000 and the total crowd equaled close to one-quarter of Worcester's Irish community. At least in part the split in Irish celebrations of the Fourth in Worcester reveals the salience of a "rough" and "respectable" divide within the immigrant working class. The most prominent difference between these two groups was their attitude toward alcohol: There were no reports of drunkenness at any of the temperance picnics. Moreover, the temperance organizations went to great pains to avoid fighting and to reassure patrons of the respectability of their gatherings. The advertisements for their 1881 picnic, sponsored by the Father Mathew temperance society, promised that the "Best of Order will be Maintained."[35]

An important means of maintaining order was the presence of clergy. At least eight priests took an active part in the 1881 temperance picnic, but there are no reports of any pastors present at any of the AOH picnics. Whereas clergymen strongly supported – and often directed – the temperance societies, they viewed the AOH with a certain amount of suspicion. The participation of more affluent and prominent members of the Irish community provided another force for discipline and hierarchy at the temperance picnics. Blue-collar workers dominated the AOH and its picnics, but about half the organizing committee for the 1882 temperance picnic held white-collar positions and the contest judges included two lawyers, a publisher, and a salesman.[36]

The combination of clerical and professional leadership obviously affected the style of the gathering. The *Worcester Daily Times* described the AOH picnic of 1882 as a "jolly good time" and its participants as "making merry." But it used the terms "orderly and well dressed" for the crowd at the Irish temperance picnic of the same year.[37] It is tempting to interpret the sober, orderly, and respectable style of the temperance picnics as evidence of the incorporation of one segment of the Irish working class into the dominant native middle-class culture. Certainly, one interpretation of American immigration history depicts immigrants as rapidly exchanging their "backward-looking" customs and values for modern American bourgeois values, centering on acquisitive individualism. And there is ample evidence that some immigrants did follow this route into the American middle class.

Many others, however, found respectability perfectly compatible with the maintenance of ethnic and working-class values. Though they shared such cultural norms as sobriety, thrift, and orderliness with the American middle class, they continued to insist upon the superiority of their own ethnic and religious values and traditions. For example, Irish priests who actively urged sober and orderly behavior also expressed doubts about the worth of the sort of material ambition and success promoted and promised by American society. They argued that Irish-Catholic religious, spiritual, and romantic virtues were more important than individual advancement. "The vast material power of the age brings war to the spirit," warned Father McCoy. Similarly, the Reverend Thomas Conaty told his parishioners: "Humility, poverty, obscurity, mortification are taught to us at the cradle. Our faith demands from us the practice of these virtues." And some Irish leaders perceived worldly success as a direct threat to these ethnic and religious virtues, pointing out that the habit of eating meat on Friday was most common among "those fairly well to do" who sought to curry favor with Protestants and that it was the rich and ambitious who were most likely to deny their Irish ancestry. Thus, respectability was not necessarily a strategy for individual advancement into the middle class. It could also be part of a world view that emphasized church, home, family, ethnic community, group solidarity, and a stable working-class identity.[38]

This distinction within the ranks of Irish promoters of respectability – between those who sought ethnic maintenance in a context of working-class stability and those who sought Americanization and middle-class acceptance – will be explored further in the next chapter's discussion of the Irish temperance movement. Its relevance to holiday celebrations, however, can be seen in the controversies of the 1880s and 1890s over celebrations of St. Patrick's Day. Whereas members of the parish-sponsored temperance societies (usually younger second-generation Irish Americans and possibly upwardly mobile) opposed public parades as leading to drunken revelry and the soiling of the image of the Irish community, both the blue-collar AOH and the Father Mathew temperance society (filled with older immigrant working-class Irishmen) favored the public demonstrations of Irish pride. Richard O'Flynn, a leader of the Father Mathew society, as well as an enthusiastic promoter of Irish history and culture, succinctly pointed up the conflict between the two groups in an 1889 entry in his journal: "It appears from the morning papers that the Irish Catholic Benevolent Society are not going to celebrate [St. Patrick's Day]. Neither are the St. Annes, Sacred Heart, or St. Peters. Too Americanized. . . . The young are a little vain perhaps." Similarly, in 1880 when Richard O'Flynn proposed celebrating Independence Day with a revival of traditional Irish sports, some temperance advocates responded by arguing that such an event would only encourage "riot and drunkenness." But the equally temperance-minded Knights of Father Mathew went ahead with the idea, and, significantly, it received active support from officers of the AOH.[39]

Such alignments suggest that at least some segments of the respectable, teetotaling, church-centered Irish working class may have actually shared more with their boisterous, nationalist, saloongoing brethren than it might appear from their division over drinking or even their varying degrees of attachment to clerical leadership. Both groups tended to retain their distinctiveness from the larger native middle-class culture. Regardless of whether their styles of celebration were "respectable" or "boisterous," they shared a common commitment to maintaining an Irish identity.

The revival of Irish sports at the 1880 picnic as well as the parades that preceded the July Fourth picnics in other years were part of this effort to demonstrate that Worcester's Irish were a people with a distinctive, autonomous, and valuable history and identity. For example, in 1882 the Knights of Father Mathew and the Volunteers of '82 led by the Worcester Cornet Band marched from downtown to the baseball grounds for their picnic, while the AOH and the Hibernian Guards led by the Worcester Cadet Band paraded to Union Station where they took the train to their field day at Lake Quinsigamond. The following day the *Worcester Daily Times* noted with obvious pride that while the day had been celebrated in the "quietest manner possible by the city government, the only displays of bands, societies and parading was by the Irish organizations."[40] Independence Day parades and picnics – whether sponsored by the AOH or the Father Mathew temperance society – became a means of symbolically asserting the public presence and social and cultural importance of the city's Irish working class.

In addition to their symbolic functions, such gatherings could fulfill economic functions within the ethnic working-class community. Recreation and celebration could be a means of financing community activities. For example the charitable St. Vincent de Paul Society raised money from the sale of food at these picnics. Similarly, two competing Irish picnics in 1890 raised funds for two different Irish-Catholic orphanages. Thus, the Irish Independence Day picnics reinforced not only an independent Irish identity but also the reciprocal bonds of mutual obligation that held together and defined the community.[41] Although the Irish working-class community divided along rough and respectable lines, it united in its commitment to a collective Irish identity, its suspicion of materialism and individualism, and its common class position.

Such common commitments do not indicate, however, a unanimity of opinion among all Irish workers, or, more important, within the Irish community in general. The conflict between upwardly mobile second-generation members of the parish temperance societies and the immigrant working-class members of the Father Mathew society points toward a gradually emerging class division within Irish Worcester. In 1880 less than 10 percent of the second-generation Irish held white-collar jobs, but twenty years later about one-fourth held such positions. One issue that split the two groups, as Timothy J. Meagher shows, was their varying degrees of support for "Irish chauvinism," on the one hand, and "Catholic Americanism," on the other hand. Yet they also differed in their style of celebrating St. Patrick's Day and the Fourth of July. In 1887 the Washington Social Club, one of the first Irish organizations with a distinctly middle-class membership, sponsored a communitywide Irish athletic tournament on the Fourth, but the following year they chose to segregate themselves from the mass of Worcester Irish by holding a private party at their lake boathouse. Similarly, more and more middle-class Irish began spending the Fourth out of town at various summer resorts around this time.[42]

It was the obvious growth of this Irish middle class with distinctive social and cultural habits that led to the increasing popularity of the phrase "lace curtain" Irish in the 1890s. Nevertheless, the emergence of class distinctions within Worcester's ethnic communities was really more of a development of the twentieth century than the nineteenth. As late as 1900 only about 13 percent of the first- and second-generation Irish held white-collar jobs. Among Worcester's two other major ethnic groups – Swedes and French Canadians – the percentage was even smaller, below 9 percent in each case.[43]

Settled living: the Swedish and French-Canadian Fourth

Some of the same emphasis on reciprocity, community, autonomy, insularity, and ethnic maintenance that marked the culture created by Worcester's Irish can be found among the city's Swedish and French-Canadian immigrants. Although the city's immigrants shared these values and a common class status, they were still generally unable to forge a common class identity, because one of those values – separatism – inhibited their collaboration.

In Worcester's Swedish community a division between rough and respectable again seems to have marked the cultural styles of the working class. However, unlike the Irish, the respectable Swedish working class clearly predominated and gave the group its public image. Swedish newspapers, for example, cultivated this reputation and reported evidence of Swedish sobriety with great pride and incidents of drunkenness with disbelief or disapproval. Central to this respectable working-class identity was the prominent role played by the city's eight Swedish Protestant churches. "It is difficult," writes a historian of the Worcester Swedish community, "to place a great enough estimate on what the church has meant to the Swedish people in Worcester." "The social life of the community," adds the author of a study of Quinsigamond Village, "centered around the churches. Courting was done between morning and evening service, and the coffee hour after the evening service was looked forward to by all as a time of social relaxation and friendliness."[44]

July Fourth celebrations reflected the cultural importance of the Swedish churches. In the 1890s their annual Independence Day picnics attracted about 4,600 participants out of a total Swedish-American population of about 11,000.[45] These picnics followed a predictable formula: services at the church; a march to the picnic grounds; religious and patriotic remarks by the minister and the Sunday school superintendent; prayer, hymn singing, lunch, ice cream, and lemonade; and finally informal games and sports. Rowdy or drunken behavior obviously had no place here; even fireworks were frowned upon.

Although these church picnics with their orderliness and seriousness resembled, in part, both the gatherings of the genteel middle and upper classes and those of Irish temperance supporters, they also had a distinctive style and purpose of their own. The speeches at these picnics, for example, usually affirmed the triple Christian, Swedish, and American identity that these immigrants sought to create and preserve. At the 1896 Independence Day picnic of the Swedish Evangelical Lutheran Church, the Reverend E. A. Zettersand spoke in Swedish on how to combine love for the "fatherland" with loyalty to the United States. A divinity student followed with remarks linking the American Revolution with Christ's bringing of liberty to the world. Often, both Swedish and American flags decorated the picnic ground, and group singing featured both hymns and "The Star-Spangled Banner."[46]

Despite their common Swedish-American pietistic identity as well as the similarity of their celebrations, the eight churches did not see July Fourth as an occasion to join together. Rather, their separate celebrations reflected their insistence upon the church as a self-contained subcommunity. On July 4, 1899, for example, the Quinsigamond Congregational Church marched down Greenwood Street led by their band. When they reached the Methodist Church, that congregation joined the parade but only until they arrived at their separate picnic grounds.[47]

The structure of the church picnics also indicates the self-contained world of the Swedish churches and their members. Whereas the activities at the Irish picnics tended to appeal most strongly to the young, and especially young men, the Swedish picnics more fully involved the entire community. For example, sports for women were as important as those for men. Despite their propriety, the picnics were also important occasions for beginning or furthering youthful romances and, thus, for perpetuating a church-centered community.[48]

Just as everyone shared in the activities, everyone shared in arranging the picnics. Overseeing the gatherings were numerous committees (including men and women), covering such diverse arrangements as transportation, lemonade, peanuts, and candy. Most often food was free and was apparently prepared collectively by groups like the Ladies Aid Society. At those picnics where families brought their own basket lunches, food was still shared. Of course, this meant that the leisure provided by the picnics rested upon a good deal of women's work. Still, the collective methods of planning and preparing the picnics meant that these occasions further reinforced the reciprocal bonds of an interdependent community of people who lived, worked, worshipped, and played together. Indeed, the collective modes reflected in the July Fourth picnics could be readily discerned in other areas of Swedish working-class life. Women's sewing circles or ladies aid societies, which were central to almost all the local Swedish churches, sustained the churches financially through the cooperative work of their female members. A similar impulse presumably underlay the establishment of cooperative groceries in the city's Swedish communities.[49]

Not all Swedes belonged to the pietistic churches or participated in their July Fourth picnics. And to some extent a division between churched and unchurched Swedes paralleled the divide between the rough and respectable Irish. The distinction between the churched and the unchurched was sufficiently strong that some of the unchurched apparently chose to live in separate neighborhoods from their more pious fellow immigrants. Still, both groups shared a commitment to maintaining their Swedish identity. The local Swedish-language newspaper probably spoke for both pietists and secularists in 1888 when it editorialized against complete Americanization and the casting away of the "vestiges of the Fatherland." Thus, secular Swedes were likely to celebrate July Fourth with fellow immigrants under the banners of the Swedish lodges of the Good Templars and the Red Men, the Svea Gille Club, the Viking Council of the Mystic Brotherhood, or even the Scandinavian Socialist Club. In the absence of pietistic prohibitions on dancing and fireworks, these gatherings took on a livelier tone than the church picnics. In 1900 the *Telegram* described the Svea Gille celebration as one of the "merriest" of the day's outings with "the usual life and enthusiasms, music, dancing, and fireworks." Yet even many of the Swedish secularists maintained a respectable and sober style. One of the most active of the secular organizations was the Good Templars, a temperance society.[50]

Worcester's French Canadians shared this preference for organizing social life within the ethnic community. French-Canadian culture, one historian notes, "was defined by language, determined by faith, and dedicated to the family." This "central trilogy" of church, language, and family probably made the French Canadians even more insular than the Irish or the Swedes. French-Canadian separatism – justified by their ideology of survivance – extended even to a suspicion of their fellow Catholics of Irish extraction as too assimilationist.[51]

July Fourth celebrations illustrate this gap between French-Canadian and American culture. Worcester French Canadians tended to show less interest in July Fourth as either an ethnic or a national celebration than did the Swedes or the Irish: Before the late 1890s there were few French-Canadian sponsored Independence Day celebrations in Worcester. French-Canadian organizations were more likely to concentrate their energies on commemorating St. Jean Baptiste Day, the French-Canadian holiday that fell ten days earlier. Having mounted a parade or picnic on June Twenty-fourth, they had little interest in mobilizing members again two weeks later.

When French Canadians did celebrate the Fourth, they generally demonstrated more of an ethnic than an American identity. On July 4, 1881, for example, French Canadians from different New England cities and mill towns gathered in nearby Southbridge with banners proclaiming: "Honor to the Canadians" and "Salute to the Glorious Children of Canada." Even more generally, Worcester French Canadians seem to have affirmed their most basic social group – the family – on the Fourth. Family-based "piques-niques" seem to have been a predominant mode of celebration.[52]

Although family gatherings remained important, by the late 1890s Worcester French Canadians were organizing more formal celebrations of the Fourth and fewer commemorations of St. Jean Baptiste

Day. June Twenty-fourth, the *Worcester Telegram* noted in 1898, "is fast losing its importance in the minds of the French-speaking people in this section of New England." At the same time French-Canadian churches and social and political organizations began to sponsor regular celebrations of the Fourth. That the Ward Three Naturalization Club was the first Worcester French-Canadian group to sponsor annual Independence Day gatherings suggests that these events presaged a gradual process of Americanization. Yet even newspapers like *L'Opinion Publique,* which strongly supported naturalization, also battled fiercely against "the numerous assimilationist elements which surround us."[53] French-Canadian adoption of American holidays or even American citizenship must be seen in the context of a larger devotion to a separate and distinct French-Canadian culture.

Thus, French-Canadian celebrations of the Fourth – like those sponsored by the Irish and the Swedes – were most important as a time to reassert ethnic ties and customs. The traditional pillars of the French-Canadian community – church and family – still took a leading role in these Independence Day celebrations. As at the Swedish church picnics and the Irish temperance gatherings, the priests superintended the day's events. And the sports contests and games had a distinctly family flavor: Married men played the bachelors in baseball; "fat" men and "old" men competed in races; and women challenged each other in nail driving and bottle breaking. French-Canadian celebrations not only affirmed the centrality of family and church but also reinforced the reciprocal bonds of community that tied French Canadians together. Church picnics often performed a crucial economic function: They were a way of raising money for parish relief activities. Indeed, throughout the year French-Canadian recreational activities – concerts, bazaars, lectures, plays – raised money for ethnic charities.[54] Recreation, in general, was a crucial means of financing group activities and charities and, thereby, of weaving a web of mutual interdependence.

Thus, as with the Irish and the Swedes, July Fourth was an arena for Worcester French Canadians to affirm and reinforce their own distinctive values and priorities: their maintenance of language, church, and family; their reciprocal ties of interdependence; and their commitment to an ethnic identity that transcended the bounds of a particular community. And other Worcester ethnic groups – English, Welsh, Scots, Germans, Finns, Armenians, Jews, English Canadians, Afro-Americans – also used the Fourth as an occasion to reassert their particular ethnic identity and values.[55]

Ethnic conflict and interclass alliances: a divided Fourth

One should not exaggerate the degree of ethnic segregation in late nineteenth century Worcester. In addition to such obvious areas of interaction as schools, factories, and neighborhoods, even some Fourth of July celebrations – commercial amusements sponsored by lakeside entrepreneurs, night-before-the-Fourth fireworks and pranks – drew multiethnic crowds. Nevertheless, working-class groups without an ethnic base had little success in developing a social life on the Fourth or on any other day. In 1879, for example, whereas huge crowds flocked to an Irish-sponsored picnic, the gathering of the United Workingmen's Association, an organization that seems to have included both Irish and native skilled workers, attracted what even the organizers conceded was a "small attendance." Although planned as a benefit for Fall River strikers, the event produced only a $20 deficit. By way of contrast, on that same day a Socialist Labor party demonstration and celebration in Detroit attracted more than 2,000 workers and their families.[56] Even on Labor Day the official trade union parade or picnic usually had to compete with often larger gatherings sponsored by Irish, French-Canadian, or Swedish organizations.

The Knights of Labor made the most ambitious and successful efforts at forging a class-based, as opposed to an ethnic-based, social and recreational world in late nineteenth century Worcester. In 1885 and 1886 when they had five local assemblies, they sponsored picnics, excursions, dances, plays, and athletic meets. Yet their social efforts, like their attempts at union organizing, had only limited and short-term successes in Worcester. As early as 1886 the anti-labor *Worcester Sunday Telegram* derided the Knights' summer excursion to Rhode Island as a "fizzle," which attracted only 300 participants instead of an anticipated 2,500. And even the pro-labor *Worcester Daily Times* lamented the inability of local Knights to organize fairs and excursions on the scale of other Massachusetts cities and towns.[57]

The overwhelmingly ethnic basis of working-class social life could foster, as well as foil, labor organizing in late nineteenth century Worcester. Given the predominantly blue-collar complexion of the city's immigrant communities, to assert an ethnic identity was also to assert a working-class identity. At least some ethnic societies both supported the labor movement and reflected class-based antagonisms. Thus, the AOH Hall provided a meeting place for many union locals as well as the setting for the founding of the Central

Labor Union. Similarly, in 1902 the AOH applauded the struggle of the coal miners against the "avarice and selfishness of a corrupt and political example of the trust system." Two years earlier an AOH-controlled local newspaper had denounced "the present Imperialistic Capitalist dynasty" in America. It is perhaps not surprising that almost half the city's labor leaders at the turn of the century were of Irish birth or extraction.[58]

But whereas the AOH might imbue its members with a message of class struggle, some leaders of ethnic communities counseled the reverse. In 1880, for example, the French-Canadian newspaper *Le Travailleur* ran a series of editorials on strikes. Although it allowed that some strikes were justified, it generally took the fatalistic view that there must be "master and servant, rich and poor, patron and worker" and that, therefore, strikes "reverse the divine order." To be sure, not all Worcester French Canadians followed this advice. But when Michael Bachand, both the president of the Barbers' Union and a leader of French-Canadian societies, defended unionism at the Franco-American Naturalization Club, he faced "strong adversaries."[59]

Even more problematic for those interested in forging a Worcester labor movement than their failure to create a class-based social life or the hostility of some ethnic leaders were the intraethnic tensions and interclass ties that an ethnically based social life fostered. Among the city's native-American working class, for example, both a hostility toward other workers (primarily those of Catholic backgrounds) and a set of connections with the middle and upper classes were readily apparent. The Protestant church was probably the most important link for Yankee workers and bosses. The social world of John F. Nourse, a boot cutter, revolved around his parents, who lived in rural Sterling, and his church, the Salem Street Congregational. Both provided direct economic benefits. His parents loaned money to him to purchase a house. When he was laid off from the shoe factory, a fellow church member and local merchant employed Nourse to paint his house.[60]

Naturally, not all Yankee mechanics spent Sundays in church with their employers, nor did they uniformly follow their leadership. For example, the local nativist newspaper of the 1890s, the *American,* opposed the election of wealthy landowner Stephen Salisbury to the state senate because "his education and associations have always kept him aloof from the workingmen." Yet the *American*'s hostility toward Worcester's "aristocratic class" did not equally dispose it toward trade unions or working-class solidarity. It attacked labor leaders as "ignorant" and "selfish," applauded the jailing of Eugene V. Debs for his role in the Pullman strike of 1894, and, of course, stereotyped immigrants as criminals and drunks. Worcester's nativists seem to have tried to construct instead a lower-middle-class Yankee social world as a way of establishing their identity in an industrial city dominated by a Yankee elite and populated largely by an immigrant working class. The nativist Order of United American Mechanics (OUAM), which held large July Fourth picnics during its heyday in the mid-1890s, reflected this lower-middle-class identity in its social composition. The membership of the Devens Council of the OUAM split fairly evenly between blue- and white-collar workers (with most of them falling into the skilled blue-collar or the lower level white-collar categories); the most common single job was foreman.[61]

Although Yankee workers could enter the social world of the native elite or middle class through the church or the nativist movement, the city's Swedish working class maintained its social and cultural distance from the native American middle and upper classes. At the same time, however, because of their Protestantism, their support for temperance and the Republican party, and their reputation for respectable behavior, the Swedes were able to forge important links with the city's industrial elite. And the manufacturers manipulated this alliance to their own ends.

Worcester employers – particularly those like Washburn and Moen who employed large numbers of Swedes – gave active support to Swedish cultural activities. Swedish July Fourth picnics sometimes took place on the Washburn and Moen grounds. In addition, the wire company contributed $300 to the building of a new chapel for the Swedish Congregationalists and Philip Moen spoke at the dedication in 1891. A few years earlier Moen purchased new uniforms for the Scandinavian Music Corps, and they responded with an evening serenade for him and his wife. There is abundant evidence that the elite's cultivation of the Swedes went well beyond some paternalist feeling for fellow Protestants. "It is a well-known fact in this community," the *Worcester Daily Times* charged in 1886, "that for some years past, Washburn and Moen have been substituting Swedes for Irishmen, on the ground that they work for less money and would worship at the same church with their employers." On another occasion the *Times* complained that employers were working "the religious racket" in order to keep Swedes within the Republican party and away from voting "for men who had sympathy with labor." The changing ethnic balance of the work force at Washburn and Moen as well as the praise heaped on the "thrifty, industrious, capable, and law-abiding" Swedes by Charles Washburn (Ichabod's grandnephew and a onetime offical of the company) in his study of *Industrial Worcester* lends credence to the *Times*'s charges.[62]

But the hostility between the Swedes and the Irish (or the Yankees and the Irish for that matter) resulted from deep-seated ethnic and religious antagonisms as well as employer manipulation. The local Swedish newspaper, for example, denounced the Irish as "unscrupulous," "worthless," and "dangerous," and stereotyped them as "gamblers," "scoundrels," and especially "drunkards." On occasion, this verbal hostility escalated into violence. In 1889, for example, Swedish and Irish gangs battled each other every Saturday for more than a month.[63] In this context, the failure of the Irish-led Knights of Labor to recruit Swedish wireworkers to their movement in the 1880s and the absence of Swedes from leadership positions in the local labor movement in the 1890s hardly seem surprising.

The division of Worcester's working class along religious lines – a division that was regularly reinforced on holidays of ostensible community solidarity like July Fourth – was the most damaging problem facing the city's labor organizers. Yet even the Catholic portion of the work force had complex internal divisions. Although *Le Travailleur* urged closer "rapport between the sons of St. Patrick and the sons of St. Jean Baptiste," it also acknowledged the "latent antipathy between the Irish and French Canadians." And this antipathy was only strengthened by the anti-Irish jokes that appeared in the French-Canadian press as well as by the entirely separate social and cultural worlds of the two groups. In 1875, for example, *Le Travailleur* complained of the unwillingness of the Irish to use its pages to invite French Canadians to Irish church bazaars.[64]

July Fourth celebrations in particular and ethnic working-class social and cultural life in general thus provided an ambiguous resource for Worcester's working class. On the one hand, these celebrations offered an occasion for workers to express their own values, affirm their ethnic and religious autonomy, escape from the oppressive burdens of the workplace, and even occasionally voice discontent. In their celebrations they expressed a vision of a better life – of a less regimented, less restrictive world. They also affirmed their commitment to values of mutuality, reciprocity, collectivity, and community. Indeed, much of the socializing and celebrating provided the economic base for the community's self-help institutions. On the other hand, this world view – admirable in so many respects – failed to transcend the insular confines of a particular ethnic group or even a particular congregation. As a result, workers found themselves divided against each other not only on the Fourth but also at the ballot box, on the picket line, and on the shop floor. Whereas working-class celebrations of the Fourth eased the pain of life under an exploitative economic system, they also suggested the difficulty of changing that system.

PART III

Conflict: struggles over working-class leisure in the late nineteenth and early twentieth centuries

4 *The struggle over the saloon, 1870–1910*

In December 1881 Worcesterites debated whether to vote "yes" (and sanction the sale of liquor under a licensing system) or "no" (and close all liquor dealers and saloons) in the first annual local option election mandated by a new state law. Prominent among the leaders of the anti-drink or "no-license" forces was Philip L. Moen, the head of the Washburn and Moen Wire Manufacturing Company as well as the son-in-law of the man who had founded the company and promoted the temperance cause a half century earlier. During the hotly contested 1881 temperance campaign Moen and forty-one other leading Worcesterites – three-quarters of them were either manufacturers or Protestant ministers – issued a broadside attack on "open drinking saloons" for "impoverishing multitudes, causing measureless misery and crime, [and] crippling our industries."[1]

The other side in the local battle over the saloon was acutely aware of the economic power and cultural prominence of the temperance forces. *Worcester Daily Times* editor James H. Mellen charged that the temperance campaign was really a vendetta against the Irish and other blue-collar workers, who lacked spacious homes and thus drank only in public saloons. According to Mellen, the "better element" behind the no-license crusade included many drinkers "who believe in drink as a luxury, and that the plebians should not be allowed to degrade the habit by participation." "Many people will vote 'no' whose cellars are stocked with liquors," he complained on another occasion, adding that this practice "savors of class legislation."[2]

The actual vote – in which the pro-license forces triumphed narrowly – confirmed Mellen's perception of temperance as a class issue. On the Irish and working-class East Side the votes ran about 2.5 to 1 in favor of licensing saloons, whereas in the elite precincts on the West Side the proportions were roughly reversed.[3] Like the movements for parks, playgrounds, and a Safe and Sane July Fourth, which also flourished in Worcester in the late nineteenth century and the early twentieth, the temperance crusade was, in part, an effort by the city's middle and upper classes to reform, reshape, and restrict working-class recreational practices. The resulting conflicts made leisure time and space into arenas where workers and industrialists struggled over the values, world view, and culture that would dominate working-class life.

Yet these recreational struggles never followed straight class lines. And nowhere were the lines of division more complex and confused than in the battle over drink and the saloon. Few Irish workers supported the no-license campaigns, but a substantial number did join their own Catholic temperance organizations. The same year that James Mellen editorialized in favor of liquor licensing, he also served as the delegate of Worcester's Father Mathew Total Abstinence Society to the Springfield Catholic Diocesan Union of temperance societies.[4] In addition, some Worcester workers – particularly Protestant workers – went beyond the self-reform program of the Catholic temperance societies and fully backed the no-license cause. In particular, Worcester's Swedish workers, who were not a political force in 1881 but rapidly became one in the 1880s and 1890s, provided many of the votes needed for the no-license victories of 1885, 1889, 1891, 1907, and 1908.

Although workers themselves took part in efforts to reform or regulate working-class recreational behavior, their goals often differed sharply from industrialists or middle-class reformers pursuing the same ostensible ends. Workers who promoted sobriety or agitated for park space sought to advance an agenda shaped by the needs and values of their distinctive working-class communities. At the same time, working-class institutions like the saloon proved highly resistant to repression or regulation. In effect, whether workers spent their evenings at the temperance hall or the saloon, they managed to defend their leisure time and space as a separate and relatively autonomous sphere of life. Whereas the temperance movement had a limited impact on the ethnic working-class saloon, the intraclass differences and interclass alliances it fostered had a profound effect on the nature of class relations in the Worcester of the late nineteenth and early twentieth centuries.

Campaigns against working-class drink places

In March 1890 Alfred S. Roe, the principal of Worcester High School, reflected on the recent license election for the readers of *Light,* a local "society" journal. No-license voters, he pointed out, held a variety of opinions about the propriety of alcohol consumption, but what united them was their "thorough agreement . . . that the saloon is here and everywhere an unmitigated evil, and that it must go." Opponents of liquor licensing repeatedly reminded voters that they sought to eliminate the *saloon,* not drinking per se. "Prohibition is not at issue," one no-license advertisement assured voters: "The Saloon is the enemy we are fighting."[5]

In focusing their movement on the saloon, middle- and upper-class temperance supporters like Roe responded to the rapid development of the saloon by the working class as its own social institution. During the last third of the nineteenth century the number of saloons in the United States had tripled.[6] That temperance crusades concentrated on this emerging "workingman's club" rather than on the individual drinker meant that the battle over the saloon often took on aspects of a "class war" over the recreational world of the industrial working class. In Worcester, at least, the generals of that class war were the city's Protestant ministers, its manufacturers, and their wives. Of course, more diverse groups enlisted in the various campaigns: to limit the total number of liquor licenses and to restrict licenses to specific areas (the springtime license petition movement); to close all drink places through the annual December local option elections (the no-license movement); and to use regulations and police enforcement to make the saloon a more orderly place. And some groups – particularly the Swedes – gradually moved into leadership postions. However, throughout the late nineteenth and early twentieth centuries the native Protestant elite staffed the command post of the war on the saloon.

After Massachusetts legalized sales in 1875 the annual springtime petition battle over license restriction, over *who* would receive a license from the city, became a major arena for conflict on the drink question. The licensing decisions of the Board of Aldermen (and after 1893 the License Commission) were the number one topic of conversation around the city for days before and after the licenses were issued. Speculation was so intense that in some factories workers formed betting pools based on predicting the winners of the licensing sweepstakes.[7]

Much of the earliest agitation for the restriction of liquor licenses came from the Protestant clergy. Hardly a year went by without petitions, sermons, and speeches by the Protestant clergy urging some general or specific license limitation. Closely allied with the Protestant clergy in license-restriction efforts were some of the city's leading industrialists. On one typical license-restriction petition from 1878, manufacturers and ministers made up the two largest occupational groups. Typically, Henry C. Graton, a manufacturer of leather belting and a member and benefactor of Grace Methodist Church, signed along with his minister.[8]

The exemplar of this clerical–industrial alliance on temperance and other major questions was Ichabod Washburn, wire manufacturer, builder of the city's first "temperance house," and secretary of a Worcester temperance society. Known locally as "Deacon Washburn" because of his position in the orthodox Union Congregational Church, he actively supported the key institutional pillars of his twin faiths in "mechanics and evangelical Christianity." He not only presided over the Evangelical Missionary Society and financed the building of its Mission Chapel but also helped found the Worcester County Mechanics Association and donated $25,000 toward the building of its magnificent Mechanics Hall. For Deacon Washburn, piety and profits went hand in hand. "If your mill owners want to make good dividends," he advised, "let them see to it that they have plenty of good orthodox preaching, a good minister well housed . . . and it will prove to be the best part of their investment; for goodliness is profitable to all things."[9]

Washburn's son-in-law, Philip L. Moen, followed him as both head of the million-dollar wire corporation and deacon of the Union Congregational Church. Although the pre–Civil War unity of Christians and capitalists could not be wholly sustained in the 1870s and 1880s, the alliance remained firm on the issue of temperance. The 1878 license-restriction petition included not only Philip L. Moen but also the Reverend George Gould, the minister of the Union Congregational Church, the Reverend William T. Sleeper, the cofounder with Washburn of the Mission Chapel and its current pastor, and the Reverend Henry T. Cheever, Washburn's brother-in-law and the former minister of the Mission Chapel.[10]

There was a remarkable continuity with the temperance movement of earlier in the century. In the 1830s the founders of Worcester's industrial economy – the mechanics and manufacturers – had led the temperance forces; now forty or fifty years later the heirs to a mature industrial economy carried the battle forward. In addition, the evangelical Protestant churches and the Mechanics Association joined together and ideologically molded both generations. Temperance men had started Worcester's Mechanics Association in the early ninteenth century, and it remained a hotbed of temperance support in the last quarter of the century: The signers of the 1878 petition included at least nine past or future presidents of the Mechanics Association.[11] The most important change in the personnel of the temperance movement actually reinforced its elite status. The wives of the manufacturers and ministers now took an increasingly active role. The signers of an 1881 license-restriction petition, for example, included the wives of Philip L. Moen, Henry Graton (the leather belting manufacturer), and the superintendents of both the wire works and the Crompton Loom Works.[12]

This petition, like many early petitions, sought to persuade the board to issue no licenses at all. But manufacturers increasingly recognized the futility of this strategy and instead sought simply to prevent the issuance of licenses in the vicinity of their factories. Beginning in 1891 Washburn and Moen annually opposed the granting of any liquor licenses south of Cambridge Street, about one mile from the company's massive South Works, and in 1895 it petitioned against "the tremendous evil" of saloons in the vicinity of their North Works. Numerous other Worcester companies followed the lead of Washburn and Moen. In 1893, for example, Crompton Loom Works, Ames Plow Company, and S. R. Heywood Boot and Shoe Manufacturing petitioned against saloons seeking to locate near their factories.[13]

In mobilizing opposition to specific saloons, manufacturers often found allies outside their own elite circles and even among their own employees. In 1883, for example, a petition against three liquor licenses in the vicinity of Lincoln Square had the backing of not just Philip L. Moen, whose North Works was located nearby, but also at least nine of his employees, including clerks, foremen, and wireworkers. Another petition from the same year, which also challenged liquor licenses in the Lincoln Square vicinity, consisted almost entirely of skilled workers from a neighboring folding-chair factory, whose owner, E. W. Vaill, actively embraced the temperance cause.[14]

Working-class opposition to specific liquor licenses also developed within particular ethnic communities. When the Finnish Temperance Society protested that a Finnish saloon would damage "the reputation of the Finnish people at large," it expressed the widespread view that an ethnic community, and not the city government, should control behavior within its own neighborhood. Worcester's Swedes were particularly active in mobilizing such communal protests. In 1899 the Swedish lodges of the International Order of Good Templars (IOGT) even petitioned against all club licenses in an effort to prevent drinking at just the Svea Gille Club, the leading Swedish-American organization in the city. Eleven years earlier Swedes had protested even more vehemently over the possibility that their fellow countryman Martin Trulson would open a saloon on the same block as the Thomas Street Swedish Methodist Church, an important social center for fundamentalist Swedes. As the Swedish-language press reported, many Swedes believed that "a Scandinavian saloon would be directly damaging to Scandinavians, especially newcomers," and that "such a saloon would tarnish the Scandinavian community's good name and reputation." Such protective sentiments struck "a deep chord" within the Swedish community, and within three days about 2,000 Swedes had signed a petition opposing liquor licenses for *any* local Swedes.[15]

Scandinavians and native Americans were the only two working-class groups to sign or circulate petitions regularly against particular saloons. When saloonkeepers retaliated against protests by passing around petitions supporting their licenses, they were more likely to pick up the signatures of Irish and French-Canadian working people. In 1887, for example, some of the native Protestant workers at the Coes Wrench Works joined with their bosses in petitioning against a Webster Square saloon that Irish and French-Canadian workers at the same factory supported.[16]

Just as licensing split the working class along ethnic and religious lines, it also may have divided the native middle and upper classes according to their place in the city's economy. Whereas Worcester's industrialists unanimously condemned the saloon, some merchants and small-business men appear to have been much friendlier. At the same time that Moen and his employees challenged the liquor license of Elijah Kennan's Exchange Hotel, nearby grocers, men's clothiers, and tobacconists came to his defense. Two other downtown saloonkeepers, who were also threatened by anti-license petitioners in 1883, mobilized even more impressive support from more than twenty-five neighboring merchants and their clerks. Downtown merchants, however, usually confined their support to the more affluent and established drink sellers like hotel owner Kennan or George Hewitt, the city's leading wholesale liquor dealer.[17] And some even denounced the drink trade as vigorously as any manufacturer or minister. Nevertheless, as was true earlier in the nineteenth century, many merchants – perhaps out of solidarity with other Main Street businessmen or out of a greater concern with consumption than with production – appear to have shied away from the temperance movement that won the allegiance of so many other members of the middle and upper classes.

Many of the same class, ethnic, and occupational lines of division on the drink question can be found in the other annual battle over the saloon: the local option vote each December over whether Worcester would license any saloons at all that year. Although a no-license victory in local option elections required the votes of the native-American middle class as well as some segments of the native and immigrant working class, the leadership of the no-license forces remained largely with the city's manufacturers and ministers. Broadsides urging "no" votes carried the signatures of these men as well as those of other prominent Worcesterites: judges, bank presidents, and leading politicians like Senator George Frisbie Hoar. Rank-and-file no-license activists included only a slightly more diverse constituency. Almost half the members of the twenty-two no-license committees organized through the Protestant churches for the 1886 election came from the upper levels of the city's white-collar work force. Only one-fifth held blue-collar jobs, and many of these belonged to the committees formed at the black Baptist and Swedish Methodist churches.[18]

Local option elections, which began in 1881 and continued until national prohibition in 1920, followed class and ethnic lines fairly closely in the 1880s. The immigrant and working-class precincts of the East Side voted "yes" by 2 or 3 to 1 margins; the native middle and upper classes voted "no" in similar proportions. In the 1890 election, for example, ethnicity and licensing sentiment correlate perfectly. Ward 5, with 67.2 percent of its adult males of foreign birth, voted 70.8 percent for liquor licensing, whereas Ward 8, with 87.5 percent of its adult males of native birth, voted 61.7 percent against licensing. These sharp ethnic and class divisions kept most license contests close and hotly contested, with victory often hinging on the degree of organization of the opposing sides or the level of voter turnout. License supporters lost only five of the forty local option votes, but their margin of victory averaged less than 5 percent annually.[19]

In part, the ethnic basis of the voting reflects strong Irish support for liquor licensing, since that group composed about 45 percent of the city's foreign-born in 1890 and an even higher proportion of the foreign-stock voting population. Even Irish temperance advocates, with only occasional exceptions, opposed the no-license position as coercive and unworkable. Worcester's French Canadians generally took the same position. Urging its readers to vote for liquor licensing in 1894, *L'Opinion Publique* called prohibition a "delusion" in densely populated areas like Worcester.[20] In the 1880s, however, the French were not a major factor in license elections since so few of them voted. As late as 1890 only 604 Worcester French Canadians were registered to vote despite a total population of about 10,000. Indeed, a local French-Canadian publication pointed specifically to the threat of no-license in trying to persuade readers to take out naturalization papers and vote.[21]

The great exception to this immigrant and working-class support for liquor licensing was, of course, the Swedes, who began entering Worcester in large numbers in the 1880s and 1890s. By the early twentieth century their impact on the license votes was unmistakable. By 1910 support for liquor licensing and foreign birth or parentage no longer correlated precisely, and the "deviant" wards (1, 2, and 6) were those with heavy concentrations of Swedish immigrants. In 1904, for example, two-thirds of the voters in the two largest Swedish neighborhoods – Quinsigamond Village and Greendale – rejected liquor licensing, whereas less than half of the voters in the city as a whole took this position.[22]

In addition to voting against liquor licensing, Worcester's Swedes played an increasingly active and vocal role in the annual no-license campaigns, particularly after the mid-1890s. Even in years when other no-license groups seemed moribund, the Swedish temperance forces could bring out thousands for no-license rallies and sermons.[23] Despite this great energy and enthusiasm, Swedish no-license efforts (like their anti-saloon petitions) – limited by problems of language and notions of ethnic autonomy – remained confined largely to the Swedish community. On a citywide basis, the Swedes entered into local option politics primarily through coalitions with the native Protestant elite.

When no-license campaigns failed, saloon opponents sought instead stricter regulations or tighter enforcement of existing rules. They advocated and won passage of rules barring Sunday sales, side- or back-door entrances, screens blocking public view into the saloon, sales after 11 P.M., and "public bars" selling drink without food. Women played a particularly active role in the struggle to enforce existing regulations. Most dramatically, in 1874, when Worcester saloons were openly violating statewide prohibition, bands of women (following the example of the Women's Crusades, which had begun in Ohio a few months earlier) marched on the city's saloons to pray, sing hymns, ask patrons to take the "pledge," and beseech proprietors to abandon their illegal and immoral business. Whether through moral example or public pressure, they also seem to have persuaded state constables to increase their seizures of illegal liquors. The "praying bands" of women apparently came from the same elite Protestant circles that championed license restriction and no-license. The members of one major committee included Elizabeth Cheever Washburn (Ichabod's widow) and the wives of at least three other manufacturers.[24]

Upper-class men spearheaded other efforts to win tighter enforcement of Worcester's liquor laws. In 1883 one hundred manufacturers, ministers, lawyers, and bankers – a virtual who's who of elite Worcester – formed the Citizens' Law and Order League to insist upon "the enforcement of the restrictive features of existing laws for the regulation of the liquor traffic and attendant vices." Three years later the Worcester Christian Temperance Union sponsored the Reverend Hugh Montgomery in a one-man vigilante crusade against liquor law violations.[25]

The ideology of the middle- and upper-class temperance movement

Worcester's manufacturers, ministers, and mothers thus commanded an anti-saloon army, whose foot soldiers included members of the native working and middle classes (with the partial exception of downtown merchants) as well as large numbers of Swedish immigrant workers. Most often, Worcester's French-Canadian and Irish communities stood on the other side of the temperance barricade. What does this social and cultural division tell us about temperance ideology in late nineteenth century Worcester? What sort of meanings did Worcesterites of different social classes and ethnic backgrounds attach to their temperance sentiments?

For the ambitious, self-improving mechanics of Ichabod Washburn's generation, temperance and evangelical Christianity were directed as much inward as outward, as much at self-control as at social control. Thus, temperance and religion both responded to and hastened an emerging industrial capitalist society; they offered optimistic solutions to both the personal anxieties and the problems of industrial discipline and social disorder brought about by such a rapidly changing society.[26] By the time of Philip L. Moen's generation, temperance ideology was gradually shifting away from its internal focus on personal reform and improvement toward a more exclusive concern with the external threat posed by working-class drinking and particularly by the working-class saloon. Washburn, after all, had begun building his wire business in a relatively homogenous town of 5,000, many of whom worked in small workshops. Fifty years later Moen presided over an established million-dollar wire corporation in a city twelve times as big with an immense immigrant working-class population that toiled in giant factories. In the intervening years this immigrant working class had developed the saloon as one of its central social and cultural institutions. To attack drinking – and especially the saloon – now became a statement with much more direct class implications.

The offensive against the saloon and its values was equally a defense of a set of bourgeois values that the saloon seemed to threaten. The urban-industrial saloon, Norman H. Clark has observed in his recent reinterpretation of American temperance, challenged "the moral values so recently articulated as the bourgeois tradition: self-confidence, conscience, sexual discipline, ambition, measurable accomplishment, loyalty, reverence, responsibility, respect." These values, rooted in what has been called the emerging "bourgeois interior" of American life, were, as Clark argues, profoundly individualistic and supported a "developing consciousness of individual, rather than communal, dignity." Just as the saloon symbolized the rejection of this middle-class world view, the middle-class home stood as its affirmation and bastion. The addition of new saloons to Webster Square, the Reverend L. W. Staples told the Worcester Board of Aldermen in 1887, menaced a "neighborhood of homes, peaceful, happy, prosperous homes." Three years later the society paper *Light* used similar language to celebrate the results of a year without liquor licenses: "Homes are today made happy by the presence of a sober father, where in times gone by tears and oaths were constant reminders of unnatural actions on the part of this same man."[27]

The middle-class home, which temperance advocates all over America sought to protect, did not exist in an economic vacuum; it rested on the economic base of industrial capitalism. Thus, the temperance movement of the late nineteenth century and the early twentieth defended not just the culture of the Protestant middle class but also the economic interests of Protestant manufacturers. The Reverend Mr. Staples, for example, appealed to both his parishioners' sentimental attachment to home and family and their rational self-interest in a disciplined work force. The elimination of the saloon, he claimed in November 1886 after Worcester's first six months under no-license, had benefited the city financially by "greatly increasing the efficiency of the city laborers, and all wage earners in the great industries of Worcester." In 1893 a temperance group similarly argued "that the men earn better wages, lose less time, do better work under no-license, while the relations between employers and workmen are more harmonious." Fifteen years later O. W. Norcross, a longtime temperance crusader and a prominent Worcester builder, echoed the same theme: "Manufacturers and employers with rare exceptions favor no-license. They report that under no-license their employees are steadier and more industrious; men are not so often absent from their work."[28]

It is difficult to untangle the degree to which middle-class and elite temperance arguments responded to actual, rather than just perceived, threats to family or factory. To be sure, alcoholism could be devastating for both middle- and working-class families. And in the context of inadequate working-class incomes, even moderate drinking could drain family finances, subvert saving for house purchases, and strain family bonds. Finally, there is ample evidence that drinking impaired work safety, discipline, efficiency, and productivity. At the same time, however, temperance ideology, as historian Harry Gene Levine has pointed out, "contained a powerful strand of fantasy" and "scapegoating." It presented abstinence as a "total solution" and alcohol as a "total cause" for much more fundamental economic and social problems rooted in the unequal distribution of power and wealth and the organization of work under industrial capitalism.[29] Indeed, even from the standpoint of pure self-interest (a concern, for example, with maintaining social order, hierarchy, and discipline) rather than altruism (a concern, for example, with poverty or alcohol-related diseases), the temperance movement was possibly misdirected. At least in Worcester, as we have seen, the saloon – the central focus of temperance venom – nurtured a working-class culture that rejected, but did not challenge, the dominant cultural and economic order.

Workers and temperance

Accurately or not, Worcester's elite perceived temperance as a defense of the industrial discipline of the factory and the cultural discipline of the middle-class home. But what about the large number of working people who shared their antipathy to alcohol? The most obvious explanation would be that these workers had absorbed the complete package of native middle-class values. Temperance, one historian argues, was "a symbol of middle-class membership" and, as another historian adds, appealed to "the aspiring workingman."[30] Some working-class temperance supporters, who might be termed "middle-class mobiles," did see sobriety as a strategy for individual advancement. But for a much larger group, which might be called "working-class respectables" or "settled livers," temperance was more of a strategy for maintaining a secure and stable way of life centered on the church and traditional ethnic institutions. And for still a third (and in Worcester quite small) group, which might be labeled "temperance radicals," anti-drink sentiment was a means for attacking the dominant power structures in the society and winning group advancement of some kind. Such analytical categories usefully recall some of the divisions in styles of July Fourth celebrations and also help to illuminate the range of working-class temperance positions. But they can distort individual experiences and values. Working-class temperance advocates could simultaneously embrace dreams of self-advancement, attachments to traditional institutions, and visions of class solidarity, just as they could fall off the wagon and rejoin their less temperate brethren in the saloon. And to complicate matters further, working-class temperance sentiment in Worcester was organized primarily through the city's ethnic communities rather than through commitments to any particular set of views on the drink question.

On October 20, 1849, the Reverend Theobald Mathew arrived in Worcester, and by the next afternoon he had administered the pledge of total abstinence to more than 400 Irish Catholics. Such rapid success would not have surprised anyone familiar with Father Mathew's prior career in Ireland. In a series of massive open-air meetings in the late 1830s and early 1840s, the charismatic reverend personally gave the pledge to more than half the population of Ireland. His American crusade yielded less spectacular, if still dramatic, results: More than a half million people took the pledge from him during his twenty-eight-month visit. Although the Father Mathew movement faded during the hard times of the late 1850s, a band of Worcester followers, who had constituted themselves as the Very Reverend Father Mathew Mutual Benevolent Total Abstinence Society in November 1849, continued to meet. They prospered sufficiently to build their own meeting hall in 1874 but attracted few other Catholics. And other Irish and French-Canadian temperance societies appear to have been short-lived.[31]

As late as 1881, then, the Father Mathew society, with about 180 members, was the only Catholic temperance society in a city with about 20,000 Irish Catholics and more than 4,000 French Catholics. In the next decade, however, Catholic temperance activity burgeoned with five of the city's seven Irish-Catholic parishes creating male temperance societies with a total membership of more than 1,000. In addition, the Catholic Young Women's Lyceum, the city's first permanent Irishwomen's organization, appeared in 1886 and centered its attention on temperance. Another three parish temperance societies appeared in the next decade, but the depression of the 1890s temporarily devastated the Irish temperance movement.[32]

Both the Father Mathew society and the more recently created parish temperance societies differed sharply from their ostensible brethren in the Protestant temperance movement in their view of liquor licensing. Seeking votes in favor of licensing, a Worcester election poem invoked the name of the founder of the city's Catholic temperance movement: "The morals plain as you may guess / had Father Mathew lived, he would vote yes." To most Irish Catholics, the no-license movement was extremely distasteful: When three of the city's Catholic priests rather tentatively recommended a "no" vote in the 1886 local option election, the city's Irish newspaper charged that "their opinions are not in accord with the majority of the Catholic clergymen of this city, nor are they binding upon the Catholics of their congregation."[33]

The author of these charges, James H. Mellen, himself a former president of the Father Mathew society, viewed persuasion, not coercion, as the proper road to temperance. The only way to meet intemperance, he editorialized, "is to inculcate into the heart of man, the love of sobriety." To achieve this goal, Irish temperance societies used two strategies: the taking of the "pledge" and the provision of recreational activities alternative to those available in the saloon. The importance of pledge taking to the Irish temperance movement indicates its primary concern with the individual drinker rather than with the social institution of the saloon – the reverse of Protestant temperance priorities. Joining a Catholic temperance society and taking the pledge was an act of self-reform, not social reform. Indeed, there was obviously a good deal of personal struggle and agony in such decisions. Members only promised abstinence for a limited period of time, usually one year. Many were unable to keep their pledge for even that period. Almost 10 percent of the members of the St. John's Temperance and Literary Guild were expelled for pledge violations in the last seven months of 1884.[34]

The taking of the pledge was an individual decision, but one carried out in a social context. It was done while kneeling before a priest and was invested with both religious and communal sanctions, which were reinforced by weekly or biweekly temperance society meetings and by attending Holy Communion as a group at least twice a year. The Irish-Catholic community both affirmed and circumscribed the action of the pledge taker, who did not proselytize for the temperance cause outside the Irish community. Even within the community their actions were limited, in the words of the pledge, to "advice and example." Members of the Catholic Young Women's Lyceum took the pledge themselves and encouraged brothers, fathers, and boyfriends to do likewise. Unlike the bands of praying women or the members of the Women's Christian Temperance Union (WCTU), they did not march on illegal saloons or leaflet against licensing.[35]

Even more central than the pledge to the Catholic temperance societies was the provision of alternative recreational facilities and activities. Most societies had well-appointed clubrooms with newspapers, domino sets, gymnasiums, card tables, libraries, and even pool tables. In addition, they usually provided such regular diversions as band concerts, minstrel shows, excursions, lectures, debates, coffee parties, and dances. Some had special paramilitary auxiliaries with elaborate uniforms and drilling routines. Almost all organized enthusiastic baseball, basketball, bowling, and track and field teams. The goal, temperance leaders believed, was to offer everything "that would tend to make the young man forget the temptations of the gilded saloon."[36]

To a surprising degree, then, the model for the temperance society was actually the saloon. The willingness of Irish-Catholic temperance societies to embrace the world of the saloon – with the obvious exception of drinking – offers a vivid contrast to the mainstream Protestant temperance movement, which rejected the saloon in its entirety. Indeed, in 1892 when social reformer Frank Vrooman, pastor of Worcester's Salem Congregational Church, attempted to provide pool tables and other facilities as "a substitute to the evil surroundings of the saloon," he met strong opposition from conservative church members. Thus, whereas Protestant temperance supporters sought to distance themselves from the world of the saloon, Catholic temperance supporters sought to narrow that gap. At least the Father Mathew society embraced the ethnic character of the saloon by participating actively in Irish celebrations and contributing to Irish nationalist causes. And all the temperance societies tried to imitate the masculinity of the saloon by sponsoring "manly sports."[37]

In the same way that many went to the saloon for the companionship more than the beer, some probably joined a temperance society for the sports or the plays more than for the support in abstinence from liquor. Yet for many, temperance was a purposeful choice representing a serious decision – or at least an aspiration – about the current or future direction of their lives. Was this a decision for upward social mobility as some historians have argued? For at least some members of the parish temperance societies, who, as previously indicated, tended to be young, single, second generation, and more Americanized, a desire for material or occupational success may have figured in their decision to shun alcohol. The notion that "excessive drinking blocked a man's chances for self improvement," as Timothy J. Meagher points out, was certainly a central theme of Catholic temperance publications and sermons in Worcester. The Catholic Young Men's Lyceum proclaimed in 1900 that it stood "not only for temperance but everything that tends toward the advancement of its members and that it created in them a "desire to improve . . . [their] condition in life." And such visions of upward mobility actively shaped the behavior of some of Worcester's young Irish-Catholic abstainers. Stephen Littleton, an Irish laborer's son who later became a lawyer, joined actively in the Catholic temperance movement and filled his diary with reminders to "spend my leisure time to some advantage to myself." The temperance societies also tried to advance concretely the careers of young men like Littleton through libraries, lectures, debates, and even courses on subjects like bookkeeping.[38]

Yet the quest for self-advancement existed within a context of an intense Catholicism, which also could proclaim a "gospel of acceptance." The Catholic priests who organized and led the parish temperance societies both promised material success and warned against unbridled ambition. Moreover, the reality of the temperance societies did not always meet the socially mobile aspirations of some of their members. The St. John's Temperance and Literary Guild nicely captured this contradiction when it announced a series of lectures by members of the society on their own trade or calling: "Many of our people are excellent journeymen, but few are masters; and we think that the reason is found in the fact that most of us rest satisfied with fair wages and ordinary knowledge and skill. We desire to see some of our men go further than this, and we are sure that such study such as is had in the preparation of the lecture, will stimulate a deeper study, and the young men will become through it, master mechanics." Yet even the author of this announcement was not willing to insist that social mobility was the only purpose of the society. "Study in winter and athletics in summer is the rule," he concluded.[39]

The social composition of the temperance societies confirms the complaint that "most of us rest satisfied with fair wages and ordinary knowledge and skill." Only about 11 percent of those who joined the St. John's temperance society between 1884 and 1888 held white-collar jobs. However, although the percentage of white-collar workers among new members had almost doubled by the turn of the century, the level of occupational attainment remained about the same as that for second-generation Irish Americans as a group. The contrast between working-class jobs and middle-class aspirations may be partially explained by the youthfulness of the membership: In 1898 the median age of those joining St. John's was only twenty-two.[40]

The members of the Father Mathew temperance society may have lacked even the aspirations toward middle-class status that marked at least some members of the parish temperance societies. They were older, married men representing the first generation of Worcester Irish. In 1880 almost 90 percent were immigrants, about 85 percent were married or widowed, and their median age was forty. For them, temperance may have signified a desire for a settled and stable life within the Irish community rather than an aspiration for individual mobility out of that community. As noted in the discussion of July Fourth celebrations, the members of the Father Mathew society emphasized the preservation and celebration of their Irish heritage to a much greater degree than did their counterparts in the parish societies. In addition, an analysis of the social composition of the Father Mathew society lends some support to an interpretation of its members as "settled livers" rather than "middle-class mobiles." Not only were the Father Mathew members largely working class (only 13 percent held white-collar jobs in 1882, for example), but individuals experienced little occupational advancement. About equal numbers of the 1882 members moved up and down the occupational scale during a ten-year period. Rather than occupational mobility, the Father Mathew members demonstrated a remarkable residential stability. Almost three-quarters of the 1882 members of the society still lived and worked in Worcester ten years later. By way of contrast, of a random sample of 226 Irish laborers drawn from the 1881 *Worcester Directory*, only 36 percent remained after ten years.[41]

For the Father Mathew society members, then, stability and community may have been the watchwords, not mobility and individuality. Interestingly, one historian has argued that the Father Mathew movement in Ireland lacked the commitment to individualism that marked the English and American temperance movements. Linked closely to Daniel O'Connell's efforts to repeal the union between Ireland and England, it offered a utopian vision of national liberation. Thus, the self-improving, purposeful strand of the Father Mathew movement – the commitment to sobriety, thrift, prudence, industry – was directed at "improvement of the entire country" more than at improvement of the isolated individual.[42]

Whether or not this collective and utopian vision continued to animate the Father Mathew movement after its transplantation to America is difficult to determine, but the presence of so many Irish immigrants in the society points toward some possible connection. "Mutuality," for example, played a crucial role within the society. The full name of the organization included the words "mutual benevolent"; benefits provided during times of sickness and death constituted a central purpose of the society; and one of its slogans was "We visit the sick and bury our dead."[43] Such mutual benefits simultaneously fulfilled a crucial economic need, bound the members together in reciprocal obligation, and institutionalized the reciprocity that informally pervaded the saloon.

To some extent, then, the Irish temperance societies stood outside the values supported by the Protestant industrial elite. But did they ever directly – rather than implicitly – challenge those values or the economic and political power that stood behind them? In some cities, temperance was clearly used as a tool of movements seeking radical change of some kind. Paul Faler and Alan Dawley, for example, have identified a group of workers in Lynn, Massachusetts, whom they call "rebel mechanics" because they viewed temperance as evidence of self-pride and independence as well as a vehicle for advancing workers as a class.[44]

In Worcester, however, where trade unionism and radicalism were weak, temperance radicalism was also weak. In late nineteenth century Worcester, its primary exponent was James H. Mellen. Worcester born of Irish immigrant parents, Mellen worked as a molder in the 1860s and 1870s; but by the end of that decade, he had entered Democratic party politics and begun to publish the city's only Irish Democratic newspaper, the *Worcester Daily Times*. As both a state representative and newspaper editor in the 1880s, Mellen backed a variety of Irish national and labor reform causes. In the words of his enemies on the conservative *Worcester Telegram*, Mellen was a "labor agitator and office seeker . . . demagogue and sand-lot orator" with "communistic ideas about labor." Mellen's radicalism was not inconsistent with strong temperance sentiment. Mellen belonged to both the Father Mathew society and the St. John's Temperance and Literary Guild. And he was not alone in seeing the union hall and the temperance hall as mututally reinforcing institutions. Terence Powderly, who, like Mellen, was both a leader of the Knights of Labor and a member of the Father Mathew society, told a Boston audience that "one hundred thousand or fifty thousand sober, honest, earnest men . . . will wage the battle of labor more successfully than . . . twelve million . . . men who drink either moderately or drink to excess."[45]

In some cities such as Denver temperance radicalism could make bedfellows of socialists and prohibitionists. But Worcester's James H. Mellen, as well as the local Knights of Labor, refused to endorse no-license or to work with groups like the WCTU. Mellen complained that the WCTU was "condescending" and asked rhetorically: "Did anybody ever hear of a prohibitionist taking an interest in the cause of labor?" For Mellen, temperance was only a means to labor reform, not an end in itself. And he similarly lashed out against saloonkeepers when he felt they were obstructing working-class causes. In 1889, for example, he denounced "the dictatorial conduct of the rum bosses" and their refusal to support "labor reform." Mellen believed that the liquor dealers were ready to sell out not just workers but also the city's Irish population to protect their own interests. In 1882 he charged that the saloonkeepers were involved in secret dealings to deliver the Democrats into the hands of "republicans or know nothings, from whose red hands the blood of many a democrat and foreigner is still dripping." So angered was Mellen that on this one occasion he threw his last-minute support to the no-license cause in his home ward.[46]

Despite such occasional defiance, Mellen had little choice but to work with the saloonkeepers and liquor dealers. They were the financial mainstays of the Democratic party, and there was very little support locally for an alternative workingman's party. Moreover, his own newspaper – always a shaky financial proposition – needed their advertising and financial support. Liquor dealers allegedly provided funds to keep him in business through the 1886 election; by 1888 liquor dealer George Hewitt held the mortgage on his presses.[47]

Temperance radicalism in Worcester, then, was as tenuous as the finances of the *Daily Times,* and there is little evidence of this position after that paper folded in 1889. In fact, during the depression years of the 1890s the Ancient Order of Hibernians (an organization with ties to the city's saloonkeepers) was much more likely to take pro-labor, anti-corporate positions than were the temperance forces. The Catholic temperance movement, with its ideology of social mobility and its conservative economic views, lost members during the hard times of the nineties.[48] Temperance sentiment continued within the Worcester labor movement, which often publicized the personal sobriety of its leaders, but it existed in the context of a conservative craft unionism. The new business agent of the Carpenters'

Union in 1897, for example, proclaimed himself both a total abstainer and a proponent of "law and order" committed to fighting the "hot heads" in his union and working "quietly" with the bosses. Moreover, whether radical or conservative, Worcester trade unionists never organized for temperance on a class basis. In 1899 both the Irish-born vice president of the Plumbers' Union and the native-born vice president of the Central Labor Union were temperance men, but the former belonged to the St. Paul's Total Abstinence Society and the latter was a member of the Worcester Reform Club.[49]

The Reform Club, founded in 1876 by Susan ("Mother") Gifford, one of the leaders of the Women's Crusade, was only one of Worcester's many Protestant temperance societies, but its predominantly working-class character made it unusual. At the turn of the century about three-quarters of the members held blue-collar – mostly skilled – jobs. As perhaps befits this amalgam of blue-collar and Protestant members, the Reform Club adopted a mix of temperance strategies that reflects the approaches of both middle-class and working-class temperance societies. Unlike the Catholic societies, the Reform Club gave vigorous support to the no-license cause. In 1899, for example, the Worcester Temperance Federation solicited the help of Reform Club members in getting "shopmates" to vote "no." Despite the Reform Club's participation in the no-license campaign, it shared with the Catholic temperance societies a primary concern with the self-reform of the drinker, particularly through pledge taking and mutual support. Meetings included personal testimony on the positive effects of abstinence and discussions of what to do about fallen members. The anniversary of a member's taking of the pledge called for a big celebration with friends gathering for singing, testimony, and the presentation of gifts.[50]

The degree to which the skilled workmen of the Reform Club shared the cultural assumptions of the Protestant elite is difficult to determine given the limited evidence. Nevertheless, there were close organizational connections between those native Protestant workers committed to temperance and the elites who dominated the city and the temperance movement. As previously noted, some native skilled workers signed anti-saloon petitions sponsored by their employers – even when fellow immigrant workers supported the saloonkeeper. In addition, the Reform Club seems to have had close ties to the manufacturers, ministers, and women who led the middle- and upper-class temperance movement. Women from the praying bands helped start the club, ministers like the Reverend Gould of the Union Congregational Church spoke at their meetings, and manufacturers like Philip L. Moen gave strong backing to their efforts. Thus, as with the Protestant church, the temperance society may have been a means of forging social and cultural ties between Protestant workers and their employers, and such ties may have offered concrete economic benefits. In 1907, for example, the Worcester No-License Correspondence Committee included eight employees of Graton and Knight, whose pro-temperance owner was one of the leading manufacturers in the city. Among the eight were the factory superintendent and two foremen – all three of whom had started out as belt makers for Graton and Knight.[51]

The close ties between the native Protestant workers and their employers make it difficult to discuss them as a distinct group. Much more visible and more important in the city's temperance movement were Swedish Protestants. Indeed, the evidence of Swedish temperance sentiment is so abundant that it is possible to forget that not all Worcester Swedes supported the dry crusade. Although temperance predominated within the Swedish community, alternative views seem to have gained in acceptability during the course of the late nineteenth century. Whereas the protest against granting a license to Martin Trulson struck a "deep chord" within the Swedish community in 1888, by the early 1890s there appears to have been no systematic protest against his license. During these same years the local Swedish newspaper also gradually dropped its support for no-license. By 1890 *Skandinavia* somewhat tentatively recommended that its readers vote "yes." And within another ten years it strongly favored liquor licensing and even criticized no-license advocates as "fanatical."[52] Perhaps one-third of Worcester's Swedish voters shared *Skandinavia*'s convictions and voted in favor of licensing.

Of course, *Skandinavia*'s editors, as well as many other Swedes who supported liquor licensing, continued to oppose drinking. But some Swedes gave more wholehearted support to the saloon through their patronage. In most years after 1888 Worcester had one or two saloons under Swedish management. Even before that year some non-Swedish saloonkeepers attracted Swedish customers by hiring a Swedish bartender. Moreover, many Swedes preferred to do their drinking within their ethnic clubs, and by the turn of the century Svea Gille and the Engelbrekt Boat Club, two popular Swedish social clubs, held licenses. Other organizations did not bother with such legal formalities. "Every inhabitant of our beloved city (especially the police officers and city marshal)," complained one Worcester Swede in 1888, "knows what kind of entertainments there used to be at Mystic Brother's hall [a headquarters of local Swedish fraternal organization] when the mystic influence of liquor had awakened their Viking blood." For the one period for which such figures are available, the 1930s, Swedes made up a disproportionate share of those arrested for drunkenness in Worcester.[53]

How do we reconcile heavy drinking with "fanatic" temperance views? In fact, both drinking and temperance have roots within Swedish history and culture. In early nineteenth century Sweden drink held a central, almost sacred, place. "What won't a German do for money and a Swede for a drink" goes an old Swedish saying. Virtually every landowning farmer operated a still to produce the fiery *brännvin,* or Swedish brandy, generally considered an integral part of the Swedish diet. Per capita alcohol consumption in early nineteenth century Sweden reportedly exceeded that of all other European nations. At around the same time that temperance and evangelical Christianity swept America, however, a similar combination of movements reshaped Swedish drinking habits. A popular anecdote told by the pietists, or *läsare,* emphasized the close relation between religious revivalism and temperance in nineteenth-century Sweden. A crown official, upon hearing that the pietists, who opposed the State Lutheran Church, were holding a secret bible reading, hastened to the scene, but finding "only a table laden with bottles, glasses, and playing cards, the officer of the law exclaimed: 'There are no *läsare* here; these people are good Lutherans!' "[54] Such conflicts between the brännvin-drinking, card-playing Lutherans and the teetotaling, Bible-reading pietists divided early nineteenth century Sweden as it would late nineteenth century Worcester.

Although in Sweden religious dissenters composed only a small percentage of the total population, in Worcester pietism and temperance were the dominant Swedish creeds. Such a configuration should suggest that pietism dominated the Swedish migrants to Worcester. Yet, though historians of Swedish emigration acknowledge that some sects such as the Baptists were more likely to immigrate to America, they argue against any general religious impact on migration patterns.[55] What explains this apparent paradox? It seems that the popularity of pietism among Worcester Swedes grew out of both transplantation and what religious historian Timothy Smith has called the "theologizing" impact of immigration. In particular, as Smith argues, the strength of temperance sentiment among some immigrants can be seen as a "perfectionist" reponse to the prospect of settling a new land.[56]

Worcester's Swedish Methodist Church, the city's first Swedish church, reflects this combination of transplantation of earlier beliefs and intensification of religious experience in a new home. "This congregation," a local church historian wrote of the Swedish Methodist Church in 1908, "has its origin in Sweden in 1867." The unpublished history then recounts the growth of Methodist sentiment in Degerfors, Vårmland, the migration of some church members to Ishpeming, Michigan, and the subsequent migration to Worcester in 1875 to seek employment in the wire works. When a Methodist congregation was officially formed in 1878, thirty-six members were admitted as transfers from the Methodist churches of Michigan and Sweden. But another twenty-three probationary members had no prior Methodist connection. From the start, therefore, Worcester's Swedish Methodist Church both drew on transplanted pietists and attracted new members not previously committed to pietism. Consequently, Swedish Methodists had adherents in almost two-thirds of the Swedish families in Quinsigamond Village by 1880.[57]

By the 1890s the Methodists faced substantial competition from Swedish Baptists and Congregationalists as well as Swedish Lutherans. Methodist Church membership among Quinsigamond Village Swedish families dropped below one-third, but overall the pietists still dominated. In 1908 less than one-third of the city's Swedish church members belonged to one of Worcester's two Swedish Lutheran churches. The rest attended the six Baptist, Methodist, and Congregational Swedish churches. Moreover, even the Lutherans – members of the Augustana Synod, a body with a distinct identity from the Swedish State Lutheran Church – were more pietistic and temperance-minded than their State Church counterparts in Sweden. Since Swedish immigrants were not required to join the church, as they had been in Sweden, only the more pious tended to affiliate. Indeed, at least half of Worcester's Swedes appear to have eschewed church membership altogether.[58]

It seems likely, then, that the "unchurched" Swedes continued to drink their brandy, while the pietistic, churchgoing Swedes campaigned to stop them. In addition, some of the more secularized Swedes – in particular, the three lodges of the International Order of Good Templars (IOGT) – joined the pietists in voicing disapproval of the drink trade. As a secret organization, however, the IOGT drew the ire of many Swedish ministers on the grounds that it "would undermine Christianity." Thus, the Swedish Good Templars advocated religious toleration and avoided religious discussions. Indeed, when the English-speaking, native-American IOGT lodges in Massachusetts, which operated more or less as "auxiliary organizations of their churches," criticized Sunday meetings of the Swedish-speaking lodges as "sacrilegious" and forbade their continuance, the Swedish lodges withdrew and formed their own Swedish-speaking Grand Lodge.[59]

Some of the pietistic disapproval of the Good Templars stemmed from the willingness of the IOGT to embrace more active recreational alternatives to the saloon. Both pietists and Good Templars participated in the no-license movement, but the IOGT also favored the "counter-attractionist" strategies used by the Catholic temperance societies. They strongly encouraged drama, singing, and gymnastics as well as lectures and study circles. Comfortable clubrooms provided a congenial gathering place for members, who were overwhelmingly blue-collar workers and included a roughly equal mix of men and women. In the words of their historian, the Good Templars sought "to fill up the emptiness of . . . existence" faced by new immigrants and to prove that "total abstinence was fun as well as seriousness."[60]

In addition to the "counter-attraction" strategy of the Catholic temperance societies, at least some IOGT members appear to have also adopted the temperance radicalism of a few Catholic temperance supporters like James H. Mellen. Such views may have had roots within the Swedish temperance movement, which also played a role in challenging the dominant social and economic order in Sweden. Indeed, the radicalism of these IOGT members focused more on Swedish than on American issues. In 1907, for example, most Worcester Swedes celebrated Swedish Prince Wilhelm's visit to Worcester as "their greatest day since coming to the land of the free," but the Quinsigamond Village Lodge of the IOGT refused to join the festivities: "This is a fraternal organization and as such, [we] regard all men as equal. Another thing, the members feel that the Prince has not done anything toward the temperance cause, and therefore should not be accorded any more honor than any ordinary man." Two years later, the Eastern Scandinavian Grand Lodge (to which the Worcester IOGT was affiliated) endorsed the resolution of Olof Bokelund of Worcester, expressing "warm sympathy" for "our fighting brothers" involved in the Swedish general strike. By World War I at least one faction of the IOGT supported a "New Sweden" reform movement, which linked "capitalism" and "the drink evil" as two major obstacles to the "pursuit of happiness."[61]

For these Swedes, then, temperance became part of a life-style and ideology directed at reforming, if not overthrowing, capitalism. Although their major interest was Swedish politics, they did not ignore American politics entirely. Theodor Osberg, for example, was not only chief templar of Worcester's Monitor Lodge of the IOGT and grand secretary of the Eastern Scandinavian Grand Lodge; he also ran in 1900 as the Socialist Labor party candidate for alderman in Worcester. In the same year Olof Bokelund, who later introduced the general strike resolution and helped lead the "New Sweden" faction, ran as a Democratic Socialist candidate for the same office. Yet the results indicate that their anticapitalist politics did not interest most voting Swedes. Neither got more than 3.5 percent of the citywide vote, and although both ran ahead of their tickets in Quinsigamond Village, their combined vote in that Swedish district was only 54, or about 14 percent of the ballots cast.[62] Still, even such limited support was significant in a city where Socialists rarely attracted more than 2 percent of the total vote.

Worcester's pietistic Swedes showed little evidence of this temperance radicalism. Indeed, their crusades against the saloon tied them closely with the city's elite as fellow participants in the no-license and license-restriction movements. Despite these links, the pietists did not embrace the full set of values promoted by the native Protestant elite. Rather, their temperance views grew out of their cultural heritage as "Christians and Swedes," as one Swedish minister put it. In other words, temperance gained its strength within Worcester's Swedish community as part of a world view with a separate integrity of its own, not out of some imitation of the values promoted by the city's leading industrialists. Moreover, Swedish temperance efforts remained largely, although not entirely, focused on the Swedish community. Petitions were aimed at *Swedish* saloons, and rallies were most often conducted in Swedish. Finally, temperance efforts could be part of larger patterns of communal self-help. During the 1893 depression, for example, the Swedish temperance union contributed all its funds to employing jobless Swedes.[63]

The drink question thus spawned a bewildering array of positions in late nineteenth century Worcester. The Protestant industrial elite and their native middle-class allies attacked the saloon for a combination of cultural and economic reasons. Some workers – particularly native skilled workers and Swedish immigrants – joined these crusades, although their actions often grew out of distinct ethnic, religious, and class perspectives. Few Catholic immigrants joined in this assault on the saloon, but some of their number did attack drinking as a problem that faced their communities. In addition, the Catholic temperance movement actually incorporated a variety of motives: a search for middle-class respectability, an interest in a stable and settled ethnic community, and a desire for social change. The saloon and the temperance movement thus became intense battlegrounds buffeted by the powerful and complex forces of class, gender, and ethnicity. But what was the impact of these clashes both on the saloon and on social and political life in Worcester?

The struggle over the saloon and its consequences

"The question is often asked," Worcester City Marshal James Drennan noted in his 1870 Annual Report, "why don't the police officers put a stop to these beer nuisances and prevent the sale and drinking of beer Sundays?" But Drennan scoffed at such bothersome complaints, equating them with the question "why don't the officers stop the rivers from descending on their course to the sea?"[64] Such fatalistic reminders of the irrepressibility of working-class drinking habits did not, of course, stop a generation of opponents of the saloon from fighting to limit the number of liquor licenses, to close all drink places through local option, or to use regulations or police powers to make the saloon a more orderly place.

In a city with a strong industrial elite and a weak working-class labor and radical movement one might assume that these class-based attacks on the saloon would prove quickly successful. In fact, they quickly failed. For the most part, Worcester working-class saloongoers simply ignored or evaded the regulations so carefully wrought by their antagonists. Through such evasions, workers frustrated the efforts of Worcester industrialists to extend their hegemony to recreation as well as work. Worcester workers generally succeeded in preserving their right to use their leisure time for "what we will," even if that meant drunkenness.

On the surface, petitions against liquor licenses yielded some concrete victories. In the late 1870s the Board of Aldermen, under pressure from elite and religious groups, cut the total number of legal licenses in half. But such cuts could do little about those who chose to stay in business without legal sanction.[65] Illegal drink sellers, City Marshal Drennan complained, "retired very slowly under the pressure of the law." The R. G. Dun and Company records indicate, however, that many unlicensed sellers did gradually abandon the drink trade. Moreover, a more professional and better equipped police force seems to have had an increasing impact on illegal sales in the 1880s and 1890s. In 1882 Drennan admitted that he had only managed to close about one-third of the illegal drink places that the police department actually knew about. Yet by 1890 his successor as city marshal claimed that "this evil is being gradually circumscribed" by the "great vigilance" and "perseverance" of the police. Reports from around the turn of the century suggest increasing, but far from total, police effectiveness in shutting down illegal sellers.[66]

Petition drives against particular liquor sellers were most successful in neighborhoods that were distant from downtown and that strongly supported temperance. The Board of Aldermen and the License Commission (which issued licenses after 1893) were most likely to be guided by such petitions, and the police were most able to enforce the ban on liquor sales in such neighborhoods. Thus, the middle-class West Side was also the city's most prominent liquor-free zone during the late nineteenth and early twentieth centuries. The experience of Washburn and Moen in campaigning against liquor licenses in the vicinity of its two major plants – the South Works in Quinsigamond Village, about two and a half miles from downtown, and the North Works, a short walk from downtown – supports this point. Its petitions against liquor licenses in Swedish and pro-temperance Quinsigamond Village were almost always granted, but its protests about saloons in Lincoln Square and the North End, neighborhoods near the downtown business district with a large Irish working-class population, met only intermittent approval. Even when these latter petitions were approved, they were much more likely to have been rendered ineffective by illegal liquor sellers.[67]

The victories of the movement to close all saloons through a "no" vote in local option elections were at once more sporadic, more complete, and more fleeting than those of the license-restriction campaigns. In December 1885, 1889, 1891, 1907, and 1908 Worcester voters gave the no-license forces narrow election victories. The ban on liquor sales was obviously more complete than those won through license-restriction petitions, but the overall result was even more widespread violations and evasions of the law. In the first of the no-license years, City Marshal W. Ansel Washburn mobilized "every means at my disposal to enforce this law." Prompted by temperance preacher Hugh Montgomery, Washburn served almost 1,400 search and seizure warrants and confiscated more than 4,000 gallons of liquor. Despite this "warfare on liquor," Washburn admitted that "I never knew the time when there were so many private families selling rum as there are today." Although one-third of the seventy-man police force was already pursuing liquor violators, Washburn felt that he needed another thirty men to attack the illegal drink trade adequately.[68]

Similar stories of widespread violations mark reports of Worcester's subsequent no-license years. Aided by the newly developed electric streetcar, many Worcesterites simply traveled to nearby towns that had not banned liquor. Even larger numbers ordered their liquor from express companies on the legal fiction that they were purchasing liquor from out of town. Between two-thirds and three-quarters of the city's liquor wholesalers used this dodge to remain in business in 1909. Between May 1908 and May 1910, the two-year period of no-license, more than 2 million gallons of beer and liquor were brought into the city. Large numbers of saloonkeepers were able to remain open on the pretext that they were selling soft drinks or 3 percent beer when actually they were selling stronger stuff fairly openly. Perhaps the most persuasive evidence of the persistence of alcoholic consumption was the high level of drunkenness arrests during no-license years. Drunkenness arrests never dropped more than 40 percent during a no-license year; in some years the decline was barely perceptible.[69] Still, it would be a distortion to say that no-license had no impact. The effect on the saloon, for example, was probably greater than on drinking itself. Generally, enforcement and compliance was strongest at the beginning of a no-license year, but violations grew more flagrant as the year proceeded.[70]

Efforts to enforce liquor laws and create more orderly saloons also had mixed effects. Yet what is most surprising, given the political and economic power of those advocating stricter enforcement, is, again, the widespread evasion of the regulations. To evangelical Protestants, the prohibition against Sunday liquor sales was obviously one of the most cherished provisions of the liquor law. But this regulation clashed with even more deeply ingrained working-class patterns. For many workers, Sunday was both their only day of leisure and the day after payday. Consequently, despite regulations to the contrary, Sunday was "the great business day" for saloonkeepers. Indeed, according to City Marshal Washburn, some proprietors apparently even left "the city during the six working days, and returned to their homes and business only on the Sabbath." Illegal Sunday sales accounted for about one-quarter of all liquor complaints between 1875 and 1879. Even more commonly violated than the Sunday ban was the law against "public bars" or drink places dispensing only liquor. Most saloonkeepers made only token compliance with the 1878 law, which required that they have "the necessary implements and facilities for cooking, preparing, and serving food." One saloonkeeper purchased an elegant range and good quality crockery, but told a reporter that "he had not had a fire in his stove and at the end of the year it would be sold for what it cost; as it would not be second-hand." Ultimately, the police gave up on enforcing the prohibition against "drink-only" establishments. "No attempt has been made to close the open bar on account of public opinion," Marshal Washburn admitted in 1879.[71]

The working-class leisure patterns that defeated the Sunday drink prohibitions and the "public opinion" Washburn cited as preventing enforcement of the public bar regulations provide the key to understanding why Worcester elites were never able to dominate effectively the nonwork lives of the immigrant working class. Drinking and the saloon were too much an integral part of Worcester's ethnic working-class world to be easily repressed by legal means. Police officials cited community opposition as the primary explanation for their failure to enforce the liquor laws. Reflecting on the difficulties of enforcing the 1886 no-license law, City Marshal Washburn wrote: "As the law is now recognized, the officers have not only to fight the liquor dealers, but a large share of the community." Two years earlier City Marshal Amos Atkinson had similarly blamed the lack of "moral support of the community at large" for his failure to eliminate unlicensed liquor establishments.[72]

Community residents subverted the enforcement of liquor laws by alerting liquor sellers to possible police raids, by helping dealers hide the illegal goods, and especially by directing popular pressure at police officers. "An officer taking the stand to testify in an ordinary liquor case," grumbled City Marshal Washburn in 1883, "goes there knowing that all the suspicions ever leveled at any mortal are to be directed at him, and it is not to be wondered at that many of them shrink from too much prominence in this business." According to Washburn, other forms of detective work were not considered "dishonorable," but "the minute war is waged upon illegal rum-selling, gambling, and kindred evils, that minute, officers become 'spotters,' 'informers,' 'peelers' and their social degradation is sure and rapid."[73]

Worcester police feared ostracism because so many of them belonged to the same Irish working-class community as did the liquor sellers and their customers. By the mid-1880s first- and second-generation Irish, primarily from blue-collar backgrounds, made up about one-half of the police force. Despite efforts to create a "temperance" police force, many officers drank. In 1874, for example, Michael McNamara was almost dismissed from the police force for getting drunk during the Father Mathew Total Abstinence Society's trip to Boston.[74]

Community pressure and police sympathy did not, however, protect all liquor law violators from apprehension and prosecution. Nevertheless, even those arrested usually escaped any immediate fine or imprisonment; jail sentences were extremely rare even for repeat offenders.[75] Such light sentences partially reflect the expert legal assistance of some of the city's smartest lawyers. "No class of offenders," wrote City Marshal Washburn of liquor law violators, "are so . . . ably defended." Local Democratic politicians like John R. Thayer and M. J. McCafferty devoted a good deal of their law practices to representing Worcester drink sellers. "All the eloquence that the 'Bar' can procure," Washburn noted bitterly, "is brought to *condemn the officer* and *condole the offender*." Where eloquence failed, time-consuming appeals did the trick. Between 1880 and 1881 almost three-quarters of those convicted in the lower Central District Court appealed to the Worcester County Superior Court. And, according to Washburn, "not over twenty percent of the appealed cases have ever been heard of since, or ever will be." The sympathetic views of the judges and juries in the superior court further benefited saloonkeepers.[76]

Legal restrictions on searches of private dwellings (where most illegal drink traffic centered) and requirements that police actually witness an illegal sale also protected liquor sellers. In 1879, for example, one policeman related how he and a fellow officer spent Sunday afternoon watching forty people come and go from a particular home. When they actually approached the house, "they heard the price of drinks for a party asked and stated; and heard money drop upon the floor." When they entered the house, they "found sixteen persons within. There were beer mugs with beer in them, tumblers with the remnants of whiskey and sugar in them, wet places on the floor where the beer had foamed over, and other evidences of the illegal traffic." However, when the violators were brought to court, "the prisoner and friends swore that it was only the visit of a few friends and the beer and liquor was given away." Since the police officers had not actually witnessed a sale, the judge dismissed the case. "There are hundreds of complaints made . . . that amount to nothing because of the requirements of the law," complained City Marshal Edward Raymond in a "Statement to Business Men."[77]

Thus, the law provided protection for boisterous and collective recreational styles that were vehemently opposed by the dominant economic group in Worcester. Even saloonkeepers, as property holders, or at least tenants, enjoyed the safeguard of the law's regard for private property. Through evasion, group pressure, and use of the legal system, saloongoers and saloonkeepers were able to defend one of the central institutions of working-class life from the attacks of some of the most powerful people in Worcester. But to conclude on this note would be to overstate both the strength of working-class culture and the impotence of elite attacks on that culture. Evaluated in another way, the struggle over the saloon suggests some of the important weaknesses of Worcester's ethnic working-class culture.

To state the obvious, the defense of the saloon involved no explicit challenge to power relations in Worcester. For the most part, workers overcame the law by ignoring it, not by confronting it in a formal or "political" way. In the annual no-license votes, the saloon was rarely defended as a working-class "right." Instead, supporters of liquor licensing usually argued their position on the grounds that no-license simply did not work.[78] Even the maneuvering over legal protections rarely raised broader issues of popular rights. Resistance to the attacks on the saloon was, like ethnic working-class culture, defensive and inward looking. Although saloongoers did not accept the dominant individualistic and competitive ethos of the industrial elite, neither did they mount an explicit challenge to that ethos. They simply ignored it. The unwillingness or inability of the police to use substantial force to ensure compliance with the liquor laws made it less likely that the alternative culture of the saloon would be transformed into an oppositional culture that directly attacked the larger system of class inequality. The likelihood of a class-wide mobilization growing out of the conflict over the saloon was further lessened by the cross-class alliances that the actual struggle created.

The defense of the saloon – both against license-restriction petitions and no-license crusades – involved workers in collaboration with those outside their class. Whereas most proprietors of small saloons had close ties to surrounding ethnic working-class communities, many of the larger liquor dealers and brewers did not. George Hewitt, the city's leading liquor dealer, was a wealthy businessman who belonged to the Masons, an organization that Catholics suspected of nativism. Many of the lawyers and politicians who defended the liquor interests also participated in a social world very different from that of saloongoers. Liquor lawyer and Democratic politician John R. Thayer hunted foxes with members of the West Side social elite, represented East Side workers on the Board of Aldermen, and defended their saloonkeepers in court.[79]

On the surface such alliances had no particular political significance. When examined more closely, however, it becomes evident that they tended to work against the development of working-class politics in Worcester. For the saloonkeepers in general and the large liquor dealers and brewers in particular, the defense of their economic interests was their overriding political goal. They sought, therefore, the defeat of no-license campaigns and the election of a sympathetic Board of Aldermen, which would freely issue liquor licenses, and a friendly city government, which would not enforce the liquor laws too rigidly. Since the liquor dealers were the financial mainstay of the city's Democratic party, they usually tried to manipulate party politics in service of these particular goals rather than of any larger social interests.[80] To this end they often – particularly in the 1870s and 1880s – backed coalition "Citizens'" candidates rather than straight Democratic tickets in the mayoralty elections. In effect, they helped to elect men tied to the city's social and economic elite who were also willing to tolerate the liquor interests. In 1883 and 1884, for example, they strongly backed mayoralty candidate Charles C. Reed, a carriage-wheel manufacturer, a member of the Mechanics Association and the Board of Trade, and a Republican in state and national politics. Even when the liquor dealers backed regular Democratic candidates, they often supported members of "the aristocratic element" of the party.[81]

Although other factors also militated against the development of a working-class political movement in Worcester, the activities of the liquor dealers seem to have been significant in preventing working-class candidates or candidates avowedly committed to working-class causes from emerging even within the limited confines of the Worcester Democratic party. In 1879, for example, H. H. Bigelow, a businessman who had the reputation of having supported labor causes, ran as a Democratic, pro-labor candidate for mayor. Liquor dealers and their close ally John R. Thayer, however, backed the more moderate Citizens' candidate, who won the election. The division within the Democratic ranks also led to the election of Republican manufacturer Matthew Whittall as the school committeeman for the working-class Fifth Ward. In 1882 a similar split between the Protective Liquor League, on the one hand, and pro-labor and pro-temperance Democrats, on the other hand, resulted in victory for the liquor interests, who were able to better command local working-class loyalties through the influence of the saloonkeepers. "Workingmen," exclaimed James H. Mellen, "you have been sold out to your enemies by a few of the liquor dealers in the city."[82]

But if the defense of the saloon inhibited the emergence of avowedly pro-labor candidates, the attack on the saloon proved even more damaging to working-class interests, albeit in very different ways. The emergence of a strong body of working-class temperance sentiment in the 1880s and 1890s made the liquor issue a potentially divisive one within the Worcester working class. More important, temperance offered a bridge for workers to unite culturally with their employers and against other workers. The particular political and social impacts of the working-class temperance movement varied, however, along with the ethnic variations in that movement.

The cross-class alliances and working-class divisions spawned by the Catholic temperance movement were limited in scope, since most Irish temperance advocates refused to back the no-license movement. Occasionally, some Irish temperance society members did join with the no-license and Republican forces out of their temperance convictions, thus further fracturing the Democratic party. But for most pro-temperance Catholics, like pro-labor voters, there was usually no choice but to remain within the Democratic party. The moral suasionist stance of the Catholic temperance movement also seems to have limited the support and patronage it received from industrialists and public officials. Although manufacturers contributed a few dollars to the Father Mathew building fund and although city officials appeared at their celebrations to praise their good work, a large gap separated working-class Catholic and elite Protestant temperance forces committed to the same ostensible cause.[83]

It was in the late 1880s and the 1890s with the entrance of large numbers of Swedish immigrants into Worcester that a much more powerful alliance between working-class and elite temperance forces developed. Whereas the Catholic and elite temperance movements appear to have operated on entirely separate tracks, the Swedes climbed aboard the elite train, even if they were not always seated in the first-class compartments. Although Philip L. Moen could spare only $5 for the Father Mathew building fund, his company contributed the entire $150 needed to fix up a cabin for the use of the Quinsigamond Good Templars – many of whom were his own employees. Whereas Irishwomen worked for temperance among their own relatives, Swedish wives and mothers joined their Yankee sisters at the polls urging "no" votes on election day. Whereas Irish temperance supporters rarely petitioned against specific liquor licenses, Swedish workers – particularly those employed at Washburn and Moen – regularly joined with their bosses on such petitions. Whereas even Irish cops feared social ostracism for testifying against liquor dealers, Swedes willingly worked as "spotters" of illegal dealers during no-license years. Whereas Irish temperance societies took no part in citywide no-license coalitions led by the Protestant elite, Swedish temperance societies and pietistic churches played a crucial role in such movements.[84]

These close ties forged in the temperance movement and reinforced through the Republican party and the Protestant churches had both economic and political implications. Swedish workers appear to have received favored treatment in both hiring and promotion from some leading companies. Yankees, according to the *Worcester Veckoblad,* expressed "respect" for Swedish workers but found the Irish "worthless and dangerous." From the perspective of Irish radicals like James H. Mellen, however, the favoritism shown toward Swedes stemmed rather from their alleged docility and willingness to work for lower wages. The "church going hypocrites" at Washburn and Moen, Mellen charged, imported Swedish workers because of the company's "low, selfish, and covetous desire to amass great wealth with rapidity. If the Chinese had a knowledge of iron working and would do it cheaper than the Swedes, the wire monopolists would send their agent, Mr. Morgan, to China."[85]

Although one might quarrel with some of Mellen's characterizations, this employer strategy does appear to have helped subvert unionization. "The ability of the Swedish workingman to get along with his employer," writes a historian of Worcester Swedes, "is witnessed by the lack of unions and strikes in such industries as Norton's and Morgan's, by the words of commendation for the Swedish workingman by John P. Higgins of the Worcester Pressed Steel Company, and Alden Reed of the Reed and Prince Manufacturing Company and by the long lists of veterans of Swedish lineage found" in many Worcester plants. In 1880 Swedish workers did briefly strike at Washburn and Moen, but they carefully explained that their complaint was against a Swedish foreman and not "Mr. Booth the good and beloved Superintendent." Seven years later when twenty-five women workers at the North Works of Washburn and Moen struck, the three Swedes among them broke ranks almost immediately and returned to work.[86]

Yet Worcester Swedes evinced divisions over trade unionism just as they did over temperance. In 1892 when Swedes took jobs as scabs during a freight handlers' strike, "150 Scandinavians met at Svea Gille Hall . . . to condemn the action of . . . their countrymen." Naturally, Swedish socialists took a favorable view of trade unionism and, although they had little success, vowed to organize the Swedish wireworkers. And during the 1915 machinists' strike Swedes appear to have been only slightly underrepresented among union members, although very few took leadership roles. In fact, Swedes rarely appeared as trade union leaders in turn-of-the-century Worcester: In 1899 no Swedes headed unions affiliated with the Central Labor Union, and only two held such positions twelve years later.[87]

At most times in the late nineteenth and early twentieth centuries the Swedish–Yankee alliance held, thereby ensuring not only labor peace on the shop floor but also Republican dominance in City Hall. Indeed, the integration of the Swedish working class into the Republican party – an allegiance forged largely through the temperance issue – goes a long way toward explaining both the local predominance of the Republican party and the absence of mayors or other political leaders from working-class backgrounds. Such an elite-controlled political system had important – and damaging – implications for those seeking to organize the city's workers or even to win equal treatment from the city government. Thus, whereas Worcester workers usually preserved their control over their nonwork lives – whether they wanted to drink at the corner saloon, shoot billiards at the Father Mathew Hall, or sew with the Swedish Ladies Aid Society – they less often triumphed at the ballot box or on the picket line. The resilience of the saloon in the face of the temperance crusade was an important victory, but given the compromises it involved and the internal divisions it exacerbated, it could not be translated into increased power in other realms.[88]

5 *The struggle over recreational space: the development of parks and playgrounds*

"You may take my word for it," landscape architect and horticulturist Andrew Jackson Downing wrote of parks in 1848, "they will be better preachers of temperance than temperance societies, better refiners of national manners than dancing schools and better promoters of general good-feeling than any lectures on the philosophy of happiness." For more than a century social reformers have depicted parks as weapons in the same moral crusade against working-class disorder, degeneracy, and drinking as the temperance movement. "No one who has closely observed the conduct of the people who visit Central Park," boasted Frederick Law Olmsted, the most distinguished and influential landscape architect of the middle and late nineteenth century, "can doubt that it exercises a distinctly harmonizing and refining influence upon the most unfortunate and lawless classes of the city – an influence favorable to courtesy, self-control, and temperance."[1]

The obvious motives of social control and the overt class biases evident in such statements have earned park and playground reformers the disdain of subsequent historians. "Thus it was," charges the author of a recent history of playground reform, "that a movement desiring to release the city's young from the harsher aspects of urban life became one which seemed to prepare them to accept their fate uncomplainingly." Social control was certainly an important and persistent motivation for many reformers, but to focus exclusively on this aspect of the park and playground movement reduces them to rationally calculating social engineers when actually their motivations were much more complex.[2] Early park reformers, for example, were also sparked by naturalistic visions of society, fears about urban disease, and infatuations with European public gardens as well as by the desire to uplift and quiet the masses.

More important, proponents of the social-control formula suggest that the object of reform designs – the urban worker – was both inert and totally pliable. By viewing park reform exclusively from the "top down," they ignore the possibility that workers might have taken an active part in conceiving or advocating parks and assume that workers uncritically accepted the park programs handed down by an omnipotent ruling class. Even Worcester's ethnically and culturally divided working class was able to resist reform schemes and even sometimes to reshape them to their own ends.

The birth of the park system

On January 11, 1870, the Worcester City Council appointed Edward Winslow Lincoln to the Commission on Shade Trees and Public Grounds. Almost immediately Lincoln became secretary and chairman of that body, and for the next quarter century he almost singlehandedly shaped and controlled Worcester's parks. So complete was his domination of the commission that his death in 1896 necessitated, for the first time, the hiring of a full-time park superintendent. A member of a leading Worcester family, Lincoln spent most of his first forty years seeking a suitable career, first in law and then in journalism. Beginning around 1860, however, he discovered his true vocation in horticulture and devoted most of his subsequent thirty-six years to the Worcester County Horticultural Society and the city's Parks Commission.[3]

In his elite background, as well as in his career instability and his idiosyncratic personality, Lincoln resembled Frederick Law Olmsted. More important, Lincoln seems also to have shared the conservative social assumptions of Olmsted and other Gilded Age genteel reformers, who insisted on a well-ordered and tranquil society based on hierarchy and professional leadership. Parks, in this view, would, in the same way as tariff or civil service reform, promote social cohesion and order. The quiet contemplation of a park's rural scenery, Olmsted believed, would calm the "rough element of the city" and "divert men from unwholesome, vicious, destructive methods and habits of seeking recreation."[4] But Olmsted's elegant vision of public parks and Lincoln's own less articulated views were not primarily centered on controlling the urban workers. Their main concern was the middle-class urban dweller, whose frayed nerves and exhausted body could be refreshed and renewed by the contemplation of a carefully crafted landscape.

Initially, at least, Lincoln had scant opportunity to implement this Olmstedian vision of the scenic park, for, upon becoming head of the Parks Commission in 1870, he found he had little to rule. Worcester's parkland consisted of an "unsightly" eight-acre Common and a larger twenty-eight-acre tract known as Elm Park, which primarily served as "a handy dumping ground for the Highway Department . . . [and] the casual job-wagon or wheelbarrow."[5] Such inelegant and inadequate public grounds offended Lincoln's horticultural sensibilities; he found them lacking the beauty of the elaborate European public gardens, fountains, and boulevards that he admired so much. Such grounds also failed to accord with Olmsted's view of parks as instruments of conservative social reform that might defuse social tensions.

Influenced by these aesthetic and moral visions, Lincoln fought for and won the appropriations needed to begin to shape Elm Park into a fair approximation of the Olmstedian contemplative ideal. Gradually, the land was cleared and drained; broad stretches of grass were planted; azaleas, rare trees, and exotic shrubs were artistically arranged; elaborate pools were constructed and arched by intricate wooden bridges.[6]

In pursuit of this ideal, Lincoln sought to banish active uses of Elm Park. Circuses, which had earlier lost their home on the Common, were banned in 1875. Three years later, the soon-to-be-familar "keep off the grass" signs were given legal sanction. Baseball playing was left undisturbed, but Lincoln hoped that this "dreary amusement" would soon be removed from his cherished Elm Park to specially designated playing fields in "different sections" of the city. Presumably, these fields would be placed closer to the homes of working-class Worcesterites who lived in the southeastern part of the city, not in the more exclusive West Side where Elm Park was located.[7] Lincoln was not necessarily opposed to what Olmsted called the "boisterous fun and rough sports" of the working classes. He simply felt that such activities did not belong in a scenic park.[8] The rowdy, exuberant, collective style of play that characterized working-class celebrations of the Fourth was the antithesis of what Lincoln and Olmsted had in mind for their scenic parks.

This clash between what environmental historian J. B. Jackson calls "two distinct and conflicting definitions of the park" – "the upper-class definition with its emphasis on cultural enlightenment and greater refinement of manners, and a lower-class definition emphasizing fun and games" – continued throughout Lincoln's park regime.[9] His annual Park Reports provide some guarded hints of this class conflict over park usage. In 1876, for example, he petitioned for police patrol of the Common and Elm Park, declaring, "this Commission will exact and enforce that decent behavior from all who frequent the Public Grounds, which is not only seemly in itself but is rightfully expected by the community." Repeated complaints describe correct park behavior as "peaceful," "inoffensive," and "quiet," whereas misbehavior was seen as "rude and boorish" or "disorderly and obscene." The *Worcester Spy* captured Lincoln's notion of proper park usage when it reported approvingly on Elm Park as a "resort for nurses and fond mamas, the former arrayed in the usual white cap and apron, who have brought out the babies for an airing."[10]

This conflict between different styles of park design and usage climaxed in the 1880s as two contrasting groups asserted new interests. On the one hand, the city's industrialists worked out new, more utilitarian arguments for park development that went beyond the contemplative ideal of Lincoln and the old gentry elite who made up the Parks Commission. They urged additions to the city's parkland for reasons of fire protection, health, civic pride, real estate development, paternalism, and social control. On the other hand, a large and rapidly growing immigrant working class raised its own demands for space suited to its more active, play-centered park models. Out of this clash emerged a spatial solution that allowed both groups a measure of autonomy within which to develop their own approaches to park usage and play.

In January 1884, 231 members of Worcester's elite, including several ex-mayors and many leading manufacturers, petitioned the City Council to purchase Newton Hill, a sixty-acre tract adjoining Elm Park. Their motivation, however, was not entirely aesthetic or recreational. They also saw Newton Hill as an ideal spot for a reservoir that would provide fire protection for their fashionable West Side homes.[11] Such political muscle could not be easily resisted. But an unlikely political alliance proved capable of at least temporarily obstructing the Newton Hill acquisition. On the one hand, fiscal conservatives on the Board of Aldermen opposed any new expenditures of public funds. On the other hand, representatives of the so-called lower wards, the immigrant and working-class southeastern section of the city, threatened to block the purchase in retaliation for the earlier defeat of their own efforts to secure public parkland for their constituents.

Residents of the East Side confronted the problem of finding play space in a city increasingly crowded by thousands of new immigrants. The expansion of the physical city could not keep pace with such rapid population growth. Before the expansion of streetcar service in the late 1880s and the electrification of the lines beginning in 1891, Worcester workers were sharply limited in their choice of residences. Between 1870 and 1890 the city's population jumped 206 percent, whereas its platted area grew only 29 percent. Consequently, the number of residents per platted acre increased by more than 50 percent.[12]

The effects of this increasing density were felt most strongly on the working-class East Side. The intensification of land use and the concurrent increases in property values encouraged the development and enclosure of vacant land previously used as play space. In 1882 the city marshal reported that in the absence of "public grounds for children and others for play and amusement, especially in the Southern section of the city . . . boys are driven from streets and fields, and private lands, by the officers." Although Worcester's East Side never approached the overcrowding of New York's Lower East Side, in the 1880s play space in that district was clearly losing ground to housing and commercial development. At the same time workers also found themselves barred from slightly more distant play areas that they had traditionally used. "Our suburban retreats," complained a letter writer to the *Worcester Daily Times,* "are dotted all over with notices to 'Keep off under Penalty of Law.'" Noting that only the rich could afford excursions to "seashore and mountain," the letter writer asked: "Where then are the masses of people to seek for rest and recreation, sunshine and the refreshing breezes of summertime?"[13]

Worcesterites of differing social backgrounds were acutely conscious of the class dimensions of these spatial developments. For its part, the city's elite was determined to prevent working-class encroachments into its West Side precincts. When a single family of French Canadians settled on Elm Street in the 1880s, it disturbed "the social serenity of the neighborhood," according to the *Worcester Sunday Telegram.* Soon a "terrible fear" swept "West-side society" in response to a rumor that a "cheap tenement block" filled with "the representatives of all nations" would be erected on the same spot. Only when manufacturer Philip W. Moen (the son of Philip L. Moen) purchased the property in 1889 did West Siders heave a sigh of relief. "Elm Street Set in Ecstacy: Philip W. Moen has Removed a Long-Time Nightmare," the *Telegram* headlined its story.[14]

While West Siders sought exclusivity, working-class East Siders complained about unequal treatment. James H. Mellen, the editor of the *Worcester Daily Times,* repeatedly accused the city government of favoritism and "deference" toward the "well-to-do people" of the

West Side, while it ignored the sewers, streets, and park space of the "workingmen's district." Noting the prevalence of diphtheria among the "cooped up" and "huddled together" East Siders, Mellen demanded municipal action: "We want more outside room, we want every inch of space the city can afford us."[15]

In the context of these class perceptions of spatial inequality, an indigenous movement developed among residents of the Irish working-class East Side (centered in the Fifth Ward) to demand public play space. As early as 1879, letter writers to the *Worcester Evening Star,* then the city's only pro-labor newspaper, complained about the attention lavished on Elm Park – derisively labeled "Lincoln's Patch" – whereas the more accessible (to the working class) Common was neglected. "One who had to stand" maintained that "the people's seats" had been removed from the Common and placed in Elm Park, which he called a "desolate spot where nobody will use them excepting the crows." Another letter writer, similarly perturbed about unequal treatment and impatient with the shaping of Elm Park into a scenic landscape, lampooned Lincoln as "the Earle of the frog ponds" and the "grandiloquent Earle of model pools."[16]

By 1882, however, East Siders began to demand not just better care of the Common; they also demanded their *own* park. Irish temperance and civic leader Richard O'Flynn called a meeting "with the thought that interest could be aroused for the establishment of public playgrounds." Around the same time, he gathered the signatures of almost 140 neighbors on a petition asking the City Council to acquire "a few acres of land" for "the less favored children." Desiring recreational space more congenial to active use than that of Elm Park, the petitioners declared, "there is no public ground in that vicinity [the Fifth Ward] where children or young men can resort, either for health or amusement."[17]

The signers of the O'Flynn petition contrasted sharply with the elite Newton Hill petitioners. Their only real social relation to these leading Worcesterites was as employees. Of the ninety-five signers who could be identified, seventy-five held blue-collar jobs. Even the twenty white-collar signers had little in common with the Newton Hill petitioners: Six of them, for example, ran provision or grocery stores and another three kept saloons.[18] Whereas the West Side industrial elite sought a park reservoir, their East Side Irish employees wanted a play space for themselves and their children.

So strong was the perception of the class basis of Worcester's spatial inequities that the park campaign united sometimes antagonistic segments of the Irish working-class community. Temperance leader O'Flynn led two major petition drives, which netted the signatures of not only local saloon keepers but also the Bowler brothers, the city's leading brewers. *Times* editor Mellen, a bitter enemy of O'Flynn's, also gave the park drive his enthusiastic support: "A playground for the children is needed, and the work people require an outdoor place of resort, near their homes."[19]

Even more vital backing for the park movement came from the city's two Democratic aldermen, John R. Thayer and Andrew Athy, both of whom at times had been at odds with O'Flynn and Mellen. Indeed, Thayer and Athy were themselves a study in contrasts. Thayer was a wealthy lawyer from old New England stock, an Episcopalian, and a member of the Worcester Fox Club, whereas Athy, a native of Ireland and an ardent Irish nationalist who had joined the abortive Fenian invasion of Canada in 1866, was a former bootmaker who had helped lead the Knights of St. Crispin strike of 1869–70.[20] Despite these differences, both men united in response to pressure from their working-class constituents to hold Newton Hill hostage for the East Side park. When the Board of Aldermen maintained that it lacked the power to purchase East Side parkland and even refused to rent a vacant lot, Athy and Thayer joined with fiscal conservatives on the board to block the Newton Hill acquisition. "If the city is not willing to provide a breathing spot for women and children who are forced to live in the thickly settled tenement houses . . . they [the East Siders] shall certainly oppose any addition to the already spacious park areas on the west side where every family has its own door yard and children's playground," reported the *Boston Sunday Herald*.[21]

Thus, the political conflict experienced by the Board of Aldermen reflected the deeper class conflict over the provision, design, and use of public space in Worcester. A letter to the *Worcester Sunday Telegram* contrasted the needs of the city's "wealthy" and its "toilers" and left little doubt about the class basis of the struggle for play space in Ward 5:

> Our wealthy citizens live in elegant homes on all the hills of Worcester, they have unrestricted fresh air and perfect sewage, their streets are well cleared and lighted, the sidewalks are everywhere, and Elm Park, that little dream of beauty, is conveniently near. The toilers live on the lowlands, their houses are close together, the hills restrict the fresh air, huge chimneys pour out volumes of smoke, the marshy places give out offensiveness and poison the air, the canal remains uncovered, the streets are differ-

> ent, the little ones are many. While the families of the rich can go to the mountains or to the sea during the hot months of summer, the families of the workers must remain at home.[22]

Whereas conflict over the drink question tended to inhibit class-wide mobilization, the struggle over park space fostered at least a neighborhood-based form of class consciousness and class conflict.

The temporary resolution of this conflict was found in a political compromise: the passage of a new Park Act in 1884, which provided funds and authority for acquiring parkland, and two years later the formulation of a comprehensive plan for Worcester parks. The trade-off between East Side and West Side park interests was central to the overwhelming support that Worcesterites gave to the Park Act and the park plan, but other interests – social uplift and control, public health, real estate development, and civic boosterism – also helped infect the city with what one contemporary diagnosed as "Park Fever."[23]

In the summer of 1884 (before the vote on the Park Act) Horace H. Bigelow and Edward L. Davis donated 100 acres to the city to establish a park on the shores of Lake Quinsigamond. There is no specific evidence of the motives of either man, but in a general way such gestures of civic generosity reinforced a paternalist social structure, which gave dominant roles to men like Davis and Bigelow, both of whom were heavily involved in local manufacturing, business, and politics.[24] In addition, some manufacturers and businessmen believed that parks would actually reshape the public behavior of their employees. Hence, Parks Commissioner Lincoln, in accepting the gift of Lake Park, noted the commission's duty "to see that it is made to promote popular enjoyment; to develop a taste for the beauties of nature; and to refine and soften, by cultivating, humanity itself." But such increased refinement might do more than just lessen internal conflict. To many, civic beauty and civic growth were inextricably linked, since a properly arranged city might attract new business. "It will not do," Lincoln wrote, comparing Worcester parks with those in New York and Chicago, "to lag in the rear and fall behind our rivals in the race for supremacy."[25]

For Bigelow, the donation of Lake Park may have gone beyond civic boosterism. As the proprietor of several lakeside amusement enterprises, the operator of the Worcester and Shrewsbury Railroad (the only transportation line to the lake), the owner of extensive lakeside property, and the builder of Lake View cottages, he stood to benefit from growing public use of Lake Quinsigamond.[26] In his Annual Parks Reports Commissioner Lincoln had pointed out that real estate values of land adjoining public parks had skyrocketed in other cities. Indeed, Lincoln, whose family had extensive landholdings in the area around Elm Park, may himself have benefited from the "greening" of the city's parks.[27] Whether or not real estate speculation prompted Bigelow's gift, he seems to have gained financially from his generosity. Between 1870 and 1890 weekend attendance at the lake jumped from 100 to about 20,000 per day. In addition, in the two years following his donation, land parcels on the eastern shore of the lake reportedly shot up in value from $35 to $500 per acre.[28]

The public enthusiasm for parks sparked by the gift of Lake Park further ensured the almost unanimous approval – 5,094 to 181 – of the Parks Act in the fall 1884 election. With this mandate and continued prodding from East Siders, the newly established Parks Commission developed a comprehensive park plan, which it unveiled in the fall of 1886. Impressive, in part, because it was one of the first examples of citywide park system planning in the United States, the plan was of even greater local importance because it resolved the class and sectional conflicts over the function and location of Worcester's parks.[29] In effect, if not in intent, the Parks Commission opted for a scheme of separate development: The East Side would have its playgrounds; the West Side, its scenic parks.

The language of the 1886 park plan reflected the growing commitment of many to the notion of parks as instruments of both social uplift and social control. It argued, for example, that parks might help mold the industrial work force: "Whatever will elevate and refine . . . [the workers'] taste or enlarge their intelligence will increase the excellence of their work." The report also endorsed parks as a setting for "healthful recreation," but it seemed more concerned with social hygiene than with the active fun and games demanded by working-class users. For Lincoln, it was the fear of disease that probably offered the most persuasive reason for the spread of parks to working-class neighborhoods.[30]

The report's conservative social vision notwithstanding, the Parks Commission, in practical and spatial terms, did not impose its view of recreational space on the Worcester working class. Of the six parcels recommended by the report, the two located on the working-class East Side – Crompton Park and East Park – were specifically designated as "playgrounds" rather than as public gardens. In these play areas, workers would have the space to use their leisure time as they pleased. Hence the enthusiastic working-class support for park reform should not necessarily be seen as an endorsement of the conservative social values of the park reformers. "Even where workingmen made extensive use of the language and concepts of middle-class reformers," labor historian David Montgomery writes in another context, "they infused those concepts with a meaning quite different from what the middle class had in mind."[31] Worcester workers had developed their own distinctive brand of park reform, just as they had of temperance reform.

In the next few years the park plan was gradually implemented with few modifications and little opposition. And subsequent additions to the city's parklands generally followed the pattern set by the original park plan.[32] Donations provided the city with additional, larger, and more "scenic" parks, whereas play areas for residents of the most densely populated working-class sections of the city came only after petition drives like those that won the original East Side parks. In the late 1890s residents of the Swedish wireworker community of Quinsigamond Village began campaigning for a park in their vicinity. As with Irish East Siders in the 1880s, the Swedish wireworkers did " not want an elaborate park, simply a playground in the center of the village." When the city finally yielded and purchased Greenwood Park in 1905, the newspapers proclaimed "This Park for Sport" and noted that "no especial attention will be paid to flowers or shrubbery." As befit the ethnic character of the neighborhood and the struggle for the park, the July Fourth picnic of the Swedish Methodist Church marked its opening.[33]

Other Worcester ethnic working-class neighborhoods also mounted campaigns for local play space. In 1901, for example, 165 South Worcester residents, more that four-fifths of them blue-collar workers and many of them English carpet weavers employed by the Whittall Carpet Company, petitioned for a playing field on College Hill.[34] Whereas the temperance issue had pitted ethnic communities against each other, the parks question tended to focus conflict between workers and elites or between neighborhoods and the city government.

Conflicts over park space and park behavior

Although Worcester workers generally won the recreational space they sought in the late nineteenth and early twentieth centuries, struggles continued over issues of park maintenance and behavior. The "separate but equal" parks faced the same problem as did schools founded under that rubric: In a stratified society separate can never be equal. "Most of the park money," charged labor leaders, "has been expended upon parks where the wage workers and their children are least seen, while in East Park, Crompton Park, and the Commons where the most good would be accomplished, the least money is expended and the least improvements made."[35] Even park enthusiasts admitted that Crompton and East parks were "dumps," and one Republican alderman astutely noted that Worcester had created a system of "class parks."[36] But better maintenance alone could not change this basic inequality, since working-class park users also faced overcrowding. "If you want the use of a baseball diamond at Crompton Park, you must sleep on the ground the night before to secure it," one local resident complained in 1904.[37] Such crowding was largely the structural by-product of an industrial city in which large numbers of workers huddled in a small area, and smaller numbers of manufacturers and managers resided in more spacious surroundings. The system of "class parks" meant both autonomy and inequality for Worcester workers.

Moreover, when Worcester workers used parks outside their own neighborhoods, the battle over proper park behavior continued. In the East Side parks, working-class park behavior was usually, but not always, condoned or ignored. But particularly in the parks that drew users from all sections and classes of the city, such as the Common, Lake Park, and Green Hill Park, conflict raged over correct park usage and behavior. Since Worcester's civic and business leaders had sold the public on parks on the grounds that such areas would teach workers "respectable habits" and cultivated manners, they fretted continuously about the obvious persistence of loafing, drinking, and similar habits in these spaces. Parks, they feared, were providing a setting for precisely the sort of behavior they were supposed to inhibit.

As the city's most central and visible park, the Common became the object of repeated middle-class complaints upon improper use, particularly by working-class patrons. Generally, these commentators grumbled about "dirty unkempt people," "bums," and "idlers" who "loiter," "loaf," and even "sleep off drunks." The implication was that these offenders against public decency were habitual drunks or transient hoboes. Although a few probably were homeless drunkards, many seem to have been unemployed workers. During the depression of 1893, for example, one labor sympathizer counted more than 400 jobless men on the Common on an average afternoon. Indeed, Worcester civic leaders actually confirmed this picture of the Common's patrons when they wanted to stop the building of a new post office on the Common. "This breathing space in the very centre of the city," proclaimed Senator George Frisbie Hoar, Worcester's best-known political leader, "is the comfort and luxury of the very poorest of the people; women who can snatch a few moments from work. . . men out of work and waiting for work." Perhaps, then, the usual complaints about loafing on the Common reflected middle-class blindness to the large-scale, recurrent joblessness of those years as well as a broader hostility to any public socializing by the city's workers. Worcester laborers, complained a letter writer to the *Worcester Daily Times,* were insulted with "the epithet of 'loafer'" when using the Common "for the very purpose . . . for which it was given us." Except when expedient, midafternoon relaxation by workers in the city's most visible park space might be defined as unacceptable park behavior, subject to offical repression, including the removal of park benches.[38]

Just as idleness was a common experience for nineteenth-century workers, so was drinking an often indispensable part of their popular culture. Olmsted and other park advocates liked to boast that parks promoted temperance and even put saloons out of business, but drinking actually accompanied workers into the parks. Relatively few users of the Common were drunkards, but more moderate drinking and even covert liquor sales could be readily found in this public space.[39] In addition, reunions and outings at Lake Quinsigamond were usually lubricated by ale and beer – sometimes donated by brewers eager to advertise their products. To reduce drinking at the lake, the Board of Aldermen on several occasions refused to issue liquor licenses to lakeside establishments. But the main impact seems to have been to encourage whiskey drinking, since flasks were more easily transported and concealed than beer kegs.[40]

Naturally, drinking was much more prevalent in the East Side parks, given their proximity to most of the city's saloons. Yet such drinking was less often complained of, in part, because middle-class Worcesterites rarely witnessed it. "Crompton Park," noted a newspaper reporter in 1898, "is a place that many people in Worcester have but slight occasion to visit." Consequently, complaints about drinking in East Side parks often emanated from temperance-minded local residents. In 1901, for example, the Reverend James Tuite of St. Anne's Catholic Church urged the Liquor License Commission to restrict the sales of a Shrewsbury Street liquor dealer. Otherwise, he feared, the area would be turned into a "place of orgies . . . on account of the proximity to East Park, which has been and will be made a place, both night and day, by men, women, and boys of carousal, and drunkenness to be avoided by all decent people."[41]

Working-class traditions of collective public leisure as well as the absence of spacious homes and apartments placed working-class drinking in public places like saloons and parks. Similarly, the lack of privacy in many tenements and three-deckers probably pushed some sexual activities into the public parks. In 1879, for example, the *Worcester Evening Star* reported that a twenty-two-year-old Irish immigrant had become pregnant after a "too intimate" acquaintance with a young man in Elm Park. Some years later the *Labor News* guardedly hinted of similar youthful sexual adventures when it reported that "young people of both sexes" resented the lighting of North Park.[42]

If parks failed to eradicate patterns of public socializing and drinking, they were even less likely to alter the ethnic basis of working-class social life, despite the Americanization claims of some park promoters. On the contrary, Worcester parks probably supported existing ethnically based leisure patterns by providing a convenient location for the outings of ethnic and church organizations. In the early twentieth century, for example, the Chandler Hill and Draper Field sections of East Park seem to have been divided between Swedes and Italians. Chandler Hill, located near the Swedish working-class community of Belmont Hill, was the scene of Swedish temperance rallies. The growing Shrewsbury Street Italian community, on the other hand, dominated the adjoining Draper Field. As recalled by Louis Lomatire, a retired streetcar conductor, it was a "center of activity" for Worcester Italians, with festivals, concerts, fireworks, sledding, skating, and swimming.[43] Green Hill Park offered picnic facilities for a wide array of ethnic groups. However, it was not a place for ethnic intermingling: Worcester immigrant picnickers remained segregated into their own fraternal or church organizations. If the parks ever served as a melting pot, it was a rather violatile one. The custodian of the men's bathhouse at the lake warned against overcrowding in the locker rooms: "You take a fellow from French Hill and double him up with a fair haired [Swedish] boy who lives on Belmont Hill, and there will be a fight right away."[44]

The introduction of parks did not "remake" the Worcester working class in the image desired by industrialists and reformers. Neither did it precipitate a new class solidarity or consciousness. While the struggle to win an East Side park had transcended some of the divisions within the Irish working-class community, the actual use of parks revealed continuing antagonisms between ethnic working-class communities. Basically, parks provided a leisure space in which workers expressed and preserved their distinct ethnic cultures. And although these immigrant workers carved out a way of life distinct from that prescribed by the native-American middle and upper classes, they rarely mobilized as a class or directly challenged the economic and political dominance of the city's Yankee elite.

The discovery of play

Ironically, at around the same time that Worcester workers were finally winning play space suited to active recreation, the city's middle and upper classes were gradually adopting some of the same preferences for sports and play over repose and contemplation. Although most middle-class people were not sufficiently aware of immigrant, working-class recreation to allow for a process of conscious imitation, occasional exposures could prove revealing. For example, in his memoir of growing up in the native-American cultural milieu of the 1890s, literary critic Henry Seidel Canby recalls that the immigrant working people represented the "reality of passion freely expressed which fascinated us." Similarly, in *The Damnation of Theron Ware,* a best-selling novel of the same decade, the book's protagonist, a small-town Methodist minister, is "bored" by his church's annual camp meeting. He drifts over to a nearby Irish-Catholic picnic and witnesses, "in mingled amazement and exhilaration," the "universal merriment" of football, horseshoe tossing, swimming, swinging, dancing, and especially beer drinking. "It is a revelation to me," he tells the Catholic priest with excitement and envy, "to see these thousands of good, decent, ordinary people, just frankly enjoying themselves like human beings. I suppose that in this whole huge crowd there isn't a single person who will mention the subject of his soul to any other person all day long."[45]

Whether it came as a "revelation" or as part of a process of gradual realization, the genteel upper and middle classes were increasingly shedding their old Calvinist suspicion of play – and particularly of active and public recreation. "The immense growth of public sentiment in favor of strictly amateur athletics, as being a healthy occupation for mind and body, is apparent on every hand," observed Worcester's society paper, *Light,* in 1890, "and the chances are that inside of another decade the number of people in the moral and intellectual classes if they may be so styled, who openly favor athletic sport will have doubled." *Light*'s comments proved prescient; the 1890s turned out to be the years in which America's middle and upper classes passionately embraced competitive sports and outdoor recreation. But, of course, the change in middle-class and elite attitudes toward leisure was neither begun nor completed in the 1890s. For a sense of the complex and generational process of change, we can turn to Worcester's Washburn family.[46]

In the early nineteenth century Ichabod Washburn established the family fortune in the wire business and led an intensely pious life centered on evangelical Christianity. When his nephew, Charles F. Washburn, settled on the West Side of Worcester, "Ichabod," according to a family memoir, "prayed aloud . . . that Charles . . . not be led out of the Kingdom by his worldly associates in the western part of the town. . . . Even then the spectres of dinnner-jackets, the dance and the decolleté stalked before him." Although Charles abandoned Ichabod's religiously proper Union Congregational Church for the socially proper All Saints Episcopal Church, he still strictly observed the sabbath, taught Bible classes, and quietly "spent his leisure hours in the library." The more dramatic change in leisure attitudes and practices came with Charles F. Washburn's son, Robert, who grew up on the West Side in the 1880s and 1890s. Robert joined enthusiastically in the elite, active, and secular world of the Quinsigamond Boat Club, the Worcester Club (which scandalized some with its allowance of liquor), the Bohemian Club, and the Grafton Country Club.[47]

An even more enthusiastic exponent of these new, more approving elite attitudes toward sport and active recreation was Robert Washburn's next-door neighbor and boyhood friend Harry Worcester Smith. The scion of an old New England cotton manufacturing family, Smith helped found the Grafton Country Club in 1895 in an effort "to bring within the reach of the West Side, wholesome English out-door life, riding, shooting and hunting." The club's motto, Each to His Pleasure, marked out a "leisure ethic" that contrasted sharply with the Protestant work ethic of the men of Ichabod's generation or even that of his nephew, Charles. Indeed, in occupation, as well, Harry Smith marked out the transition to the new generation and century. Like Ichabod, he was a skilled mechanic, tinkerer, and inventor, but, unlike the deacon, his wealth came not from building up new industrial enterprises but from combining existing ones. He was known nationally as "a 'harmonizer' of industries," a euphemism for his skill at arranging corporate mergers and creating monopolies. Harry Smith also differed from Deacon Washburn in how he chose to spend his money. Rather than financing an evangelical mission, the Mechanics Hall, or other Christian charities,

Smith devoted his fortune to his huge country estate, where he was known as "The Master of Lordvale," and to his passion for horses, hounds, and fox hunting.[48]

Smith brought this new upper-class enthusiasm for active sports with him into public life. In 1916 he was appointed to the Worcester Parks Commission, and he almost immediately organized a lavish "Sportsmen Dinner" to honor local track, golf, and tennis stars and to mark a new acceptance of active and competitive sports in the city's parks. Mayor George Wright told the "society" crowd that Worcester's parks were no longer just "sacred spots, places merely to be looked at, they are used . . . [they] are coming more and more to be places of recreation as well as places of rest." To symbolize the new official view, the Parks Commission was reconstituted as the Parks *and Recreation* Commission the following year.[49] In part, this new upper- and middle-class embrace of active recreation reflected a triumph of older working-class leisure attitudes. But important differences remained. The working class valued active play as part of a process of public socializing, as an end in itself. The middle and upper classes were more concerned with the product, with active play as a means to an end.

This *instrumental* view of play partially emanated from a concern with middle-class behavior. Through more energetic sports and leisure, it was argued, white-collar workers would not only find some release from the tensions and burdens of an urban, industrial society but also learn to cope with, and compete in, that society. Some members of the elite – particularly those like Harry Smith who found their social models among the European aristocracy – probably did not worry as much about the functionality of recreation as did members of the central middle class and their ministers. Still, even among Smith and his circle we can find instrumental notions about play and sport, particularly as embedded in the growing cult of "strenuosity" and competitive sport. It was no coincidence that the man who popularized the notion of "The Strenuous Life" – Theodore Roosevelt – was hosted by Harry Smith in a 1916 visit to Worcester's parks. Men like Smith and Roosevelt believed that athletics would teach young people the ideal of competition and bring America to "true national greatness." Yale students could learn Social Darwinist ideology on the football field under Coach Walter Camp just as they learned it in the classroom from his brother-in-law, Professor William Graham Sumner. "The cult of strenuosity and the recreation movement grew together," historian Daniel Rodgers writes, "minimizing the distinctions between usefulness and sport, toil and recreation, the work ethic and the spirit of play."[50]

Having accepted recreation as a means of self-development and self-control for themselves, the middle and upper classes began – rather more slowly – to perceive its possibilities as a means of social control. Thus, the emerging instrumental view of play also partook of a concern with working-class behavior, a belief that proper play behavior would ensure proper behavior in other areas of social life. In the early 1890s Worcester's middle- and upper-class Protestants denounced the efforts of one of their ministers, Frank Vrooman, to provide supervised recreation for the city's workers, but by the early twentieth century a variety of groups had embraced the notion of providing supervised leisure through Boys' Clubs, neighborhood social centers, company-sponsored sports teams, and especially playgrounds.[51] Having finally liberated play from its Puritan cage, middle-class leaders felt it must now be kept on a tight rein, not only for their own class but especially for the working class.

One of the central figures in creating and publicizing this new instrumental view of play was a prominent Worcester resident, G. Stanley Hall, the president of Clark University and one of the founders of American psychology. Hall urged that children's play was essential to normal child development. In his warnings against both the repression and the misdirection of play, Hall revealed the tension between freedom and regimentation common to many play advocates. They sought to eliminate existing constraints on play, but they also sought to impose new constraints of their own devising.[52]

Early psychologists like Hall were not the only writers to urge a more instrumental view of play. Environmentalist social reformers at the turn of the century saw play facilities as part of the social environment that could be reconstructed as a means of reshaping social behavior. They believed that the correct management of the juvenile life cycle and the proper provision of play facilities would socialize children into the roles, behaviors, and values expected of modern urbanites.

Playgrounds and social reform

The conjunction of these new ideas about play and adolescence with growing concern about the urban, immigrant working class made play reform a central project of progressive reformers. Jane Addams, Jacob Riis, and Lillian Wald, as well as such former students of G. Stanley Hall as Henry Curtis, helped found and staff the Playground Association of America, the leading organization of the play reformers.[53] By concentrating on children and the playground, these reformers believed they could both attack the immediate problem of juvenile delinquency and socialize children into their proper adult roles as workers and citizens. Not only had the studies of Hall and his followers persuaded reformers of the essential role of play in normal child development, but child-centered reform provided a more acceptable outlet for a broader concern with social behavior in general. As Robert Sklar writes in a slightly different context, since reformers "could deal only indirectly or covertly with the issue of class conflict, they made their case on the ground of protecting the young."[54] For many reformers, the entire working class appeared as a group of children whose behavior needed to be reshaped and controlled.

Despite such middle-class goals, in Worcester the first demands for city-sponsored play space came from within the working class. As we have seen, Irish workers in the 1880s sought play areas within the context of the parks system, and such demands escalated around the turn of the century. Growing working-class neighborhoods such as South Worcester, New Worcester, Quinsigamond Village, and Vernon Hill also petitioned the Parks Commission and City Council for playgrounds. Some of the city's most recent immigrants even began to take matters into their own hands. When Jewish residents of an East Side tenement went on a rent strike, one of their complaints was the lack of play space for children amid the tenements. Lithuanians considered buying their own enclosed park for the "exclusive use of their people."[55]

Gradually, the parks commissioners began to endorse calls for more public play space in the immigrant wards as well as in the more affluent areas of the city. The turning point in their acceptance of municipal sponsorship of playgrounds came in 1907. Late that year Parks Commissioner Obadiah Hadwen died, and his death marked the final passing of the old guard of the Worcester Parks Commission. Along with Edward Winslow Lincoln and James Draper, who had died earlier the same year, Hadwen had been a shaping influence on Worcester's Parks Commission for almost forty years. All three men came from elite, landed families and were dedicated horticulturalists with strong ties to groups like the Worcester Horticultural Society, the Grange, and the Massachusetts Fruit Growers' Association. Both Draper and Hadwen made their livings from horticulture.[56] Although they at times supported more active uses of parkland, their deaths in 1907 marked the symbolic close of the era of the contemplative, scenic park.

Manufacturer Peter Baker replaced Draper on the board and Swedish ticket agent Sven Hanson took Hadwen's seat. In general, the commission remained in the hands of the city's elite families, but the members tended to be manufacturers rather than men whose wealth was in land and whose primary interests were in horticulture.[57] Such men brought with them a more utilitarian view of parks. They would no longer simply serve as "breathing spaces" and natural retreats but also as a structured and controlled environment for play.

Little more than two months after Hadwen's death, James Logan, general manager of the U.S. Envelope Corporation and the newly elected mayor of Worcester, emphasized in his inaugural address "the necessity of playgrounds" and argued that "modern industry and commerce should bear its share of the cost in providing a suitable place, conveniently located near the home of the workman, where, after the day's toil is ended, he can with his wife and children breathe a little of God's pure air." The general population of Worcester seems to have shared Logan's excitement about playgrounds; later in 1908 voters overwhelmingly (14,570 to 4,849) endorsed the Massachusetts Playground Act, which mandated that cities provide at least one playground for every 20,000 residents.[58]

This growing enthusiasm for play and playgrounds was not confined to the acquisition of new parklands. Beginning around 1905, sections of existing parks were specifically set aside as playgrounds. In conjunction with this development, the Parks Commission began constructing special play facilities for park users, such as baseball fields, tennis courts, wading pools, outdoor gymnasiums, picnic groves, swings, sandboxes, and seesaws. The commission had first installed primitive playground equipment in Crompton Park in 1898, and by 1909 it was experimenting with the latest steel gymnastic apparatus.[59]

The provision of playground equipment and play facilities encouraged and fostered play, but it also structured and directed play. In contrast to the original parks, which had simply provided open space, these newer facilities dictated their own use. Carefully graded and laid-out regulation tennis courts could not be easily used for anything but that sport. Nor could children confronted with metal swings and gymnastic apparatus use this equipment or the space on which it stood for anything but its intended purpose. These years also saw the inauguration of an elaborate system of park permits for picnic grounds, ball fields, and tennis courts; the asphalting of parkland; the segregation of play areas by age of users; and the fencing of play spaces. "On the vacant lot we can do as we please," one playground advocate noted disapprovingly, but "when we have a fenced playground it becomes an institution."[60]

The playground promoters' desire to contain and regulate play was usually only implicit in the design and equipping of early twentieth century playgrounds. It became explicit, however, in the drive to hire playground supervisors. In 1908 the parks commissioners in their annual report had urged "competent supervision" to make playgrounds "educational centers and not mere resorts." "Mere playgrounds without intelligent and sympathetic supervision of the play of children will be barren of the best results," they declared. Concerned with similar issues, G. Stanley Hall convened the "Worcester Conference for Child Welfare" later the following year, and it immediately organized a subcommittee on play and playgrounds. With the help of the Board of Trade, this committee launched the Worcester Playground Association in March 1910.[61]

The new Playground Association had the support of a diverse coalition. Whereas the Parks Commission as of 1910 had only included one non-WASP (a Swede), the directors of the Playground Association included prominent Worcesterites from Irish, Jewish, and French-Canadian as well as Swedish backgrounds. The rising ethnic middle class, based in the second generation of immigrants, joined the native middle class in its enthusiasm for play reform. The "new" professional middle class – particularly schoolteachers and school principals – also played a leading role in the playground movement. Of course, many of the members of the new middle class had roots in the old elite as well as in the emerging group of ethnic entrepreneurs. Lizette Draper, the principal of Bloomingdale School and the daughter of former Parks Commissioner James Draper, was a Playground Association director, as was Ellen Murphy, a local schoolteacher and the daughter of the city's first Irish alderman. While some children of the elite joined the Playground Association out of their professional commitment to teaching through play, others apparently signed on because of their enthusiasm for active sports. For example, Samuel E. Winslow, the son of the skate manufacturer and former mayor, was an early leader of Harry Smith's Grafton Country Club as well as a star of the Harvard baseball team.[62]

Although the Playground Association managed to attract ethnics, women, teachers, manufacturers, lawyers, businessmen, sportsmen, priests, and ministers, it was not composed of a cross section of the city. No blue-collar workers, trade unionists, or representatives of the city's recent Italian, Polish, and Lithuanian immigrants were among the approximately thirty directors of the association. Worcester's working class had joined actively in movements for public play space, but it took no part in the movement to supervise and control play.

To build broader public support and to raise money for a summer program of supervised playgrounds, the association hired playground activist Henry S. Curtis to spend five weeks in Worcester. With the assistance of the movement's leading local boosters, like the *Worcester Gazette* editor, George F. Booth, and the St. Anne's Church pastor, John J. McCoy, Curtis generated substantial support and enthusiasm for the playground idea among local businessmen and clergy and helped raise more than $10,000.[63]

The success of Curtis's playground crusade enabled the Playground Association to undertake an ambitious program of supervised play in the summer of 1910 at twenty different locations around the city – half of them school yards and the rest parts of existing city parks and playgrounds. A paid staff of fifty and eight volunteers oversaw a diverse play program, which included organized athletics, ring and singing games, gardens, caning, basketry, raffia, sewing, drama, folk dancing, and storytelling. More than 6,500 children daily joined in these activities during the two-month playground season.[64]

For all the fanfare, the Playground Association added little additional play space to the existing Worcester park system. The essential new ingredient was *supervision*. "The playground is something more than a mere means of pleasant diversion," explained George Booth in a *Worcester Gazette* editorial. "It is, in fact, a school, where instruction of no less value than that of the school proper is given." And there was little that these play schools would fail to teach. Loyalty, courtesy, justice, helpfulness, friendship, courage, sympathy, morality, cleanliness, citizenship, seriousness, patience, honesty, mutual understanding, and higher ideals were among the virtues promised for Worcester playground graduates.[65] Such catalogues of proper conduct and high moral standards tended to be rather vague, and playground advocates thus claimed three more specific benefits of their work: a decrease in juvenile delinquency, an improvement in work habits, and the rapid assimilation of immigrants.

The specter of juvenile crime was a staple of the playground movement from its inception. Movement leaflets luridly asked: "Shall We Provide a Playground? Or Enlarge the Jail?" Such arguments found a ready echo in Worcester. "Experience has shown," proclaimed Mayor James Logan, "that when city children are playing in the places prepared for them, under proper supervision, they are not on the back alleys learning to become criminals."[66]

In addition to becoming law-abiding citizens, playground users would become compliant workers. "In our playground we did not forget to teach children to work as well as to play," Father McCoy reported at the end of the first Worcester playground season. In part, play leaders sought to teach specific job-related skills. The aim of the playground sewing course, according to its instructor, was "to teach the girls high standards, habits of accuracy and thrift so much needed when the girl enters the business life or becomes a homemaker." But playground advocates also believed that playing itself would make better workers. "As a child plays," noted Booth, "so will he later work."[67] "The boy without a playground is the father to the man without a job" became a leading slogan of the playground movement.

In these objectives, playground reformers revealed their preoccupation with working-class conduct. Juvenile delinquency in Worcester was almost entirely concentrated in the poor, working-class district known as the Island. Proper assembly-line demeanor hardly needed to be taught to middle-class children headed for business or the professions. But it was the playground movement's obsession with Americanization that most suggested its interest in reforming and controlling the working class, since in Worcester immigrants were the predominant constituents of that class. Thus, the effort to Americanize immigrants was a frontal assault on the dominant characteristic of their defensive culture: the separateness and impermeability of the ethnic worlds within which they lived. "We have got to make Americans of these children," insisted Booth. Although other twentieth-century Americanizers saw the schools or evening citizenship classes as the shortest route to assimilation, in Booth's assessment only the playground would "bring pure gold out of the melting pot." Even Irish pastor McCoy assented: The public school (a hostile environment for many Catholics) was not always a successful Americanizer, "but he who says that the *playground* is the 'melting Pot' will tell the absolute truth."[68]

Playgrounds and working-class behavior

There is little doubt then that Worcester playground advocates promised to reshape not just children's play but play in general, not just working-class play but working-class life in general. Their success in achieving these goals is more questionable. The limited available evidence suggests that instead of being reshaped by playgrounds, workers and their children actually reshaped the playgrounds (as they had the parks) according to their own needs and values.

Despite the many proclamations to the contrary, the Worcester playground system, at least initially, did not serve as a "great melting pot." Quite the opposite, it seems to have offered play space for the preexisting, separate, ethnic communities to affirm their own national identities. On August 26, 1910, the Playground Association took a census of that day's playground users. The census showed that the playgrounds were quite effective in reaching their intended immigrant constituency. Fully 85 percent of that day's 3,400 playground users were of foreign background, although only 71 percent of the total city population was also of foreign stock in 1910.[69] Immigrant children came to play at Worcester playgrounds but not with the children of different immigrant groups. Of the twenty playgrounds in operation in 1910, fifteen were dominated by a single immigrant group. In some cases other immigrant groups were all but excluded. For example, Greenwood Park was 86 percent Swedish, Institute Park 79 percent Irish, and Ledge Street School Yard 75 percent Jewish. In part, these figures reflected Worcester's ethnic neighborhood structure: Greenwood Park was located in heavily Swedish Quinsigamond Village, Ledge Street School Yard in the midst of the Providence Street Jewish ghetto. Since 82 percent of the children who attended a particular playground lived within a quarter mile of it, Worcester playgrounds necessarily mirrored their surrounding communities. Regardless of the cause, the effect was still the same: Worcester playgrounds, although intended to break down ethnic exclusivity, actually reinforced the existing pattern of immigrant enclaves.

A further analysis of the 1910 Playground Census suggests that this ethnic exclusivity may have been a matter of choice as well as a product of social geography. Comparing playground attendance by nationality with the overall 1910 census figures suggests that some ethnic groups were overrepresented on the city's playgrounds, whereas others were underrepresented. Significantly, it was the city's largest ethnic groups (Irish, French Canadians, Swedes, and Jews) that were overrepresented and its smaller ethnic groups (Italians, Germans, Finns, English Canadians, and Scots) that were underrepresented. What this pattern may indicate is that those ethnic groups that had sufficient numbers in a particular locality to dominate a playground adopted it as a local institution, whereas smaller ethnic groups, fearful of being outnumbered on the playground, tended to stay away.[70] The city's largest immigrant group, the Irish, was also the group that most heavily patronized the playgrounds.

Although the playgrounds did not promote ethnic intermingling, they may have had a more subtle and more limited Americanizing and assimilating impact. It is possible that the patriotic songs, the American games, and the Anglo-American folk dances taught at the playgrounds helped to bring immigrant working-class children closer to the American mainstream or at least made them more aware of its existence. It is intriguing to note the important role played by second- and third-generation immigrant young people – particularly Irish Americans – as playground supervisors and teachers. These college students and recent college graduates may have served as intermediaries in the long-term process of partially integrating immigrants and their children into the dominant American culture.[71]

Although the impact of the playgrounds on Americanization remains unclear, it is evident that Worcester playgrounds never diminished juvenile crime. Since arrestable offenses were socially determined and might include loitering on the streets, playgrounds could immediately lower the arrest rate simply by shifting the location of juvenile activity. But Worcester playgrounds failed to produce even a lower arrest rate. In 1933 sociologist Paul Shankweiler, a professor at Clark University, concluded that "in Worcester supervised summer play activities have little or no bearing on the incidence of juvenile delinquency."[72]

The persistence of ethnic segregation and juvenile delinquency points to the rather unsurprising conclusions that manipulating or controlling play would not alter working-class behavior and that neither children's play in general nor working-class children's play in particular was as easily reshaped as playground reformers had anticipated. As one recent student of the history of play has pointed out, "there is evidence that children are not easily influenced and select elements from the adult culture to fit their particular needs and values."[73] In Worcester, at least, this subversion of the intentions of play reformers appears to have been the general rule.

In 1912 the *Worcester Telegram* ran a series of articles critical of the Worcester playgrounds as a needless extravagance aimed at taking the fun out of play. The *Telegram* articles included what purported to be twenty interviews with children who had used the city's playgrounds. In all cases, the children expressed disdain for the adult efforts to teach them how to play, and many said that they either no longer paid any attention to play leaders or had stopped attending the playgrounds altogether. "I can't go to the playgrounds now," complained one eleven-year-old living near Crompton Park. "They get on me nerves with so many men and women around telling you what to do." "I can't see any fun playing as school ma'ams say we must play," explained a fourteen-year-old boy. One group of boys asserted their independence by organizing their own baseball team outside the playground league and proclaimed that their team could "defeat the playground baseball team with its paid umpires and balls furnished by the city." Often the children's disdain for the playground coexisted with an outward compliance with external forms. Some children found the playground storytelling inane but still applauded the stories since they were told they must. Others told of being drafted into the annual playground festival because of a shortage of performers. Even some behavior that playground advocates promised to eliminate seems to have flourished on its grounds. A fifteen-year-old resident of the Island neighborhood reported that he had never seen an ambulance at Crompton Park until the playground began. "They say they don't let the kids fight," he grumbled. But "I know [a] . . . kid that got swiped over the bean with a beer bottle some of the bums had left from the night before."[74]

As with the parks, the efforts of social reformers to uplift, refine, and control the working class through the provision of supervised playgrounds did not significantly diminish the autonomy Worcester workers exercised over their leisure time and space. Indeed, in both cases, Worcester workers were able to turn reform efforts to their own advantage. Parks provided them with free space within which to pursue their active conception of leisure activity. Within that unstructured context, workers were able to affirm their ethnic cultures and their alternative values. Even the tighter supervision and reform designs of the playground advocates were often ignored or subverted by Worcester workers and their children. Working-class recreational space and recreational behavior thus remained largely under working-class control.

Given the nature of economic relationships and power in Worcester society, however, this working-class recreational autonomy existed only within limited boundaries and under substantial constraints. East Side parks, for example, never received the appropriations and the care lavished on the West Side equivalents; hence, working-class park space in Worcester was often poorly maintained and heavily overcrowded. In addition, although the various attempts to mold working-class recreational behavior were never fully successful, some of these efforts, such as the removal of park benches from the Common, the banning of liquor sales at the lake, the establishment of a permit system for baseball and picnics, and the structuring of play space through the provision of steel apparatus and the asphalting of grounds, did have an impact on working-class life. Workers could, for example, smuggle liquor to the lake but that was neither as simple nor as pleasant as purchasing it there.

The most fundamental constraint on working-class recreation, however, was work itself. In 1890 the *Worcester Evening Gazette* described in detail how Worcester workers played freely in Institute Park during lunchtime:

> Before the 12:05 whistle blows, the crowd begins to arrive from Washburn and Moen's, the envelope shops, electric light station, and many other establishments north of Lincoln Square. After eating, a good romp is indulged in by the girls, running and racing about, with now and then a scream of laughter when some mishap, a fall perhaps, occurs to one of their numbers. Some of them wander about in pairs or groups, exchanging girlish confidences, or indulging in good-natured banter with their masculine shop-mates. Occasionally a boat is secured by some gallant youth, who rows a load of laughing maidens about the pond, the envied of their less fortunate friends.
>
> The younger men try a game of base ball or a little general sport, jumping, running, etc., while their elders sit about in the more shaded spots, smoking their pipes. But when the whistles blow previous to 1 o'clock there is a general stampede to the shops and in a few minutes all of those remaining can be counted on one's fingers.[75]

No matter how much autonomy Worcester workers achieved in their leisure space and time, they still had to confront the factory whistle. Its sound returned them to a sphere of life in which power and control resided outside their class.

6 *The struggle over the Fourth: The Safe and Sane July Fourth movement and the immigrant working class*

"The vacant national holiday," Luther H. Gulick, president of the American Playground Association, declared in 1909, "needs to be utilized as much as the vacant lot."[1] Contrary to Gulick's rhetorical flourish, neither the empty lot nor the national holiday was truly "vacant." Just as the playground movement had confronted – and tried to reshape – existing and autonomous traditions of working-class play, so the effort to reform Independence Day celebrations – what came to be called the Safe and Sane July Fourth movement – sought to repress and replace the distinctively boisterous and ethnic commemorations by the working class of the nation's birthday. Although the two movements shared not only objectives but also personnel, an examination of the Safe and Sane crusade in Worcester highlights some important additional factors that were only implicit in the discussion of playground reform. By the early twentieth century newer immigrants from southern and eastern Europe had joined the Irish, French Canadians, and Swedes in the city's factories and working-class neighborhoods. At the same time, some of the children and grandchildren of earlier immigrants were gradually joining the middle class and leaving those same factories and neighborhoods behind. These two developments shaped not just the fate of the local Safe and Sane July Fourth movement but also the nature of class relations in early twentieth century Worcester.

Reforming the Fourth

Throughout the late nineteenth century Worcester police made repeated efforts to ensure order and quiet on July Fourth. They routinely hired as many as sixty special police to supplement the regular force; issued periodic ordinances banning "chinese crackers," toy cannons, and firecrackers more than three inches in length; and prohibited the use of fireworks and noisemakers before certain hours. Such efforts had intermittent success at best. Illegal fireworks were often available, and if not, merchants would market new devices not yet outlawed. Similarly, in 1890, though the police tried to stop noisemaking from commencing before 4 A.M. on the Fourth, loud celebrations continued through the night. In 1892, for example, the *Worcester Telegram* reported that boys with horns, firecrackers, torpedoes, and revolvers were on the streets before midnight and that soon thereafter "Main St. was full of men and boys." All night stores and stands peddled fireworks and lemonade to the crowd.[2]

In the late nineteenth century these police efforts found only limited support in the local press. In 1875 the *Worcester Daily Press* complained of the "ignominious toot of the tin horns" and asked: "Isn't it about time to begin the inauguration of a grand 4th of July Reform?" But most Worcester newspapers remained remarkably indulgent. "The boy who is not inclined to make a noise on the Fourth of July is scarcely worth raising," the *Worcester Sunday Telegram* proclaimed in an 1886 editorial, which was typical of many in the 1880s and 1890s. The local society publication, *Light,* agreed: "What manner of a Fourth would it be without the smell of powder and noise, and lots of racket generally?"[3] Those irritated by noisy celebrations seem to have simply avoided them. "Among people of refined tastes and sensitive nerves," social reformer Julia Ward Howe noted in 1893, " 'Going out of town to avoid the Fourth' has been a phrase so common in my time that it ceases to awaken attention, and is taken as a matter of course."[4] This tendency of the middle and upper classes "to disperse" on the Fourth made it less likely that a reform movement would develop in the late nineteenth century. Only in the new century did growing fears about fires and vandalism, immigrant mobs, and injuries and accidents, as well as broader social and cultural concerns, coalesce into the Safe and Sane July Fourth movement.

Property owners led the way in focusing critical scrutiny on the way Worcesterites celebrated the Fourth. Whether the problem of fire and vandalism or only the perception of the problem actually got worse, Worcester newspapers clearly reflected a heightened concern by the turn of the century. In 1876 the *Worcester Evening Gazette* casually suggested that "doing justice" to a Centennial Fourth required acceptance of the fire hazards posed by the firecrackers. By 1899, however, local newspapers headlined Independence Day fires and prominently listed the number of fire alarms turned in. Two years later, after a spectacular fire at the Walker Ice Company, which attracted a crowd of 20,000, the press pointedly blamed fireworks set off by workers from the ice company and the nearby American Steel and Wire (formerly Washburn and Moen) North Works for the blaze. Two other manufacturers suffered fire damage from firecrackers and bonfires that same day. Reflecting the growing fears of businessmen, *Worcester Magazine,* the organ of the Board of Trade, complained that "people who have property on the Fourth are obliged to remain at home and protect it." The old middle-class strategy of leaving town to avoid Fourth of July noise and heat seemed in jeopardy. Some people, however, tried to maintain their distance by seeking police protection for their property. By 1903 twenty-five special officers patrolled residential sections of the city, "protecting property at the request of citizens."[5]

That year, at least, the police patrols curbed fires and vandalism on the middle-class West Side of Worcester. The diminished threat of business and residential property damage, however, only served to focus attention on what to many appeared to be a more ominous danger: mob rule of the downtown streets. "For several years past," the *Worcester Sunday Telegram* wrote in its lurid account of the 1903 festivities, "the night before the Fourth celebrations have been growing wilder and more lawless, and more unrestrained, but the climax was reached Friday night when all previous records for lawlessness and disorder were eclipsed." According to the *Telegram,* "rough elements," many of them drunk, used "firearms and powerful explosives" with "utter abandon," hurling dynamite crackers at streetcars and shooting Roman candles into crowds.[6]

Such sensational accounts suggested to readers that July Fourth celebrations threatened not only to destroy property but also to unleash an uncontrollable mob. "Police Negligence Invites the Burning Up of the City in a Single Night" was the *Telegram* headline of that day. Worcester's chief fire engineer warned "citizens and property owners" that "we have passed the dangerpoint." Those who failed to connect the dual July Fourth threats of mob rule and property damage had only to read another *Worcester Telegram* article headlined "Mob Runs Town of Marlboro," which reported on July Fourth fires, assaults on police, and the bombarding of the home of a judge in that nearby community.[7]

The fears of public disorder and mob rule did not focus on just any mob but specifically on the city's growing immigrant population from southern and eastern Europe. In these years thousands of Jews, Italians, Poles, and Lithuanians were supplementing Worcester's already established Irish, Swedish, and French-Canadian communities. The number of southeastern European immigrants in Worcester multiplied more than four times in the first fifteen years of the twentieth century. Between 1900 and 1910 Worcester's Italian community increased almost five times, and it nearly doubled again in the next decade.[8] This flood of seemingly unassimilable foreigners became the particular focus of native and middle-class fears and provided the most important impetus for the rise of the Safe and Sane movement.

Worcester newspapers and magazines were not reticent about blaming the city's most recent immigrants for July Fourth disturbances. Referring to the 1903 disorders, *Worcester Magazine* wrote of "recent importations from other parts of the world hurling dynamite crackers at motormen and defenseless women." Similarly, the *Worcester Evening Post* complained that the fifty-one people arrested on July 4, 1902, included "foreigners who had no earthly business to be celebrating the Fourth of July." The *Worcester Telegram* was even more pointed in 1907 when it reported that a twenty-four-year-old Lithuanian arrested for firing a revolver "showed but a scant knowledge of the English language and couldn't for the life of him tell why he was celebrating except that he was told that the time was ripe for fun by men he knew who had been in the country a longer time." Another item on the very same page was headlined: "Italian Celebrates: Couldn't Speak English but Could Fire Revolver Shots."[9]

This new focus on immigrants as the source of July Fourth noise and disorder represented a shift in popular thinking. Although the Irish had been often depicted as the inevitable source of July Fourth drinking and fighting, earlier views of loud celebrating had represented young "boys" as primarily responsible and had thus embodied nostalgic recollections of the writer's own youth or indulgent feelings about his or her own children. Now the noise appeared to emanate from a much less familiar and less easily controllable source, albeit one that the middle class continued to depict in childlike terms. Just as the playground movement was to teach immigrant children how to play, a combination of police and reformers would teach immigrant adults how to celebrate the Fourth. "The education of the masses," a mayor told the Sons and Daughters of the American Revolution in January 1904, "particularly of the large and increasing foreign element, ignorant of our history and constitutional principles, must not be overlooked in a proper celebration of Independence Day."[10]

Whereas local middle-class fears of fire and immigrant mobs were undoubtedly exaggerated, the national concern about July Fourth deaths and injuries was more legitimately based. In 1899 the *Chicago Tribune* began compiling and publicizing statistics showing that 30 to

50 people died and that 2,000 to 3,000 were injured in July Fourth accidents each year. Other newspapers across the country – including those in Worcester – copied the list as well as the more comprehensive figures that the *Journal of the American Medical Association* began assembling in 1903. Such publicity fueled reform efforts.[11]

Few people besides fireworks manufacturers openly opposed a movement that promised to reduce deaths and injuries. There is no evidence of immigrant working-class attitudes on this subject, but it seems likely that workers supported increased safety since they and their children were the most common victims of July Fourth accidents. Still, it is a mistake to take the movement at its face value – as some historians have done – and assume that the Safe and Sane movement was entirely a response to "the slaughter of children."[12] In Worcester, at least, a more diverse set of concerns – including not only fears of property damage and immigrant mobs but also broader goals of social reform – governed as a more formal July Fourth movement emerged in early 1904.

In April of that year Jeanie Lee Southwick, a local artist and art teacher, spoke to forty-six members of the Worcester Twentieth Century Club, a reform-oriented group composed largely of teachers, social workers, and other professionals, on "A Rational Celebration of the 4th of July." "People having valuable property interests at stake," she declared, "have become alarmed at the growing tendency in modern celebrations." As a result of the meeting, the Twentieth Century Club formed a committee to see the mayor, the police chief, and the press about tighter enforcement of existing ordinances. Responding to this pressure, Police Chief William Stone "issued orders in ten different languages" that before-the-Fourth celebration "must be dispensed with." Although noisemaking was permitted after midnight, the cautious crowd that gathered in 1904 dispersed after forty-five minutes. A smiling Chief Stone told reporters: "It pays to advertise." *Worcester Magazine* praised the new orderliness in an editorial entitled "As it Should Be": "Worcester's Fourth of July . . . was dignified, rational, and quiet."[13]

The police pressure on disorderly conduct and noise continued in subsequent years, although not always with as much success. In 1906, for example, the police confiscated bushels of fish horns, guns, blank cartridges, and giant firecrackers. Nevertheless, the newspapers reported that after "midnight the lid was off in real earnest." In general, the police seem to have had intermittent success with relatively quiet years being followed by noisier ones. At the same time, "night before" rowdiness often shifted to Lake Quinsigamond in the face of increasing police surveillance downtown. In 1906, for example, while police concentrated their manpower downtown, a riot broke out at the lake at 3 A.M. with a crowd of 300 throwing whiskey bottles and stones at officers who tried to arrest a man for disturbing the peace and firing a revolver. In addition, whatever the location, heavy drinking continued to be an integral part of celebrating the Fourth. Even in 1908 and 1909 when liquor sales were ostensibly banned in Worcester, the Fourth remained an occasion for heavy drinking. In 1908 express companies brought 8,000 gallons of beer into Worcester on the day before the Fourth and drunkenness arrests were more numerous than the previous year when liquor sales were legal. The next year, with the city still under a no-license regime, the pre-Fourth liquor deliveries doubled.[14]

Despite the lingering problems of noise, disorder, and drunkenness, a new fireworks ordinance, which went into effect in 1910, did substantially reduce the number of July Fourth injuries. Between 1907 and 1909 injuries averaged around forty-five per year, but in the next six years they *totaled* only twenty-three.[15] If the sole concern of the reform movement had been the "slaughter of children," it could have closed up shop in 1910. Instead, reformers shifted their agenda from repression to reform from ensuring order to promoting new forms of celebration. The initial movement had focused only on the boisterous and rowdy Fourth; the expanded movement concerned itself with those "settled-living" immigrants who celebrated quietly but within their own ethnic communities. Even more than before, the focus of the reform movement was the immigrant, particularly the more recent immigrant. While the movement continued to operate on the local level, it increasingly drew its specific program from national progressive organizations.

In May 1909 representatives of forty-five cities gathered at the annual meeting of the Playground Association of America to discuss how to promote a "Safe and Sane Fourth." As a solution to the problem of arranging "civic celebrations" in the multiethnic "modern city," they particularly recommended the pageants and processions arranged by Springfield, Massachusetts, in which "representatives of each National group in the city have depicted some event in the history of its fatherland or some contribution it had made to American civilization." The Springfield celebration did not insist that immigrants discard their ethnic identity, but it did require that they abandon the autonomy and separatism that had almost always marked immigrant social life. Moreover, as historian David Glassberg has noted of other recreational reformers, a "professed cosmopolitan stance" often masked a covert goal of assimilating "immigrants into Anglo-American tradition and American nationality."[16] At best, the Safe and Sane movement walked a thin line between Americanization and a diluted form of cultural pluralism. While acknowledging ethnic (but not class) differences, these progressives sought to dissolve those differences into a new "community consciousness" based on idealized notions of preindustrial village life.

Progressives thus saw July Fourth celebrations – like playgrounds – as potential tools in forging a new social and cultural order. "There is no way," wrote Luther Gulick in a 1909 article on "The New and More Glorious Fourth," "in which a community can be brought together and made to feel and act as a unit so well as by playing together." Recognizing the barriers to social solidarity in the hierarchical industrial workplace but ignoring those implicit in a stratified social and cultural order, he argued that communitywide consciousness would grow out of celebrations and play since "we can choose those with whom we play to a far greater extent than we can those with whom we work."[17]

The Safe and Sane gospel spread from the 1909 Playground Association meeting to hundreds of cities and towns. According to the Child Hygiene Department of the Russell Sage Foundation, another spearhead of the movement, between 1909 and 1911 the number of cities with "Sane" celebrations jumped from 20 to 161. In 1911 Worcester joined the bandwagon: Public and private contributions financed the city's first celebration that included flag raisings in the public parks, a military and civic parade, sports and games for young people at ten parks, and city-sponsored fireworks in Elm, East, and Crompton parks. The Worcester Safe and Sane movement moved even closer to the Springfield model in the next two years, sponsoring pageants, parades with nationality floats, and patriotic and athletic exercises for children at the city's recently opened playgrounds. Although the local committee extensively quoted the national leaders of the movement, showed their film *A Sane Fourth of July,* and followed the models set out in their publications, they were less clear on the links of their movement to progressive notions about community solidarity. They often fell back on more traditional ideas about patriotism, local boosterism, and the melting pot to justify their efforts.[18]

The Worcester Safe and Sane movement shared many supporters with the kindred playground crusade but had fewer representatives from the city's elite. Educators, the owners of small factories, merchants, and clerks, rather than industrialists, dominated the actual Safe and Sane organizing committee. To a greater degree even than the playground movement, the ethnic middle class proved enthusiastic supporters. The presence of four Irish Americans, three French Canadians, two Swedes, two Jews, and one Italian among the twenty-five committee members gave the city's ethnic communities close to a majority of the movement's governing body. At the same time, the city's leading industrialists did not ignore the Safe and Sane crusade. Mayor James Logan, who was also the head of the U.S. Envelope Corporation, gave it energetic backing; his company distributed free paper cups to the children on the playgrounds; the Board of Trade enthusiastically promoted the movement in its magazine; and industrialist Harry Stoddard solicited financial support from local manufacturers. More important, Donald Tulloch, the secretary of the Metal Trades Association, the city's most powerful employers' organization, served as secretary of the Safe and Sane Committee.[19]

Not surprisingly, given the leading role played by Tulloch – the bitterest enemy of organized labor in the city – Worcester trade unions viewed the Safe and Sane movement with suspicion and distaste. At a March 1911 City Council hearing, which discussed appropriations for the Safe and Sane committee, the president of the Central Labor Union (CLU), Charles A. Cullen, "criticized those who thought too much noise marked past celebrations and sarcastically remarked that they 'should go down to Bunker Hill and read the inscriptions on the monument.'" Then, he turned to the women present and "appealed to them not to confine their interest in women and children for only one day in the year, but to cooperate with the labor movement in working for the betterment of conditions of those who toil in factories and work shops and who need the cooperation of those in better circumstances."[20]

After the initial excitement, the Worcester Safe and Sane movement waned somewhat in 1914 and 1915.[21] It also followed the general pattern of progressivism nationally and began to veer away from its original pluralist goals toward more conservative ones centered on Americanization and preparedness for war. In 1915, when Frederic C. Howe, commissioner of immigration at the Port of New York, urged mayors across the country to make July Fourth an "Americanization Day," Worcester was one of the many cities to respond. Its "Americanization Day Services" attracted 1,000 people to Mechanics Hall. "The next time you hear a man complaining about this country or desiring to transplant the animosities of the old world into the soil of this country," corporate leader and former Mayor James Logan told the crowd, "raise a subscription for a third class ticket and ship him back."[22]

The following year, as the country edged closer to war, the Americanization ceremonies expanded. Eight thousand Worcesterites marched through the city to demonstrate their patriotism. Unlike previous civic parades, neither ethnic associations nor floats emphasizing immigrant heritages and contributions to America dominated. "Thousands who saw the procession noted how many United States flags were in the parade and how few flags of other nations were seen showing that it was in no sense a hyphenated parade," the *Telegram* reported. The message of Americanization and labor–management harmony became even more explicit and strident in the 1917 celebration, which gathered 10,000 Worcesterites in front of City Hall for a "Ceremony of Citizenship." The assembled crowd recited a "civic ritual," which included a pledge of labor–management cooperation.[23]

Along with this growing conservatism came a slight shift in leadership. Harry Worcester Smith, inventor, industrialist, English fox hunter, and organizer of multimillion-dollar industrial mergers, took charge of the celebration. Such other major industrialists as Swedish-American George Jeppson of Norton Company and George Crompton of Crompton and Knowles (and Smith's father-in-law) also joined the organizing committee. Members of the ethnic middle class continued their strong support: Irish Americans made up 15 percent of the organizing committee. The local labor movement, however, became more vehement in its objections. The CLU denounced the "preparedness craze" and urged trade unionists to boycott the July Fourth parade. It maintained that "preparedness" like "efficiency" was simply a scheme by employers to make more money.[24]

Not all Worcester workers heeded the warnings of the CLU and the *Labor News*, however. While not flying the flags of their native lands, some of the city's more recent immigrants – particularly Poles, Syrians, and Italians – marched in the parade as members of ethnic societies. Worcester Swedes indicated an industrial, rather than an ethnic, loyalty as they marched in the 950-person delegation of the Norton Company, the largest in the parade. This procession, led by the Norton Company police and including the top officials of the company, had a particular significance, given the defeat of the company's machinists in a bitter strike only seven months earlier.[25] The message of class harmony in the national interest seems to have penetrated at least some segments of the working class.

Whereas the organizers of the preparedness parades touted them as instruments of patriotism and Americanization, the *Labor News* suspected them as tools of industrialists seeking to imitate the English aristocracy. It titled one editorial against the 1916 parade "Autocracy, Snobbishness and Arrogance in Preparedness Craze" and complained that reform was simply a guise for Harry Worcester Smith's Anglophilia: "They have taken all the pep out of the glorious fourth and instead of rousing old celebration with cannon salutes from the crests of Worcester's seven hills, we get instead Harry . . . Smith riding horseback and the leftovers from the rookies camp. Why is all the ginger taken out of our national holiday? Is it because we are afraid to celebrate on account of the English government? Looks like it. Safe and Sane! Piffle. It's lack of Americanism and a toadyish fawning toward the hams-across-the-sea."[26]

By 1917, however, the *Labor News,* which had only reluctantly gone along with the American war effort, gave guarded support to the Safe and Sane celebration on the patriotic grounds that it would save gunpowder. The CLU joined the Metal Trades Association and the Chamber of Commerce in the "Business" delegation to the Ceremony of Citizenship.[27] Just as the flush of victory in the Civil War in 1865 had created a unified July Fourth celebration, so had the pressure of wartime conformity fifty-two years later. At least momentarily, the Safe and Sane movement had forged a community solidarity of sorts.

The limits of reform: reformers, immigrants, and the ethnic middle class

The elaborate parades, pageants, and ceremonies of the Safe and Sane movement soon faded along with progressivism. In 1919, for example, only 200 people turned out for the municipal-sponsored celebration. Nevertheless, the movement left some lasting changes in the way the Fourth was celebrated. The new fireworks regulations permanently reduced July Fourth deaths and injuries both locally and nationally. In addition, the city took over some Independence Day events that had traditionally been part of private and ethnic celebrations. Under city auspices, the playgrounds, for example, provided games and sports that had been included in ethnic and church picnics. They also offered some of the "treats," like free ice cream, that had attracted children to those picnics. Organizers of the Safe and Sane celebrations even worried that children were coming for only the ice cream and not the patriotic ceremonies. In 1919 the director of the Lamartine Street playground tried to "nab" children who got several free ice creams by moving from one East Side playground to another. The city also started providing massive fireworks displays, particularly in working-class neighborhoods, as part of its Safe and Sane program. Displays in East Park and Crompton Park often attracted 25,000 to 50,000 people.[28] The city's provision of fireworks and ice cream can be interpreted in different ways. Reformers and city officials may have seen them as a triumph of social control, but working people may have simply viewed them as a new benefit they had won from a municipal government that gave them very little.

The city government thus assumed a greater responsibility for both policing and entertaining its people on the Fourth. Although the holiday seems to have become safer, it is questionable whether the reforms affected some of the other features of the day that had troubled middle-class property owners. Drunkenness, for example, remained a constant part of celebrations with 106 arrests recorded in 1918. Similarly, some of the night before rowdiness that was repressed in downtown Worcester simply shifted to Lake Quinsigamond. Fireworks did come under control, but they were replaced by the new problem of bonfires. As the number of July Fourth accidents went down, the number of fires went up. In the first decade of the twentieth century July Fourth fire alarms usually ranged from ten to fifteen each year; in the second decade they averaged closer to forty-five.[29]

Just as the Safe and Sane reformers failed to extinguish fires and drunkenness on the Fourth, they also proved unable to eliminate the ethnic insularity that many of them found troubling and potentially subversive. At the same time, however, the structure of ethnic Worcester – as seen on the Fourth – did change, albeit in incomplete and uneven ways. The most recent immigrants generally proved the most resistant to change, whereas those immigrant groups that had produced a large second generation or, more important, a middle class revealed at least ambivalent signs of Americanization or acculturation.

There are no precise figures on the size of the emerging ethnic middle class, but it seems likely that at least 15 to 20 percent of the city's Swedes, Irish, and French Canadians had achieved this status by 1915. And there is abundant evidence of the growing importance of these groups among Worcester's professionals, politicians, and businessmen and of their appearance in more affluent, non-ethnic neighborhoods.[30] Not surprisingly, this ethnic middle class began to adopt some of the July Fourth habits of the native middle and upper classes. More affluent Swedes, for example, appear to have dominated the Worcester Yacht Club, which held annual races on July Fourth in the early twentieth century. The numerous boat clubs that surrounded Lake Quinsigamond were often important gathering places for the better-off members of Worcester's different ethnic groups. Not only did Worcester's middle-class ethnics imitate the native middle class by creating their own private clubs, they also began to follow the habit of leaving town on the Fourth. By 1911 the newspaper lists of those taking out-of-town vacations on the Fourth contain large numbers of Irish names.[31]

The ethnic middle class followed the lead of the native middle class not only in leaving town on the Fourth but also in promoting the opposite: the revival of civic-sponsored communitywide celebrations under the auspices of the Safe and Sane July Fourth movement. Irish, French-Canadian, Swedish, Jewish, and Italian store owners, lawyers, editors, teachers, and politicians lent their names and prestige to the Safe and Sane crusade even as some of their working-class compatriots – at least those represented by the local labor movement – reacted more suspiciously. It was this emerging middle class that was most likely to look favorably on patriotic and assimilationist schemes such as those promoted by playground and July Fourth reformers. For example, Richard H. Mooney, a second-generation Irish American who became a school principal and married a woman from an "old New England" family, served on the Safe and Sane committees of both 1911 and 1917. Some middle-class ethnics like Mooney apparently saw themselves as intermediaries who could help to narrow the gap that had long existed between the immigrant working class and the native middle class. Explaining why Mooney did not belong to ethnic societies or other voluntary organizations, a biographical sketch commented: "Everything is subordinated with him to the great work of turning out good, intelligent, *patriotic* citizens."[32]

Although Mooney devoted all his Americanist energies to his work as a schoolteacher, other Irish Americans of his generation and class joined organizations like the Knights of Columbus (K of C) in both a personal commitment to such ideals and a social commitment to spreading them to others. Organized in 1894, the K of C soon became the city's largest Irish-Catholic organization by attracting the burgeoning Irish middle class to its ranks: Between 1905 and 1915 almost three-quarters of its new members were either white-collar workers or students. Members of the K of C, like army officer Thomas Foley, participated actively in the Safe and Sane movement. In addition, the organization sponsored its own July Fourth celebrations, which won praise from the local political and economic leaders, who had greeted the earlier celebrations of the Ancient Order of Hibernians with only criticism or indifference. The K of C also enthusiastically supported the American war effort in World War I, raising $5,000 locally for recreational facilities for servicemen. Although predominantly an Irish organization, the K of C avowed a Catholic, rather than an Irish, identity and explicitly sought to assimilate more recent Catholic immigrants into that Catholic-American identity. In 1915, for example, it organized night classes to teach English to immigrant adults. While the K of C was less aggressively assimilationist among other Worcester Irish than among the more recent immigrants, its Catholic Americanism – what Timothy J. Meagher defines as a combination of patriotism, allegiance to the Catholic church, and moderate to conservative economic and political views – had apparently become the dominant perspective in Worcester's Irish community by the time of World War I.[33]

Worcester's ethnic politicians also played an important role in transmitting this patriotic ideology to the ethnic working class and in helping to bring that working class closer to, although not within, the mainstream of Worcester society. The ethnic middle class might separate itself from the working class for social purposes, but it also sought to lead the working class for both ceremonial and political purposes. Certainly, the participation of Swedish-American Mayor Pehr Holmes in the 1917 Safe and Sane celebration in Quinsigamond Village must have helped to attract thousands of Swedes to that occasion.[34] Similarly, the inclusion of Irish and French-Canadian politicians on the Safe and Sane organizing committees ensured greater acceptance of the reform movement within those ethnic communities.

Yet the leadership of ethnic middle-class professionals and politicians did not guarantee the transformation of the social and cultural views of Worcester's ethnic communities. Catholic Americanists, for example, faced a continuing challenge in the Irish community from people Meagher calls ethnic "chauvinists" who remained committed to Irish nationalism and more class-conscious economic and political positions.[35] Certainly, on the Safe and Sane issue the local labor movement was not prepared to follow the leadership of the ethnic middle class if that meant also parading behind men like Donald Tulloch and Harry Worcester Smith. Indeed, some men and women who were perceived as ethnic leaders by the surrounding society might be viewed much more ambivalently *within* the ethnic community. As the wealthiest Jew on the East Side, comb manufacturer Samuel Wolfson probably appeared to be the logical Jewish representative for the Safe and Sane committee. Yet while poorer East Side Jews envied Wolfson's wealth and possessions, they also deeply resented his pretensions, his aloofness, and his Boston-centered social life. Behind his back, they contemptuously referred to him as a "*Grober Jung,*" or "gross fellow," who had plenty of money but little knowledge of the Talmud and other spiritual matters.[36]

Thus, in at least some instances internal "class" struggles flared within Worcester's ethnic communities over issues of assimilation, tradition, unionization, and politics. And even the ethnic middle class often embraced the values of the larger American society with some misgivings or ambivalence. Worcester Swedes may have enthusiastically participated in the Safe and Sane movement, but the location of their celebrations in Quinsigamond Village and the use of the Swedish language in some of the speeches gave the events a strongly Swedish flavor. Even in 1917 Swedish churches went ahead with their traditional picnics in preference to the citywide ceremonies and the Swedish-dominated Safe and Sane celebration in Quinsigamond Village. Although the Swedish churches lost some of the predominance they had in the late nineteenth century, members of the second generation and the emerging middle class still preferred Swedish secular organizations as the venue for their Independence Day festivities. In a similar fashion, W. Levi Bosquet, a French Canadian and a former president of the Board of Aldermen, may have participated in the Safe and Sane movement, but as part owner of *L'Opinion Publique,* he also had a vested interest in encouraging the retention of the French language among French Canadians.[37]

Worcester's middle-class Irish Catholics were particularly ambivalent about their assimilationist views. On the one hand, they sought to exchange their ethnic identity (as Irish) for a more acceptable religious one (as Catholics); they patriotically endorsed American policies at home and abroad; they championed American capitalism and denounced "foreign" socialism; they promoted sober and respectable behavior (no saloonkeepers could belong to the Knights of Columbus); and they energetically worked to spread these ideals throughout the Catholic community. On the other hand, they viewed the larger Protestant society with intense distrust and militantly insisted upon their distinct Catholic identity.[38] Middle-class Irishmen and -women served as intermediaries, models, and pioneers for a changing Irish community, but their trek toward the mainstream of American society led them only to the sidelines.

Despite their middle-class leadership, then, Worcester's older ethnic communities remained ambivalent about the dominant Yankee society; its newer immigrants, however, were more likely to be indifferent or even hostile – to re-create some of the patterns that had marked the Swedes, French Canadians, and Irish in the late nineteenth century. As did their predecessors, Worcester's Italians, Poles, and Lithuanians sought to celebrate July Fourth according to their own communities' traditions. Many of the newer immigrants maintained their Old World festivals and saints' days in the New World. At the same time, they celebrated an American holiday like the Fourth according to preexisting customs. Worcester Italians, for example, set off massive fireworks displays in East Park not only on the feast days of St. Anthony and Santa Maria but also on Independence Day. Among Poles and Lithuanians, the Fourth apparently provided an occasion for exuberant wedding celebrations. On July 4, 1910, for instance, there were six Polish and six Lithuanian weddings in the working-class Island district. The festivities of the evening "opened with several large bonfires built in the middle of [Lamartine] street." The receptions, held in vacant storefronts on the same street, included lots of beer and native dances.[39]

As in the late nineteenth century, early twentieth century native middle-class observers viewed such rowdy and boisterous celebrations with disapproval. Peter Roberts found a July Fourth "beer parade" in a Pennsylvania coal community as evidence of "a lower type of civilization." In Worcester, the July Fourth arrests of an Italian, Luthianian, or Pole would be the occasion for similarly nativist comments. Indeed, even some of the older immigrants joined in the complaints against more recent arrivals. In 1915 Swedish Quinsigamond Village residents protested a Lithuanian July Fourth picnic in their section of the city because of the beer drinking, band playing, and general "racket." With the partial exceptions of 1916 and 1917, the more recent immigrants simply went their own way on the Fourth, ignoring civic-sponsored ceremonies and being ignored by the dominant social groups. Worcester Lithuanians, for example, saw the Fourth primarily as an occasion to affirm group ties, particularly through regional celebrations. Such celebrations, one longtime resident recalls, "were the kind of things that kept the Lithuanians together."[40]

As of 1920, then, Worcester's immigrant workers had resisted the efforts of July Fourth reformers to remake their holiday celebrations just as they had evaded or subverted similar efforts by temperance and playground advocates. The entrance of tens of thousands of southern and eastern European immigrants into Worcester around the turn of the century actually reaffirmed preexisting patterns of celebrating the Fourth in a boisterous or ethnically isolated manner. To the extent that working-class holiday festivities – or indeed working-class social life in general – were transformed, it was in response not to the designs of reformers but to the leadership of an emerging and often American-born ethnic middle class – and to the new attractions offered by the amusement park operator or the movie theater owner.

PART IV

Culture, conflict, and change: the working-class world of the early twentieth century

7 *The commercialization of leisure: the rise of a leisure market and the persistence of the saloon*

In August 1912 *Worcester Magazine,* the official organ of the Board of Trade, reflected enthusiastically on the city's recent Safe and Sane July Fourth celebration. "In no other city in this great country," it exulted, "was there a better, safer or more complete celebration of the Signing of the Declaration of Independence." To substantiate its claim, the magazine boasted of the success of the day's parade, pageant, and patriotic exercises, as well as the water sports sponsored by the Safe and Sane Committee "at Lake Quinsigamond where fully 30,000 people congregated during the day." Although *Worcester Magazine* implied that 30,000 Worcesterites had gathered for the Safe and Sane lakeside festivities, the *Worcester Telegram*'s reporter had found only "an impatient and bored crowd of 3,000" at those events.[1]

Was *Worcester Magazine* lying? Not entirely: Thirty thousand people did go to Lake Quinsigamond on the Fourth, but only one-tenth of them bothered to attend the events sponsored by the Safe and Sane Committee. Most of the others spent the day at one of the two commercially owned amusement parks operated on the shores of Lake Quinsigamond. Indeed, the lakeside celebration began the night before the Fourth as a record-breaking crowd of 35,000 thronged the dance halls, amusement parks, and lake boat clubs. Even at the peak of the Safe and Sane movement, then, amusement park operators proved more adept than social reformers in organizing successful and popular July Fourth celebrations. And by 1920 most Worcesterites would have agreed with the advertisement for the White City Amusement Park that proclaimed it "The Real Place for 'July Fourth' Fun."[2]

The triumph of the amusement park operator over the July Fourth reformer was not an isolated phenomenon. Whether they ran amusement parks, operated saloons, or owned movie houses, recreational entrepreneurs played an increasingly important role in defining and controlling the leisure lives of Worcester workers in the twentieth century. Historical accounts of the "commercialization of leisure'' have sometimes depicted this process as the story of omnipotent capitalists of leisure time who quickly and without resistance dissolved long-standing ethnic and working-class cultures in the early twentieth century through the magic wand of the marketplace. Such accounts have also often implied that the same process ''co-opted'' the working class, incorporated it into a ''bourgeois hegemony,'' and rendered it politically impotent. The next two chapters, which examine the development of a leisure market as seen at the amusement park, the continuing importance of the saloon in a commercialized leisure world, and the rise of the movie theater as a center of interclass entertainment, argue instead that the commercialization of leisure has been a slow, gradual, and not always one-directional process with roots that developed well before the twentieth century. Not only did established institutions, traditions, and cultures – the saloon, the church, and the ethnic community, for example – survive the ''onslaught'' of commercial leisure; they also helped to shape the commercial ''products'' – the amusement park or the movie theater, for instance – in line with popular customs and modes of play. Finally, while the commercialization of leisure has had some deleterious effects on working-class life – the loss, for example, of communal control over popular recreation – it has also fostered new opportunities for class solidarity across ethnic lines and ultimately new challenges to the status quo.

Horace Bigelow and the emergence of a working-class leisure market

In abstract terms, the rise of a working-class leisure market required the emergence of producers – entrepreneurs of leisure – and consumers – workers with money and time to purchase leisure products or ''fun.'' In the real world, of course, the process was a good deal more complex as suggested by the following account of the activities of one man (Horace H. Bigelow) at one place (Worcester's Lake Quinsigamond) on one day (July Fourth) between the 1870s and his death in 1911. This discussion reveals the earlier roots of commercialized leisure, the tensions implicit in marketing amusement in a Protestant culture, and the ways the marketplace both accommodated and altered the sorts of popular July Fourth recreational traditions discussed in previous chapters. Most important, it points up some of the forces of change – the activities of recreational entrepreneurs, the shifts in middle-class attitudes toward leisure, the improvements in working-class incomes, and the appearance of

American-born ethnic workers – that would gradually alter the working-class world of the nineteenth century.

In the 1850s and 1860s partisans of horse racing and enthusiasts of collegiate rowing dominated summertime and July Fourth use of Lake Quinsigamond, the long, narrow body of water located about two and a half miles east of downtown Worcester. More popular and extensive use of the lake and its shores did not develop until after 1873 when J. J. Coburn completed the Worcester and Shrewsbury Railroad (known as the "Dummy" because of its narrow gauge), which provided a quick ten-cent ride to the lake shores, where Coburn owned considerable land. In 1875 a hot July Fourth brought a record-breaking crowd of about 7,000 to the lake to picnic, ride the lake steamboats, partake of the clambakes offered at various privately run picnic groves, and shoot billiards, bowl, and drink beer at the one hotel. By the following year, Coburn had transformed his "Coburn's Grove" – located conveniently at the terminus of the Dummy – into "Lincoln Park," a fenced ground that offered celebrators boat rentals, a shooting gallery, "flying horses," and refreshments.[3]

Coburn pioneered the commercial exploitation of the lake and the Fourth, but it was Horace H. Bigelow who had the vision and the capital to take full advantage of the entrepreneurial opportunities offered by a scenic location and a public holiday. Known later as the "Great Amusement Caterer," Bigelow's early career followed in the mold of Worcester's self-made manufacturers like Ichabod Washburn. Growing up in a family of fourteen, he began as a shoemaker in a little shop on his father's farm, but soon his experiments in subdividing the work in shoemaking, his knack for inventing shoe machinery, and his skill at organizing convict labor made him a wealthy boot and shoe manufacturer. In 1875 the forty-eight-year-old Bigelow retired from the shoe business and began to invest in Worcester real estate. He gradually bought up Coburn's lakeside holdings as well as Lincoln Park and the Dummy railroad.[4]

As an amusement entrepreneur, Bigelow drew upon the same innovative methods that had made him a wealthy manufacturer. In effect, he transferred the techniques of mass production and vertical and horizontal integration from manufacturing to leisure. Bigelow understood the simple axiom that maximizing patronage of his railroad and his lakeside enterprises would maximize profits. Soon he began sponsoring boating regattas, band concerts, balloon ascensions, and fireworks at the lake to stimulate travel on his railway, patronage of his refreshment stands, hotel, and Lincoln Park, and purchase of the Lake View cottages he was building. Naturally, July Fourth was a central occasion for Bigelow's amusement businesses. On July 4, 1885, for example, he helped sponsor a major boating regatta, which brought 20,000 people to the lake and, not coincidentally filled Bigelow's Dummy railroad well beyond its capacity. Not only did Bigelow profit from transporting the crowd, but he also secured control of Regatta Point for the Fourth and erected grandstands for those willing to pay for a more comfortable spot from which to view the race.[5]

Bigelow's application of mass marketing to recreation was even more evident in "Bigelow's Gardens," his combination skating rink and amusement emporium, located in downtown Worcester. Charles Lalime, who had first opened a skating rink at this spot in 1878, had tried to attract only "the best people in Worcester." In response to complaints of high prices at Lalime's rink, the *Worcester Evening Star* explained "that the reason for charging the established admission was not so [much] for profit . . . as to *exclude* an undesirable element from the place. None but the better portion of our citizens have congregated there, and have done so without any annoyance from the general rabble that would have packed the building had the price of admission been less."[6]

Bigelow, who took over the rink in 1881, did not have any biases about whose money he would accept. Particularly after he expanded the rink and built his surrounding Gardens the following year, Bigelow saw the need for a mass audience. As the *Worcester Daily Times* reported in 1882, "he is taking immediate steps to provide amusement for the pleasure seekers of Worcester on a larger scale than has ever before been undertaken by anyone here." In line with this new approach, Bigelow lowered skating prices by about one-third and kept admission to the Gardens at fifteen cents. The strategy worked. At the time of his purchase of the skating rink, one source notes, "this form of amusement was but little enjoyed; by a wise policy of low prices, band concerts and various attractions offered from time to time[,] he was able to furnish pleasant amusements to thousands at a cost whole families could afford to pay." On July 4, 1882, Bigelow's first Independence Day in business, his provision of a spectacular fireworks display as well as the usual flying horses, fountains, comic opera, and refreshments attracted 2,000 customers. Having succeeded with mass appeal, vertically integrated amusement enterprises, Bigelow expanded "horizontally" and opened a chain of skating rinks throughout New England.[7]

Although Bigelow aggressively sought a mass audience, he did not want to lose the patronage of the upper and middle classes, and so he tried to create a controlled and respectable environment that would attract a range of patrons to his Gardens. Bigelow surrounded the grounds with a high fence and filled the inside with some of the accoutrements of the scenic park – shade trees, fountains, landscaped lawns, "everything that taste will suggest and money will provide." Most significantly, Bigelow, a teetotaler himself, conducted the Gardens on strict "temperance principles."[8]

At the lake, Bigelow had a different solution to the problem of attracting the working class without losing the middle class. Instead of mixing classes, he encouraged the development of separate areas. Whereas Lincoln Park catered to the "masses," Bigelow built summer homes and exclusive boat clubs for the "classes." By the late 1880s people of "great wealth and prominence" were purchasing Bigelow's Lake View cottages as summer homes, and others, mostly young men from the same class, were joining one of the three elite boat clubs on the shores of the lake. "Young men of the highest social standing" assembled at the Quinsigamond Boat Club, a contemporary publication noted. Only a slightly less affluent group met at the "elegant" Lakeside Boat Club, built by Horace Bigelow and presided over by his son. And not to be outdone, Worcester's most successful Irish Americans spent their summers lakeside at the Washington Social Club.[9]

Although Bigelow managed to accommodate both workers and employers within his diversified amusement empire, it was an uneasy kingdom. The economic imperatives of seeking the largest audience and the largest profit did not always accord with the dominant middle-class cultural assumptions. Commercially sponsored recreational spots, which attracted immigrant working-class crowds, could not be conducted entirely according to the precepts of native middle-class culture. Entrepreneurs like Bigelow tried to create a controlled social environment, but working-class patrons often used these spaces in accordance with their own active and exuberant recreational styles. The spirit (and the reality) of the "greased pig," which characterized AOH picnics, also invaded some of the commercially sponsored celebrations of the Fourth.

In 1879, for example, Quinsigamond Park, a lakeside private park, advertised a gala July Fourth celebration with such attractions as horse races, clambakes, footraces, the climbing of greased poles, and the chasing of greased pigs. The public responded enthusiastically to promises of "Fun for the Million," and by 2 P.M. "the shores of Lake Quinsigamond were thronged by thousands of working people," according to the local papers. These blue-collar workers of Irish, French-Canadian, and native-American backgrounds proceeded to celebrate the Fourth in a boisterous and – from the perspective of the middle class – excessive manner. Even the prolabor *Worcester Star* criticized the "drunkenness and rowdyism" of the lake crowd.[10]

Heavy drinking marked lakeside celebrations, despite regular police patrols and intermittent bans on liquor sales in the vicinity of the lake. Although a teetotaler, Bigelow indirectly aided the drink merchants. In 1885, for example, overheated spectators at his July Fourth regatta, who had journeyed there in his overcrowded railroad cars, proved eager patrons for W. C. Blos, the holder of the only liquor license at the lake. When no-license ostensibly prevailed in Worcester, visitors to the lake could still quench their thirst in the woods or on the less well policed Shrewsbury (eastern) shore.[11]

Not surprisingly, drunken and rowdy working-class behavior at commercial lakeside resorts provoked middle-class complaints. In 1896 several boat clubs petitioned for better police protection at the lake, complaining that "there are a certain class attracted here who care nothing for law and order and who conduct themselves in such ways and manners as to terrorize, annoy and disgust the law abiding citizens and destroy and depreciate our property." One city councilman, who was also a lake-area resident, pointed to the prominence of drinking, liquor selling, and women of shady character and maintained that "it is impossible to take ladies there without their being insulted." Almost a decade later the *Worcester Evening Gazette* found similar conditions prevalent. "Vice and Crime Run Riot at Lake" screamed one front-page headline in 1907. "The atmosphere reeks with rottenness and pollution, which is fast driving away respectable people and giving this beauty spot to the wicked, lawless, and ignorant," the *Gazette* added in a boxed front-page comment.[12]

Most middle-class complaints centered on alleged "improper" users of the lake. Yet occasionally observers placed the blame on supposedly sinful entrepreneurs who, in their quest for profit, had attracted the "wicked, lawless, and ignorant" to the lake in the first place. On April 30, 1877, a letter appeared in the *Gazette* addressed "To the General Christian Public of Worcester" and signed by leading Protestant ministers and their wealthiest parishioners – men like wire manufacturers Charles F. Washburn and Philip L. Moen. They expressed "regret" that lakeside proprietors "should deem it wise or necessary in providing for the public recreation to make *intoxicating drinks* of various kinds in saloons, hotel, grove and beer garden so large an element on their bill of popular attractions." Even more vehemently, they protested the plans of these same men to "build their hopes of pecuniary profits so largely – as they undeniably do – on the utter *disregard and desecration of the New England Sabbath.*" Their protest directly confronted the contradiction between the dictates of the market and those of Christian morality. "Have Christian stock owners in our dummy railroad no responsibility," they asked, "in the turning of this natural paradise into a modern Sodom of license and riot?"[13]

To the ministers and industrialists, popular use of the lake posed a grave moral problem. But a "Liberty Loving Citizen," who responded to their letter in the next day's *Gazette*, saw the issue as primarily one of class inequality. He joined with the ministers and manufacturers in "condemning the sale and use of intoxicating drinks" and deploring "bad conduct at any time or place." On the issues of sabbath observance and *control* over leisure time, however, he passionately dissented:

> I question very much the right of one class of people to dictate to another class the manner in which they shall worship God or spend the Sabbath. It may indeed be very well for people of ample means, who have plenty of leisure on week days to ride around and enjoy the country air and scenery, to attend church and worship God there on Sunday, but these gentlemen must bear in mind that all the good people of Worcester are not thus favored. A very large majority of all who visit the Lake on Sunday are people who are confined to shops ten hours in a day, six days in the week, myself among that number. Now, if the gentlemen were to have their way, when should we ever see our beautiful Lake jewel, to bathe in its limpid waters, to glide over its glassy surface, or ramble in its groves or upon its verdant shores? Do these gentlemen think that working people have no love of the beautiful, have no admiration for God made manifest in the flowers, grass, or trees? Must my appetite be satiated by church ceremonies when it craves the broad open fields, the waving trees, the fragrant flowers and God's pure air and azure sky, filled with its myriad warblers who know no Sunday, but praise Him as loudly at one time as at another?[14]

As the "Liberty Loving" workingman realized, the moral issue of sabbath observance was also a class issue of equal access to recreation and relaxation. Yet, as the Protestant ministers understood, in a commercializing leisure world the working class had gained some powerful allies in their struggle against restraints on Sunday recreation – entrepreneurs who made their living amusing the working class. Not surprisingly, then, Horace Bigelow, although descended from the same Puritan stock as those who defended the New England sabbath as "the foundation of the American character," actually sided with the "Liberty Loving" workingman. In July 1882, shortly after he opened Bigelow's Garden, he shocked the elite of the community by holding Sunday evening band concerts there. Even after he was arrested and fined for his violation of the "blue laws," he defended his actions on principle. He argued that "he had a right to operate his swings, run the horses and have a band concert," since "it was no worse for a poor man to ride a wooden horse on Sunday than it was for a rich man to ride behind a living animal." Moreover, Bigelow pointed out that most of those who were "shut up in the workshops and stores for six days in the week" did not attend church on Sunday. Consequently, he told a Congregationalist minister that "by providing a place free from all objectionable features, where under the open sky and in the enjoyment of God's pure air, those who wish may gather together quietly and peaceably, I think that I am practically working with you in the same direction."[15]

Despite the "populism" and the deism implicit in Bigelow's defense of his Sunday amusement enterprises, one could easily argue that the real issue for him was money not principle. Since working people had only Sundays free, business on that day was essential to the success of not only Bigelow's Gardens but also his Dummy railroad and Lincoln Park.[16] Yet Bigelow's defense that "rational recreation is next to religion" was not necessarily a cynical cover for his quest for profits. Bigelow may have become a populist and free thinker because it served his economic interests, but it is more likely that those radical views enabled him to become a recreational promoter in the first place.

Bigelow was an outsider to elite Worcester before his heyday as an amusement caterer. In 1878, for example, the R. G. Dun and Company credit report called him " a keen shrewd businessman but not well regarded socially in some quarters." Four years later, after describing in glowing terms the economic success of Bigelow's six skating rinks, the credit service noted that "personally [he] is regarded a peculiar man of radical ideas in politics and religion which makes him rather unpopular." Bigelow may have been unpopular among his elite West Side neighbors, but the working-class East

Siders who patronized his businesses regarded him rather differently. In 1879, when he ran for mayor as a pro-labor Democrat, the *Worcester Daily Times* touted him as "a laborer, a mechanic, an honest workingman." And Bigelow sought to return the compliments paid to him by Worcester's workers. In 1886, for example, he announced plans to mount at the lake a medallion of "heroic size . . . representing in bas relief the workingman's family."[17]

While Bigelow's radicalism was undoubtedly sincere, his populism and free thinking benefited him as a recreational entrepreneur. Only someone so situated at the margins of the dominant culture could fully exploit the economic opportunities of the leisure market by disregarding the dictates of a traditional Protestant culture. Oddly, it was Bigelow's radicalism that enabled him to pursue the logic of capitalism. But Bigelow's position – like that of the Irish saloonkeepers who exploited the same market – became less marginal as the nineteenth century turned into the twentieth. In part, the dominant culture itself was changing; it gradually came to accept active recreation, even on Sunday. But the arguments of the market were probably even more persuasive in changing elite and middle-class views of Bigelow and other recreational promoters. Horace Bigelow was obviously a very rich man, who had done even better as an amusement entrepreneur than he had as a shoe manufacturer. And, as those who rushed to imitate, rather than condemn, Bigelow realized, the leisure market that he had first exploited in the 1870s and 1880s had grown substantially by the 1890s and early twentieth century.[18] Working people had more money and more free time to spend it in.

In these years working-class incomes continued their modest but steady growth. Average real wages for nonfarm employees increased by more than half between 1870 and 1900. Although blue-collar workers did not share fully in this prosperity, their incomes increased along with those of the rest of the labor force. Nationwide, manufacturing wages increased another 25 percent in the next two decades.[19] Equally vital to the success of Bigelow and his competitors was the growth in leisure time. As with wages, average figures conceal great variations, but the general trend was toward shorter hours. According to one estimate, the nonagricultural workweek, which had already dropped by about 3 percent per decade in the second half of the nineteenth century, plummeted an additional 10 percent in the first ten years of the twentieth century – from 55.9 to 50.3 hours. Average hours in foundries and machine shops – important Worcester industries – dropped 15 percent, from 59.8 to 50.4

hours, between 1890 and 1928. Finally, not only were workers more likely to have free hours in the evening for commercial entertainment, but the growing number of firms that required only a half day's work on Saturday and the increasing numbers of legal holidays – from five in 1870 to nine in 1920 – made visits to amusement parks and other commercial entertainment arenas at least an option for working-class Worcesterites.[20]

That more and more Worcester businessmen were eager to exploit this expanded working-class leisure market is well illustrated by a quick look at July 4, 1920. While, as we have seen, July Fourth had been a profitable day for leisure entrepreneurs back in the 1870s and 1880s, the dominant focus had been on the events sponsored by the ethnic societies and churches. By 1920, however, the balance had begun to shift. On July 4, 1920, workers could attend at least ten different movie and vaudeville theaters – now more attractive to summertime crowds because of the addition of fans and cooling systems. The Rialto on the working-class East Side offered a special July Fourth program of *Every Mother's Son* and Jack Dempsey in episode six of *Daredevil Jack.* Poli's movie and vaudeville house advertised itself as "the FIRST place" to "celebrate the FOURTH." In addition, several thousand baseball fans packed Boulevard Park to watch Worcester play Springfield.[21]

Lake Quinsigamond promised the greatest diversity of amusements. In 1920 the lake offered dancing, canoeing, fishing, merry-go-rounds, skating, penny arcades, bowling, tearooms, musical theater, and "Japanese Amusement Parlors." Even more appealing was the lakeside amusement park called White City, which had been opened in 1905 by the aging Horace Bigelow. Like Coney Island and other amusement parks that were sweeping the country around this time, White City offered a vivid contrast to conventional society through its carnival atmosphere, its sideshows ("freak animals," a "snake den," and a "foolish house") and its rides ("shoot the shoots," circle swings, merry-go-round, flying boats, and roller coaster). These attractions had an immediate appeal. On its first July Fourth in business, 30,000 people paid the ten-cent admission charge. In subsequent years it attracted equally large crowds as well as imitative competitors.[22]

The gradual spread of commercialized leisure between 1870 and 1920 is obvious, particularly when viewed from the vantage point of Lake Quinsigamond on the Fourth of July. Through the efforts of H. H. Bigelow and other entrepreneurs, the Fourth had become a "festival of consumption" and the lake and its amusement parks arenas for the buying and selling of "fun." But despite this growing penetration of market relations into leisure time, Worcester's ethnic working-class cultures – at least based on the evidence of Fourth of July celebrations – were only transformed in very limited and incomplete ways in the first two decades of the twentieth century.

In this period, commercialized working-class leisure still rested on a tenuous economic base. Although industrial wages did rise, many working-class families still lacked adequate financial resources. As late as 1929 more than one-fifth of American families lived in what contemporary economists defined as "poverty," with "inadequate diet, overcrowding, and no resources for unexpected expenses."[23] Even those workers comfortably above the poverty line could still only spend limited amounts on recreation. When Robert Coit Chapin surveyed working-class living standards in New York in 1907, he found that 10 percent of the families studied made *no* expenditure for recreation. The percentages were even higher in the lowest income categories: Of those families with annual incomes under $600, 28 percent spent no money on recreation, and of those with incomes under $800, 15 percent refrained from recreational expenditure. Typically, investigators recorded on their reports of those families: "Never go any place at all except to the woman's parents who live across the way." Even for those working-class families that could afford recreational expenditures, the amounts were relatively small: less than $8.50 per year for all families studied.[24] Many more working-class families could now afford to spend the Fourth of July and a few other summer weekends at White City, but they could not make such outings on a weekly basis. Furthermore, recessions and depressions – a regular fact of life for working people in these years – could eliminate even modest recreational expenditures. On July 4, 1894, during the nationwide depression, there were only "scattered hundreds" at the lake in contrast to the many thousands of previous years. "People had no money to spend in these times," the *Telegram* explained.[25]

While working-class incomes inhibited the degree of participation in commercial leisure, ethnic cultures limited and shaped the nature of that participation. Commitment to an ethnic community was often stronger than interest in amusement parks or movie theaters. In the late nineteenth century ethnic-sponsored events remained more important than commercial amusements on the Fourth of July. In the twentieth century, when the recreational entrepreneurs multiplied and gained in influence, many of the city's newer immigrant groups still kept their members together on the Fourth. The central social event of the summer for Providence Street Jews, S. N. Behrman remembers, was the Independence Day picnic of the Jewish Maccabee Club.[26] But Worcester's first- and second-generation immigrants also infused commercial leisure spaces with elements of their culture. The rides and sideshows of White City were new to Worcester, but the boisterous, exuberant carnival atmosphere was familiar to the 1880s patrons of the picnics of the Ancient Order of Hibernians.

Although the amusement park built upon and even reinforced ethnic working-class cultures, it also undercut those same cultures. In effect, the rise of the amusement park eroded some of the traditional bases of authority in Worcester's ethnic communities. The ethnic July Fourth picnics had been held under the watchful eyes of community leaders, particularly priests and ministers. At White City or Lincoln Park the dominant figure was Horace Bigelow, a man on the margins of the Worcester elite but still a very wealthy businessman of old Yankee stock who lived in large mansions on the West Side and at the lake. Bigelow was interested in attracting the largest possible crowds to ride on his railroad or visit his amusement parks, not in maintaining valued traditions, practices, or structures of authority. Nor was he concerned with fostering the kinds of ethnic solidarity that were forged and reinforced at church and immigrant July Fourth picnics.

Thus, as historian John Kasson notes, "the amusement parks and the emergent mass culture offered an opportunity to participate in American life on a new basis, outside traditional forms and proscriptions." Worcester workers who spent their holidays at White City as *individuals* or members of family units, rather than with the AOH or the Swedish Methodist Church as part of a group, took an important, but often unconscious, step away from the insular and restrictive world of their ethnic communities. Of course, this did not amount to an entrance into some homogenized middle-class culture, as some historians have imagined. Indeed, the middle and upper classes began to shun places like White City when they became havens for working-class celebrators. Rather, the commercialized amusement places – along with such other forces as the public school system and the breakdown of linguistic barriers with the growth of a second (American-born) generation – fostered the creation of a multiethnic working-class culture. Perhaps one small indication of this very gradual development is the increasing frequency of intermarriages between Worcester Catholics of different ethnic backgrounds.[27]

The increasing popularity of places like White City not only challenged the cultural authority and insularity of the ethnic communities but also threatened their economic base. The ethnic picnics had often been a means of financing immigrant organizations, churches, and charities, which were crucial to the infrastructure of the community. Money spent at or on church and ethnic celebrations remained largely within the ethnic working-class community. At first this money shifted to locally based entrepreneurs. But by the 1920s national corporations increasingly reaped the profits of holiday celebrating, and the Fourth became at least partially integrated into a national "leisure industry" and a national consumption economy.

In effect, working-class amusement park customers in these years were learning to be consumers of a commercialized leisure. The process of change, of course, was slow, halting, and never unaffected by the consumers themselves. Still, by July 3, 1911 – as Horace Bigelow died and more than 20,000 Worcesterites gathered to welcome in the Fourth at the lakeside amusement parks – the commercialized leisure business that Bigelow had fathered in Worcester had entered its adolescence.

Commercialization and the saloon: continuity and change, 1910–1920

The gradual emergence of new centers of commercialized leisure like the amusement park and the movie theater did not spell the end of older institutions like the saloon. Nevertheless, the same leisure market that had given rise to, and shaped, the amusement park and the movie house also affected the saloon. As a result, it did not remain fixed in its late nineteenth century form but became increasingly businesslike, orderly, and well regulated. At the same time, the opposition to the saloon shifted: The elite and the native middle class began to accept drinking, if not the saloon, and some members of the emerging ethnic middle class joined the no-license forces. By the time of national prohibition the Worcester saloon had become increasingly respectable and acceptable to the city's middle class and thus no longer appeared to offer as clear a threat to the dominant culture as it had in the late nineteenth century. Still, the saloon had not fully entered the mainstream of Worcester life. Those saloons patronized by the city's most recent immigrants remained particular objects of distaste and attack.

From its start, the saloon had been a commercial leisure business. Yet its commercial character was limited: The proprietors were small, often marginal, operators who often earned little more than a typical blue-collar worker; the saloons and saloonkeepers were closely tied to particular local ethnic working-class communities; the physical setting and ethos of the saloon drew upon and reinforced the cultural norms of working-class life. Over the fifty years between 1870 and 1920, however, the saloon gradually became much more of a conventional commercial enterprise.

The crucial agents in this commercializing process were, of course, the saloonkeepers and brewers. For many saloonkeepers, the liquor trade was a route out of the working-class communities that supported their business. By 1918 almost three-quarters of all Worcester saloonkeepers held some assessed real estate, a gradual increase from the 65 percent of 1900 and a dramatic increase from the 40 percent of 1870. In addition, saloonkeepers advertised their increasingly respectable status by moving away from the areas in which their saloons were located to the middle-class West Side of the city. In 1880 more than 90 percent of the saloonkeepers resided within a half mile of their saloons; by 1918 less than 40 percent lived that close. The common practice of living in the same building or next door had all but disappeared over this forty-year period. Although some of the residential changes simply reflected the physical growth of Worcester and the development of an electric street railway, they primarily stemmed from the growing affluence of the saloonkeepers. By 1918 at least six saloonkeepers lived on Pleasant Street, whereas none had chosen this middle-class West Side street eighteen years earlier. Another nine saloonkeepers populated Vernon Street in the "lace curtain" Irish community of Vernon Hill.[28]

Not only were saloonkeepers becoming increasingly distant – literally and socially – from their customers, but many saloons actually came under the control of the city's two large brewers, Bowler Bros. and the Worcester Brewing Company. The growth of brewer control over local saloons seems to have begun in 1889 with the inauguration of stricter limits on the number of licenses and the imposition of extremely high annual fees for those licenses. Faced with license fees of $1,000 to $2,000 per year many saloonkeepers agreed to sell only a particular brewer's product in return for financial assistance. In some cases, the brewer effectively took over the saloon. In 1909, for example, one saloonkeeper admitted that his saloon had merely been a front for the Worcester Brewing Company; which paid all the bills and reaped all the profits. Given the secrecy of these arrangements, the degree and nature of brewery control is difficult to determine. But it seems likely that by the early twentieth century the two breweries paid at least the license fees of about half the city's saloons.[29]

The passage of control over Worcester saloons to more affluent saloonkeepers working in partnership with corporate brewers encouraged a more businesslike and orderly saloon. Saloonkeepers with increasingly large investments in equipment and fixtures and brewers with huge manufacturing plants as well as interests in many saloons wanted some insurance that they would be able to stay in business. They were much more willing to follow the new License Commission rules than had been the more marginal operators of forty years earlier. Mayor George Wright, a businessman himself, understood this logic when he urged in 1914 that liquor licenses be automatically renewed: "Liquor dealers are engaged in a business which requires extensive equipment; and they are entitled to full consideration for a continuance of that business, providing they conduct it in accordance with the law."[30]

The willingness of Worcester saloonkeepers to comply with license regulations had grown in 1910 when Worcester returned to liquor licensing after two no-license years. Apparently fearful that open disregard of the law would lead to a return to no-license, saloonkeepers and brewers decided to pay closer attention to the rules established by the License Commission. Brewer John Bowler reportedly kept "a close watch on his saloons" and told the proprietors that they must follow the new regulations. More stringent police and License Commission surveillance reinforced this tendency toward self-regulation. In 1910 the commission intensively screened license applicants, paying particularly close attention to their financial standing and any previous liquor law violations. Those who actually received licenses realized, according to the *Worcester Gazette,* that things were "different than formerly" and that "a simple violation of the law means, if they are detected, a temporary shutup." By 1910 possible infractions included not only old rules against Sunday sales but also new prohibitions against providing free lunches, treating customers, selling to women, and cashing paychecks.[31]

The overall impact of these external licensing regulations and procedures and the internal changes in the management of the saloon was to put the saloon on "business lines," as Mayor Logan had urged in 1910. Only the more affluent and well-established saloonkeepers could survive the more stringent licensing process. And only those who abandoned some of the old reciprocal customs – treating customers, providing free lunches – were free from police harassment. "Gone are the days," one Worcester saloonkeeper commented in 1915, "when the barkeep can shake dice with his customers, and it's now as much as a man's life is worth to offer a customer a drink. Gone are the days when one could drop into a saloon and hear the latest melodies played. Music is barred, and even one place on Pleasant St., to make sure that order is preserved, has a sign over the mahogany reading: 'Nix on the conversation; this place is neutral.'" Other observers noticed a similar waning of the earlier casual and communal atmosphere. "In the old days," the *Labor News* wrote in 1913, the saloon was "run haphazardly . . . bums were allowed to lounge around, and most places were notorious for their filthy appearance. The proprietors in those days, for the most part, were sports . . . Most of their time was spent at the horse track, the baseball field or the prize fight, their business was left in charge of someone who either couldn't or didn't choose to run things in the proper way." Now, the *Labor News* explained, saloonkeepers had become "real businessmen." Even such critics of the saloon as the former secretary of the citizens' No-License Committee agreed that it was more orderly: "That the saloon in our city is regulated just as well as a saloon can be regulated, none, I think will deny."[32]

While both saloongoers and saloonkeepers may have regretted the loss of some of the more communal and reciprocal features of the late nineteenth century saloon, most saloonkeepers knew that better regulated and more businesslike establishments were less likely to attract controversy and face shutdowns under local option. After the improved regulations and conditions took effect around 1910, many Worcesterites seem to have stopped considering no-license as a viable option. For the next ten years, as the nation was moving toward prohibition, about 60 percent of Worcester voters annually endorsed liquor licensing – although support had averaged less than 54 percent over the previous thirty years. And just as the formerly contentious issue of local option now stirred only apathy among most Worcester voters, the issuance of licenses no longer dominated local conversations in mid-April. The same newspapers that had previously run banner headlines announcing the winners of the annual licensing "sweepstakes" no longer even published the names of the successful applicants. After 1910 few licenses changed hands from year to year and by 1915 the License Commission actively discouraged new applicants. The saloon had become a stable, orderly business, not so different from a clothing store or grocery. A reporter for the *Labor News* captured the new atmosphere: Worcester saloons, he wrote, had changed from "sporting and loafing centres to places where men go and buy what they want, pay for it and get out, just as they do any other commodity."[33]

Of course, it is a mistake to exaggerate the magnitude or the completeness of the transformation of the saloon or the attitudes of middle-class Worcesterites. To be sure, the personal abstinence from liquor that was so common among Worcester's leading citizens in the 1870s and 1880s had gradually faded, particularly with the birth of a new, less Calvinist generation. By 1895 the *Worcester Telegram* noted that many of the "best people" drank beer and wine. And by the turn of the century many of the city's leading social clubs – the Worcester Club and the Tatnuck Country Club, for example – held liquor licenses.[34]

The personal drinking habits of Worcester manufacturers, however, were changing more quickly than their attitudes about drinking among their employees. Corporations continued to petition against saloons in the vicinity of their factories and to campaign against drinking by their employees. Worcester's American Steel and Wire Company (the successor to Washburn and Moen) even ordered its employees to resign from clubs that sold liquor – an order that apparently did not extend to corporate executives who belonged to the Worcester Club or the Tatnuck Country Club. And in 1914, 250 leading Worcester businessmen and manufacturers attended an Anti-Saloon League meeting chaired by G. Stanley Hall to listen to speakers explain how to "promote sobriety, safety, and efficiency of employees."[35]

Despite their support for the Anti-Saloon League, Worcester manufacturers tended to concentrate more on keeping saloons away from their factories and stopping employee drinking on the job than on promoting the no-license and prohibition causes. After 1910 the local stalwarts of the no-license movement came largely from the Swedish pietist churches. And they were aided by at least some members of the emerging Irish middle class. In 1909 the *Catholic Messenger,* which after 1906 had come to represent the views of Americanized, second-generation, upwardly mobile Irish Catholics, broke with the traditional Catholic moral suasionist position and called for "no" votes in the local option election. Although the growing and heavily white-collar Knights of Columbus did not also take this radical step, they did bar liquor dealers from their ranks.[36]

Although the city's leading ministers and manufacturers no longer played as active a role in the no-license movement, they still instinctively checked the "no" box in the annual local option election as did 40 percent of all Worcesterites in the decade before prohibition. And the no-license and license-restriction movements continued to focus on working-class drinking and the working-class saloon, particularly since it was those saloons that catered to the poorest workers and the newest immigrants that proved least susceptible to the trend toward more businesslike and orderly operations. Saloons "patronized mainly by laborers" and located in the working-class East Side districts – now increasingly populated by Poles, Lithuanians, Jews, and Italians – the *Worcester Sunday Telegram* reported in 1912, were the most likely to violate the rules against treating and free lunches.[37]

The focus of the temperance movement remained the working-class saloon, but the patrons of the saloon had changed somewhat during the forty-year interim period. For one thing, they had aged. Many who had made the saloon a social center in the 1880s still used it in the same way in the 1910s, but now they were in their sixties rather than their thirties. A social survey of a working-class neighborhood of Columbus, Ohio, in 1919 found that it was primarily among the "older men" that the saloon served as a "social club." The younger men favored the more active recreation offered in the poolroom or the opportunities for meeting women offered in the dance halls. In Worcester, local union officials similarly noted the popularity of automobiles, dance halls, and other commercialized leisure centers among "young workers." A local saloonkeeper, reflecting on the competition from new commercial amusements like the movies, commented in 1915 that "it isn't the natives of Worcester who are doing the drinking nowadays."[38]

The most important exception to this apparent aging of the saloon clientele, as this same saloonkeeper knew, was "the fellows from Europe." In the early twentieth century a vast number of immigrants from southern and eastern Europe entered Worcester and many of these workingmen made the saloon into their own social centers. Arguing for the impracticality of no-license in Worcester, lawyer John H. Meagher noted in 1912 that Worcester "is made up of people from every country in the world" who "maintained their customs and habits as lived in the countries of their birth." While many immigrants brought their drinking habits along with them, some re-created social patterns that did not involve alcohol or the saloon. Worcester's Greeks, Turks, and Albanians, for example, centered their social life in coffeehouses. Jews found drugstores more congenial gathering places than saloons. Among Poles and Lithuanians, however, two of the city's largest immigrant groups, the saloon apparently had an importance comparable to its significance among Worcester's Irish in the 1880s.[39]

Poles and Lithuanians followed the Irish into the Worcester saloon, but their experiences there were not identical to those of their predecessors. Whereas Irish saloongoers had patronized Irish-run saloons, the new immigrants did not enter the saloon business in the same numbers. Barred by rules against the granting of licenses to noncitizens and, even more important, by Irish control of most of the city's available liquor licenses, the drink trade offered the more recent immigrants few opportunities. As late as 1918, only about one-eighth of Worcester's saloonkeepers were from southern or eastern European backgrounds. Most of the rest were Irish or Irish Americans.[40] The early twentieth century saloon was thus not as closely tied to specific ethnic working-class communities as had been the late nineteenth century saloon.

For all these reasons – the growing commercialization and regulation of the saloon, the gradual shift in middle-class attitudes, the ethnic division between owner and patrons – the Worcester saloon was less likely to come into conflict with the dominant society by 1918. In Worcester, at least, the drastic solution posed by national prohibition was probably not necessary. By the time it was imposed, the saloon was no longer perceived so clearly as a fundamental threat to Worcester society.

Indeed, by 1920, some people began to wonder whether it had ever been a threat at all, to realize that the saloon, after all, had nurtured a form of *alternative,* rather than *oppositional,* culture, and to see that it had failed to directly challenge the dominant political economy. One such perceptive observer was the aging Worcester resident G. Stanley Hall, by then retired as president of Clark University. By 1920 Hall had begun to reevaluate the opposition to the saloon he had demonstrated by his leadership of the 1914 Anti-Saloon League rally. Perhaps, in the wake of the 1915 Worcester machinists' strike, he had started to wonder whether there were not more serious threats to the industrial economy than the saloon. Certainly, the Russian Revolution had given him further pause to reconsider his position on prohibition.

Thwarted drinkers, Hall now feared, might look outside the saloon to vent their feelings. With the imposition of strict prohibition, Hall told a Worcester audience, "the former would-be drinker turns against capital, employers and the industrial system, or at least is more ready to listen to the advocates of radical views . . . Deprived of the conviviality of the saloon he finds a proxy for it in strike meetings, where the common cause brings him very close to his fellow-men." The mob, then, replaced the bottle as a source of excitement for the worker, and "the discontent of his alimentary tract is projected outward upon his general social and industrial environment."

However, Hall did see a glimmer of hope. Perhaps "the mild excitement of the movies, prize-fights, and our great national game" might serve as "vents to compensate men for the long repressions that society and the mores always impose."[41] And, indeed, as America entered the "dry decade," the movies, the prizefights, and our great national game increasingly did become the long-sought-after substitutes for the saloon.

8 *From rum shop to Rialto: workers and movies*

G. Stanley Hall was not alone in pointing out the close connection between the decline of the saloon and the rise of the motion pictures. "Often when a moving picture house is set up," Vachel Lindsay wrote in 1915 in his study of *The Art of the Moving Picture,* "the saloon on the right hand or the left declares bankruptcy." Movies, according to Lindsay, had emerged as "the first enemy of King Alcohol with real power where that King has deepest hold." Saloonkeepers ruefully conceded Lindsay's point. Almost from the opening of the very first movie theaters in 1905, they had "protested excitedly against the nickelodeon as a menace to their trade," according to one national magazine. What saloonkeepers bemoaned, temperance leaders celebrated. "I believe the movies now occupy the attention of a great many persons who would otherwise be in a saloon," exulted a prominent Worcester no-license crusader and building contractor.[1] While the Worcester saloon had already begun a process of internal transformation, the development of a new form of working-class leisure – the movies – proved to be a much more potent force in the displacement of the saloon from the center of ethnic working-class life.

Of course, the nickelodeon's triumph over the saloon was never as complete as temperance and movie promoters liked to believe. Analyzing the results of a detailed 1910 study of the leisure-time pursuits of 1,000 New York workingmen, a temperance reformer cautioned that the five-cent show "hasn't quite put the saloon out of business." But the balance had shifted: Of the men in the study, 60 percent patronized the movies, whereas only 30 percent frequented the saloon. And certainly by the dry decade of the 1920s the movies had triumphed as the most popular form of public working-class recreation. But by that time the movies were no longer merely the private preserve of the urban, immigrant working class. They had become a truly mass entertainment, attracting a weekly attendance of well over 50 million – equivalent to half the total U.S. population.[2] This dramatic emergence of the movie theater as a center of interclass, nationally distributed mass entertainment and its impact on the late nineteenth century working-class world of the saloon and the holiday picnic forms the subject of this chapter.

The movies come to Worcester

As in most cities, moving pictures first appeared in Worcester in the late 1890s as a sporadic novelty. By 1904, however, they had found a regular spot on the program of two of the city's vaudeville theaters. The next year movies acquired their first full-time outlet when Nathan and Isaac Gordon converted a Main Street furniture store into a "penny arcade," which they filled with Edison peep-show machines. In the fall of 1906 the Gordon brothers joined with local theater managers P. F. Shea and Alf T. Wilton in opening the city's first full-fledged movie theater. With the Gordons' machines in the lobby, Shea and Wilton transformed the Palace Museum, a 1,000-seat showcase for low-priced vaudeville and Friday-night wrestling, into the Nickel Theatre, which premiered on September 24, 1906, with a program of motion pictures and illustrated songs. Other Worcester theaters continued to exhibit films as part of vaudeville programs or as special presentations, but only the Nickel offered the continuous shows and the "democratic" seating and pricing that characterized the nickelodeons, which were rapidly proliferating throughout the nation's cities.[3]

The prices and programs proved a local success; the Nickel claimed 10,000 customers in its first week of business. Although it faced both criticism and censorship early in 1907 for showing *The Unwritten Law,* a film about the sensational Thaw–White murder case, the Nickel soon found itself surrounded by imitators. Within a few months in the spring of 1907, three other Worcester theaters, which had previously presented melodrama or vaudeville, switched to so-called pictorial vaudeville. Of course, the separation between these two entertainments was not always absolute – some theaters mixed live vaudeville and motion pictures. But the movies were now leading the way. "The unusual demand for moving pictures shows has caught the people of Worcester as it has those in every other city and town in the country," the *Worcester Gazette* reported.[4]

Although the "nickel madness" that gripped the country equally infected Worcester, the precise pattern of growth differed from that of the largest cities. Entrepreneurs in metropolitan centers like New York and Chicago, spurred by licensing regulations, had established small storefront theaters usually seating fewer than 300 people. Only later did they open larger and more centrally located theaters.

But in Worcester the movies came first to the full-sized downtown theaters and only spread to three smaller cinemas over the next two and a half years. Even more than the city's first movie houses, these smaller theaters had an ethnic or working-class management, an immigrant, working-class clientele, and the lowest prices in the city.[5]

In 1909 John W. Raymond, a former machinist, opened the 350-seat Majestic Theatre in what had been a downtown variety store. Later Aduino Feretti and Carmine Zamarro, who ran an employment and steamship ticket agency, took it over. Also in 1909, a Jewish shoe operator, Max Graf, launched the 300-seat, five-cent Pastime Theatre. Subsequently, "Gaspard and Charlie," two French Canadians who performed between film reels, reportedly took charge. Finally, in early 1910, the larger Bijou opened its doors on the site of what ten years earlier had been Michael McGaddy's saloon. For the first time in Worcester a theater had located itself well outside the city's central business district. Significantly, the Bijou chose Millbury Street, the heart of the city's multiethnic, working-class East Side. "At Last – A High Class Amusement Temple for the East Side" its advertisements proclaimed.[6]

Thus, by 1910 Worcester had about 4,250 seats devoted exclusively to moving pictures. Furthermore, in the first ten years of the twentieth century the total number of seats in Worcester available for all forms of commercial entertainment – theater, burlesque, vaudeville, and movies – had almost tripled from 3,438 to 9,338. In the process, the number of Worcester residents for each theater seat dropped sharply from thirty-four to fewer than sixteen.[7] The most important explanation for the rapid expansion in theatrical seats lies with the opening of the new, cheap movie houses and the development of a working-class movie audience.

Workers go to the movies

In 1912 Clark professor and social reformer Prentice Hoyt scrutinized Worcester's three cheap movie theaters, the Bijou, the Family (formerly the Nickel), and the Majestic. "All the world of a certain class meets together for an hour or two a day" at these theaters, Hoyt concluded. The poorest immigrants dominated at the Bijou, while "the slightly better class of workmen and their wives and children" filled the Family. The Majestic, located only a few steps from the Family, drew a similar crowd. Hoyt's analysis of Worcester's movie audiences confirmed the patterns found in other cities.

In 1910, for example, a Russell Sage Foundation study found that in New York City blue-collar workers made up only 2 percent of the audiences at theaters showing live dramatic productions but almost three-quarters of moving picture audiences. Around the same time, a Columbia University sociology graduate student, writing his doctoral thesis on the leisure activities of New York workingmen, discovered that only reading newspapers or socializing with family or friends occurred more frequently or occupied more spare time than moviegoing for most workers. "Motion pictures," John Collier explained to a middle class suddenly noticing this new amusement, "are the favorite entertainment today of the wage earning classes of the world." And journalists and other commentators penned such phrases as "the academy of the workingman," the "drama of the multitude," "the workingman's college," and the "true theater of the people" to dramatize the new development.[8]

While reformers, sociologists, and journalists rushed to report on this new working-class movie audience, few paused to ask where it had come from. In part, the crowds that flocked to the early nickelodeons had simply transferred their allegiances from the existing varieties of cheap commercial entertainment. As early as the 1870s, the Worcester Theatre, while primarily offering dramatic productions aimed at the city's "well-to-do," occasionally presented minstrel shows and plays appealing to Irish and German audiences. But the high tariff charged at the Worcester Theatre kept away many blue-collar workers. By 1883 Bristol's Dime Museum gave them Bohemian glass blowers, comedy sketches, ventriloquists, acrobats, and human-faced chickens at a much more affordable price. In the following decade those with only ten cents to spend could sit in the gallery of Lothrop's Opera House and watch melodramas and minstrel shows or visit the nearby Front Street Musee for burlesque or vaudeville. And such outlets for cheap amusement multiplied further in the first decade of the twentieth century.[9]

The lower prices, the "democratic" seating, the novelty, and the excitement of the five-cent movie houses appealed strongly to the patrons of these cheap theaters. With the coming of the movies, actors in local melodramas – what a historian of Worcester theaters referred condescendingly to as "dramatic pablum of the masses for two generations" – reported "the loss of gallery patronage." Thousands of theatergoers voted with their nickels and dimes for the new entertainment sensation. Movies benefited not only from the patronage of those who had always attended the city's lower-priced theatrical amusements but even more from the general expansion of the leisure market in early twentieth century Worcester. The amusement parks discussed in the preceding chapter are one example of that boom. And the four "dime museums" featuring a combination of melodrama, farces, vaudeville, and wrestling, which opened on Front Street between 1900 and 1905, are another. Thus, even before the nickel madness of 1907 swept through Worcester, the number of theatrical seats in the city had more than doubled.[10] In effect, a good portion of the new movie audience had found its way to older, live entertainments in the years immediately preceding the birth of the nickelodeon.

Why was commercial entertainment enjoying such prosperity around the turn of the century in both Worcester and the rest of the country? As previously noted, the rise in real incomes and the decline in work hours crucially fueled the expansion of the leisure market. Yet, significantly, movies, with their low admission price and their short programs, were also regularly accessible to workers who still had low wages and long hours. Thus, in 1912 when a Worcester labor lawyer worked out a relatively generous budget for a working-class family, he could only find room in it for a weekly expenditure of about twenty cents for amusements. In this context, the five-cent movie house had a decisive edge over not only the twenty-five-cent gallery seats at the Worcester Theatre but also the ten-cent melodrama in competing for the working-class entertainment dollar (or quarter).[11] Similarly, nickelodeons, because their shows were continuous and short, proved compatible with long work hours. Although the U.S. Steel Corporation, a major employer in both Worcester and Pittsburgh, maintained the twelve-hour day for some workers until 1923, investigators for the 1908 Pittsburgh Survey still encountered long lines of overworked steel-mill hands at that city's nickelodeons.[12]

Part of the success of the movies thus rested on their ability to attract the underpaid and overworked as well as those who were gaining a bit more disposable income and a few more free hours in the early twentieth century. By accommodating both kinds of schedules and pocketbooks, the movie theater managed to become – like the saloon, the church, and the fraternal lodge – a central working-class institution that involved workers on a sustained and regular basis.

Yet there was an even more obvious source for the growth in movie audiences: more people. America's cities were booming and Worcester was no exception. Its population grew by 72 percent between 1890 and 1910. Immigrants, of course, played a disproportionately large part in that population growth. In those twenty years, the city's foreign-born increased by 82 percent, adding almost 22,000 immigrants to Worcester's already substantial foreign population. These new immigrants – almost entirely non-English speaking and often from southern and eastern Europe – proved particularly important to the growth of Worcester's movie theaters. "It doesn't matter whether a man is from Kamchatka or Stamboul, whether he can speak English or not. He can understand pictures and he doesn't need to have anyone explain that to him," commented a Worcester movie theater manager in accounting for the burgeoning of the movies. The silence of the movies beckoned immigrants unable to comprehend so many other facets of American life. "Its very voicelessness," one student of popular amusements wrote of the new medium in 1909, "makes it eloquent for Letts, Finns, Italians, Syrians, Greeks, and pigtailed Celestials. It has pulled down the Tower of Babel, abolished the hyphenated dictionary, and fulfilled the Esperantist's dearest dream."[13]

For many Worcester immigrants – circumscribed by their language to the social institutions of their own ethnic communities – movies offered their first nonwork contact with the larger American society. "I never saw a movie in Italy," recalls Fred Fedeli, who arrived in Worcester in 1907 at age thirteen. "I was on the farm; when I came here I got interested in going to the movies." In his limited spare time from his sixty-hour per week factory job, Fedeli would spend part of the sixty cents he had left each week after paying room and board to attend the newly opened Nickel Theatre. In 1912, realizing the appeal of the new medium for his fellow immigrants, Fedeli, along with his older brother and a cousin, leased the Bijou Theatre on Millbury Street in the heart of Worcester's immigrant, working-class district. "The [Bijou] audiences," commented Professor Hoyt, "are of every nationality under the sun, every type which has its home in the region around Vernon Square." As a moviegoer and an immigrant himself, Fedeli understood this audience well. Explaining the popularity of silent films, he recalls: "My people, the Polish people and the Lithuanian and Jewish people . . . didn't talk any more English than I did."[14]

Of course, some observers probably exaggerated the ease with which the most recent immigrants adapted to the new entertainment medium. A Worcester woman wrote that it was only through evening English-language classes that she had learned to "red a newspaper and to red de moving pekses."[15] Reading movie captions was much less likely to be a problem for the children of immigrants, and this second generation took to the movies with even more enthusiasm than their parents. Virtually all observers of early movie theater audiences noted the presence of large numbers of children and young people. "The nickelodeon," wrote one in 1908, "is almost the creation of the child, and it has discovered a new and healthy cheap-amusement public." "Children are the best patrons of the nickelodeon," added a trade press correspondent that same year. So great was the hold of the movies on immigrant children, according to reformer Jane Addams, that a group of young girls, "accustomed to the life of a five-cent theater, reluctantly refused an invitation to go to the country for a day's outing because the return of a late train would compel them to miss one evening's performance. They found it impossible to tear themselves away not only from the excitements of the theater but from the gaiety of the crowd of young men and girls invariably gathered outside discussing the sensational posters." Children, a range of different studies agreed, composed about one-quarter to one-half of the new movie audience.[16]

As Edward Chandler told the First Conference on Child Welfare in Worcester in 1909, the "simplest reason" why so many children and young people found their way to the movies was "the low price. A nickel or a dime is far easier to get than a quarter." But for the children of immigrants, movie houses may have had a particular attraction: freedom from the surveillance mandated by a constricted and conservative family life. One woman, a New York Italian garment worker brought up by strict parents, recalls that "the one place I was allowed to go by myself was the movies. My parents wouldn't let me go out anywhere else, even when I was 24." Another woman of the same background recalls meeting her future husband on the sly at the local movie house.[17]

While some immigrant teen-agers relished the freedom provided by the movie house, much moviegoing was actually done in family groups. Reformer Frederic Howe noted with satisfaction that "men now take their wives and families for an evening at the movies where formerly they went alone to the nearby saloon." Mary Heaton Vorse visited a movie house on Bleecker Street in the heart of New York's Italian section and reported: "Every woman has a baby in her arms and at least two children clinging to her skirts." Whereas Worcester's Deputy Sheriff James Early complained that a mother "should be at home, attending her household duties," not patronizing "this popular form of amusement," the *Labor News* leapt to the defense of "these overworked women" who take advantage of the few hours' time during which "the older children are at school or at the playgrounds" to attend the movie theater, "very often carrying a babe in arms."[18]

Worcester movie theater managers assiduously courted this female patronage. Press releases from the newly opened Nickel Theatre announced the management's intention "to cater especially to the patronage of women and children," and its advertisements labeled it "The Ladies and Children's Resort." After its first week of operation, it claimed that women and children made up 60 percent of the audience.[19] The young workingwoman joined working-class mothers in this new female audience. In the early twentieth century, increasing numbers of women took jobs outside the home. In Worcester, which mirrored national trends, women's labor force participation rates went from 19.5 to 23.7 percent between 1890 and 1910. As Elizabeth Butler documented in the Pittsburgh Survey, these women – especially those living alone in cheap rooming houses – had few outlets for their hard-earned leisure time and money. Often "the only relief for nervous weariness and the desire for stimulation" was the picture show.[20]

The working-class movie audience thus drew on a variety of sources. The movie house attracted former patrons of other cheap amusements as well as tapped what one contemporary reporter called "an entirely new stratum of people." It appeared at a moment when workers had more time and money for leisure, but its low price and convenient time schedule made it available to workers who still remained poorly paid and overworked. Finally, it had particular appeals for the non-English-speaking immigrant who was effectively shut out of other entertainment forms; the child with only a nickel to spend; the immigrant teen-ager seeking freedom from restrictive family life; and the wife and mother, who had traditionally shunned, or been barred from, many other working-class social centers. "As a business, and as a social phenomenon," writes historian Robert Sklar, "the motion pictures came to life in the United States when they made contact with working-class needs and desires." "The art of the photo-play," the *Nation* concluded in a similar contemporary comment, was "created for the masses and largely by them."[21]

Moviegoing as working-class culture

Working-class audiences were decisive in the early success of the movies. But did the new medium actually reflect the values and traditions of its new patrons? Analyzing the relationship between audience and movies before 1920 is fraught with more than the usual difficulties of popular cultural analysis. Prewar films, unlike those popular in the 1920s, seem to have "dealt mostly with the working man and his world," according to one prominent film historian. Yet even this general characterization of movie content remains open to debate, given the paucity of films surviving from this period. Additionally, even if we could see all the films produced in these years, how would we know which ones particularly appealed to working-class viewers or how they responded to the picture on the screen? D. W. Griffith's *The Fatal Hour,* which was shown at Worcester's Nickel Theatre in September 1908, may have offered a moralistic attack on the white slave trade, but working-class viewers may have simply seen it as an action-packed melodrama.[22]

With these difficulties in mind, it may be more fruitful to focus on the moviegoing experience, rather than movie content. Whatever the degree of control of the middle and upper classes over movie content, the working class was likely to determine the nature of behavior and interaction within the movie theater. Although theater managers mediated the audience's self-determination, they were, like saloonkeepers, usually cut from the same cloth as their customers. They shared similar backgrounds, values, and perspectives, and even, as with Fred Fedeli, a similar language disadvantage. Together, the immigrant working-class movie manager and the immigrant working-class audience developed a style of moviegoing that accorded with, and drew upon, earlier modes of public working-class recreation.

Working-class movie theater conduct built on a long tradition of crowd behavior that could be found at a variety of earlier popular amusements from melodramas to saloons to July Fourth picnics to working-class parks. Indeed, such patterns of public sociability and boisterousness can also be discerned in eighteenth-century French and English middle- and upper-class theater audiences. But by the mid-nineteenth century, historian Richard Sennett notes, "restraint of emotion in the theater became a way for middle-class audiences to mark the line between themselves and the working class." The "silence" that descended over bourgeois public behavior in the nineteenth century did not also blanket working-class public life.[23] Modes of conviviality, active sociability, and liveliness remained the norms for the working class. And workers brought these behavior styles with them when they entered the world of commercial amusement.

Working-class audiences at the melodramas, minstrel shows, and burlesque acts of the late nineteenth and early twentieth centuries gave repeated evidence of interactive, lively, and often rowdy public behavior. Even when the upper-class men and women of the theater boxes maintained a restrained decorum, the lower-class inhabitants of the gallery could be counted on for vocal and high-spirited spontaneity. "In all theaters," writes a historian of early nineteenth century melodrama, "the gallery was the place most suitable for rowdyism, the best point from which to bombard disliked actors, members of the orchestra who failed to play popular tunes, or even the helpless 'middling classes' ensconced in the pit." Similarly, despite a placard proclaiming "no guying, whistling, or cat-calls," the gallery of the early twentieth century urban burlesque house would rage with "whistling, stamping, and hand-clapping."[24]

Naturally, in theaters that drew exclusively working-class patronage such lively behavior was not confined to the gallery. In the late 1890s drama critic John Corbin described the friendly and expressive audiences that filled the Teatro Italiano on New York's East Side: "They would speak to you on the slightest pretext, or none, and would relate all that was happening on the stage . . . At the tragic climaxes they shouted with delight, and at the end of each act yelled at the top of their lungs." Making the reverse comparison, a letter writer to a Yiddish newspaper pointed out that "the English Theater" is "not like our Jewish theater. . . . I found it so quiet there . . . There are no cries of 'Sha!' 'Shut up!' or 'Order!' and no babies cried – as if it were no theater at all!"[25]

Although ethnic theater companies made only occasional stops in a medium-sized industrial city like Worcester, audiences at its other low-priced commercial entertainments revealed these same patterns of theatrical behavior. At melodrama productions in the 1880s, most of the action took place "down stage," a local historian comments laconically. The "dime museums," which sprang up on Front Street in the early twentieth century, attracted particularly lively working-class crowds. At the always popular Amateur Night, singers met shouts of "If you can't sing get off the stage" and persistent howls and hisses from an audience filled with friends of their competitors. Only the presence of "several policemen in full uniform in the building put a quietus on what may have easily terminated in a miniature riot," the *Worcester Sunday Telegram* reported after one Amateur Night. Professional companies at Worcester's ten-cent music halls faced equally demanding and vocal audiences. Charles Baker, the man charged with writing, directing, performing in, and even selling tickets for productions at the Palace Museum, noted that stale jokes would never wash since "the dime audience knows more about a good joke than half of the two dollar theatre patrons." "If it isn't a go," the opening-night audience would quickly let him know, and a new production would have "to be written before the next afternoon for two o'clock."[26]

The Nickel movie theater inherited not only the actual building of the Palace Museum but also the lively and demanding crowds that had filled it and such other centers of working-class sociability as the saloon, the fraternal lodge, and the cheap theater. Indeed, the particular structure of the moviegoing experience – especially prices, seating arrangements, time schedules, and internal conditions – reinforced and heightened preexisting behavior patterns. The lack of seating differentiation by price at the early movie house exemplified its egalitarian social style. Whereas the Worcester Theatre carefully stratified patrons according to their ability to pay, the Nickel Theatre placed all customers on an equal plane. Even many other cheap forms of commercial entertainment such as the melodrama or vaudeville had often resisted this radical "leveling."

This "democratic" pricing fostered what one critic called an "atmosphere of independence" and " a kind of proprietorship in the playhouse" and along with that an air of informality and relaxed socializing at early movie houses. The lack of a structured time schedule further encouraged these tendencies. Workers could casually stop at the movie theater on their way home from work or shopping and catch all or part of the twenty- to sixty-minute show. Since no single item on the program lasted very long, there was little pressure to arrive at a specific time. Workers, already burdened with exacting time demands on the job, undoubtedly appreciated this lack of structure. The slogan "Stay as Long as You Like," from an early Nickel Theatre advertisement, captured the casual spirit of the enterprise.[27]

This informality sanctioned a wide variety of behaviors that were disdained at most higher-priced theaters. Commenting on the timelessness of movie shows, a reporter for the *Moving Picture World* noted that some patrons watched the same performances all day and into the night, eating their lunch in the theater along the way. In Worcester, the use of the movie house as a lunchroom brought complaints from the middle-class press: "One can go into any theatre in town prior to the noon hour and find at least one-half of the women patrons nibbling lunch biscuits, cakes, or sweet meals of some kind," one reporter grumbled. Even less acceptable to middle-class observers was drinking alcohol or exhibiting drunken behavior. Part of the job of the ticket taker at the Nickel Theatre was keeping out intoxicated patrons. Despite his efforts, "a choice collection of drunks" could be found in the back rows, perhaps sleeping off a binge. Still others undertook more animated, if still less acceptable, pursuits. "The very darkness" of the movie house, observed Jane Addams, "is an added attraction to many young people, for whom the place is filled with the glamour of love making." Newspapers labeled the last row of Worcester movie theaters "lovers' lane" and youths filled these seats well before those that provided better views.[28]

Such unacceptable public behavior – eating, drinking, sleeping, necking – was actually incidental to the larger function of the movie house as a vehicle for informal socializing. The Bijou, for example, apparently served as a social center for Worcester's immigrant working-class East Side – "the gathering place of the women of the neighborhood with their babies and little children, a crude sort of tea-room gossiping place," according to Professor Hoyt. Similarly, in 1915, the theater correspondent of the *Worcester Sunday Telegram* complained of some Irish women at the Family Theatre who "substitute seats in the orchestra for seats at the tea table." In New York in 1909 a movie house visitor similarly observed "regulars" who "stroll up and down the aisles between reels and visit friends." "The five-cent theater," Jane Addams reported from Chicago that same year, "is also fast becoming the general social center and club house in many crowded neighborhoods . . . The room which contains the . . . stage is small and cozy, and less formal than the regular theater, and there is much more gossip and social life as if the foyer and pit were mingled."[29]

Overall, then, moviegoing was far from the passive experience that some critics accused it of being. The working-class audience interacted volubly not only with each other but also with the entertainment presented. The large number of children at the movie houses reinforced this boisterous atmosphere. "When the hero triumphs during a children's performance, shouting, whistling, and stomping combine in a demonstration which at times is most remarkable," noted the *Worcester Telegram.* Various nonmovie features also encouraged audience participation. The illustrated song used as a "filler" between movie reels promoted group singing with its injunction: "All Join In The Chorus." Amateur Night, of course, stimulated audience participation, with friends and neighbors shouting for their favorites and the crowd usually selecting the winner. Other forms of working-class recreation from bike racing to wrestling complemented movie shows and stimulated audience cheering.[30]

Not only did movie theater conduct grow out of traditions of working-class public recreational behavior based on sociability, conviviality, communality, and informality, but movie theater conditions also accorded with the realities of working-class life. The movie house might offer some relief from crowded urban tenements or three-deckers, but it did not offer a radically different environment. Unlike the ornate movie palaces of later years, recalls an old-time Worcester manager, the early and cheaper movie theaters were just "four walls." Another early manager remembers the closely packed wooden seats. But a former patron paints an even less flattering picture. He recollects the old Gem Theatre as nothing more than a "shack" and remembers rats from the city's sewers scurrying under his seat while he was watching movies at the Bijou.[31]

Spartan, and even unsanitary, conditions made little impression on working-class moviegoers; such surroundings were part of their daily lives. But middle-class commentators reacted with horror. "A room that is stuffy and congested is not a proper place for a growing child to be, and it doesn't look at first glance as if it were the place for the mother either," Worcester Deputy Sheriff James Early asserted. Only the word "filth" could adequately describe these theaters according to Professor Hoyt: "The floors are dirty and the air is stagnant and charged with the vileness and disease that is poured into it."[32]

But part of the shocked reaction of middle-class observers was not to the actual physical conditions of theaters themselves but simply to the presence of large numbers of working-class people, who acted, looked, and smelled differently from themselves. The *Worcester Sunday Telegram* drama correspondent, for example, was obsessed by the odors of theaters: "Unclean persons should be influenced to respect the rights of others. The best ventilating system made will not rid playhouses of odors which have become component parts of individuals." Despite this pessimism, he offered such remedies as distributing soap to patrons or burning incense. On one occasion he recommended that patrons who "eat garlic and spread their breath promiscuously should be given seats on the roof or in the alley." In the early twentieth century odors had important class and cultural implications. Indeed, Rollin Lynde Hartt, the author of a 1909 study of *The People at Play,* whimsically suggested that "some modern sage might devote study to the graded aromas of our entertainments." Whereas Hartt characterized the opera as "the breath of roses," he labeled burlesque "an unwashen odor, mitigated with vile tabacco" and the dime museum "the same and more of it, though unfortunately without the tobacco." "With the nose we knows," Hartt concluded.[33] And so observers like the *Telegram*'s drama correspondent could not only see and hear working-class movie audiences, they could also smell them.

Conflict over the working-class movie theater

As the "odor issue" indicates, the development of a new entertainment medium with a distinctive working-class presence and style occasioned a variety of social and cultural conflicts. On the one hand, the forces of middle-class reform, morality, and order perceived the movie house as a barrier to their efforts not only to control and redirect working-class leisure but also to shape changing middle-class leisure patterns. On the other hand, the movie theater also challenged the prevailing working-class culture and its twin institutional pillars, the saloon and the church. Accordingly, over the next twenty years advocates of the status quo within both the middle and working classes struggled to control, restrict, regulate, and redirect the new medium. In effect, both the middle and working classes split over their willingness to accept the emerging mass culture. Nevertheless, the efforts of both groups had only limited impact. More influential in transforming the movie house were those actually assembled there: the theater owner, the working-class audience, and the new, developing middle-class audience.

In January 1910 the *Worcester Telegram* began a series of sensationalized front-page stories about the city's juvenile gangs, which stressed that many of the gangs' allegedly immoral activities centered around the city's movie theaters. According to the *Telegram*, female gang members with their "short, close fitting dresses" and "paint on their faces" could usually be found at "the opening matinees" of the downtown theaters, and male gang members also "hung about the cheap moving picture places on Front Street." The police responded swiftly to this ostensible problem of immorality and movies. Noting that girls involved in the alleged "orgies" had "confessed that their early tendencies toward evil came from seeing moving pictures . . . and from certain houses where conditions were permitted that made temptations easy," Police Chief David Matthews appointed Police Lieutenant George Hill, who had been serving as head of the police liquor squad (a job made less necessary by the impending end of no-license), as movie censor.[34]

Just as he had fought to control working-class drinking habits, Police Censor Hill zealously battled to bring Worcester movies in line with his own narrow conceptions of propriety. Within his first two weeks as police censor in 1910, he scissored out the duel and hell scenes from *Faust*, the murder of Julius Caesar from the Shakespeare play, and a scene from a labor film in which strikers murdered a scab. The police went beyond the picture on the screen to regulate conduct within the theater. In late January, for example, Chief Matthews banned standing in theaters. And in March, Censor Hill stopped the Nickel Theatre's popular and lively Amateur Night because it "attracted lots of young girls and boys, . . . [and] it was thought best to . . . keep the girls and boys at home."[35]

Such censorial zeal did not meet with uniform approval. The Worcester *Labor News* commented that "Hill might make an excellent rum sleuth, but that as a censor of picture films, he is an out-and-out failure," and suggested "that someone with more brains might have been selected for the position." But opposition was not confined to the labor press. The *Worcester Evening Gazette* ran a satirical poem, which commented that "the picture shows don't have a thrill / since censored by Lieutenant Hill. / There'll be no kissing scenes, you bet / no Romeo and Juliet! / . . . No bar-room scenes – ten nights or one – / are all cut out – are simply done." The poem concluded with the suggestion that his excesses might drive movie patrons back to the saloons, which were soon to reopen with the end of no-license.[36]

While some voices of native-American middle-class public opinion, like the *Gazette*, opposed zealous censorship, some representatives of ethnic constituencies, like the *Catholic Messenger*, gave it wholehearted support. As early as 1907 it had denounced moving pictures as "The Devil's Lieutenants." When the city closed *The Unwritten Law*, the paper congratulated the police, urging them to carry on an "axe raid" on the moving picture shows, particularly the Gordon Brothers' penny arcade machines. Can the mayor and City Council, they asked, "permit on Main and Front Streets a public nuisance which is being driven from the Tenderloin and the Bowery of New York?" Again, in the 1910 controversy the *Catholic Messenger* called for even more drastic action than the city had taken: "Since these shows are the breeding places of a moral plague far worse than any physical ills, why hesitate to close them?"[37]

The *Catholic Messenger* of these years spoke more for the emerging middle-class and second-generation Irish American than it did for the laborer or the recent immigrant. Nevertheless, even such a well-known champion of the Worcester worker as the now aging James H. Mellen apparently shared the *Messenger*'s distrust of the new medium. In 1910 he urged a state investigation into the moving picture business, maintaining that "the corruption these places breed is great." "Motion pictures rightly conducted," Mellen declared, "could be made a great educational and instructive institution but the business has degraded [fallen] into the hands of men without any moral conception and the main idea is to make money at the sacrifice of the community." Mellen's moralistic strictures about popular entertainment were not simply a product of his old age. Twenty-five years earlier, as editor of the *Worcester Daily Times,* he had bitterly denounced the Worcester Theatre for posting "show bills about the city . . . bedaubed with disgusting pictures of shameless women . . . exhibiting their limbs in a series of indecent gyrations."[38]

The Swedish evangelical churches with their large immigrant working-class congregations shared Mellen's long-standing and morally based suspicion of uncontrolled commercial amusements. But they were even more absolute in their condemnation of the latest entertainment sensation. Swedish ministers considered attendance at movies, like card playing and dancing, a serious sin. So strong were the denunciations that one Swedish woman recalls that "some youngsters developed a morbid fear just walking by a movie theater." The daughter of a Swedish foundry worker who grew up in Quinsigamond Village at the beginning of the century similarly recounts how her father gave her five cents every Saturday to prove that he was not cheap but forbade her to use the money to go to the movies.[39]

As with temperance, the motives of working-class critics of moviegoing often differed from those of their middle-class counterparts. For workers, the threat was from within rather than from without; it was an issue of maintaining ethnic and religious traditions, not controlling a disorderly mob. One Slovak commentator explained that with "a public school education" children are "lost completely to the Slovaks. Their idea of life is a breezy and snappy novel, a blood curdling *movie* and lots of money."[40] The movies, like the amusement park, challenged traditional cultural authorities both inside and outside the ethnic working-class community.

Despite this lingering distrust, controversy over the content of movies shown in Worcester soon faded. Compulsory local censorship boards, such as that set up in Chicago in 1907, as well as the voluntary National Board of Review established in New York in

1909, began to bring movies under outside surveillance, if not total control.[41] At the same time, the red pencil of the accountant often had more impact on film content than the blue pencil of the censor. "It is an expensive business, the making of films only to have them thrown away," noted one 1910 commentator. Indeed, as early as the 1907 controversy over *The Unwritten Law,* the nascent trade press urged the withdrawal of the film *"for the sake of the future prosperity of the five cent theaters,* all of whom are now menaced by public opinion."[42] For businessmen interested in building a national market, self-censorship appeared to be the most prudent – and profitable – course.

Such commercial considerations also operated powerfully on the local level. "Those interested in the moving picture business realize that it is to their advantage to have pictures of the highest type," the manager of the Majestic Theatre commented in 1910. Not only did managers begin to cooperate with Police Censor Hill, but they also carefully watched other sources of public disapproval. Bijou proprietor Fred Fedeli, for example, recalls that "we were amongst six [Catholic] churches in them days, and if you played a movie, that wasn't fit to be seen, they could crucify you by saying 'don't go and see it.'" So when Fedeli feared possible clerical criticism, he immediately canceled the offending film and repeated an old one. He recounts that "you would put a slide on the screen: 'By Popular Demand This Picture Brought Back.' And we were the one that was demanding it, because we were afraid; after all, you had to be careful."[43]

Thus, by 1912 movie content rarely caused trouble in Worcester. Professor Hoyt noted that while a 1909 report on Worcester movies had revealed "a coarseness and . . . a suggestivness of crime and sin that was frankly appalling . . . now, thanks to the most careful censorship of films we get little note of criticism." But the elimination of what he called "the story of clever vice and of trickery triumphant" did not eliminate conflict over moviegoing. "As we turn to the consideration of the conditions existing in the theatres themselves," Hoyt warned, "there is another story to tell." The reform-oriented Worcester Public Education Association agreed: "The chief weakness of the moving picture lies in the conditions of presentation rather than in the picture itself. The halls and buildings are very dirty and poorly ventilated, and the audiences [are] under no *supervision* or *surveillance* as to age or character." Other middle-class commentators also complained about poor ventilation, odor, dirt, eyestrain, and darkness at movie houses.[44] As the now-censored films became palatable to middle-class critics, they increasingly focused their disapproval on the conditions of the theaters and the behavior of their patrons. Just as anti-saloon agitators concentrated their attacks on the saloon, not alcohol, movie reformers increasingly concerned themselves with the cheap movie theaters, not the movies. It was autonomous working-class institutions and behavior that troubled the middle class.

The middle class goes to the movies

Middle-class complaints about theatrical conditions and behavior reflect, in part, fears about a hidden and unknown working-class culture and a desire to control that culture and limit its autonomy. But behind all the talk about filth and body odor lay the entrance, in large numbers and for the first time, of middle-class people into movie houses and their forced encounters with a resident working-class audience, which smelled and acted in ways that jarred middle-class standards of decorum. It was the emergence of this new middle-class audience – and the theater managers' fervent efforts to cultivate it – that led to an alteration of some of the basic characteristics of the early moviegoing experience.

As late as 1914 the Worcester working class still seems to have dominated the city's movie houses. The controversy that burst forth early in that year over Sunday moving pictures confirms this alignment. Whereas the city's Protestant establishment – virtually all the Protestant ministers, the Women's Christian Temperance Union, as well as most city officials – vehemently denounced this desecration of the sabbath, "those favoring Sunday shows," according to the *Worcester Telegram*, "were composed mostly of the working class of people and persons directly or indirectly connected with the Worcester playhouses and moving picture places." To those who fought over Sunday movies, the reason for this division was obvious: "The movies always was and always will be the poor man's amusement," declared one Worcester theater manager.[45]

Yet this very controversy also suggested that the association of the working class with the movie house was neither timeless nor total. Some of the more moderate ministers insisted that they opposed a commercialized Sunday, not moviegoing per se. "We believe in moving pictures . . . it is not moving pictures that we oppose," the Reverend Francis Poole told his Union Church congregants. Furthermore, the city's manufacturers – aligned with the Protestant clergy on issues like drinking – do not seem to have joined in the attack on Sunday movies. Donald Tulloch, secretary of the Worcester Metal Trades Association, endorsed the idea of "well-regulated, suitable movies Sunday afternoon, leaving the forenoon and evenings entirely to the Church services and home life."[46]

These new, more approving attitudes toward movies by middle-class Worcesterites reflected not only the success of earlier censorship efforts but also the growing appeal of movies for middle-class audiences, a trend increasingly evident in pre–World War I Worcester. In December 1913 the *Worcester Sunday Telegram*'s drama correspondent noted that Worcester theaters had suffered a bad season, and he blamed the competition of moving pictures. He pointed out that the movie version of *Quo Vadis* had attracted more Worcesterites in three days than had its live version in an entire week. "Whether the play be popular priced or of a higher scale," he concluded, "the moving pictures are drawing bigger." Vaudeville suffered less directly from the competition of movies, since many movie houses offered vaudeville acts in addition to their film programs, and most vaudeville bills included some moving pictures. Still, the balance seemed to be shifting in favor of movies. In February 1914 Sylvester Poli, Worcester's leading vaudeville promoter, recognizing "the prominent part that moving pictures have come to play in the amusement world," added feature films to the program at his flagship theater. By the following year, the *Worcester Sunday Telegram*, distressed by the dismal quality of vaudeville shows, wondered whether "the silent drama" had given vaudeville "the count."[47]

By the end of World War I movies had not only captured many theater and vaudeville patrons but also expanded the market for commercial entertainment in general. Between 1910 and 1918 the number of theatrical seats in Worcester nearly doubled, going from about 9,300 to about 17,600. The rate of increase greatly exceeded even Worcester's rapidly growing population; the number of people for each theatrical seat declined sharply from sixteen to ten. Even more significantly, the percentage of seats devoted primarily to moving pictures almost doubled. In 1910 moving picture houses contained only 44 percent of Worcester's theatrical seats, whereas eight years later they included 82 percent. Since moving picture houses usually had continuous or multiple performances and legitimate theater, stock, and vaudeville offered only two shows per day, these figures actually understate the ascendance of moving pictures. By 1919, according to conservative estimates, more than 128,000 Worcesterites attended the movies each week.[48]

The burgeoning of the Worcester movie audience indicates the expansion of moviegoing into the city's middle class and the creation of the first medium of regular interclass entertainment, a development that local observers increasingly noticed around World War I. In 1917, for example, the *Worcester Telegram* observed that the new Strand movie theater was "catering to the best class of theatrical patronage in Worcester." Pointing to the "long line of touring cars and limousines" parked in front of the theater every night, it concluded that "society folks have acquired the movie habit."[49]

How had middle- and upper-class Worcesterites found their way into the previously disdained movie theater? In part, the theater managers and movie producers brought them there.[50] The search for larger markets, which had motivated the movie industry to accept censorship from without and promote self-censorship within, also encouraged the quest for a middle-class audience. In pursuit of these new customers, exhibitors modernized their theaters, and producers experimented with different kinds of films. The cries of reformers to improve movie theater conditions and conduct had gone largely unheeded, but the quest for a larger and more respectable audience accomplished the same purpose: the transformation of the shabby nickelodeon into the opulent movie palace.

After 1913 Worcester movie theaters became increasingly lavish. At first the changes were rather modest. The Pleasant Theatre, reopened in November 1913 after a fire, simply advertised itself as "safe" and "clean." But a further remodeling three years later involved more extensive alterations, such as "new carpets of the finest Wilton velvet," a "colorful electric fountain," and a large rooftop electric sign. The *Worcester Telegram* theater correspondent enthusiastically celebrated this "real high-class house of feature photoplays" with its "elegance," "refinement," and "dignity." The building of the Strand Theatre in 1917 culminated the trend toward lavish theaters – until the still more impressive structures of the 1920s. Lauded as a "modern photoplay house," it included "red plush seats," no obstructed views, frosted ceiling globes, a "rich chandelier," drinking fountains, a gold fiber screen, "luxurious carpets," loges for private parties, "rich velour curtains," marble pillars, an advanced ventilating system, a $15,000 Austin organ, and, most important, "finely appointed toilet rooms."[51]

The more elaborate accouterments of the newer Worcester theaters were often complemented by more professional theatrical management, which brought greater internal order to the theaters. Early Worcester movie managers were often local men from immigrant backgrounds who went directly from working-class jobs or small businesses to movie management. Increasingly after 1915, however, Worcester movie theaters came under the control of theatrical chains and the direction of professional theater managers, men with long experience in theaters in different cities, who had worked their way up to the position of manager.[52]

These more professional managers – often college graduates – hired large and well-disciplined staffs to impose order on their theaters. By way of contrast, the East Side Bijou had a staff of only four, mostly relatives. Discipline within the theater was far from tight. Fred Fedeli, who served as usher in the theater's early days, complained that "you would call people in the aisle where there were the seats and they would go the other way." But the newer and more elegant movie houses employed large corps of ushers, who strictly enforced standards of decorum. At the Plaza Theatre ushers donned summer uniforms of "military coats, white trousers and white oxfords." The military attire was perhaps deliberate, an effort to assure middle-class patrons that this was a well-run and well-ordered establishment. Indeed, by 1928 theaters like Worcester's new Plymouth were hiring army officers to drill their ushers in "bearing and discipline as well as in courteous handling of the public." The thrust of all these efforts to improve theater conditions and control theater behavior was, as historian Lary May has observed, to remove any "unease" the middle class might have over entering the previously "disreputable movie house."[53]

While the movie exhibitor pursued middle-class patrons with carpeting and well-disciplined ushers, the movie producer enticed them with feature films, which approximated the form and length of theatrical production. By 1914 feature films had met with such success that the Paramount Pictures Corporation, the first national distributor of feature films, could guarantee exhibitors two features each week. Worcester's Pleasant Theatre, for example, immediately signed up with Paramount, believing that the combination of longer films and well-known stars would win "a patronage that will be quality and quantity combined." The exhibition of *The Birth of a Nation* sealed the marriage of middle-class audiences and movies. "It is the greatest thing I have ever seen in the way of a moving picture," Worcester's Mayor Wright declared.[54]

Wright's enthusiasm for *The Birth of a Nation* represented a radical departure from the disapproving stance he took in the 1910 controversies. In this shift he followed the path trod by many other middle-class Worcesterites in these years. Initially perceiving movies and movie houses as a threat to the social fabric, by 1916 he joined in the hometown frenzy over the local filming of *A Romance in Worcester*. Wright even agreed to play the role of the father of the heroine, but when the Republican National Convention took him out of town, the president of the Board of Aldermen replaced him.[55]

Mayor Wright's newfound passion for the movies reminds us of the relatively recent recognition by the middle class of its own need for non-instrumental recreation, for "fun." In going to the movies, as in playing more active sports, the middle class at least partially adapted some of the leisure patterns that characterized working-class life. As Lary May has argued, the movie theater, with its mixing of sexes and classes, its lack of formality, and its intimacy, represented a radically new experience for the native middle class.[56] Thus, in many ways the development of moviegoing habits was a sharper break in middle-class culture than it had been in working-class culture. Moreover, it was a shift toward working-class norms.

But the process was hardly one way. The entrance of the middle class into the movie houses had altered moviegoing conduct and conditions. The new and more lavish movie theaters represented a more distinct change from the everyday conditions of working-class life than had the old storefront, five-cent theaters. More important, the new environment prescribed a more formal and structured moviegoing experience. Ushers instructed by handbooks of theater management carefully controlled conduct within the new theaters and politely guided customers to a specific seat. The longer programs made necessary by the feature films meant specific show times and even sometimes reserved seats. In effect, the new moviegoing experience was both more public and informal than that normally expected by the native middle class but also more privatistic and formal than that traditionally followed by the immigrant working class.[57]

Still, the experience of class mixing remained limited. Many working-class people continued to view movies within their own neighborhood theaters, which more closely reflected the behavior patterns, conditions, and ownership of the early movie days. Generally, these theaters charged lower prices, showed "second-run" films, and attracted local, ethnic, and working-class crowds. Despite their downtown locations, the Family and Majestic drew what the *Worcester Telegram* called "more of a neighborhood patronage." The Family and Columbus theaters drew heavily on the Shrewsbury Street Italian community; the Gem on Quinsigamond Village Swedes; the Court on Belmont Hill Swede-Finns; and the Bijou and

Vernon on the multiethnic working-class neighborhood surrounding Vernon Square. In 1917 half the city's fourteen movie theaters could be classified as "neighborhood" rather than "first-class."[58]

Despite the strength and persistence of these neighborhood theaters, the balance was gradually shifting. Although there were equal numbers of neighborhood and first-class theaters in 1917, the larger downtown theaters held almost three-quarters of the movie seats. Moreover, whereas the ethnic working class increasingly patronized the first-class theaters, the middle-class West Siders shunned the neighborhood houses. Fred Fedeli recalls that his customers might visit the first-class theaters but that the "people uptown [i.e., middle-class West Siders] wouldn't come to us." Similarly, when the *Labor News* wrote about his cousin and partner, Jim Greeko, they felt obliged to note that "uptown folks mayhap are not acquainted with him." At the same time, however, the neighborhood theaters were becoming less Spartan. In 1918 Greeko and the Fedeli brothers opened the much larger and better appointed Rialto Theatre across the street from the Bijou. Comparing the 600 wooden seats of the Bijou with the 1,250 red-plush, spring-cushioned seats of the air-conditioned Rialto Theatre, Fedeli notes "that was a big change." The combination of the Rialto and the more lavish downtown houses forced out many of the smaller neighborhood theaters; the Bijou, Gem, Columbus, and Vernon theaters all disappeared in the next two years. "The Rialto licked them all," Fedeli recalls.[59]

The emergence of a middle-class movie audience and the development of more lavish and formal movie houses did not, however, drive away working-class customers. Indeed, in the years during which theater owners built a middle-class clientele, the movies increasingly penetrated those working-class groups initially resistant to the lure of the nickelodeon. For example, churchgoing Irish Catholics, whose initial suspicion of the new medium was presented so vehemently by the *Catholic Messenger,* seem to have gradually warmed to it. Annual discussions in the press of whether Lent would adversely affect the movie trade were one indication of the centrality of churchgoing Catholics to the local movie audience. The competition of movies even curtailed the activities of church-affiliated groups like the Catholic total abstinence societies. This development found symbolic expression in 1914 when the Crescent movie theater temporarily took over the auditorium of the Father Mathew society.[60]

Movies also attracted workers attached to that other pillar of traditional working-class culture: the saloon. "It is generally conceded by all," the *Worcester Sunday Telegram* reported in 1915, "that, since the increase in the number of moving picture houses, there has been somewhat of a correspondent reduction in the amounts expended for . . . booze." "Where a man was in the habit of passing much of his time in a saloon," explained the manager of the Family Theatre, "now he passes a portion, if not all of it, in the moving picture houses. They stay as long as they want to. The price is five cents. That is the cost of one beer." Particularly with Worcester's saloons under the stricter regulations imposed after 1910, the movie theater proved an increasingly enticing alternative. "Between the movies and the rigid rules of the city government our profits are cut out considerably," complained one liquor man. The situation was hardly this dismal, but one local merchant estimated that the movies had captured as much as 25 percent of the saloon trade.[61]

Within the working class the Worcester Swedes, particularly the members of the evangelical churches, were perhaps the group least affected by the movies. But even here some signs of change could be discerned. In 1915, movie theaters opened for the first time in Worcester's two major Swedish neighborhoods. That same year the editors of *Skandinavia* noted that many Swedes still considered movies "sinful" and corrupting. But after a Saturday-night visit to the new Royal Theatre, they advised their readers that "we believe that the movies will serve our young people well."[62]

By the 1920s, then, the movies had penetrated virtually all segments of American society and touched the lives of people who had little else in common. In 1921, for example, Socialist leader Eugene V. Debs, who languished in jail for his opposition to World War I, received a letter from a friend in which she noted that Debs and President Warren Harding shared an affection for cowboy movie star Tom Mix: "I feel sure the President will appreciate your desire to see Tom. Someday, dear Gene, we shall see Tom do his stunts and you can laugh all you want."[63]

If Gene Debs and Warren Harding could agree on the movies, so could most Worcesterites. Thus, in 1922 Worcester voters rejected a state referendum on censorship of motion pictures by a vote of better than 3 to 1.[64] The movie theater had become enshrined as a major mainstream cultural institution. An advertisement for Poli's Theatre summarized the new position: "As important to a city as its churches and schools is the theatre to which is entrusted the play hour of its citizens and children." Indeed, by the late 1920s new movie houses seem to have been given greater importance than new schools or churches. "As New York notes an opera opening, so does

Worcester note the opening of a new movie house," the *Worcester Sunday Telegram* reported on November 25, 1928, after the premiere of the ornate, Egyptian-style Plymouth Theatre. "Its 3000 seats," the *Telegram* continued, "were filled with a moving, pulsing, vivid, throng; bankers in evening dress and newspaper men in clean collars. The city government, including the Democrats, was there."[65] The Worcester movie house had clearly arrived.

Continuity and change in working-class culture

Cultures do not change overnight or even over fifty years. But over long periods of time, we can watch them slowly, and often incompletely, transforming themselves, taking on new shape and substance. The birth and triumph of the movies heralds this slow, gradual, and incomplete process of change for ethnic working-class culture. It would be foolish to see the movies as the triggering device for this glacial process of change. Deeper social and economic forces – the coming of age of second- and third-generation immigrants, the emergence of an ethnic middle class, the development of mass-production and mass-marketing techniques – are at the root of the transformation of working-class culture.[66] Although movies themselves did not change working-class culture, the movie theater of the 1920s can serve as an important indicator of the nature and extent of changes in that world.

Like the popularity of the White City Amusement Park or the development of more businesslike saloonkeepers, the emergence and triumph of motion pictures did not signal the total obliteration of older or "residual" forms of working-class culture. Many people, for example, disdained or simply ignored the new medium. Even into the 1950s, members of Worcester's Swedish evangelical churches – particularly the Mission Covenant Church – viewed moviegoing as sinful. Age or generation could be an even more important, if less absolute, bar to movie attendance. Phyllis Williams reported in her study of New Haven Italians in the 1930s that whereas the younger generation attended the movies frequently, the older generation did not approve of this "waste of money" and was "reluctant to have any part in it." A social survey of Worcester's small black community in the 1920s found similarly that "many are positively opposed to moving pictures, but in some families the young people go as often as once or twice a week."[67]

Even where the practice of moviegoing was wholeheartedly embraced, it often occurred within the context of an older ethnic culture. The neighborhood theater continued to foster an active and lively style of public sociability, and it often retained clear ethnic ties. When "talkies" came in, some neighborhood theaters offered foreign-language films. The Columbus Theatre on Shrewsbury Street in the heart of Worcester's Italian neighborhood was owned by Italians, who seem to have encouraged local Italian groups to meet in their theater. The Fedelis' Rialto Theatre on Millbury Street took special pains to cater to its multiethnic clientele. In 1931, when financial straits forced the theater to discontinue advertising in the daily newspapers, it continued to run ads in the local Lithuanian weekly. It even recognized religious holidays, offering *Passion Play from the Life of Jesus* for Easter-time viewers.[68]

The persistence of ethnic patterns points to the simple fact that moviegoing did not destroy all other forms of working-class leisure; it was simply an additional – albeit particularly important – recreational option. Working people continued to go to their saloon, church, or ethnic club. Only now such activities might be punctuated by, or mixed with, visits to the movie theater. "When a man emerges from a saloon in an intoxicated condition," the *Worcester Telegram* complained in 1917, "he usually decides on one or two objective points, the retracing of his footsteps back to the saloon or going to a theatre." Fraternal and ethnic organizations often entered into a different sort of symbiotic relationship with the movie theater. Since Sunday movie shows were only permitted if classified as "benefits," such performances often assisted groups like the Lithuanian Women's Alliance, the Jewish School, the Polish Naturalization Club, and the Italian Soldiers Suffering from Tuberculosis Caused by the War.[69]

If moviegoing coexisted with many elements of the older ethnic working-class culture, what about the actual pictures on the screen? In *Hollywood in the Twenties,* David Robinson argues that producers abandoned the "characteristically working class" settings of prewar films and "now showed predominantly a wholly imaginary leisured class, with lovely homes and lovely clothes and lovely cars and lovely lives." But given the paucity of available films from the twenties and the unreliability of existing film plot summaries, such sweeping generalizations may be open to question. Chaplin's 1920s films, for example, revolved around working-class settings and attacked the premises of middle-class life.[70] Moreover, judging from a sample of about thirty films shown during February and March 1928 at the Rialto Theatre, Worcester's leading working-class theater, films of that era dealt not simply with the rich but with the lower class's relationships with the rich. Most commonly, the film plots seem to have revolved around the problems and possibilities of interclass and intercultural relationships. In *Spring Fever,* for example, Jack Kelly, a "wisecracking shipping clerk, secures a card to an exclusive country club, and meets Allie Monte, who after some wooing reciprocates his love."[71]

In the films shown at the Rialto success and wealth came through marriage or such leisure-oriented careers as prizefighting, dancing, music, and baseball. Upward mobility did not even require the adoption of a middle-class life-style. In *The Babe Comes Home* (starring Babe Ruth), for example, the Babe's working-class manners (exemplified by tobacco chewing) prove intrinsic to his success as a ballplayer.[72] Thus, neither the picture on the screen nor the behavior in the theater caused, or even necessarily represented, a sharp or sudden abandonment of an embedded ethnic working-class culture. Yet movies did presage some important, if gradual, changes in working-class life. In the shadows of the movie theater one can catch glimpses of the waning of the older ethnic, insular working-class culture and the emergence of a new outward-looking working-class culture.

The movie palace of the 1920s broke down much of the informality and communality that characterized the ethnic working-class saloon, the July Fourth picnic, and even the dime museum and the nickelodeon. The lavish setting, the militarily attired and drilled ushers, the fixed starting times, the disinfected air, the lighted clocks, and the "finely appointed toilet rooms" had all made moviegoing a more controlled, structured, and anonymous experience. Whereas before patrons might mingle in the aisles, now the nattily attired ushers directed them to a specific seat. The advent of the "talkies" heightened this trend toward formality and privatism by making in-theater conversation unacceptable. The new movie houses also imposed a more rigid time discipline than had the nickelodeon, with its slogan Stay as Long as You Like. An item from the movie page of the *Worcester Sunday Telegram* of 1925 exemplified the new moviegoing style: "*Come Early:* Are you careful to learn the starting time of a movie feature before you leave home for the theatre? . . . Every week about 20,000,000 movie cash customers see movies backward because they're too lazy to telephone for the 'starting time of the features' and to get to the theatre at the right time."[73] No longer was the movie theater a working-class refuge from the time discipline of the factory.

Naturally, the neighborhood theaters retained much of the old informality and communality with their amateur nights and perennial giveaways of dishes, linens, and turkeys. But in the downtown movie palaces, which were more likely to be attended by second-generation teen-agers than by their parents or their younger brothers and sisters, recreation became a more formal and less collective experience.

Not only did moviegoing lack the boisterous and communal style of the saloon, it also failed to challenge the legal order or the work ethic in the same way as had the rum shop. In the nineteenth century, drunkenness and liquor law violations had been the most common Worcester crimes. But, unlike the saloongoer and the saloonkeeper or even the overly exuberant July Fourth celebrant, the moviegoer and the theater owner rarely ran afoul of the law. The early movie houses came into conflict with police authorities and reformers over film content, moviegoing conduct, and theater conditions, but by the 1920s such conflicts were rare. In 1929 the Worcester Board of Motion Picture and Theatre Review, reporting on its first thirteen years of operation, noted "a steady improvement in the nature of released films" as well as the amicable cooperation of the city's theater managers.[74]

Worcester's manufacturers also expressed satisfaction with the new medium. Both Mayor Wright, a leading wire manufacturer, and Donald Tulloch, spokesman for the city's leading industrialists, enthusiastically embraced the movies by World War I. The reasons for such approval are not hard to find: Moviegoing posed no threat to work discipline as had the saloon. Movies encouraged neither hangovers with their absenteeism nor on-the-job drunkenness with its accidents and decreased work efficiency. With these changes in the style of working-class recreation as well as the middle- and upper-class shifts in leisure habits and attitudes, working-class recreation declined as an arena of social conflict.

A related reason for this lessening of conflict was that the movie theater lacked the sort of ominous working-class autonomy and control that had worried reformers concerned about the saloon. Movies, because of their production by a small number of large, vertically integrated corporations and their national market, were vulnerable to national censorship, as well as market and social pressures. Even the theaters themselves were much less localized and individualized than the saloons, which were always much greater in number and more diverse in ownership. Increasingly, Worcester theaters came under the control of regional and national chains, and patrons had limited influence on their operations. E. M. Loew's take-over of the Olympia and Family theaters in 1930 illustrates this waning of control of the working class over its recreational institutions. Up to that time Worcester movie houses had generally been unionized. Within two weeks, however, Loew fired his union workers and hired scabs at lower wages. Both picketing and a labor boycott failed to reverse Loew's policy. Significantly, thirty years earlier a similar boycott of Bowler Bros. beer had won a closed union shop for its employees.[75] The more local and more exclusively working-class saloon business had been more susceptible and responsive to the pressures of Worcester's organized workers.

The nationalization and centralization of the leisure industry affected what workers saw at the movies even more than how the theaters were run. When Charles Baker wrote farces for the Palace Museum in 1904, he closely followed "the varying tastes of customers" and made sure to add "a Worcester setting" to his songs and sketches.[76] By the 1920s even such a sporadic novelty as the local filming of *A Romance in Worcester* was inconceivable. As the production of popular culture receded from both local control and local view, the pictures on the screen were less likely to speak to the everyday lives of Worcester workers.

The loss of local working-class control over its leisure was also manifest in economic terms – a pattern noted in relation to the amusement park. Much of the money spent at the nineteenth-century saloon remained within the ethnic, working-class community in the form of wages paid to brewery workers and bartenders, profits earned by locally resident saloonkeepers, and rents paid to small landlords. Even more important, money collected at entertainments and picnics sponsored by ethnic churches, clubs, and lodges financed local charities as well as the activities of those bodies. The profits of the movie industry, however, were increasingly expropriated by oligopolistic movie corporations and national and regional theater chains located outside Worcester and its working-class neighborhoods. In such an economic structure there was little room for the reciprocity and mutuality that had characterized the saloon and the mutual benefit society. Increasingly, a national market insulated from local pressures had intruded itself into the everyday lives of working people.

The movie theater's challenge to the intense localism of the saloon also fostered the erosion of the central feature of the older working-class culture: its focus around inward-looking, ethnic separatist communities. By the 1920s the movie theater, unlike the saloon, was not the exclusive province of a specific ethnic group nor of the working class in general. Instead, it was an arena for the mixing of ethnic groups, classes, age groups, and sexes. Even the working-class-dominated neighborhood theater sometimes operated counter to the ethnic separatist communities because they mixed several ethnic groups as with the Jews, Poles, and Lithuanians who mingled at the Rialto. Of course, ethnic tensions remained strong in Worcester; the rise of a local Ku Klux Klan in the 1920s, for example, pitted not just natives against immigrants but Swedes against Irish.[77] Still, as the rising intermarriage rate indicates, the walls of ethnic Worcester were no longer as impermeable as they had once been.

The decline of ethnic separatism and insularity had a particular impact on women. Movie theaters, unlike the saloon, courted the patronage of women. When middle-class reformers celebrated the ways that the photoplay "reunite[d] the lower class families," they failed to perceive the strains that moviegoing could create in the strongly patriarchal immigrant working-class family. Both movie content and the experience of taking leisure outside the home or the ethnic community challenged old patterns and assumptions. For many women, as Elizabeth Ewen has pointed out, the movies could mean a shift from "the constricted family-dominated culture to the more individualized values of modern urban society." But, Ewen adds with irony, "new authorities replaced the old. In the name of freedom from tradition, they trapped women in fresh forms of sexual objectification and bound them to the consumerized and sexualized household."[78]

In the long run, of course, the greatest changes can be detected among the young, the new generations, whether male or female. They were the most regular moviegoers and the least tied to the older ethnic culture. The "models for the consumption economy" that so many recent historians have detected in 1920s films like *Charge It* and *Ladies Must Dress,* which celebrate "the new joys and pitfalls of consumption," probably had their greatest impact within the working class on the rising second and third generations. Certainly, the personal accounts of moviegoing in the 1920s collected from students and young workers by sociologist Herbert Blumer suggest that movies may have helped reorient working-class youths outward to middle-class consumer society rather than inward to Old World ethnic ties and practices. "The day-dreams instigated by the movies consist of clothes, ideas on furnishings and manners," reflected one high school student. "After seeing a wonderful picture full of thrills and beautiful scenes, my own home life would seem dull and drab," wrote another.[79]

The ethnic industrial working class was thus moving gradually from the margins to the mainstream of American life – following, in effect, the same path marked out by the transition from the shabby neighborhood five-cent movie house to the opulent downtown movie palace. And the children and grandchildren of Worcester's immigrant working class were leading the way. Playwright S. N. Behrman, himself a son of immigrant Worcester, captured the mood of transition in his recollections of how he gradually abandoned his neighborhood gathering spot (Elkind's drugstore) for one downtown (Easton's): "The trek from the soda fountain at Elkind's to the soda fountain at Easton's was a long leap in evolution because Easton's was the centre of the world . . . The displacement of the password for rendezvous from 'meet you at Elkind's' to 'meet you at Easton's' signalized the transition from periphery to the core, from provincialism to worldliness, from naivete to sophistication."[80]

Of course, while the children and grandchildren of the immigrant working class could join the middle class at Easton's or at the ornate Plymouth Theatre, the trek downtown only went so far. The path to full participation in the "commodity culture" advertised on the movie screen remained blocked. In another account collected by sociologist Blumer, a high school senior noted poignantly: "Fashionable pictures make me long for fine clothes. I could not see why my parents were not able to buy me all the clothes I wanted." "The movies have often made me dissatisfied with my neighborhood," added a black high school freshman, "because when I see a movie, the beautiful castle, palace, . . . and beautiful house, I wish my home was something like these."[81] By 1930 the movie theater had brought workers closer to the mainstream of American society, but the assembly line – particularly in non-unionized, unsafe, low-paying factories – kept them out of it.

Conclusion

Writing in his autobiography, *My Life and Work,* Henry Ford sought to explain why the machines in his auto plants were "closer together than in probably any other factory in the world." "To a stranger they may seem piled right on top of one another," Ford conceded. But efficiency and the maximization of profits dictated that they be "scientifically arranged" in this crowded fashion. After all, Ford argued, "our factory buildings are not intended to be used as parks." The dichotomy Ford drew between factories and parks, between workplace and play space, was axiomatic by the time he wrote his autobiography in 1922. Only a century earlier, however, Ichabod Washburn had been regarded as something of an eccentric when he insisted upon the same separation of work and play by refusing to provide any rum to the builders of his house. Yet by 1890, when Washburn's son-in-law, Philip L. Moen, presided over the Washburn and Moen Wire Manufacturing Company, the distinction between these spheres was quite marked: The sound of the North Works' 1 P.M. factory whistle could quickly empty Institute Park of the workers who had spent their lunchtime there playing ball, socializing, or just sitting in the shade smoking their pipes.[1]

Labor historians have paid a good deal of attention to the factories operated by men like Ford, Washburn, and Moen but much less to the parks, saloons, or movie houses populated by their workers. They have focused on trade union struggles over the conditions of factory life to the exclusion of cultural struggles over the conditions of the park or the existence of the saloon. It would be foolish to stand labor history on its head and to argue that parks and saloons are more important than factories and unions. Yet it is equally foolish to try to understand the working-class experience in all its complexity without examining the realm of leisure. For what Worcester workers did in Institute Park, or in Alice Dignan's illegal kitchen dive, or at the Swedish Methodist Church's July Fourth picnic, or in Horace Bigelow's White City Amusement Park, or at Fred Fedeli's Bijou movie theater had a good deal of bearing on what happened inside the city's wire factories, its union halls, its voting booths, and even in the neighborhoods of its wealthiest citizens.

This book has proceeded from the premise that the study of leisure can also tell us about these broader spheres of social, economic, and political experience because the history of working-class recreation directly illuminates three questions that are central to understanding the largest dimensions of life in industrializing America: (1) What was the nature of working-class culture – the basic values, beliefs, and traditions of workers – in the late nineteenth century? (2) What was the character of class relations – the bonds and antagonisms between workers and their employers – in the late nineteenth and early twentieth centuries? (3) How did both working-class culture and class relations change as workers entered the more commercialized leisure world of the twentieth century? The evidence from one medium-sized industrial city – especially in the absence of solid comparative data from other locales – can only resolve these questions about class and culture in tentative ways. Nevertheless, it might be useful to close this study with a review of the preliminary answers we have discovered to the three questions just enumerated, which were addressed in Parts II, III, and IV of this book.

One of the persistent myths about late nineteenth century America (and other eras of our past as well) has been the notion that most people accepted the same general package of beliefs and values centered around acquisitive individualism. While some divergences from the mainstream are acknowledged, they are usually dismissed as fringe (i.e., radical) or temporary (i.e., the views of quickly assimilated immigrants). The conventional practice of talking about an undifferentiated "American culture" embodies this view that almost everyone shared the same set of values. A look at the late nineteenth century saloon – or late nineteenth century celebrations of our nation's birthday, for that matter – calls into question this myth of cultural consensus. In the saloon, Worcester's immigrants created a distinctive social institution that symbolized not only a rejection of some of the cornerstones of the dominant culture (e.g., mobility, sobriety, thrift, competition) but also an endorsement of alternative public modes of mutuality, conviviality, and collectivity.

To argue for the existence of a distinctive working-class culture may appear on the surface to erect a new mythology of a fully class conscious American proletariat plotting against the industrial system in their saloons. Rather than support either of these views of American workers, however, this study has argued that the culture of the Worcester saloon was *alternative* – separate and distinct from the dominant society – but not *oppositional* – not a direct challenge to that society. Working-class saloongoers may have disliked or distrusted the acquisitive individualism that characterized late nineteenth century American society, but they were unlikely to organize against the capitalist system, which nurtured competition and the quest for profits. Even had they been so inclined, class-wide mobilization would have been inhibited by one of the central features of the alternative culture found at both the Irish working-class saloon and the Swedish working-class church picnic: an insularity or ethnic separatism. Ironically, when Worcester workers celebrated the Fourth, they revealed shared commitments to values of communality and mutuality, but the way they actually carried out those celebrations – separated by church or ethnic group – made it unlikely that those common values could become the basis of a movement to alter the balance of political and economic power in the city.

The insular and divided nature of late nineteenth century working-class culture did not, however, protect it from attack. The line between alternative and oppositional cultures, Raymond Williams notes, is often "very narrow," and "the same meanings and practices can be seen by the dominant culture not merely as disregarding or despising it, but as challenging it."[2] Although some observers like G. Stanley Hall might perceive the alternative, rather than oppositional, character of the saloon, many industrialists tended to focus on the ways that drinking and the saloon subverted work discipline and thereby impinged upon the pursuit of profits. For many members of the middle and upper classes, it was simply the visibility of many forms of working-class recreation – saloongoing and public celebrating, for example, more than private or home-centered socializing – that made them so threatening. They saw workers who celebrated the Fourth by unhinging the gates of West Side mansions or by taking over downtown streets as a menace to public order and private property. Similarly, they viewed workers who "loafed" or drank on the Common as affronts to propriety and decorum. Indeed, just the public existence of a separate and relatively impermeable sphere of working-class leisure time and space worried a number of more affluent Worcesterites.

The middle and upper classes thus perceived at least some forms of working-class recreation as challenges to the dominant culture, to family and factory, to patriotism and property. And they responded to this ostensible challenge with a variety of campaigns aimed at reshaping or restricting working-class leisure practices through temperance reform, the parks and playground movements, and the Safe and Sane July Fourth crusade. As a result, even in Worcester where the conventional expressions of class conflict – unions, strikes, radical political parties – were muted, leisure time became an arena of class struggle in which workers and industrialists fought over who would control life outside the workplace. If we fail to examine these recreational struggles, we might (like Emma Goldman) be deceived into thinking that Worcester was a city without class conflicts. Yet, whether or not Worcester workers were conscious of themselves as a class, they acted in class ways in these conflicts over recreational space and behavior.

Worcester workers won some important victories in these struggles to shape their own play, to have their "eight hours for what we will." They constantly subverted or evaded efforts to close or tightly regulate their drink places. They pressured the city to give them badly needed play space and used that space in line with their own recreational conceptions rather than those of park reformers. They made the Fourth of July into a release from the regimentation of the workplace and a moment to affirm the ties of their ethnic communities. Overall, Worcester workers managed to maintain control over their own leisure time and space, to mitigate and meliorate the effects of an exploitative and oppressive economic system, to maintain ethnic traditions and communities. Yet these victories also exacted a price. Whereas recreational struggles – such as the movement for a working-class park in Ward 5 – might unite a particular ethnic working-class community, they never brought together all workers under one banner. Nor did resistance to, say, temperance ever involve an articulation of working-class "rights" or a direct challenge to the centers of power.

Even more damaging from a working-class perspective was that struggles over recreation – particularly the struggle over the saloon – fostered intraclass hostility and interclass alliances. On the liquor question, Swedish wireworkers who belonged to evangelical Protestant churches had more in common with their employers than they did with fellow Irish or French-Canadian wireworkers who belonged to Catholic churches. Even Irish-Catholic workers did not all agree on temperance, and their disagreements sometimes subverted working-class political movements. The Catholic–Protestant divide, however, proved particularly troublesome, especially since the city's manufacturers were able to manipulate it to their own advantage. There were other reasons why Worcester was known as a "scab hole" and a notorious open-shop town – the unity of the city's industrialists, the success of their blacklists, the diversity of the city's industrial structure are just three – but cultural divisions certainly added to the difficulties of the local labor movement.

Slowly and unevenly, however, the cultural patterns and class relations that characterized late nineteenth century Worcester began to change in response to a variety of forces: the shifting attitudes of the middle and upper classes, the emergence of an ethnic middle class, the arrival of new immigrants from southern and eastern Europe, the gradual increase in working-class incomes and the decrease in the workweek, and more basic changes in the structure of the economy. In the realm of leisure the most important change was the increasing importance of commercialized forms of amusement. Yet this development did not represent as sharp a break in working-class experience as it might at first appear. The saloon itself had always been a commercial leisure institution, albeit one on the fringes of respectability and sometimes even profitability. In addition, workers took a hand in making or at least in shaping the newer commercialized leisure places. Both the amusement park and the early movie house reflected working-class traditions of boisterousness and public sociability. The Nickel and Bijou movie houses inherited not just the locations but also the traditions of lively and active socializing that had characterized the Palace Museum and Michael McGaddy's saloon. At the same time, the new commercialized leisure did not immediately destroy these older centers of working-class social life: The saloon and the church, for example, remained vital pillars of the ethnic working-class communities, particularly those populated by the city's most recent immigrants.

The recreation of Worcester's workers was not entirely remade by 1920, but the leisure-time activities of the working class nevertheless revealed evidence of how class relations and working-class culture were changing. By the end of World War I leisure had become much less of an arena of contention between classes. Middle- and upper-class Worcesterites who played active sports at the Grafton Country Club on Sunday or attended Saturday shows at the Plymouth Theatre were much less likely to condemn working-class amusements that were identical or at least superficially similar. In addition, the recreational entrepreneur – whether the amusement park impresario seeking the largest possible crowds, or the business-minded saloonkeeper worried about no-license votes, or the movie theater operator concerned about censorship – proved to be a more effective regulator of popular amusements than the understaffed and harassed city police had ever been. That the working class increasingly spent its leisure time in the movie house – an amusement place also patronized by the middle class and controlled by national corporations – rather than in a grog shop located in a working-class kitchen and controlled by an immigrant widow made working-class recreation appear much less immediately threatening to the guardians of public morality. This change did not signal the end of class conflict in Worcester, but popular recreation – or indeed cultural issues in general – would never again be as central an arena of such conflicts as had been true in the late nineteenth and early twentieth centuries.

Intimately related to this lessening of conflict over issues of leisure and culture were the very gradual changes that were occurring in working-class culture itself. Ethnic working-class culture was slowly losing its older separatist and inward-looking perspective and becoming more oriented toward the larger society. Some of this shift was the result of the leadership of an ethnic middle class, which promoted a limited form of Americanization for its working-class compatriots. Although the impact is difficult to gauge, the Swedish politicians who spoke at Safe and Sane July Fourth rallies, the second-generation and white-collar Irish Catholics who taught classes at the playgrounds and the night schools, the members of the Knights of Columbus who preached patriotism and temperance, all helped to reshape working-class culture more than the native middle-class progressive reformers with whom the ethnic middle class sometimes worked. Even more important in fostering change, however, were the working-class children and grandchildren of earlier immigrants who had been through the schools, had learned English, and had spent their evenings or weekends at the movie theater and the amusement park. In the process, they had become less suspicious of other workers from different ethnic and religious backgrounds and had become attracted by the material promise of American life that flashed before them on the movie screen.

Understanding the implications of these changes in class relations and cultural patterns is difficult, particularly when based on a case study that stops with 1920. Nevertheless, even by that time two future – and somewhat contradictory – directions could be discerned. As many have argued, the allures of the dominant culture – the fashions seen at the movies, the appliances advertised in mass-circulation magazines, the pursuit of fun offered at the amusement park – could divert workers from seeking more fundamental changes. In the 1920s, for example, Worcester labor leaders complained that "young workers of all nationalities" spend their time in "automobiles . . . dance halls and cheap amusement places, to the exclusion of union meetings and union business."[3] Yet the labor leaders of the 1920s failed to perceive the countervailing forces that were perhaps operating at those very dance halls and amusement places.

At the Rialto more than at the rum shop, young workers were likely to meet members of other ethnic groups and these recreational associations could begin to facilitate some of the workplace organizing that had proven so difficult in earlier decades. In addition, although desires for fashions and furnishings might divert workers from the labor movement, the frustration of those desires by an unequal social and economic system might prompt some questioning of that system. Finally, the worker's new perception of themselves as "Americans" could lead them to expect a good deal more than their parents had ever received from the larger society. Consequently, workers who had spent their time in the movie theater in the 1920s might find their way to the union hall in the 1930s and 1940s, as they sought to achieve what the movies promised but the larger society failed to deliver and as they became increasingly able to make common cause with workers from different ethnic and religious groups. In particular, the shock of the Great Depression could provide the spark to provoke these young workers not just to demand access to the commodities they had seen in movies and advertising but also to demand full power and participation in American society, to demand treatment as "decent *American* citizens." Having already made the transition from the rum shop to the Rialto, at least some workers now made the more important and more difficult shift from the cinema to the CIO.[4]

Abbreviations used in notes

AAS	American Antiquarian Society, Worcester, Mass.
CSP-AC	Community Studies Program of Assumption College, Worcester, Mass. (files available in Community Studies Program office)
HCC	College of the Holy Cross Archives, Worcester, Mass.
Mass. BLS	Commonwealth of Massachusetts, Bureau of Statistics of Labor, Boston, Mass.
WHM	Worcester Historical Museum, Worcester, Mass.
LN	*Labor News*
WAT	*Worcester Aegis and Transcript*
WDP	*Worcester Daily Press*
WDT	*Worcester Daily Times*
WEG	*Worcester Evening Gazette*
WEP	*Worcester Evening Post*
WES	*Worcester Evening Star*
WS	*Worcester Spy*
WST	*Worcester Sunday Telegram*
WT	*Worcester Telegram*

Notes

Introduction

1. *WT*, Dec. 3, 1889; Oct. 28, 1915; *LN*, June 7, 1913. On "Eight Hours," see Philip S. Foner, *American Labor Songs of the Nineteenth Century* (Urbana, Ill., 1975), 222–4; William Brooks, "Liner Notes," *The Hand That Holds the Bread: Progress and Protest in the Gilded Age* (New World Records, NW 267, 1978).
2. U.S. Congress, Senate, *Committee of the Senate Upon the Relations Between Labor and Capital, Hearings*, 4 vols. (Washington, D.C., 1885), 3:386.
3. David Riesman, "Some Observations on Changes in Leisure Attitudes," *Antioch Review* 12 (Dec. 1952):417; Gregory S. Kealey, "Introduction," in Gregory S. Kealey and Peter Warrian, eds., *Essays in Canadian Working Class History* (Toronto, 1976), 7. A recent assessment of Commons's work is Maurice Isserman, "'God Bless Our American Institutions': The Labor History of John R. Commons," *Labor History* 17 (Summer 1976):309–28. David Brody discusses Philip Taft as the "authentic embodiment of the Wisconsin school of labor scholarship" in "Philip Taft: Labor Scholar," *Labor History* 19 (Winter 1978):9–22.
4. It is impossible to acknowledge here the work of literally dozens of American working-class historians who have reshaped the field and greatly influenced my own work. For recent reviews of the literature, see David Montgomery, "To Study the People: The American Working Class," *Labor History* 21 (Fall 1980):485–512; David Brody, "The Old Labor History and the New," *Labor History* 20 (Winter 1979):111–26; Charles Stephenson, "A Gathering of Strangers? Mobility, Social Structure, and Political Participation in the Formation of the Nineteenth-Century American Working Class," in Milton Cantor, ed., *Working-Class Culture* (Westport, Conn., 1979).

   My work has benefited greatly from not only the exciting work of recent American scholars of working-class culture but also the extremely thoughtful British scholarship on popular recreation and working-class culture. Some of the important studies of English popular recreation include E. P. Thompson, *The Making of the English Working Class* (New York, 1963), 401–17; Keith Thomas, "Work and Leisure in Pre-industrial Society," *Past and Present*, no. 29 (Dec. 1964):50–66; Brian Harrison and E. J. Hobsbawm, "Work and Leisure in Industrial Society," *Past and Present*, no. 30 (Apr. 1965):96–102; Brian Harrison,

"Religion and Recreation in Nineteenth-Century England," *Past and Present*, no. 38 (Dec. 1967):98–124; Robert Malcolmson, *Popular Recreations in English Society, 1700–1850* (New York, 1973); Gareth Stedman Jones, "Working-Class Culture and Working-Class Politics in London, 1870–1900: Notes on the Remaking of a Working Class," *Journal of Social History* 7 (Summer 1974):460–508; E. P. Thompson, "Patrician Society, Plebeian Culture," *Journal of Social History* 7 (Summer 1974):382–405; Douglas A. Reid, "The Decline of Saint Monday, 1766–1876," *Past and Present*, no. 71 (May 1976):76–101; Robert Storch, "The Policeman as Domestic Missionary: Urban Discipline and Popular Culture in Northern England, 1850–1880," *Journal of Social History* 9 (Summer 1976):481–509; Peter Bailey, *Leisure and Class in Victorian England: Rational Recreation and the Contest for Control, 1830–1885* (London, 1978); James Walvin, *Leisure and Society, 1830–1950* (London, 1978); Hugh Cunningham, *Leisure in the Industrial Revolution, 1750–1880* (New York, 1980). The autumn 1975 conference of the Society for the Study of Labour History, at the University of Sussex, offered a number of excellent papers around the theme "The Working Class and Leisure: Class Expression and/or Social Control." See the "Conference Report," *Bulletin of the Society for the Study of Labour History* 32 (1976):5–18. For a perceptive critique of the papers presented at this conference, see Gareth Stedman Jones, "Class Expression Versus Social Control? A Critique of Recent Trends in the Social History of 'Leisure,'" *History Workshop*, no. 4 (Autumn 1977):163–70. The literature on British working-class culture is too vast to even superficially summarize here. For a good introduction to the field, see John Clarke, Chas Critcher, and Richard Johnson, eds., *Working-Class Culture: Studies in History and Theory* (London, 1979).

5. Kealey, "Introduction," 7–8.
6. Herbert Gutman, in particular, has stressed the local orientation of the nineteenth-century worker; see his "Class, Status, and Community Power in Nineteenth Century American Industrial Cities: Paterson, New Jersey, A Case Study," in Frederick Jaher, ed., *The Age of Industrialism: Essays in Social Structure and Cultural Values* (New York, 1968), 263–87; his "The Worker's Search for Power," in H. Wayne Morgan, ed., *The Gilded Age*, 2nd ed. (Syracuse, N.Y., 1970), 31–54; and his collected essays in *Work, Culture, and Society in Industrializing America* (New York, 1976). On this same point also see Bryan D. Palmer, "Most Uncommon Common Men: Craft and Culture in Historical Perspective," *Labour/Le Travailleur* 1 (1976):21.
7. This is W. Lloyd Warner's claim in his "Yankee City" study. For Warner, Newburyport was "to serve as a microscopic whole representing the total American community." Quoted in Colin Bell and Howard Newby, *Community Studies: An Introduction to the Sociology of the Local Community* (New York, 1972), 103.

8. Clifford Geertz, "Thick Description: Toward an Interpretive Theory of Culture," in Clifford Geertz, *The Interpretation of Cultures: Selected Essays* (New York, 1973), 22.
9. Despite the importance of the saloon and July Fourth celebrations to late nineteenth century working-class leisure, a discussion of them does not exhaust the recreational expressions of working-class culture in that era. A more comprehensive treatment of this subject would require an examination of churches, fraternal lodges, ethnic associations, dime museums, participant and spectator sports, pool halls, card playing, and informal visiting patterns. Moreover, a focus on *public* recreational forms fails to illuminate fully the leisure patterns of working-class women. My treatment of the saloon and July Fourth is intended as illustrative rather than exhaustive. It is hoped that subsequent research will carry the analysis into other forms of recreation.
10. Other similar efforts to reform working-class leisure that might be profitably studied include sabbatarianism, company-sponsored recreational programs, the YMCA and YWCA, night schools, boys' clubs, settlement houses, and public libraries.

1. Workers in an industrial city, 1870–1920

1. Emma Goldman, *Living My Life,* 2 vols. (1933; rpt. New York, 1970), 1:82. See also Richard Drinnon, *Rebel in Paradise: A Biography of Emma Goldman* (Boston, 1961), 39–54; *WT,* July 27, 1892.
2. Goldman, *Living My Life,* 1:83–6.
3. *WT,* July 27, 1892; Goldman, *Living My Life,* 1:81–8; *A Columbian Tribute by the City of Worcester* (Worcester, 1894), 69; Robert A. Roberge, "The Three-Decker: Structural Correlate of Worcester's Industrial Revolution" (M.A. thesis, Clark Univ., 1965), 48. Around 1900 American Steel and Wire (the successor to Washburn and Moen) had about 3,000 employees and the Homestead plant had about 3,800 workers; Michael T. Neary, "The Industrial Development of the American Steel and Wire Company" (M.A. thesis, Clark Univ., 1933), 43; David Brody, *Steelworkers in America: The Nonunion Era* (1960; rpt. New York, 1969), 59.
4. S. N. Behrman, *The Worcester Account* (London, 1954), 132–3.
5. Ibid., 30. For examples of communities in which skilled workers built a culture centered, in part, around their trade unions, see Francis G. Couvares, "Labor and Leisure in Pittsburgh: Some Tendencies in Late Nineteenth Century Working Class Culture" (paper presented at Social Science History Association Meeting, Ann Arbor, Mich., Oct. 1977); Robert S. Lynd and Helen Merrell Lynd, *Middletown* (1929; rpt. New York, 1956), 76. On radical political parties as a force in organizing working-class life, see the articles in the special issue on "The Origins of Left Culture in the U.S., 1880–1940," *Cultural Correspondence,* no. 6–7 (1978).

6. Albert Farnsworth and George B. O'Flynn, *The Story of Worcester, Massachusetts* (Worcester, 1934), 129; U.S. Bureau of the Census, *Tenth Census, 1880,* 22 vols. (Washington, D.C., 1883–8), 1:538.
7. Roberge, "Three-Decker," 9, 11; Franklin P. Rice, ed., *The Worcester of Eighteen Hundred and Ninety-Eight* (Worcester, 1899), 449–55. For overviews of Worcester history, see Charles A. Nutt, *History of Worcester and Its People,* 4 vols. (New York, 1919); John Nelson, *Worcester County: A Narrative History* (New York, 1934); Margaret A. Erskine, *Heart of the Commonwealth: Worcester* (Woodlands Hills, Calif., 1981). Although all these works are extremely useful, there is no comprehensive or academic history of the city. A good annotated bibliography to some of the sources for nineteenth-century Worcester history can be found in Joshua Chasan, "Civilizing Worcester: The Creation of Institutional and Cultural Order, Worcester, Massachusetts, 1848–1876" (Ph.D. thesis, Univ. of Pittsburgh, 1974), 491–503. On population growth, see Rose Zeller, "Changes in the Ethnic Composition and Character of Worcester's Population" (Ph.D. thesis, Clark Univ., 1940), chap. 4.
8. *Celebration of the Two Hundredth Anniversary of the Naming of Worcester* (Worcester, 1885), 149; *Tenth Census, 1880,* 2:402, 410, 445. The percentages for industrial output are computed in Walter S. Foley, "Heterogeneity of Population as Correlated with Diversity of Industries in Worcester and Other Massachusetts Cities" (M.A. thesis, Clark Univ., 1910), 37. The calculations on percentages of wage earners employed by "other industries" are drawn from the "Manufactures" volumes of the U.S. Census. See also Charles Washburn, *Industrial Worcester* (Worcester, 1917), 299–300.
9. Donald Tulloch, *Worcester: City of Prosperity* (Worcester, 1914), 13. See compilations of census figures in Rice, *Worcester of Eighteen Hundred and Ninety-Eight,* 449–55, and Foley, "Heterogeneity of Population," 37.
10. Neary, "Industrial Development," 6, 43; Nutt, *History of Worcester,* 2:1069; Washburn, *Industrial Worcester,* 152–68.
11. U.S. Bureau of the Census, *Fourteenth Census, 1920,* 13 vols. (Washington, D.C., 1923), 9:662–5; Rice, *Worcester of Eighteen Hundred and Ninety-Eight,* 449–55. On Royal Worcester Corset, see Tulloch, *Worcester,* 137. For overviews of Worcester industry, see Washburn, *Industrial Worcester; Celebration of the Two Hundredth Anniversary,* 149–65; Herman L. Nelson, "Some Aspects of Manufacturing in Worcester" (Ph.D. thesis, Clark Univ., 1954); Charles C. Buell, "The Workers of Worcester: Social Mobility and Ethnicity in a New England City, 1850–1880" (Ph.D. thesis, New York Univ., 1974).
12. *Celebration of the Two Hundredth Anniversary,* 149. On early manufacturers, see Buell, "Workers of Worcester," 18–46; Washburn, *Industrial Worcester.*
13. The figures for the average size of manufacturing establishments probably overstate the change between 1880 and 1919, because in 1910 the Census Bureau stopped including handicraft industries in its tables.

Tenth Census, 1880, 2:445; *Fourteenth Census, 1920,* 9:662. The eight largest companies were calculated on the basis of assessed value of their buildings; Roberge, "Three-Decker," 48–52.

14. Roberge, "Three-Decker," 48–52; *WT,* Apr. 2, 1912; Robert H. Binstock, "A Report on Politics in Worcester, Massachusetts," Joint Center for Urban Studies of Harvard University and M.I.T. (mimeographed, Cambridge, Mass., 1960), chap. 6:6.
15. On Wyman-Gordon, see Mildred M. Tymeson, *The Wyman-Gordon Way* (Worcester, 1959), 47; Erskine, *Heart of the Commonwealth,* 200; Rae MacCollum Spencer, *The Gift of Imaginative Leadership: Harry Galpin Stoddard* (Worcester, 1972), 50; Washburn, *Industrial Worcester,* 299–300. On the tight control of banks, see Timothy J. Meagher, " 'The Lord Is Not Dead': Cultural and Social Change Among the Irish in Worcester, Massachusetts" (Ph.D. thesis, Brown Univ., 1982), 177, 510–12. On interconnections among industrial leaders, see Nutt, *History of Worcester,* 2:1068–79 and vols. 3 and 4. On Smith and on social elite, see *WEG,* Apr. 6, 1945; R. M. Washburn, *Smith's Barn: "A Child's History" of the West Side Worcester, 1880–1923* (Worcester, 1923), 88–96; Edwin Theodore Weiss, Jr., "Patterns and Processes of High Value Residential Districts: The Case of Worcester, 1713–1970" (Ph.D. thesis, Clark Univ., 1973); Paul R. Swan, "Personal Histories of Worcester's Social and Industrial Leaders with Certain Sociological Interpretations" (M.A. thesis, Clark Univ., 1929); and the numerous biographies in Rice, *Worcester of Eighteen Hundred and Ninety-Eight* and Nutt, *History of Worcester,* vols. 3 and 4.
16. Washburn, *Smith's Barn,* 113; Tulloch, *Worcester,* 157; Lester P. White, "Elements Affecting Organized Labor in Its Relationship with the Worcester Branch National Metal Trades Association Since 1916" (M.A. thesis, Clark Univ., 1924), 26. See also Washburn, *Industrial Worcester,* 308–9. In 1905 about one-third of the members of the elite Worcester Club were born outside Worcester; Meagher, " 'Lord Is Not Dead,' " 347.
17. *WS,* May 8, 1892; *WT,* June 16, 1902; Nutt, *History of Worcester,* 2:1059–61; Tulloch, *Worcester,* 189–239; White, "Elements Affecting Organized Labor," 4–8, 19–22; Harry Elmer Barnes to Upton Sinclair, Oct. 14, 1922, Sinclair MSS, Manuscripts Department, Lilly Library, Indiana University, Bloomington; *LN,* Apr. 8, 1916. (Neil K. Basen directed my attention to Barnes's scathing indictment of the NMTA.)
18. Charles C. May, *Indian Hill: An Industrial Village for the Norton Company* (n.p., n.d., but probably 1916 or 1917), WHM. See also the excellent collection of excerpts from the *Norton Spirit* (Aug. 1914 to Dec. 1919), selected and compiled by Kevin L. Hickey, CSP-AC; Tulloch, *Worcester,* 298; Neary, "Industrial Development," 62–84. For the national context, see Daniel Nelson, *Managers and Workers* (Madison, Wis., 1975), 101–21. For positive and negative working-class responses to

these schemes, see *WES*, May 31, 1879; *LN*, May 3, 1918; July 11, 1919; *WDT*, Mar. 8, Dec. 2, 1886; White, "Elements Affecting Organized Labor," 23.

19. Loomis is quoted in Herbert Gutman, "Work, Culture, and Society in Industrializing America, 1815–1919," *American Historical Review* 78 (June 1973):561; U.S. Bureau of the Census, *Twelfth Census, 1900, Special Reports, Occupations* (Washington, D.C., 1904), 760–3.
20. Buell, "Workers of Worcester," 112, 146, 174.
21. Esther M. Wahlstrom, "A History of the Swedish People of Worcester, Massachusetts" (M.A. thesis, Clark Univ., 1947), 179; Nancy Mayo Waterman, "The Evolution and Delimitation of Quinsigamond Village" (M.A. thesis, Clark Univ., 1952), 56; Neary, "Industrial Development," 65.
22. Neary, "Industrial Development," 65; Bryan Thompson, "Settlement Ties as Determinants of Immigrant Settlement in Urban Areas: A Case Study of the Growth of an Italian Neighborhood in Worcester, Massachusetts, 1875–1922" (Ph.D. thesis, Clark Univ., 1971), 80, 94, 95; Jesse May Thornton, "Character, Composition, and Distribution of the Southeastern Europeans in Worcester" (M.A. thesis, Clark Univ., 1934), 67, 79, 80, 94, 95; Joseph Talamo, "A Preliminary Social Survey of the Jewish Population of Worcester" (M.A. thesis, Clark Univ., 1915), 19 and unnumbered tables.
23. Paul Shankweiler, "A Sociological Study of the Child Welfare Program of Worcester, Massachusetts" (Ph.D. thesis, Univ. of North Carolina, 1934), 43; Meagher, "'Lord Is Not Dead,'" 225–38; *WS*, Mar. 5, 6, 1892; *Skandinavia*, Mar. 10, 1892; Mass. BLS, *Labor and Industrial Chronology of the Commonwealth of Massachusetts, Report for 1901* (Boston, 1901), 79; *WDT*, May 6, 1880; *Twelfth Census, 1900, Occupations*, 760–3.
24. Alan Dawley, *Class and Community: The Industrial Revolution in Lynn* (Cambridge, Mass., 1976), 215.
25. *LN*, Apr. 28, 1906, Feb. 11, 1916, Dec. 18, 1915. For similar earlier complaints, see *WDT*, Jan. 6, 1881; *WT*, Dec. 13, 1897. The biographies of the mayors were examined in Rice, *Worcester of Eighteen Hundred and Ninety-Eight*, and Nutt, *History of Worcester*, vols. 3 and 4. I identified the names and occupations of aldermen and council members in the relevant volumes of the *Worcester Directory* (Worcester, 1885, 1890, 1895).
26. Leon Fink, "Politics as Social History: A Case Study of Class Conflict and Political Development in Nineteenth-Century New England," *Social History* 7 (Jan. 1982):43–58; Leon Fink, "Workingmen's Democracy: The Knights of Labor in Local Politics, 1886–1896" (Ph.D. thesis, Univ. of Rochester, 1977); Charles Francis Adams, Jr., *Three Episodes of Massachusetts History* (Boston, 1892), 988–96. On the political failure of the Knights in Worcester, see, for example, *WDT*, Jan. 10, 1883, Jan. 2, 1885.

27. Henry Bedford, *Socialism and the Workers in Massachusetts, 1882–1912* (Amherst, Mass., 1966), 118; Nutt, *History of Worcester*, 1:398. Of course, voting statistics do not fully gauge immigrant support for socialism. See, for example, *LN*, Mar. 23, Oct. 10, 1908, May 6, 1916; *WT*, Dec. 13, 1897, Mar. 31, Apr. 1, 1912; Sirkka Tuomi Lee, "Radical Finns Respond to America: 1910–60" (paper presented at Mid-Atlantic Radical Historians Organization Conference, New York, N.Y., Apr. 17, 1977).
28. Charles Francis Johnson, "The Organized Labor Movement as a Social Force in Worcester, 1888–1913" (M.A. thesis, Clark Univ., 1935), 23–6.
29. Steve Miller, "The Boston Irish Political Machines," Working Paper 15, *Boston: Studies in Urban Political Economy* (mimeographed, Waltham, Mass., 1974); James R. Green and Hugh Carter Donahue, *Boston's Workers: A Labor History* (Boston, 1979), 72–93; *WDT*, Mar. 31, 1885; Nutt, *History of Worcester*, 1:396–8. See also Chapters 3 and 4, this volume.
30. *Scandinavia*, Apr. 13, 1888; *Le Travailleur*, Nov. 5, 1880, Oct. 24, 1882. French Canadians apparently tended to shift to the Republican party after 1896. See, for example, *L'Opinion Publique*, Nov. 5, Dec. 3, 1900, Dec. 5–7, 1901.
31. *WST*, Nov. 28, 1886; *WDT*, Dec. 6, 1879; *WT*, Dec. 13, 1911; *LN*, Dec. 4, 11, 1915. The following discussion of labor activity in Worcester does not consider working-class resistance on the shop floor. Such resistance was undoubtedly significant, but there is not sufficient evidence to document it from the few available company records. For one example in the metal trades, see White, "Elements Affecting Organized Labor," 4.
32. *WT*, Dec. 3, 1889; Johnson, "Organized Labor Movement," 6–7.
33. Call, quoted in *LN*, Sept. 3, 1910; *WDT*, Dec. 2, 1884, Mar. 8, 1886, June 30, 1885. See also *WDT*, Jan. 12, Mar. 10, Apr. 30, Sept. 4, 1886; *WST*, Aug. 1, 1886; *WT*, Sept. 20, 1886; *Worcester Commercial and Board of Trade Bulletin* (Aug. 1892), WHM.
34. John Laslett, *Labor and the Left* (New York, 1970), 146; *LN*, May 14, 1910. See also William Edward Zeuch, "An Investigation of the Metal Trades Strike of 1915" (M.A. thesis, Clark Univ., 1916); *WT*, Apr. 9, 1901.
35. Alice V. Emerson, "The Failure of Organized Labor in Worcester (1930–1940)" (M.A. thesis, Clark Univ., 1966), 11–18; Johnson, "Organized Labor Movement," 40–2; *LN*, Mar. 22, 29, 1913, Mar. 14, May 16, 1914.
36. This comparison is based on the data presented by Jonathan Ezra Garlock in "A Structural Analysis of the Knights of Labor: A Prolegomenon to the History of the Producing Classes" (Ph.D. thesis, Univ. of Rochester, 1974). Garlock's data is incomplete, but I have assumed that Worcester and Lynn are equally undercounted. For contemporary comments suggesting the same pattern, see *WDT*, June 30, July 3, 1885.

37. For U.S. figures, see Albert A. Blum, *A History of the American Labor Movement* (Washington, D.C., 1972), 14. The U.S. figure is for the nonagricultural work force, whereas the Massachusetts city and state figures are for the entire work force. In a highly industrialized state like Massachusetts, however, the two are almost equivalent.
38. *WDT*, July 9, 1887, Apr. 29, June 13, 1886; *WS*, May 4, 1890. For later examples of the same practice, see *WT*, June 18, 1902, Nov. 6, 1913; *LN*, Feb. 21, 1918.
39. Commonwealth of Massachusetts, State Board of Conciliation and Arbitration, *Thirtieth Annual Report for Year Ending December 31, 1915* (Boston, 1916), 206; *Labor News*, quoted in Zeuch, "Investigation of the Metal Trades Strike," 25. See also *LN*, Oct. 6, 1915, May 24, 1917, Sept. 20, 1918; White, "Elements Affecting Organized Labor," 5; Emerson, "Failure of Organized Labor," 17; Joshua Chasan, *Human Rights in Worcester* (Worcester, 1972), 16.
40. *WT*, June 5, 1902; *WEP*, July 1, 2, 5, 1902; *WT*, Mar. 31, 1912; Drinnon, *Rebel in Paradise*, 130; Goldman, *Living My Life*, 1:455–6; *LN*, Oct. 4, 11, 1918. Goldman spoke on the lawn of a private home. While in Worcester, she attended Sigmund Freud's famous address at Clark University.
41. "Advantages of Worcester as a Manufacturing Center," *Worcester Magazine* 4 (Dec. 1902):204; *WEG*, Nov. 1, 5, 8, 1870; Mass. BLS, *Second Annual Report, 1871* (Boston, 1871), 126–31. For other examples of immigrant strikebreakers, see *WDT*, Mar. 31, Apr. 22, 1885, Apr. 26, May 3, 6, June 13, 25, July 27, 30, 1886; *WT*, July 3, 1893; *WS*, Jan. 6, 1899. On the rapid turnover of population in Worcester in this period, see Sune Åkerman, "Stability and Change in the Migration of a Medium-Sized City: The Case of Worcester, Massachusetts," in I. Semmingsen and P. Seyersted, eds., *Scando-American Papers on Scandinavian Emigration to the United States* (Oslo, 1980), 65–94.
42. Emerson, "Failure of Organized Labor," 18; Johnson, "Organized Labor Movement," 15, 17; Mass. BLS, *Labor and Industrial Chronology for Year Ending September 30, 1904* (Boston, 1905), 239.
43. *WT*, June 8, 1902, Apr. 30, 1917; *WEG*, Jan. 3–5, 7, 10, 15, 21, 22, 25, 27, Feb. 1, 8–10, 19, Mar. 9, 10, 23, 1870; *WDT*, Apr. 23, 27, 28, May 1, 3, 4, 6, 1880; *WEG*, Apr. 30, May 3, 5, 1880; *WT*, July 7–12, 14, 16, 17, 29, 31, 1919. For a good illustration of how ethnic working-class communities mobilized in strike situations, see Victor Greene, *Slavic Community on Strike: Immigrant Labor in Pennsylvania Anthracite* (Notre Dame, Ind., 1968).
44. For some examples of recollections of earlier unsuccessful strikes, see *WEP*, May 3, 1899; *L'Opinion Publique*, May 1, 1899; *WST*, June 20, 1897; *LN*, Dec. 14, 1915. For an example of a community where a strike defeat appears to pervade the collective memory, see Tamara K. Hareven and Randolph Lagenbach, *Amoskeag: Life and Work in an American Factory-City* (New York, 1978).

45. Zeuch, "Investigation of the Metal Trades Strike," 2, 13; *WT*, Oct. 14, 1915. On the "deskilling" of machinists and "workers' control" struggles, see Harry Braverman, *Labor and Monopoly Capital: The Degradation of Work in the Twentieth Century* (New York, 1974), 85–123; David Montgomery, "Workers' Control of Machine Production in the Nineteenth Century," *Labor History* 17 (Fall 1976):485–509.
46. *WT*, Dec. 23, Oct. 6, 1915; *LN*, Oct. 9, 1915.
47. Zeuch, "Investigation of the Metal Trades Strike," 34–6. The history of the strike can be traced in the *Labor News*, the *Worcester Telegram*, and Zeuch's thesis.
48. Vincent E. Powers, "Irish," in James E. Mooney, ed., *Worcester Massachusetts Celebration, 1722–1972* (Worcester, 1972), 44, 46. See also Meagher, "'Lord Is Not Dead'"; Vincent E. Powers, "The Irish and Worcester," in *Commemorating the 150th Anniversary of the Irish Community in Worcester* (Worcester, 1977), 21–35; Vincent E. Powers, "'Invisible Immigrants': The Pre-Famine Irish Community in Worcester, Massachusetts, From 1826 to 1860" (Ph.D. thesis, Clark Univ., 1976).
49. Richard Sorrell, "The Sentinelle Affair (1924–1929) and Militant *Survivance:* The Franco-American Experience in Woonsocket, Rhode Island" (Ph.D. thesis, State Univ. of New York at Buffalo, 1976), 399. For an overview of sources on French Canadians, see Richard Sorrell, "Franco-Americans in New England," *Journal of Ethnic Studies* 5 (Spring 1977):90–4. On Worcester French Canadians, see Harold Franklin Creveling, "The Pattern of Cultural Groups in Worcester" (Ph.D. thesis, Clark Univ., 1951), 139–40; Nutt, *History of Worcester,* 1:311–23; Alexandre Belisle, *Livre d'Or des Franco-Américains de Worcester, Massachusetts* (Worcester, 1920); and the excellent materials gathered by the CSP-AC.
50. Meagher, "'Lord Is Not Dead,'" 33, 159, 400–56. In terms of adult population, the second generation did not outnumber the first until 1900. The discussion of Worcester's ethnic communities provided here is intended only as a very brief overview of some of the largest groups and some major themes. For a more comprehensive survey, see Morris H. Cohen, *Worcester's Ethnic Groups: A Bicentennial View* (Worcester, 1976).
51. On Swedes in Worcester, see Wahlstrom, "History of the Swedish People"; Waterman, "Evolution and Delimitation of Quinsigamond Village"; Karl J. Karlson, "The Swedish Population of Worcester: A Study in Social Survey" (M.A. thesis, Clark University, 1910); Thure Hanson, *Swedish-American Souvenir: Settlement, Growth, and Progress of the Swedish People in Worcester* (Worcester, 1910); H. N. Orup, "The Swedes of Worcester," *Light* 1, 2 (Apr. 26, Oct. 16, 1890):9, 16. A variety of studies touching on Swedes in Worcester have been undertaken under the project "Sweden and America after 1860," centered at Uppsala University in Sweden. See, in particular, Harald Runblom

and Hans Norman, eds., *From Sweden to America: A History of the Migration* (Minneapolis, 1976). Professor Steven Koblick of Pomona College, Claremont, California, is directing a major project on Swedes who migrated to Greendale and worked at the Norton Company. Finally, the Community Studies Program of Assumption College has uncovered and made available a large volume of primary sources on Worcester Swedes.

52. U.S. Bureau of the Census, *Fourteenth Census, 1920, Bulletin Population: Massachusetts* (Washington, D.C., 1922), 15; Thompson, "Settlement Ties," 147. Of course, some people who were foreign-born or who were of foreign parentage did not belong to any ethnic community. For example, although there was a strong English immigrant community surrounding the Whittall Mills in South Worcester, many English immigrants lived in other parts of the city and were well assimilated into the native-American population. On Italians, see also interview with Louis Lomatire, Worcester Bicentennial Oral History Project, 1976 (typescript of interview in author's possession); John J. Capuano, *A Brief History of the Italian Americans of Worcester from 1860 to 1978* (Worcester, n.d.).
53. William Wolkovich-Valkavičius, "Lithuanians of Worcester, Massachusetts: A Socio-Historic Glimpse at Marriage Records" (paper, Boston College, 1978, WHM), 17; Creveling, "Pattern of Cultural Groups," 94, 142. See also Elaine Kokernak, "The Lithuanian Immigrant in Worcester" (Sufficiency Paper, Worcester Polytechnic Institute, May 1980); Anthony M. Miner, "Lithuanians," in Mooney, ed., *Worcester, Massachusetts Celebration*, 9.
54. William Harold Somers, "A Socio-Historical Study of the Jewish Community of Worcester, Massachusetts" (M.A. thesis, Clark Univ., 1933), 38. On Jews, see also Talamo, "Preliminary Social Survey"; Behrman, *Worcester Account;* Goldie Michelson, "A Citizenship Survey of Worcester Jewry" (M.A. thesis, Clark Univ., 1936). On Armenians, see Thornton, "Character, Composition, and Distribution of the Southeastern Europeans," 25–6; Robert Mirak, "On New Soil: The Armenian Orthodox and Armenian Protestant Churches in the New World to 1915," in Randall M. Miller and Thomas D. Marzik, eds., *Immigrants and Religion in Urban America* (Philadelphia, 1977), 141–7.
55. Waterman, "Evolution and Delimitation of Quinsigamond Village," 42; interview with Mary Savage Mason, Worcester Bicentennial Oral History Project, 1976 (typescript of interview in author's possession); Emerson, "Failure of Organized Labor," 27. For further discussion of ethnic tensions and conflicts, see Chapters 3 and 4, this volume.
56. For a discussion of the common features uniting ethnic working-class communities and life-styles, see Herbert Gans, *Urban Villagers: Group and Class in the Life of Italian-Americans* (New York, 1962), 229–62.
57. Irwin T. Sanders et al., *Worcester, Massachusetts: A Community Social*

Profile (Boston, 1975), 28. On three-deckers, see Roberge, "Three-Decker"; Marilyn Spear, *Worcester's Three Deckers* (Worcester, 1977). On residential segregation, see Weiss, "High Value Residential Districts"; Buell, "Workers of Worcester," 87–90, 112, 127–8, 147, 164–5, 175; Shankweiler, "Sociological Study of the Child Welfare Program," 21; Meagher, "'Lord Is Not Dead,'" 400–56.

2. The rise of the saloon

1. Rev. Henry T. Cheever, ed., *Autobiography and Memorials of Ichabod Washburn* (Boston, 1878), 56–7. (Reference courtesy of Gary Kornblith.)
2. Joshua Chasan, "Civilizing Worcester: The Creation of Industrial and Cultural Order, Worcester, Massachusetts, 1848–1876" (Ph.D. thesis, Univ. of Pittsburgh, 1974), 148–62; C. E. Goodrich, "Story of the Washburn and Moen Manufacturing Company, 1831–1899" (typescript, 1935); "Regulations to be Observed by all Persons in the Employ of the Washburn and Moen Manufacturing Company" (Apr. 11, 1871); "Washburn and Moen M'F'G Co. 1869 Time Table"; Goodrich, the regulations, and the timetable can be found in the American Steel and Wire MSS, Baker Library, Harvard University Graduate School of Business Administration, but were made available to me through the generosity of the Community Studies Program of Assumption College, Worcester.
3. The development of the saloon as a distinct leisure institution is only one example of a very long-term and gradual process through which "leisure" emerged as a separate sphere of life. For discussions of this general process in non-American contexts, see Michael Marrus, ed., *The Emergence of Leisure* (New York, 1974); E. P. Thompson, "Time, Work-Discipline, and Industrial Capitalism," *Past and Present*, no. 38 (Dec. 1967):56–97; Keith Thomas, "Work and Leisure in Pre-industrial Society," *Past and Present*, no. 29 (Dec. 1964):50–66; James Walvin, *Leisure and Society* (New York, 1978); Robert Malcolmson, *Popular Recreations in English Society, 1700–1850* (New York, 1973); Hugh Cunningham, *Leisure in the Industrial Revolution, 1750–1880* (New York, 1980).
4. Paul Faler, "Cultural Aspects of the Industrial Revolution: Lynn, Massachusetts Shoemakers and Industrial Morality, 1826–1860," *Labor History* 15 (Summer 1974):379; Paul Johnson, *A Shopkeeper's Millennium: Society and Revivals in Rochester, New York, 1815–1837* (New York, 1978), 56–7. See also W. J. Rorabaugh, *The Alcoholic Republic* (New York, 1979), 14; Ian R. Tyrell, *Sobering Up: From Temperance to Prohibition in Antebellum America, 1800–1860* (Westport, Conn., 1979), 103; Herbert Gutman, "Work, Culture, and Society in Industrializing America, 1815–1919," *American Historical Review* 78 (June 1973):557; Harry Gene

Levine, "Industrialization and Worker Drinking" (paper presented at the National Academy of Science, National Research Council Conference, Washington, D.C., Mar. 8–10, 1982).

5. Margaret A. Erskine, *Heart of the Commonwealth: Worcester* (Woodland Hills, Calif., 1981), 53; George Potter, *To the Golden Door: The Story of the Irish in Ireland and America* (Boston, 1960), 320; Richard Stivers, *A Hair of the Dog: Irish Drinking and American Stereotype* (University Park, Pa., 1976), 140; Richard O'Flynn, "Rumsellers of Worcester," Folio 2, 553–83, Richard O'Flynn MSS, HCC. See also Vincent E. Powers, " 'Invisible Immigrants': The Pre-Famine Irish Community in Worcester, Massachusetts, From 1826 to 1860" (Ph.D. thesis, Clark Univ., 1976), 122–3.
6. Rorabaugh, *Alcoholic Republic*, ix; Paul Mange, *Our Inns From 1718 to 1918* (Worcester, n.d., but probably 1918), 16.
7. Rorabaugh, *Alcoholic Republic*, 232; Massachusetts General Court, *Reports on the Subject of a License Law by a Joint Special Committee of the Legislature* (Boston, 1867), Appendix (testimony), 15. Emory and Ichabod Washburn were not related. On the beginning of the temperance movement, see Tyrell, *Sobering Up;* John A. Krout, *The Origins of Prohibition* (New York, 1925). (I have not yet seen Robert Hampel's recently published *Temperance and Prohibition in Massachusetts, 1813–1852* [Ann Arbor, Mich., 1982].)
8. Tyrell, *Sobering Up*, 96–7, 98, 272. On workers and temperance elsewhere, see Bruce Laurie, *Working People of Philadelphia, 1800–1850* (Philadelphia, 1980), 40–2, 53–66, 119–24; Faler, "Cultural Aspects of the Industrial Revolution"; Jill Siegel Dodd, "The Working Classes and the Temperance Movement in Ante-Bellum Boston," *Labor History* 19 (Fall 1978):510–31; Johnson, *Shopkeeper's Millennium*, 79–83, 113–15, 121–2, 130–5.
9. Tyrell, *Sobering Up*, 108; *Reports on the Subject of a License Law*, Appendix, 461; U.S. Congress, Senate, *Committee of the Senate Upon the Relations Between Labor and Capital, Hearings*, 4 vols. (Washington, D.C., 1885), 2:1110; herafter cited as *Relations Between Labor and Capital.*
10. *WEG*, Sept. 6, 1898; Mass. BLS, *Third Annual Report, 1872* (Boston, 1872), 386; hereafter cited as Mass. BLS, *Report, 1872*; Mass. BLS, *Report, 1881*, 414; Hyman Feldman, *Prohibition: Its Economic and Industrial Aspects* (New York, 1930), 200–1. See also *Relations Between Labor and Capital*, 1:746, 2:1110; Tyrell, *Sobering Up*, 297–8; Mass. BLS, *Report, 1870*, 228; John Fitch, *The Steel Workers* (New York, 1910), 226–7.
11. Mass. BLS, *Report, 1881*, 455; U.S. Commissioner of Labor, *Twelfth Annual Report: Economic Aspects of the Liquor Problem* (Washington, D.C., 1898), 69–72.
12. Joseph G. Rayback, *A History of American Labor* (New York, 1966), 59–60; Johnson, *Shopkeeper's Millennium*, 42; Marion Cotter Cahill, *Shorter Hours: A Study of the Movement Since the Civil War* (New York,

1932), 40; George Gunton, "The Economic and Social Importance of the Eight-Hour Movement," as reprinted in Leon Stein and Philip Taft, eds., *Wages, Hours and Strikes: Labor Panaceas in the Twentieth Century* (New York, 1970), 12–13. For an excellent overview of the eight-hour movement, see David Montgomery, *Beyond Equality: Labor and the Radical Republicans* (New York, 1967), 230–60. (I have only been able briefly to examine David Roediger's important recent study of "The Movement for a Shorter Working Day in the U.S. Before 1866" [Ph.D. thesis, Northwestern Univ., 1980].)

13. U.S. Bureau of the Census, *Tenth Census, 1880,* 22 vols. (Washington, D.C., 1883–8), 20:187; Charles E. Persons, "The Early History of Factory Legislation in Massachusetts," in S. M. Kingsbury, ed., *Labor Laws and Their Enforcement* (New York, 1911), 41; Norman Ware, *The Industrial Worker, 1840–1860* (Boston, 1924), 160. See also Thomas Dublin, *Women at Work* (New York, 1979), 108–31.
14. Montgomery, *Beyond Equality,* 236; *WES,* July 1, 1879; Jurgen Kuczynski, *A Short History of Labour Conditions in the United States of America, 1789–1946* (1943; rpt. New York, 1973), 45; Mass. BLS, *Report, 1883,* 239. At Washburn and Moen the official workday was 11¼ hours (9¼ on Saturday) in 1869, but 10 hours by 1870; see "Time Table" and "Regulations" cited in note 2. Nevertheless, based on an examination of the Time Books for the North Works (available in the American Steel and Wire MSS), at least some workers apparently worked much longer days in the 1870s, 1880s, and 1890s.
15. Lawrence Levine, *Black Culture and Black Consciousness* (New York, 1977), 202–17.
16. Tyrell, *Sobering Up,* 27. See also Mange, *Our Inns;* Alexander H. Bullock, "Discourse on Early Worcester Taverns" (paper, 1880, available at AAS); Charles A. Nutt, *History of Worcester and Its People,* 4 vols. (New York, 1919), 2:596.
17. Charles C. Buell, "The Workers of Worcester: Social Mobility and Ethnicity in a New England City, 1850–1880" (Ph.D. thesis, New York Univ., 1974), 60; *Illustrated Sketch of the Police Service of the City of Worcester* (Worcester, 1888), 20; Franklin P. Rice, ed., *The Worcester of Eighteen Hundred and Ninety-Eight* (Worcester, 1899), 23; *Reports on the Subject of a License Law,* Appendix, 350, 8.
18. Herbert M. Sawyer, *History of the Department of Police Service of Worcester* (Worcester, 1900), 27–9; Powers, "'Invisible Immigrants,'" 252, 422 (see also 315); *Reports on the Subject of a License Law,* Appendix, 17; see also 19–20, 23, 31, 87, 105, 107, 216. On the shebeen in Ireland, see K. H. Connell, *Irish Peasant Society* (Oxford, 1968), 1–50. Paul Johnson finds similarly that in early nineteenth century Rochester working-class drink places "were not great beer halls and saloons (they would arrive much later in the century) but houses and little businesses where workmen combined drinking with everyday social transactions"; *Shopkeeper's Millennium,* 58.

19. Mass. BLS, *Report, 1875,* 275.
20. *Annual Report of the City Marshal, Year Ending, November 30, 1876* (Worcester, 1877), 23; hereafter cited as *City Marshal, 1876; WEG,* Apr. 5, 1875; *WDT,* Dec. 4, 1888; Arrest Cards, James Drennan MSS, WHM.
21. *City Marshal, 1876,* 24; *WEG,* Apr. 22, 1879; *City Marshal, 1875,* 51.
22. *Reports on the Subject of a License Law,* Appendix, 12. "When drinking was done at home, women played an important part in liquor sales"; Perry R. Duis, "The Saloon and the Public City" (Ph.D. thesis, Univ. of Chicago, 1975), 205. About one-quarter of those arrested for illegal liquor sales in the spring and summer of 1870 were women; *WEG,* May–Aug. 1870.
23. Connell, *Irish Peasant Society,* 18; *WT,* Mar. 10, 1896; *WDT,* Jan. 15, 1883. See also *WEG,* Mar. 21, 1874. Such arguments were not confined to the Irish; see *L'Opinion Publique,* Mar. 3, 1893.
24. First- and second-class licenses – those permitting on-premise drinking – accounted for about three-quarters of the annual licenses. Grocers, whose fourth-class licenses entitled them to sell liquor only for off-premise consumption, received most of the other licenses; *WEG,* May 7, 1879, May 1, 1880.
25. *WES,* May 9, 1879 (emphasis added); see also May 17, 1879. The earlier credit ratings of thirteen saloonkeepers who lost their licenses in 1879 or 1880 contained the term "worthless" or an equivalent; Massachusetts volumes of R. G. Dun and Co. Collection, Baker Library, Harvard University Graduate School of Business Administration; hereafter cited as RGD.
26. *WEG,* Apr. 26, 1880; *Le Travailleur,* May 7, 1881. The effort to foster *public* drinking is a major theme of Duis, "Saloon and the Public City," 207–11, 327–9.
27. *WES,* May 9, 1879; Arrest List and Arrest Cards, James Drennan MSS. Even as late as 1882, more than one-quarter of those similarly prosecuted had lost their licenses in the cutbacks. Significantly, more than one-third (thirty-two of ninety-three) of those prosecuted were women, and of these, close to two-thirds were listed as "widows" in the *Worcester Directory.* The Dignans are sometimes listed as Degnan, Deignan, and Dignon in the *Worcester Directory* and the newspapers. The James Drennan MSS contain other accounts of raids, many of them on Irish liquor sellers. Groceries were also an important outlet for illegal sales.
28. Although it is difficult to compare precisely, turnover was substantially slower for a comparable group of licensed dealers, who were also checked in the R. G. Dun and Company records. Data on liquor violation arrests are from the annual *City Marshal Reports.* Joshua Chasan discusses the increasing professionalization of the Worcester police beginning in 1867 in "Civilizing Worcester," 75–6. For an example of the impact of a liquor seizure on one liquor seller, see entry on Patrick J. Welch, RGD, 104:793.

29. Clarence Long, *Wages and Earnings in the United States, 1860–1890* (Princeton, N.J., 1960), 61–8.
30. John Modell, "Patterns of Consumption, Acculturation, and Family Income Strategy in Late-Nineteenth-Century America," in Tamara K. Hareven and Maris A. Vinovskis, eds., *Family and Population in Nineteenth-Century America* (Princeton, N.J., 1978), 212–14.
31. Modell, "Patterns of Consumption," 217; of Irish families earning between $200 and $299, 36.9% spent money on both alcohol and tobacco, and 52.6% of those earning more than $600 showed similar spending. Among native families, the figures were 19.9% and 35.5%, respectively; Michael R. Marrus, "Social Drinking in the *Belle Epoque*," *Journal of Social History* 7 (Winter 1974):132; *Relations Between Labor and Capital*, 2:671, see also 537, 1360. Friedrich Engels, *The Condition of the Working Class in England*, trans. and ed. W. O. Henderson and W. H. Chaloner (Stanford, Calif., 1968), 141–4, offers a classic statement of the pathology of drink among workers.
32. RGD, 99:204; 100:72; 104:633, 911. See also *WDT*, June 6, 1885; *WT*, Apr. 30, 1889; *WST*, July 24, 1910.
33. RGD, 102:21, 371; *WST*, July 4, 1886; Mass. BLS, *Report, 1889*, 377. For earlier failures in brewery business, see RGD, 104:782, 783; Mange, *Our Inns*, 28.
34. *WST*, Dec. 13, 1885, July 4, 1886; RGD, 101:33. See also O'Flynn, "Rumsellers of Worcester."
35. See, for example, RGD, 97:756–8, 808; 99:469; 101:285. On the use of these records for studying immigrant business people, see David Gerber, "Ethnics, Enterprise and Middle Class Formation: Using the Dun and Bradstreet Collection for Research in Ethnic History," *Immigration History Newsletter* 12 (May 1980):1–7.
36. O'Flynn, "Rumsellers of Worcester." On the term "saloon," see Mitford M. Mathews, ed., *A Dictionary of Americanisms on Historical Principles* (Chicago, 1951), 1448; Jim Marshall, *Swinging Doors* (Seattle, 1949), 170. As late as the early 1870s, the term "grog shop" seems to have been more common than "saloon." See, for example, Mass., BLS, *Report, 1871*, 594.
37. *WST*, Apr. 26, 1885; *WDT*, Apr. 20, 1885.
38. U.S. Manuscript Census, Worcester, 1880; Powers, "'Invisible Immigrants,'" 430. If second-class licenses (beer and wine only) had been included, the Germans would have been even more overrepresented. Additional data on the ethnic composition of the saloon trade in the published censuses for 1880 and 1885 tend to be somewhat contradictory, because of the manner of presentation.
39. RGD, 104:842; 99:342; Addison V. Newton, *The Saloon Keeper's Companion* (Worcester, 1875).
40. *WT*, Apr. 23, 1891. See also *WEG*, May 18, 1880; Petition in Favor of Innholder License for Napoleon Guertin, May 7, 1883, Board of Aldermen MSS, Worcester City Hall; *L'Opinion Publique*, Apr. 21, 1893.

O'Flynn, "Rumsellers of Worcester," mentions the Christopher brothers. The number of French-Canadian saloonkeepers can be discerned from annual listings in the *Worcester Directory* and the French-Canadian press. Between 1883 and 1885, the total number of licenses issued to French Canadians fluctuated between eight and thirteen, but these included pharmacies, groceries, and hotels. See *Le Courrier de Worcester,* May 4, 1883; *Le Travailleur,* May 2, 1884, May 15, 1885.

41. *Scandinavia,* May 25, 1888. There was also drinking at the English Social Club; *WEP,* May 3, 1897; *WT,* May 8, 11, 1897.
42. For more on ethnic drinking customs, see Madelon Powers, "Faces Along the Bar: The Saloon in Working-Class Life, 1890–1920" (paper, Social Research Group, School of Public Health, Univ. of California, Berkeley, July 1979), 39–40; John C. Koren, *Economic Aspects of the Liquor Problem* (Boston, 1899), 228; O'Flynn, "Rumsellers of Worcester"; Stivers, *Hair of the Dog;* Andrew Greeley, William McCready, and Gary Theisen, *Ethnic Drinking Subcultures* (New York, 1980); Robert F. Bales, "Attitudes toward Drinking in the Irish Culture," in D. J. Pittman and C. R. Snyder, eds., *Society, Culture, and Drinking Patterns* (New York, 1962), 157–87; Thomas J. Noel, "The City and the Saloon: Denver, 1858–1916" (Ph.D. thesis, Univ. of Colorado, 1978), 118–47; James R. Barrett, "Why Paddy Drank: The Social Importance of Whiskey in Pre-famine Ireland," *Journal of Popular Culture* 11 (Summer 1977):155–66.
43. "Editorial," *Light* 4 (Nov. 7, 1891):291; RGD, 104:793; *WT,* May 2, 3, 1893. See also *WST,* Apr. 19, 1896; *WT,* June 25, 1898; *Skandinavia,* Jan. 12, 1893; Olive Higgins Prouty, *Pencil Shavings* (Cambridge, Mass., 1961), 43.
44. Group purchases evaded the law against liquor sales at private clubs. Unidentified clipping, Jan. 8, 1922, Clipping File, AAS; *WDT,* Apr. 29, 1886. See also *WDT,* May 17, 1885, May 3, 1886, Dec. 4, 6, 1888, Nov. 29, 1886.
45. For example, between 1886 and 1888, when drunkenness arrests rose 65% (because of the end of no-license), arrests of laborers swelled 81%. Arrests of wireworkers rose only 1% and of machinists 10%. Arrest statistics are from the annual *City Marshal Reports.*
46. Mass., BLS, *Report, 1881,* 477–531. See also Mass. BLS, *Report, 1895,* 1–416; lists of drunkenness arrests were drawn from the Central District Court Docket books, Central District Courthouse, Worcester.
47. The biography of Murphy is drawn from RGD, 99:14; O'Flynn, "Rumsellers of Worcester"; U.S. Manuscript Census, Worcester, 1880; and *Worcester Directory.*
48. The distance from home to saloon was calculated as a straight line rather than as actual walking distance. Data on the occupations of neighbors of saloonkeepers come from U.S. Manuscript Census, Worcester, 1880.
49. Wyckoff, quoted in Koren, *Economic Aspects of the Liquor Problem,* 239.

For a similar statement, see Royal L. Melendy, "The Saloon in Chicago," *American Journal of Sociology* 6 (Nov. 1900):291. On the social functions of the saloon, see Jon M. Kingsdale, "The 'Poor Man's Club': Social Functions of the Urban Working-Class Saloon," *American Quarterly* 25 (Oct. 1975):472–89; Duis, "Saloon and the Public City," 509–87; Melendy, "Saloon in Chicago," 289–306; George Ade, *The Old-Time Saloon* (New York, 1931); Raymond Calkins, *Substitutes for the Saloon* (Boston, 1901), 1–24; Koren, *Economic Aspects of the Liquor Problem*, 210–40; Ronald Morris Benson, "American Workers and Temperance Reform, 1866–1933" (Ph.D. thesis, Univ. of Notre Dame, 1974), 95–120; Powers, "Faces Along the Bar," 1–50; Noel, "The City and the Saloon."

50. Noel, "The City and the Saloon," 118–47, 197–225; Powers, "Faces Along the Bar," 27–48; Robert A. Woods, ed., *The City Wilderness* (Boston, 1899), 118. On free lunch in Worcester, see *WDT*, Mar. 8, 1886; *WEG*, July 5, 1910.
51. Melendy, "Saloon in Chicago," 290; Mass. BLS, *Report, 1871*, 540; Fitch, *Steel Workers*, 226–7; Maurice Parmelee, *Inebriety in Boston* (New York, 1909), 38–9; *Relations Between Labor and Capital*, 3:631. See also Mass. BLS, *Report, 1895*, 40–1, 46.
52. Newton, *Saloon Keeper's Companion*, iii; O'Flynn, "Rumsellers of Worcester"; "In Leisure Moments," *Light* 1 (June 7, 1890):14. See also *WT*, May 2, 1893.
53. Newton, *Saloon Keeper's Companion*, 11–59.
54. Mass. BLS, *Report, 1870*, 540; Ade, *Old-Time Saloon*, 128–30. See also Marshall, *Swinging Doors*, 171–4.
55. *Worcester Directory, 1875* (Worcester, 1875), 441; O'Flynn, "Rumsellers of Worcester"; Michael Gordon, "Studies in Irish and Irish-American Thought and Behavior in Gilded Age New York City" (Ph.D. thesis, Univ. of Rochester, 1977), xxvii–viii. Massachusetts saloons were not legally permitted to offer commercial entertainment.
56. RGD, 97:758; *WT*, Dec. 6, 1885; O'Flynn, "Rumsellers of Worcester"; *WST*, May 2, 1885, Dec. 6, 1885; Ade, *Old-Time Saloon*, 32; Marshall, *Swinging Doors*, 163. James Gilrein recalls that some Worcester saloons attracted specialized crowds of sports fans: boxing at Jerry Regan's, track at Sanderson's, and harness racing at the Lincoln House; interview, Worcester, Mar. 1, 1978.
57. *WST*, Jan. 3, 1886. See also *WT*, June 6, 1886; *WST*, Apr. 12, 1897.
58. Mass. BLS, *Report, 1870*, 334, 266–7; see also Mass. BLS, *Report, 1871*, 589, 612–13; *Relations Between Labor and Capital*, 2:649; U. Waldo Cutler, "A Problem in Public Welfare," *Worcester Magazine* 12 (Sept. 1909):303. On working-class housing, see Mass. BLS, *Report, 1875*. In 1895 housing in the working-class Fifth Ward averaged .96 persons per room, whereas in the more affluent Eighth Ward it was .57. Timothy J. Meagher, "'The Lord Is Not Dead': Cultural and Social Change Among the

Irish in Worcester, Massachusetts" (Ph.D. thesis, Brown Univ., 1982), 55.

59. *Relations Between Labor and Capital,* 1:44; Meagher, "'Lord Is Not Dead,'" 123. See also *Relations Between Labor and Capital,* 1:409, 854; Mass. BLS, *Report, 1871,* 543.

60. Meagher, "'Lord Is Not Dead,'" 115; Duis, "Saloon and the Public City," 361; Parmelee, *Inebriety in Boston,* 25. Mass. BLS, *Report, 1895,* 122–3, shows that younger males dominated among drunkenness arrests (63% were between 20 and 39). For a discussion of the "bachelor subculture" and the Irish, see Stivers, *Hair of the Dog,* 51–135.

61. Cutler, "Public Welfare," 303; Mass. BLS, *Report, 1870,* 306; Jay P. Dolan, "Immigrants in the City: New York's Irish and German Catholics," *Church History* 41 (Sept. 1972):366; Ade, *Old-Time Saloon,* 99–100. According to one printer, the "thinking mechanic" abstained from church membership because of his "inability, if he has a family, to come up to the social requirements of church membership, in dress and in contributions to the various objects that the church carries along with it"; *Relations Between Labor and Capital,* 1:50. See also Walter A. Wyckoff, *The Workers: An Experiment in Reality – The West* (New York, 1899), 196–7; Fitch, *Steel Workers,* 225; George L. McNutt, "Why Workingmen Drink," *Outlook* 69 (Sept. 14, 1901): 115–18; Mass. BLS, *Report, 1871,* 591, 594–5, 606, 618; Woods, *City Wilderness,* 228–9; Marshall, *Swinging Doors,* 13.

62. "To the Voters of Worcester," Dec. 7, 1883, Broadside Collection, WHM.

63. Melendy, "Saloon in Chicago," 294; McNutt, "Why Workingmen Drink," 115, 118. Even the national field secretary of the Church Temperance Society called the saloon the "most democratic institution in America"; Clipping and Minutes, Jan. 11, 1920, Scrapbook, Twentieth Century Club of Worcester, Worcester Public Library. On reciprocity, see David Harvey, *Social Justice and the City* (Baltimore, 1972), 206–7, 209, 282; Karl Polanyi, Conrad M. Arensberg, and Harry W. Pearson, eds., *Trade and Market in the Early Empires* (1957; rpt. Chicago, 1971).

64. Bales, "Attitudes toward Drinking in the Irish Culture," 172.

65. Joseph Walker, *Hopewell Village* (Philadelphia, 1966), 381 (emphasis added); Bales, "Attitudes toward Drinking in the Irish Culture," 175. On drink customs of Irish artisans, see John Dunlop, *Artificial and Compulsory Drinking Usages of The United Kingdom,* 7th ed. (London, 1844), 84. On the twentieth-century Irish rural economy, see Conrad Arensberg and Solon Kimball, *Family and Community in Ireland,* 2nd ed. (Cambridge, 1968). On similar American economic arrangements, see Mike Merrill, "Cash Is Good to Eat: Self-Sufficiency and Exchange in the Rural Economy of the United States," *Radical History Review* 4 (Winter 1977):42–71.

66. Mass. BLS, *Report, 1895,* 41; Mass. BLS, *Report, 1871,* 540–1. See also

Kingsdale, "'Poor Man's Club,'" 480; Upton Sinclair, *The Jungle* (1905; rpt. New York, 1960), 84–5; Thorstein Veblen, *The Theory of the Leisure Class* (1899; rpt. New York, 1953), 72–3; Ernest R. Cherrington, ed., *Standard Encyclopedia of the Alcohol Problem*, 6 vols. (Westerville, Ohio, 1930), 6:2668. A recent sociological study finds that treating is still "the most general of bar forms"; Sherri Cavan, *Liquor License: An Ethnography of Bar Behavior* (Chicago, 1966), 41.

67. Jack London, *John Barleycorn* (1913; rpt. Westport, Conn., 1968), 84 (also quoted in Powers, "Faces Along the Bar," 21); Arrest Cards, James Drennan MSS (emphasis added). See also *WDT*, July 6, 1883.

68. Veblen, *The Theory of the Leisure Class*, 72–3; *Catholic Messenger*, May 17, 1907; see also Feb. 15, 1907.

69. Stivers, *Hair of the Dog*, 86–7; Rorabaugh, *Alcoholic Republic*, 151; Cavan, *Liquor License*, 43.

70. Mass. BLS, *Report, 1871*, 543; *WT*, Apr. 16, 1895. Significantly, the Knights of Labor with its emphasis on the dignity of labor and its producerist ideology was the labor organization most hostile to drinking and the saloon; see David Brundage, "The Producing Classes and the Saloon: Denver in the 1880's" (paper presented at the Knights of Labor Centennial Symposium, Chicago, Ill., May 17–19, 1979); Benson, "American Workers and Temperance Reform," 150–86.

71. Committee of Five, "A Statement to Businessmen," Nov. 17, 1893, copy of broadside found in Worcester Room, Worcester Public Library; Stephan Thernstrom, *Poverty and Progress: Social Mobility in a Nineteenth-Century City* (1964; rpt. New York, 1972), 136–37. For claims about the connection between temperance and homeownership, see *Relations Between Labor and Capital*, 2:960, 1285.

72. Meagher, "'Lord Is Not Dead,'" 201, 182. The degree to which American workers accepted or rejected "acquisitive individualism" remains a subject of debate. For contrasting positions, see, for example, David Montgomery, *Workers' Control in America: Studies in the History of Work, Technology, and Labor Struggles* (Cambridge, 1979), 4, 153, and Melvyn Dubofsky, "Hold the Fort: The Dynamics of Twentieth-Century American Working-Class History," *Reviews in American History* 9 (June 1981):250–1.

73. Kingsdale, "'Poor Man's Club,'" 485–7; Norman H. Clark, *Deliver Us from Evil: An Interpretation of American Prohibition* (New York, 1976), 13.

74. Robin Room, "Cultural Contingencies of Alcoholism: Variations Between and Within Nineteenth-Century Urban Ethnic Groups in Alcohol-Related Death Rates," *Journal of Health and Social Behavior* 9 (Mar. 1968):99–113. The Irish male death rate was two times that for women for deaths from alcoholism. However, the male rate of deaths from liver diseases (except jaundice) was only 80% that of the female rate.

75. *Reports on the Subject of a License Law*, 19, 20; Woods, *City Wilderness*, 155. Stivers notes that women in Ireland drank but not in pubs; *Hair of*

the Dog, 177. Noel found both a social and a legal taboo on women drinking in saloons in Denver; "The City and the Saloon," 242–3, 246. Legal prohibitions on women in saloons seem to have emerged gradually. In the 1880s in Boston and Chicago there was only a social taboo; Duis, "Saloon and the Public City," 221. There seem to have been some public drink places primarily for upper-class women in New York City in the 1880s, but such habits were viewed as "exotic" from the perspective of Worcester; *WST*, July 7, 1889.

76. Marshall, *Swinging Doors*, 13; Powers, "Faces Along the Bar," 16; Noel, "The City and the Saloon," 250; Stivers, *Hair of the Dog*, 86. On women (probably English immigrants) in Fall River saloons, see Jonathan Baxter Harrison, *Certain Dangerous Tendencies in American Life* (Boston, 1880) as excerpted in Alan Trachtenberg, ed., *Democratic Vistas, 1860–1880* (New York, 1970), 171–4; *Relations Between Labor and Capital*, 1:647. Cavan notes that the treating of men by women was still a taboo in the 1960s; *Liquor License*, 114, 122–3. In the Fall River example cited above, Harrison notes an asymmetrical form of treating – men treat women but not the reverse.

77. Raymond Williams, "Base and Superstructure in Marxist Cultural Theory," *New Left Review*, no. 82 (Dec. 1973):11; John Bodnar, "Immigration and Modernization: The Case of Slavic Peasants in Industrial America," *Journal of Social History* 9 (Fall 1975):44–71. See also John Bodnar, "Materialism and Morality: Slavic-American Immigrants and Education, 1890–1940," *Journal of Ethnic Studies* 3 (Winter 1976):1–19.

78. Angela Keil and Charles Keil, "In Pursuit of Polka Happiness," *Cultural Correspondence*, No. 5 (Summer–Fall 1977):8, 6.

3. Immigrant workers and the Fourth of July

1. Mass. BLS, *Second Annual Report, 1871* (Boston, 1871), 449, 612–16; hereafter cited as Mass. BLS, *Report, 1871*.
2. Ibid., 461.
3. *WEG*, July 3, 1878; *WAT*, July 8, 1865; on earlier celebrations, see Charles A. Nutt, *History of Worcester and Its People*, 4 vols. (New York, 1919), 2:665–7; Franklin P. Rice, "Independence Day," Clipping File, WHM; *Celebration by the Inhabitants of Worcester, Mass. of the Centennial Anniversary of the Declaration of Independence, July 4, 1876* (Worcester, 1876); *WS*, July 6, 1859, July 11, 1860. Civic-sponsored celebrations did not occur every year, however; see *WS*, July 8, 1857; *WAT*, July 4, 1855.
4. Stephen Salisbury III, Diary, July 4, 1865, July 4, 1868, July 3–7, 1871, AAS; see also July 4, 1870, 1872, 1873. Francis Couvares notes that in Pittsburgh the city's elite had withdrawn from leadership in July Fourth celebrations as early as 1858; "Work, Leisure, and Reform in Pittsburgh: The Transformation of an Urban Culture, 1860–1920" (Ph.D. thesis, Univ. of Michigan, 1980), 103.

5. *WES*, July 5, 1879; *WS*, July 6, 1885, *WT*, July 4, 1890; *WDT*, July 5, 6, 1887. I identified the occupations of those listed as going out of town on July 4, 1890, in the *Worcester Directory*. By that date there were even a few skilled blue-collar workers on the list. For further local comments on shifts in July Fourth celebrations, see *WEG*, July 5, 1870; *Worcester Commercial Advertiser*, July 4, 1868; *WDP*, July 5, 1875.
6. *WEG*, July 5, 1870; *WS*, July 5, 1884. On Draper, see Franklin P. Rice, ed., *The Worcester of Eighteen Hundred and Ninety-Eight* (Worcester, 1899), 607. A possible sign of the exclusivity of the gathering was the notation by a working-class neighbor of Draper's that, although invited, her family did not attend because they "did not think they wanted us very bad"; Mabel Dickinson (Pond), Diary, July 4, 1884, WHM.
7. *WES*, May 20, July 1, 2, 1879; *WS*, July 6, 1880; *WDT*, July 5, 1881; *WST*, July 5, 1891; Visitors Book, July 4, 1887, 1893, Worcester Continentals MSS, WHM. I traced the signers in the *Worcester Directory*. In 1893, for example, about 90% of the visitors held white-collar jobs; about 20% were manufacturers; and about 19% were clerks. Officers of the Worcester Continentals reflected a similar mix of clerical workers, professionals, city officials, and manufacturers (based on lists of officers from 1880 and 1890 traced into the *Worcester Directory*). On the creation of an elite "caste," see E. Digby Baltzell, *The Protestant Establishment: Aristocracy and Caste in America* (New York, 1964), 109–42. On the more exclusive character of the Worcester Club, see *WS*, Mar. 31, 1888; R. M. Washburn, *Smith's Barn: A "Child's History" of the West Side Worcester, 1880–1923* (Worcester, 1923), 96.
8. On the growth of historical and geneaological societies, see Baltzell, *Protestant Establishment*, 114–15; Wallace Evan Davies, *Patriotism on Parade: The Story of Veterans' and Hereditary Organizations in America, 1783–1900* (Cambridge, Mass., 1955).
9. *Celebration by the Inhabitants of Worcester; WT*, July 1–2, 4–5, 1892; *WST*, July 3, 1892. Of eighty members of sixteen different planning committees for the centennial, only two held blue-collar jobs, and both of them were assigned to the "tent and fixtures" committee (I traced the names in the *Worcester Directory*).
10. *WEG*, July 5, 1871, July 3, 1872; the officers of the Worcester Park Association, which sponsored the 1872 trotting matches, included a thread manufacturer, a wholesale merchant, and a lawyer; *WEG*, July 2, 1867, July 5, 1868, July 5, 1873; Salisbury III, Diary, July 4, 1867. The diaries of Catherine White Forbes (1872–84, AAS), who lived in nearby Westborough, give a good sense of the elite social world.
11. On middle-class vacations, see Neil Harris, "On Vacation," in *Resorts of the Catskills* (New York, 1979), 101–8; Hugh DeSantis, "The Democratization of Travel: The Travel Agent in American History," *Journal of American Culture* 1 (Spring 1978):1–19; Daniel Rodgers, *The Work Ethic in Industrial America* (Chicago, 1978), 106. A 1928 New York Depart-

ment of Labor study found that of 1,500 factories investigated, 91% gave paid vacations to office workers and only 18% to production workers. Harris, "On Vacation," 105–6. Even in the nineteenth century, however, there were some workers – skilled iron and glass workers, for example – who had regular summer vacations; Couvares, "Work, Leisure, and Reform," 21. For a good sense of class differences in early twentieth century vacation patterns, see "How Long Should a Man's Vacation Be," *New York Times*, July 31, 1910. (Reference courtesy of Betsy Blackmar.)

12. *WDT*, Sept. 9, 1887, July 15, 1886; *WST*, June 26, 1892. Anticipating a successful AOH picnic in 1889, the *Worcester Daily Times* noted its expectation that "many of the manufacturing establishments will shut down for the occasion"; *WDT*, Aug. 5, 1889.
13. *WST*, July 7, 1895.
14. Mass. BLS, *Report, 1871*, 591; *WT*, Jan. 1, 1913. On traditional holidays, see Kevin Danaher, *The Year in Ireland* (Cork, Ireland, 1972); Horace Miner, *St. Denis: A French-Canadian Parish* (1939; rpt. Chicago, 1963), 141–68. On January First, see *Le Travailleur*, Dec. 26, 1879; Jan. 6, 1880; Jan. 7, 1890; Jan. 6, 1891; *L'Opinion Publique*, Jan. 1, 5, 1897, Jan. 2, 1899, Jan. 2, 1901; Jacques Ducharme, *The Shadows of the Trees: The Story of French Canadians in New England* (New York, 1943), 181. For other evidence of the persistence of ethnic holiday celebrations, see Herbert Gutman, "Work, Culture, and Society in Industrializing America, 1815–1919," *American Historical Review* 78 (June 1973):547, 550; Peter Roberts, *Antracite Coal Communities* (New York, 1904), 54, 219.
15. *Worcester Veckoblad*, June 24, 1887; *Le Travailleur*, May 7, 1880; *WEG*, June 24, 1870; L'Abbé T. A. Chandonnet, *Notre-Dame-Des Canadiens et Les Canadiens Aux Etats-Unis* (Montreal, 1872; translation by Kenneth Moynihan, Assumption College, Worcester, 1977), 36–8.
16. Timothy J. Meagher, "'The Lord Is Not Dead': Cultural and Social Change Among the Irish in Worcester, Massachusetts" (Ph.D. thesis, Brown Univ., 1982), 311–12; *Scandinavia*, June 29, 1888; *Skandinavia*, June 28, 1889; *WT*, June 25, 1895. On Midsummer Day in Sweden, see Dorothy Spicer, *The Book of Festivals* (Detroit, 1969), 311.
17. Quoted in M. R. Werner, *Tammany Hall* (New York, 1931), 48. For insightful comments on Walsh, see Gutman, "Work, Culture, and Society," 572; Joshua Brown, "The 'Dead Rabbit' – Bowery Boy Riot: An Analysis of the Antebellum New York Gang" (M.A. thesis, Columbia Univ., 1976), 93–4.
18. *WDP*, July 4, 1874.
19. *WEG*, July 5, 1870; *WDT*, July 5, 1888; *WDP*, July 6, 1874.
20. *WS*, July 5, 1886; *WST*, July 4, 1886. (On July 3, 1873, the police carried out at least twenty-seven successful raids on illegal dealers; Central District Court Docket book, Central District Courthouse, Worcester.) *WS*, July 11, 1860; *WEG*, July 6, 1874. The holiday arrest figures are

drawn from the Central District Court records and the daily average is computed from the police reports. The different sources used may result in a slight overstatement of the July Fourth arrests because the court records include a small number of arrests from outside Worcester (but probably less than 2% of the total). The profile of those arrested is based on data from seven years (1871, 1872, 1879–81, 1886, 1899). In the seven years less than 2% of those arrested for drunkenness held white-collar jobs. Occupations were identified in *Worcester Directories* and ethnicity was inferred from last names. (On the propensity to stereotype Irish as drunkards and on the greater likelihood of the Irish to be arrested for drunkenness, see Richard Stivers, *A Hair of the Dog: Irish Drinking and American Stereotype* [University Park, Pa., 1976], 141, 143; George Potter, *To the Golden Door: The Story of the Irish in Ireland and America* [Boston, 1960], 526–7.) In the seven years sampled, the total percentage of skilled workers arrested for drunkenness on July Fourth was 46.3%. In June 1880 and January 1886, however, the total for skilled workers was only 26%. In a slightly later period, John Fitch noted "binge" drinking among steelworkers on holidays in Pittsburgh; *The Steel Workers* (New York, 1910), 227–8. The data on age and marital status is more tentative, since it is based on a sample of drunkenness arrests from several holidays (1879–81) and June 1880 arrestees that I traced into the U.S. Manuscript Census, Worcester, 1880. The use of the census index developed by the Community Studies Program of Assumption College greatly facilitated the tracing process.

21. Quoted in Meagher, "'Lord Is Not Dead,'" 363.
22. See, for example, *WS*, July 4, 1885; *WT*, July 4, 1887, July 4, 1895.
23. *WDT*, July 3, 6, 1885. See also, *WS*, July 6, 1880; *WT*, July 5, 1886, July 5, 1887, July 5, 1895; *WDT*, July 2, 1886; on Taylor, see Rice, *Worcester of Eighteen Hundred and Ninety-Eight*, 765–7.
24. *WST*, July 2, 1916.
25. Ibid. I traced the names mentioned in the article into the U.S. Manuscript Census, Worcester, 1870, 1880, and the relevant *Worcester Directories* and *Worcester House Directories*.
26. Visitors Book, July 4, 1887, Worcester Continentals MSS.
27. *WS*, July 6, 1885. Joyce was arrested for illegal liquor selling in 1886; *WS*, July 5, 1886. Winners of sports events were identified in the *Worcester Directory*. In 1885, seven of the eight officers of the AOH held blue-collar jobs. For a more detailed occupational analysis of the AOH, see Meagher, "'Lord Is Not Dead,'" 649.
28. *WS*, July 6, 1885; *WST*, July 5, 1885; *WDT*, July 13, 1885; Richard O'Flynn, "Rumsellers of Worcester," Folio 2, 563, Richard O'Flynn MSS, HCC. See also *WDT*, July 3, 7, 1885; *WS*, July 4, 6, 1885.
29. *WT*, July 5, 1887; *WST*, July 19, 1887; *WS*, July 5, 1883. There were seventy-one drunkenness arrests in Worcester on July 4, 1887.
30. *WT*, July 5, 1893; *WT*, July 6, 1886.
31. Patrick O'Donnell, *The Irish Faction Fighters* (Dublin, 1975), 30; David

Miller, "Irish Catholicism and the Great Famine," *Journal of Social History* 9 (Fall 1975):90–4. "Patterns" were feasts of the patron saints of the parish.

32. Meagher, "'Lord Is Not Dead,'" 281.
33. Brown, "The 'Dead Rabbit' – Bowery Boy Riot," 94; *WDT*, July 6, 1880, July 8, 1882; Michael Gordon, "Studies in Irish and Irish-American Thought and Behavior in Gilded Age New York City" (Ph.D. thesis, Univ. of Rochester, 1977), 27.
34. *WEG*, July 5, 1876.
35. *WDT*, July 2, 1881. A number of historical and sociological studies have noted the "rough" and "respectable" division within American working-class culture. Although they sometimes use different terms (e.g., traditionalist and loyalist, hard living and settled living, action seeking and routine seeking), their categories are remarkably similar. See, for example, Paul Faler, "Cultural Aspects of the Industrial Revolution: Lynn, Massachusetts Shoemakers and Industrial Morality, 1826–1860," *Labor History* 15 (Summer 1974):367–94; Herbert Gans, *The Urban Villagers: Group and Class in the Life of Italian-Americans* (New York, 1962), 28–32; Joseph T. Howell, *Hard Living on Clay Street: Portraits of Blue Collar Families* (New York, 1973), 6–7, 249–360; Bruce Laurie, *Working People of Philadelphia, 1800–1850* (Philadelphia, 1980), 33–66; S. M. Miller and Frank Riessman, "The Working-Class Subculture: A New View," *Social Problems* 9 (Summer 1961):86–97. Of course, the terms "rough" and "respectable" are most commonly used by British social historians and sociologists.
36. *WDT*, July 5, 1881; *WT*, Aug. 16, 1889; *WS*, July 6, 1882 (occupations identified in the *Worcester Directory*).
37. *WDT*, July 5, 1882.
38. Quoted in Meagher, "'Lord Is Not Dead,'" 182, 184. For similar analyses of antimaterialism among Catholic immigrants, see John Bodnar, "Materialism and Morality: Slavic-American Immigrants and Education, 1890–1940," *Journal of Ethnic Studies* 3 (Winter 1976):1–19; M. Mark Stolarik, "Immigration, Education, and the Social Mobility of Slovaks, 1870–1930," in R. Miller and T. Marzik, eds., *Immigrants and Religion in Urban America* (Philadelphia, 1977), 103–16; Jay Dolan, *Catholic Revivalism: The American Experience* (Notre Dame, Ind., 1978), 159–66. For discussions of the complex meanings of "respectability" in a British context, see, for example, R. Q. Gray, "Styles of Life, the 'Labour Aristocracy,' and Class Relations in Later Nineteenth Century Edinburgh," *International Review of Social History* 18, no. 3 (1973):428–52; Peter Bailey, "Will the Real Bill Banks Stand Up? Toward a Role Analysis of Mid-Victorian Working-Class Respectability," *Journal of Social History* 13 (Spring 1979):336–53.
39. Folio 3, 131; Folio 2, 608, Richard O'Flynn MSS. For more on St. Patrick's Day in Worcester, see Meagher, "'Lord Is Not Dead,'" 312–25.
40. *WDT*, June 19, 1880, July 5, 1882; *WS*, July 6, 1882.

41. *WDT*, June 28, 1880; *WT*, July 4, 1890. See also *Boston Sunday Herald*, July 11, 1880.
42. Meagher, "'Lord Is Not Dead,'" 156, 243; *WDT*, June 30, 1887, July 5, 1888. On Washington Social Club, see clipping, Oct. 26, 1892, Folio 1, 272–3, Richard O'Flynn MSS (this includes a membership list that was analyzed in the 1892 *Worcester Directory*); Meagher, "'Lord Is Not Dead,'" 516–19.
43. William V. Shannon, *The American Irish* (New York, 1974), 142; Meagher, "'Lord Is Not Dead,'" 155, 161.
44. *Worcester Veckoblad*, Jan. 28, 1887; *Scandinavia*, June 22, 1888; *Skandinavia*, May 26, 1892, Feb. 4, 1892; Esther M. Wahlstrom, "A History of the Swedish People of Worcester, Massachusetts" (M. A. thesis, Clark Univ., 1947), 82; Nancy Mayo Waterman, "The Evolution and Delimitation of Quinsigamond Village" (M.A. thesis, Clark Univ., 1952), 43.
45. The population of 11,000 includes first- and second-generation Swedes in 1900. The figures for attendance at picnics include estimates from both 1899 and 1900, since reports were incomplete for both years.
46. *WST*, July 5, 1896; *WT*, July 5, 1900, July 5, 1901.
47. *WT*, July 5, 1899.
48. *WT*, July 5, 1891, July 5, 1905.
49. *WT*, July 5, 1899, July 5, 1907; interviews with Grace Caldwell and Ethel Bigelow, Aug. 5, 1980, Worcester; Charles Estus, "A Swedish Working-Class Church: The Methodists of Quinsigamond Village, 1878–1900" (paper, CSP-AC, 1979), and "Quinsigamond Village Churches, 1875–1900" (paper, CSP-AC, 1978); Thure Hanson, *Swedish-American Souvenir: Settlement, Growth, and Progress of the Swedish People in Worcester* (Worcester, 1910), 13, 30.
50. *Scandinavia*, Mar. 23, 1888; *WT*, July 5, 1900.
51. Elliott Barkan, "French Canadians," in Stephan Thernstrom, ed., *Harvard Encyclopedia of American Ethnic Groups* (Cambridge, Mass., 1980), 392. On relations with Irish, see Meagher, "'Lord Is Not Dead,'" 378–82.
52. *Le Travailleur*, July 7, 1881; *Le Courrier de Worcester*, July 8, 1880.
53. *WT*, June 25, 1898; *Le Travailleur*, June 24, 1887, July 2, 1889; *L'Opinion Publique*, Jan. 27, 1893, Mar. 31, 1893, May 1, 1899, June 25, 1902.
54. See, for example, *WT*, July 5, 1896, July 6, 1897, July 5, 1899, July 5, 1900; *WEP*, July 5, 1902; *Le Travailleur*, Nov. 29, Dec. 29, 1876.
55. See, for example, *WEG*, July 3, 5, 1873, July 6, 1874, July 6, 1875; *WST*, July 5, 1891, July 5, 1896; *WT*, July 5, 1895, July 5, 1897, July 5, 1899, July 5, 1900, July 5, 1901, July 5, 1906.
56. *WES*, June 12, 18, 24, July 3, 8, 1879; *WEG*, July 5, 1879; Richard Oestreicher, "Socialism and the Knights of Labor in Detroit, 1877–1886," *Labor History* 22 (Winter 1981):16.
57. *WST*, Aug. 1, 1886; *WDT*, Mar. 18, 1886. On social activities, see *WDT*,

Apr. 23, 29, May 10, 1886; Ladies' Knights of Labor, *Program for Grand Calico Ball* (Worcester, May 14, 1886), copy available at AAS.

58. Meagher, "'Lord Is Not Dead,'" 564. On labor leaders, see Central Labor Union, *Illustrated History of the Central Labor Union and the Building Trades Council of Worcester and Vicinity* (Worcester, 1899).
59. *Le Travailleur,* Apr. 6, 1880; *LN,* Nov. 7, 1908. See also *Le Travailleur,* Apr. 9, May 7, 14, 1880, Mar. 8, 1884, Mar. 19, May 7, 1886, May 20, 1887; *L'Etendard National,* May 13, 1873; *LN,* Sept. 9, 1914. There were three labor leaders of French-Canadian background included in the 1899 *Illustrated History of the Central Labor Union.*
60. John F. Nourse, Diary 1869–1908, WHM.
61. *American* (a local newspaper published by the nativist American Protective Association, copies available AAS), Sept. 11, June 19, July 17, Feb. 6, 1894. (References courtesy of Timothy J. Meagher.) OUAM membership lists were found in National Council, Order of United American Mechanics, *Souvenir Fifty-First Annual Convention* (Worcester, 1896) in Pamphlet Collection, WHM, and were traced into the *Worcester Directory.* For more on nativism, see Meagher, "'Lord Is Not Dead,'" 360–6.
62. *WT,* July 5, 1893, *Skandinavia,* Dec. 24, 1891; *Scandinavia,* June 24, 1887; *WDT,* Apr. 29, July 30, 1886; Charles Washburn, *Industrial Worcester* (Worcester, 1917), 160, 313; Meagher, "'Lord Is Not Dead,'" 179–82. See similar charges against the wire company in *Worcester Argus,* June 3, 1886. For complaints about the replacement of French Canadians by Swedes in Worcester factories, see *Le Travailleur,* Sept. 19, 1884.
63. *Worcester Veckoblad,* Apr. 8, Apr. 15, 1887; *Scandinavia* Oct. 7, 21, 1887, Mar. 9, 16, 1888; *Skandinavia,* Aug. 2, Aug. 23, Nov. 8, 1889. See also Waterman, "Evolution and Delimitation of Quinsigamond Village," 42.
64. *Le Travailleur,* Mar. 20, 1883; *Le Foyer Canadien,* Sept. 22, 1874; *Le Travailleur,* Sept. 30, 1875.

4. The struggle over the saloon, 1870–1910

1. "Citizens of Worcester," Dec. 1881, Broadside Collection, WHM. I identified the signers of the broadside in the *Worcester Directory, 1882* (Worcester, 1882).
2. *WDT,* Dec. 5, 6, 1881.
3. *WDT,* Dec. 12, 1881. The West Side vote was actually around 2.1 to 1 against license. The wards do not precisely reflect ethnic and class divisions, because they were pie-shaped and radiated out from downtown.
4. *Constitution and By-laws of the Very Reverend Father Mathew Mutual Benevolent Total Abstinence Society of Worcester, Mass.* (Worcester, 1882), 21–2. Mellen was apparently expelled from the Father Mathew society

in 1889 for nonpayment of dues, but by 1899 he was again a prominent member and the toastmaster at their fiftieth anniversary banquet. Folio 1, 198, Richard O'Flynn MSS, HCC; Father Mathew T. A. Society, *Grand Banquet Program*, Nov. 15, 1899, Temperance Society Pamphlets, AAS.

5. Alfred S. Roe, "Temperate Worcester," *Light* 1 (Mar. 8, 1890):8; *WT*, Dec. 13, 1909. See similarly "Editorial," *Light* 4 (Nov. 7, 1891):219; "Citizens of Worcester"; *LN*, Sept. 26, 1914.
6. Norman H. Clark, *Deliver Us from Evil: An Interpretation of American Prohibition* (New York, 1976), 50.
7. *WT*, Apr. 17, 1893.
8. *WEG*, Apr. 26, 1878. Based on the occupational scheme developed in Stephan Thernstrom's *The Other Bostonians: Poverty and Progress in the American Metropolis, 1880–1970* (Cambridge, Mass., 1973), about three-quarters of the signers could be classified as "high white collar." There were twelve ministers and twenty-eight manufacturers but no blue-collar workers. I identified signers in the *Worcester Directory;* Charles A. Nutt, *History of Worcester and Its People*, 4 vols. (New York, 1919), vols. 3 and 4; and Franklin P. Rice, ed., *The Worcester of Eighteen Hundred and Ninety-Eight* (Worcester, 1899). For other clerical-led protests, see *WEG*, Apr. 26, May 1, 1875, and the annual protests recorded in the Board of Aldermen Minutes and the Board of Aldermen Petitions, Board of Aldermen MSS, Worcester City Hall; hereafter cited as Board of Ald. Minutes, Petitions. Unitarian and Episcopal ministers were, perhaps, less active than their evangelical counterparts. They were not, however, absent from the temperance campaigns, as one might expect, based on the arguments of some historians about the "pietist" and "liturgical" divide over the drink question. For a summary of this argument, see Clark, *Deliver Us from Evil*, 89–91. For the presence of Unitarians on both sides of the temperance question in early nineteenth century Worcester, see Ian R. Tyrell, *Sobering Up: From Temperance to Prohibition in Antebellum America, 1800–1860* (Westport, Conn., 1979), 110.
9. Joshua Chasan, "Civilizing Worcester: The Creation of Industrial and Cultural Order, Worcester, Massachusetts, 1848–1876" (Ph.D. thesis, Univ. of Pittsburgh, 1974), vi, 146–62; Tyrell, *Sobering Up*, 111.
10. See relevant biographies in Nutt, *History of Worcester*, for these interconnections.
11. According to Tyrell, *Sobering Up*, 102, nine of the sixteen founders of the Mechanics Association supported prohibition and only two opposed it. I checked the signers of the 1878 petition against a list of Mechanics Association presidents in Nutt, *History of Worcester*, 2:1058. See Chapter 2, this volume, on the early Worcester temperance movement.

12. Board of Ald. Petitions, Apr. 20, 1881. I identified the signers in the *Worcester Directory;* Nutt, *History of Worcester;* Rice, *Worcester of Eighteen Hundred and Ninety-Eight.* On women and temperance, see Harry Gene Levine, "Temperance and Women in 19th Century America," in Oriana Kalant, ed., *Research Advances in Drug and Alcohol Problems, Vol. 5: Alcohol and Drug Problems in Women* (New York, 1980), 25–67; Barbara Leslie Epstein, *The Politics of Domesticity: Women, Evangelism, and Temperance in Nineteenth-Century America* (Middletown, Conn., 1981), 89–146; Ruth Bordin, *Woman and Temperance: The Quest for Power and Liberty, 1873–1900* (Philadelphia, 1981).
13. *WT,* Apr. 21, 1891, Apr. 16, 1895; Board of Ald. Minutes, Mar. 16, 1891; *WT,* Apr. 18, 1893; Board of Ald. Minutes, Apr. 10, 1893. See also *WT,* Mar. 30, Apr. 9, 1901.
14. Citizens of Ward One and Two against Reissuance of License to . . . ; To Mayor and Aldermen, Apr. 1883, Board of Ald. Petitions. I identified the signers in the *Worcester Directory.*
15. *WT,* Apr. 6, 7, 1912; *WEP,* Apr. 6, 1899; *Scandinavia,* Apr. 20, 1888. See also *WT,* Apr. 18, 20, 25, 1888. For the continuing controversy over Trulson's license, see *Scandinavia,* June 1, 8, 15, 1888; *Skandinavia,* June 21, 1889; *WT,* May 2, July 2, 1889.
16. Petition Against Licenses in Webster Square or Vincinity, Apr. 21, 1887; Petition of . . . citizens and voters of New Worcester . . . in favor of Thomas H. Downes, Apr. 1887, both in Board of Ald. Petitions. The petitioners were identified in the *Worcester Directory.* I located only one example of an Irish working-class petition against a saloon. Most of the signers were women. See Petition Against Edward Leyden, Apr. 1883, Board of Ald. Petitions.
17. Petition in favor of E. L. Kennan, May 7, 1883, Board of Ald. Petitions (at least half the signers were proprietors of Main Street stores or their employees); Petition in favor of liquor license for John McGuire and John L. Truax, Apr. 18, 1883, Board of Ald. Petitions; *WT,* May 7, 1889. I identified the signers of these petitions in the *Worcester Directory.*
18. "Citizens of Worcester"; "Appeal to Voters," Dec. 1886, Politics and Propaganda file, WHM; committee members were listed in the *No-License Advocate,* Dec. 3, 1886 (copy available at AAS), and traced in *Worcester Directory.* Except for the representatives from the black Baptist Church, all the blue-collar workers were skilled. Blacks averaged less than 1% of Worcester's population between 1870 and 1920. For an excellent study of this community, see Ella L. Vinal, "The Status of the Worcester Negro" (M.A. thesis, Clark Univ., 1929).
19. *WT,* Dec. 10, 1890. I used the published U.S. Census figures to correlate the ethnic basis of the voting. For a more detailed discussion of these correlations, see Roy Rosenzweig, " 'Eight Hours for What We Will': Workers and Leisure in Worcester, Massachusetts, 1870–1930"

(Ph.D. thesis, Harvard Univ., 1978), 219–20. The victory margin was calculated from the annual licensing votes provided in the local newspapers.

20. *L'Opinion Publique,* Dec. 7, 1894. See also *Le Courrier de Worcester,* Dec. 9, 1880; *Le Travailleur,* Dec. 11, 1888, Dec. 10, 1889.
21. *Le Worcester Canadien, 1888* (Worcester, 1888; translated excerpts courtesy of CSP-AC), 58–64, 76–80.
22. *WT,* Dec. 14, 1904. Since Worcester's ward and precinct boundaries changed frequently, comparisons over time are difficult to make.
23. See, for example, *WT,* Dec. 9, 1889, Dec. 8, 1890, Dec. 11, 1893, Dec. 9, 1895, Dec. 7, 1896, Dec. 13, 1897.
24. *WT,* Apr. 12, 1895, Mar. 13, 1901; *WEG,* Mar. 18, 20, 21, 23–5, 1874. On the elite profile of women's crusades elsewhere, see Charles A. Isetts, "A Social Profile of the Women's Temperance Crusade: Hillsboro, Ohio," in Jack S. Blocker, Jr., ed., *Alcohol, Reform and Society: The Liquor Issue in Social Context* (Westport, Conn., 1979), 101–10; Bordin, *Woman and Temperance,* 163–75.
25. "Worcester Citizens' Law and Order League," Broadside, Jan., 1883, Temperance Society Pamphlets, AAS; I identified signers in the *Worcester Directory. WST,* Apr. 18, 1886.
26. On early nineteenth-century temperance ideology and evangelical religion, see W. J. Rorabaugh, *The Alcoholic Republic* (New York, 1978), 205–13; Tyrell, *Sobering Up,* 110–13.
27. Clark, *Deliver Us from Evil,* 53, 12; Letter to Mayor from L. W. Staples, Apr. 23, 1887, Board of Ald. Petitions; *Light* 2 (Dec. 13, 1890):3. On the "home protection" theme, see Levine, "Temperance and Women," 55–7; Epstein, *Politics of Domesticity,* 89–113.
28. "Six Months of No-License in Worcester," Nov. 5, 1886, Broadside Collection, WHM; Committee of Five, "A Statement to Businessmen," Nov. 17, 1893, copy of broadside found in Worcester Room, Worcester Public Library; O. W. Norcross, "No-License the Better Business Policy," *Worcester Magazine* 11 (Dec. 1908):319. See also *Solid Facts for Thinking Men,* Dec. 7, 1889 (a temperance newspaper, copy available at WHM); *Light* 3 (May 30, 1891):303; *No-License Advocate,* Dec. 3, 1886; *WT,* July 5, 1886, Dec. 13, 1909.
29. Harry Gene Levine, "Temperance and Prohibition in America" (forthcoming in a book on alcohol and drug problems edited by Griffith Edwards and Jerome Jaffe), and Harry Gene Levine, "The Birth of Demon Rum: Changing Attitudes about Alcohol in America" (paper presented at the Annual Meeting of the American Association for Public Opinion Research, Buck Hill Falls, Pa., May 1981).
30. Joseph R. Gusfield, *Symbolic Crusade: Status Politics and the American Temperance Movement* (Urbana, Ill., 1963), 5; Jay Dolan, *Catholic Revivalism: The American Experience* (Notre Dame, Ind., 1978), 155.
31. *Constitution and By-Laws,* 20; Nutt, *History of Worcester,* 2:901–2; George

Potter, *To the Golden Door: The Story of the Irish in Ireland and America* (Boston, 1960), 522, 525. In 1872 Father Primeau organized a large French-Canadian temperance society, but I have found no references to it after 1873. See *L'Etendard National*, Feb. 15, 29, 1872; Apr. 4, 1872; *Le Foyer Canadian*, July 1, 1873; L'Abbé T. A. Chandonnet, *Notre-Dame-Des-Canadiens et Les Canadiens Aux Etats-Unis* (Montreal, 1872; translation by Kenneth Moynihan, Assumption College, Worcester, 1977), 82–3, 92–3.

32. On the rise and fall of Irish temperance societies, see Timothy J. Meagher, "'The Lord Is Not Dead': Cultural and Social Change Among the Irish in Worcester, Massachusetts" (Ph.D. thesis, Brown Univ., 1982), 297–310, 570; *WDT*, Jan. 31, 1885, Apr. 26, June 2, 1886; Temperance Society Pamphlets, WHM; *Worcester Directories*. On the national movement, see Sister Joan Bland, *Hibernian Crusade: The Story of the Catholic Total Abstinence Union of America* (Washington, D.C., 1951). I found no evidence of a comparable burgeoning of French-Catholic temperance societies in the 1880s.
33. *WDT*, Dec. 4, 6, 1886.
34. *WDT*, Dec. 1, 1886; Father Mathew Pledge Card, Temperance Society Pamphlets, WHM; Membership Books, St. John's Temperance and Literary Guild, St. John's Parish Archives, Worcester (copies courtesy of Timothy J. Meagher). One study of 616 men arrested for drunkenness in Boston in 1909 found that 224 had taken the pledge at some time; Maurice Parmelee, *Inebriety in Boston* (New York, 1909), 47.
35. *Constitution and By-laws; WDT*, Apr. 26, 1886; Parmelee, *Inebriety in Boston*, 47; Meagher, "'Lord Is Not Dead,'" 249; *Light* 4 (Dec. 5, 19, 1891):315, 381.
36. Incomplete Program of St. Anne's Temperance Society, c. 1890, Folio 1, 214–5, Richard O'Flynn MSS, HCC. On temperance society activities, see the Temperance Society Pamphlets, WHM; *WT*, Dec. 14, 1888, Oct. 12, 1896, Mar. 13, Dec. 7, 1900; *LN*, June 2, 1908; *WEP*, Oct. 26, 1935; interview with Frank Nagle, Mar. 1, 1978, Worcester.
37. Ross E. Paulson, *Radicalism and Reform: The Vrooman Family and American Social Thought, 1837–1937* (Lexington, Ky., 1968), 79–91; *WDT*, Apr. 26, 1886; *Constitution of the Father Mathew Athletic Association of Worcester* (Worcester, 1904), available at AAS.
38. Meagher, "'Lord Is Not Dead,'" 173, 302–3 (Catholic Lyceum quotes); Stephen F. Littleton Diary, Mar. 22, 1890, AAS. I traced sixteen men who joined the St. John's Temperance and Literary Guild around 1884 into the U.S. Manuscript Census, Worcester, 1880. (The tracing was greatly facilitated by the use of the street index developed by the Community Studies Program of Assumption College.) About two-thirds were second generation and single; the median age was about 29 (in 1884). Timothy J. Meagher traced members of the same organization into the U.S. Manuscript Census for 1900 and found that they

were even younger and more likely to be single and American-born; Meagher, "'Lord Is Not Dead,'" 647. One of the ironies of Littleton's advancement through sobriety is that by 1908 he was the lawyer for druggists seeking to sell liquor during a no-license year; *WT*, July 6, 1908.

39. Meagher, "'Lord Is Not Dead,'" 299–300, 303; *WDT*, Apr. 26, 1886. On the "gospel of acceptance," see Dolan, *Catholic Revivalism*, 159–65.
40. I traced names from Membership Books, St. John's Temperance and Literary Guild (courtesy of Timothy J. Meagher) into the *Worcester Directories*. On the occupational distribution of the Irish in Worcester during these years, see Meagher, "'Lord Is Not Dead,'" 159.
41. I traced the members listed in the 1882 *Constitution and By-laws* to the 1880, 1882, and 1892 *Worcester Directories* as well as to the U.S. Manuscript Census, Worcester, 1880. For comparative persistence rates, see Charles C. Buell, "The Workers of Worcester: Social Mobility and Ethnicity in a New England City, 1850–1880" (Ph.D. thesis, New York Univ., 1974), 112, 115, 148, 151, 175, 179. For a more detailed discussion of the residential stability and modest property accumulation of the members of the Father Mathew society, see Rosenzweig, "'Eight Hours for What We Will,'" 249–50, 401–2.
42. Richard Stivers, *A Hair of the Dog: Irish Drinking and American Stereotype* (University Park, Pa., 1976), 34–50.
43. *Constitution and By-laws.*
44. Paul Faler and Alan Dawley, "Working-Class Culture and Politics in the Industrial Revolution: Sources of Loyalism and Rebellion," *Journal of Social History* 9 (Summer 1976): 469. For other discussions of temperance radicalism, see Bruce Laurie, *Working People of Philadelphia, 1800–1850* (Philadelphia, 1980), 71–2, 79; Jill Siegel Dodd, "The Working Classes and the Temperance Movement in Ante-Bellum Boston," *Labor History* 19 (Fall 1978):510–31. For a recent critique of Faler and Dawley's analysis, see Friedrich Lenger, "Class, Culture and Class Consciousness in Ante-bellum Lynn: A Critique of Alan Dawley and Paul Faler," *Social History* 6 (Oct. 1981):317–32.
45. *WST*, Nov. 29, 1885, Apr. 11, 1886. On Mellen, see Rice, *Worcester of Eighteen Hundred and Ninety-Eight*, 143; *WDT*, Mar. 11, 1886; *WEP*, June 16, 1910, Aug. 26, 1935; *WT*, June 17, 1910; *Worcester Directories*. Powderly is quoted in Ronald M. Benson, "'Sober Workmen': Late Nineteenth Century Enthusiasm for Temperance Reform Among American Workers" (paper presented at Organization of American Historians meeting, New Orleans, La., April 11–14, 1979). See also Ronald M. Benson, "Workers and Temperance Reform, 1866–1923" (Ph.D. thesis, Univ. of Notre Dame, 1974), 150–86.
46. David Brundage, "The Producing Classes and the Saloon: Denver in

the 1880's" (paper presented at the Knights of Labor Symposium, Chicago, Ill., May 19, 1979); *No-License Advocate,* Dec. 3, 1886; *WDT,* Dec. 6, 1885; *Worcester Argus* (Knights of Labor newspaper, copy available at AAS), June 3, 1886; *WT,* Nov. 10, 1889; *WDT,* Dec. 9, 11, 13, 1882.

47. *WST,* Nov. 21, 1886; Massachusetts Volumes of R. G. Dun and Co. Collection, Baker Library, Harvard University Graduate School of Business Administration, 101:38; 104:1337,1354; hereafter cited as RGD.

48. Meagher, "'Lord Is Not Dead,'" 553, 564, 570.

49. *WST,* June 20, 1897; Central Labor Union, *Illustrated History of the Central Labor Union and the Building Trades Council of Worcester and Vicinity* (Worcester, 1899), 173, 189. On temperance and CLU, see *LN,* Sept. 7, 1907, Feb. 7, 1914.

50. F. G. Stiles, *History of the Worcester Reform Club* (Worcester, 1906), available at AAS; Nutt, *History of Worcester,* 2:902–3; Minute Book, Oct. 16, 1899, Worcester Reform Club MSS, AAS. I identified the Reform Club members in the relevant *Worcester Directories.* About half the members were skilled workers. Violations of pledges seem to have been fairly common: About half the members broke their pledges in a sixteen-month period. On pledge anniversaries, see *WDP,* June 22, 1877; *WES,* June 20, 1879; and Minute Book.

51. Nutt, *History of Worcester,* 2:902–3; Stiles, *History of the Worcester Reform Club; WES,* June 6, 1879; *WEP,* Dec. 9, 1907. I traced the members in relevant *Worcester Directories.* Interestingly, one of the Graton and Knight foremen may have been Irish. At the same time, however, editorials in the *American* (a local newspaper published by the nativist American Protective Association, copies available at AAS) and the *Worcester Telegram* seem to suggest some tension between the very rich and the native middle and working classes on drinking habits, with lower-middle-class leaders charging that the rich failed to abstain.

52. *Scandinavia,* Apr. 20, 1888; *Skandinavia,* Apr. 24, 1891, Apr. 20, 1893; *WT,* Apr. 30, 1889; *Worcester Veckoblad,* Apr. 8, June 3, Nov. 4, 1887; *Scandinavia,* Dec. 9, 1887; *Skandinavia,* May 2, Oct. 24, 1890, Dec. 15, 19, 1900. In 1891 the paper seems to have shifted back to no-license, but it returned to support for licensing by 1893; see Aug. 6, Nov. 12, 1891, Dec. 20, 1893.

53. *WT,* Apr. 8, 1897, Apr. 8, 1899, Apr. 20, 1888. (Englebrekt may not have received its first license until 1912; *WT,* Apr. 20, 1912. The Mystic Brothers blamed other groups for the drinking at their hall; *Scandinavia,* Feb. 17, 1888); James J. McGrail, "Sociological Aspects of Drunkenness in Worcester" (M.A. thesis, Clark Univ. 1936), 117. Alcoholism rates for Scandinavian Americans are among the highest in America today; David J. Pittman and Charles R. Snyder, "Introductory

Note on Religion and Ethnicity," in David J. Pittman and Charles G. Snyder, eds., *Society, Culture, and Drinking Patterns* (New York, 1962), 154.

54. George M. Stephenson, *The Religious Aspects of Swedish Immigration: A Study of Immigrant Churches* (Minneapolis, 1932), 17, 24; Ernest H. Cherrington, ed., *Standard Encyclopedia of the Alcohol Problem,* 6 vols. (Westerville, Ohio, 1930), 6:2561–76; Clark, *Deliver Us from Evil,* 21; Rorabaugh, *Alcoholic Republic,* 10–11, 238–9.
55. Florence E. Janson, *The Background of Swedish Immigration, 1840–1930* (Chicago, 1931), 167, notes that in 1920 only 3.3% of Swedes were dissenters. Hans Norman, "The Causes of Emigration," in Harald Runblom and Hans Norman, eds., *From Sweden to America: A History of the Migration* (Minneapolis, 1976), 155, argues that "religious oppression was not a strong impetus to emigration." He disputes the earlier work of Stephenson, *Religious Aspects of Swedish Immigration,* and implicitly affirms that of John S. Lindberg, *The Background of Swedish Emigration to the United States* (Minneapolis, 1930), 212.
56. Timothy L. Smith, "Religion and Ethnicity in America," *American Historical Review* 83 (Dec. 1978):1176.
57. "History of the First Swedish Methodist Episcopal Church in Quinsigamond, Worcester, Mass." (manuscript translated by Helen Winroth, CSP-AC, 1978); Charles W. Estus, "A Swedish Working-Class Church: The Methodists of Quinsigamond Village, 1878–1900" (paper, CSP-AC, 1979). Ulf Beijbom notes a growth in pietism among Swedish settlers in Chicago in *Swedes in Chicago: A Demographic and Social Study of the 1846–1880 Immigration* (Växjo, 1971), 228–50.
58. Estus, "Swedish Working-Class Church"; Karl J. Karlson, "The Swedish Population of Worcester: A Social Survey" (M.A. thesis, Clark Univ., 1910), 4; Sture Lindmark, *Swedish America, 1914–1932: Studies in Ethnicity with Emphasis on Illinois and Minnesota* (Uppsala, 1971), 248–53.
59. The International (originally Independent) Order of Good Templars (IOGT) was founded in the United States in 1859; it spread to Sweden in 1879 and then returned to America with Swedish immigrants. *Fifty Years: The Eastern Grand Lodge* (n.p., 1946), 31, 100, 129; Stephenson, *Religious Aspects of Swedish Immigration,* 130. The churches were not uniformly opposed to the IOGT. Some Lutherans belonged to the order and at least one Methodist minister spoke to it. Nevertheless, on at least one occasion IOGT members debated whether the order was opposed to the church. The Swedish Mission Church seems to have been the most vociferously critical of the IOGT. Thure Hanson, *Swedish-American Souvenir: Settlement, Growth, and Progress of the Swedish People in Worcester* (Worcester, 1910), 14; *WT,* July 5, 1897; *Skandinavia,* Apr. 26, 1893; Janson, *Background of Swedish Immigration,* 211–12.
60. *Fifty Years,* 17, 27, 28, 100. The names of IOGT members were found in

Programbok orh Addresskalender för de Svenska Goodtemplorglogerna inom Worcester-distriktet at IOGT (Worcester, 1909) in Temperance Society Pamphlets, WHM. Of the members identified in the 1909 *Worcester Directory*, 88.4% held blue-collar jobs.

61. Sune Åckerman and Hans Norman, "Political Mobilization of the Workers: The Case of the Worcester Swedes" (paper presented at Conference on American Labor and Immigration History, Bremen, Germany, Nov. 1978); Hanson, *Swedish-American Souvenir*, 3; *WEG*, June 1, 1907; *Fifty Years*, 27, 35. In 1919 the IOGT held a joint celebration with the Scandinavian Socialists; *WT*, July 5, 1919. In Sweden, however, the Socialists and the IOGT split in 1896; Janson, *Background of Swedish Immigration*, 219.
62. *WT*, Dec. 10, 12, 1900.
63. *WS*, July 5, 1886; *Skandinavia*, Sept. 19, 1890; *Worcester Veckoblad*, Mar. 25, 1887; *Skandinavia*, Nov. 25, 1893.
64. *Annual Report of the City Marshal, Year Ending December 31, 1870* (Worcester, 1871), 12; hereafter cited as *City Marshal*.
65. *WEG*, May 7, 1879, May 1, 1880. For illegal sales, see, for example, *City Marshal, 1876*, 23; *WEG*, Apr. 5, 1875; Arrest Cards, James Drennan MSS, WHM.
66. *City Marshal, 1881*, 204; *City Marshal, 1882*, 427; *City Marshal, 1889*, 153; *City Marshal, 1890*, 134; *WEG*, Dec. 30, 1898; *L'Opinion Publique*, Dec. 7, 1901.
67. See Board of Ald. Minutes, Petitions.
68. *City Marshal, 1886*, 218; *WEG*, Oct. 20, 1886.
69. *WT*, July 25, 1892; *LN*, Nov. 30, 1908, Feb. 13, 1909; "The Question," broadside issued by Citizens No-License Committee, Dec. 1909, Broadside Collection, WHM; *WT*, May 2, 1910. Drunkenness figures are from the *City Marshal Reports*.
70. See, for example, *Skandinavia*, July 21, 1892.
71. *City Marshal, 1875*, 51; *City Marshal, 1875–1879; WEG*, Apr. 22, 1879, May 13, 27, 1878.
72. *City Marshal, 1886*, 218–19; *City Marshal, 1884*, 251. See also *City Marshal, 1889*, 154; *WDT*, July 6, 1887.
73. *City Marshal, 1884*, 251; *City Marshal, 1883*, 315–16. See also *WDT*, June 11, 1886; *City Marshal, 1892*, 171.
74. *WDT*, Feb. 2, 1885; Folio 2, 232, Richard O'Flynn MSS.
75. *WEG*, Apr. 22, 1879; *City Marshal, 1875*, 49; Arrest Lists, James Drennan MSS. According to the lists in the Drennan MSS, only six of eighty-five people convicted in 1882 received jail sentences, and most of them appealed their cases.
76. *City Marshal, 1883*, 315; Arrest Lists, James Drennan MSS; *WEG*, Apr. 22, 1879. For complaints about the Superior Court, see *City Marshal, 1875*, 50; *City Marshal, 1876*, 24; *WDT*, Dec. 13, 1880. It appears that

lawyers for the drink sellers tried to keep temperance advocates from sitting as jurors on their clients' cases; see Massachusetts Supreme Judicial Court, *Massachusetts Reports* (Boston, 1888), 145:282.

77. *WEG*, Apr. 22, 1879; "Statement to Businessmen," Nov. 17, 1893. See also *WDT*, Dec. 13, 1880, Apr. 27, 1885; *WEG*, Oct. 20, 1886; *City Marshal, 1881*, 205; *City Marshal, 1884*, 251; Arrest Cards, James Drennan MSS.
78. Occasionally, a defense was developed on the grounds of "popular right." See, for example, *WDT*, Dec. 6, 1884.
79. *WDT*, Apr. 17, June 6, 1885; RGD, 99:204, 101:72, 104:633, 911; Nutt, *History of Worcester*, 3:48–9; R. M. Washburn, *Smith's Barn: "A Child's History" of the West Side Worcester, 1880–1923* (Worcester, 1923), 127–8; *WST*, Jan. 11, 1885; *WDT*, May 9, Dec. 11, 1882. On nativism and the Masons, see Roy Rosenzweig, "Boston Masons, 1900–1935: The Lower Middle Class in a Divided Society," *Journal of Voluntary Action Research* 6 (July–Oct. 1977):119–26.
80. See *WST*, Nov. 30, 1884; *WDT*, June 3, 1886.
81. *WST*, Nov. 30, 1884; *WDT*, Dec. 6, 1879. On Reed, see Rice, *Worcester of Eighteen Hundred and Ninety-Eight*, 727–8. On the tendency of Democrats to nominate "aristocratic" candidates, see also *WST*, Nov. 28, 1886.
82. *WDT*, Dec. 2, 5, 6, 8, 10, 1879, Dec. 11, 1882. See also Dec. 7, 13, 14, 16, 21, 1882.
83. *WDT*, Dec. 3, 1883; *WST*, Dec. 13, 1885; *WT*, Dec. 11, 1889; *First Annual Report of the Trustees of the Father Mathew M.B.T.A. Society for the Year 1890* (Worcester, 1891); *WT*, Dec. 3, 1886, June 26, 1895. Industrialist Philip L. Moen gave $5 to the building fund, liquor dealer George Hewitt gave $10 and Bowler Bros. Brewery gave $15.
84. *WT*, Dec. 14, 1886; *WDT*, Dec. 4, 1886; *WS*, July 4, 1886; *Worcester Veckoblad*, Sept. 9, 16, 1887. The Worcester Temperance Federation included the Swedish temperance societies but not the Irish-Catholic groups; *Worcester Temperance Federation* (Worcester, c. 1900), Temperance Society Pamphlets, WHM.
85. *Worcester Veckoblad*, Oct. 7, 1887; *WDT*, June 25, 1886. See also *LN*, Apr. 19, 1918.
86. Esther M. Wahlstrom, "A History of the Swedish People of Worcester, Massachusetts" (M.A. thesis, Clark Univ., 1947), 221–2; *WDT*, Dec. 20–2, 27, 29, 1880; *Worcester Veckoblad*, Mar. 25, 1887.
87. *Skandinavia*, May 12, 19, 26, June 2, 1892; *WT*, May 9, 16, 18, 1892; William Edward Zeuch, "An Investigation of the Metal Trades Strike of 1915" (M.A. thesis, Clark Univ., 1916), 17–18; *Illustrated History of the Central Labor Union; LN*, Sept. 2, 1911.
88. See Chapter 1, this volume, on elite dominance of local politics. For a discussion of "worker politicians" elsewhere, see Alan Dawley, *Class and Community: The Industrial Revolution in Lynn* (Cambridge, Mass.,

1976), 194–219; Daniel Walkowitz, *Worker City, Company Town* (Urbana, Ill., 1978), 253–7. This is not to argue a direct cause and effect between a strong saloon culture and a weak labor movement. Cities like New York and Milwaukee, for example, combined vibrant saloons with active trade unions. Even in those cities, however, it seems likely that conflict over the saloon weakened the working class politically and economically. In industrial communities generally but in Worcester particularly – with its large Swedish pietist population – the drink question subverted working-class political, economic, and cultural solidarity.

5. The struggle over recreational space

1. Downing, quoted in Jon Alvah Peterson, "The Origins of the Comprehensive City Planning Ideal in the United States, 1840–1911" (Ph.D. thesis, Harvard Univ., 1967), 76. Frederick Law Olmsted, Jr., and Theodora Kimball, eds., *Frederick Law Olmsted: Landscape Architect, 1822–1903*, 2 vols. (New York, 1928), 2:171; also quoted in John F. Kasson, *Amusing the Million* (New York, 1978), 15.
2. Lawrence A. Finfer, "Leisure as Social Work in the Urban Community: The Progressive Recreation Movement, 1890–1920" (Ph.D. thesis, Michigan State Univ., 1974), 143–4. For even more sweeping indictments, see Joel Spring, "Mass Culture and School Sports," *History of Education Quarterly* 14 (Winter 1974):483; Cary Goodman, *Choosing Sides: Playground and Street Life on the Lower East Side* (New York, 1979). For discussions of parks framed in terms of social control, see Paul Boyer, *Urban Masses and Moral Order in America, 1820–1920* (Cambridge, Mass., 1978), 238, 356–7; Galen Cranz, "Changing Roles of Urban Parks: From Pleasure Garden to Open Space," *Landscape* 22 (Summer 1978):9. On the use of social-control theory by historians, see William A. Muraskin, "The Social-Control Theory in American History: A Critique," *Journal of Social History* 9 (Summer 1976):559–80; Gareth Stedman Jones, "Class Expression Versus Social Control? A Critique of Recent Trends in the Social History of 'Leisure,'" *History Workshop*, no. 4 (Autumn 1977):163–70.
3. Commission on Shade Trees and Public Grounds, Minutes, Jan. 11, 1870, Parks Commission MSS, Green Hill Park, Worcester; hereafter cited as PC Minutes. Worcester Commission on Shade Trees and Public Grounds, *Annual Report for the Year Ending November 30, 1896* (Worcester, 1897), 5; The variously titled annual reports of the Parks Commission are hereafter cited as *Park Report*. *Park Report, 1897*, 3–5; unidentified clipping, Dec. 15, 1896, Clipping File, WHM; Waldo Lincoln, *History of the Lincoln Family* (Worcester, 1923).
4. Olmsted, quoted in Geoffrey Blodgett, "Frederick Law Olmsted: Landscape Architecture as Conservative Reform," *Journal of American*

History 62 (Mar. 1976):872, 877, 878, and Roy Lubove, "Social History and the History of Landscape Architecture," *Journal of Social History* 8 (Winter 1975):274. Whether Olmsted was a "conservative" or a "democratic" thinker remains a subject of debate. Compare, for example, the essays by Geoffrey Blodgett and Albert Fein in Bruce Kelly, Gail Travis Guillet, and Mary Ellen W. Hern, eds., *Art of the Olmsted Landscape* (New York, 1981). On Olmsted, see Laura Wood Roper, *FLO: A Biography of Frederick Law Olmsted* (Baltimore, 1973); Albert Fein, *Frederick Law Olmsted and the American Environmental Tradition* (New York, 1972); S. B. Sutton, ed., *Civilizing American Cities: A Selection of Frederick Law Olmsted's Writings on City Landscapes* (Cambridge, Mass., 1971).

5. *WEG*, Sept. 15, 1870; *Park Report, 1884*, 189–90. On the state of Worcester's parks before Lincoln, see *Park Reports, 1867–70;* Walter C. Wilson, "A Financial History of Worcester, Mass., 1772–1899" (Ph.D. thesis, Clark Univ., 1939), 233–5; Zelotes W. Coombs, "Elm Park" and "More about Elm Park," *This Week in Worcester,* Apr. 10, 17, 1937 (a weekly newspaper, copies available at Worcester Public Library); John F. Adamonis, "The Historical Development of Worcester Parks" (paper, Apr. 1974, copy available at Worcester Office of Planning and Community Development).
6. See *Park Reports, 1870–85;* James Draper, "The Parks and Playgrounds of Worcester," *Worcester Magazine* 1 (Apr. 1901):239.
7. PC Minutes, Dec. 30, 1874, Jan. 23, 1878; *Park Report, 1873,* 12–13. Edwin Theodore Weiss, Jr., "Patterns and Processes of High Value Residential Districts: The Case of Worcester, 1713–1970" (Ph.D. thesis, Clark Univ., 1973), details the changing social geography of Worcester's elite residences.
8. Quoted in Blodgett, "Frederick Law Olmsted," 881. On Olmsted's hostility to active recreation in his scenic parks, see also Steve Hardy, "'Parks for the People': Transforming the Concept of Parks in Boston, 1870–1915" (paper presented at the Annual Convention of the North American Society for Sport History, Banff, Alberta, Canada, May 26, 1980); Kasson, *Amusing the Million,* 12–15.
9. John Brinckerhoff Jackson, *American Space* (New York, 1972), 214–15. See also Joseph Kett, *Rites of Passage: Adolescence in America, 1790 to the Present* (New York, 1977), 227.
10. *Park Report, 1876,* 9–10; *Park Report, 1878,* 19; *Park Report, 1880,* 10; *WS,* Apr. 19, 1885.
11. *Park Report, 1884,* 209–14. See also *Boston Sunday Herald,* June 29, 1884; *WS,* July 12, 1884. The movement for Newton Hill had begun around 1872 and early opposition appears to have centered in the working-class wards. *WDP,* Dec. 10, 1873; *Park Report, 1872,* 6; *Park Report, 1873,* 15–16; *Park Report, 1876,* 24.
12. Robert A. Roberge, "The Three-Decker: Structural Correlate of Worcester's Industrial Revolution" (M.A. thesis, Clark Univ., 1965),

19–21. On Worcester street railways, see Philip Becker, "History of the Streetcar in Worcester, Mass." (paper, copy available at AAS); Helen H. Balk, "The Expansion of Worcester and Its Effect on the Surrounding Towns" (Ph.D. thesis, Clark Univ., 1944), 75–81.

13. *Annual Report of the City Marshal, 1882* (Worcester, 1883), 427; *WDT*, July 5, 1887, see also May 5, 1883. Paul Faler describes a similar process of "enclosure" of recreational space in early nineteenth century Lynn, Mass., in "Cultural Aspects of the Industrial Revolution: Lynn, Massachusetts Shoemakers and Industrial Morality, 1826–1860," *Labor History* 15 (Summer 1974):384.
14. *WST*, July 7, 1889.
15. *WDT*, Jan. 25, June 23, Jan. 12, 6, 1885. See also *WDT* editorials of Feb. 17, Mar. 25, Apr. 30, and May 25, 1885. For a similar French-Canadian complaint, see *Le Travailleur*, Oct. 24, 1882.
16. *WES*, Aug. 5, 7, 1879. See also June 25, July 25, Aug. 1, 14, 1879; *WDT*, Mar. 18, 1881.
17. George O'Flynn, "Richard O'Flynn – A Founder," *Publications, Worcester Historical Society*, n.s. 2 (Apr. 1936):55; Petition of Richard O'Flynn et al., Aug. 10, 1882, Board of Aldermen Petitions, Board of Aldermen MSS, Worcester City Hall; hereafter cited as Board of Ald. Petitions.
18. I identified the occupations of petitioners in the *Worcester Directory*.
19. *WDT*, Dec. 3, 1883. On tension between O'Flynn and Mellen, see Richard O'Flynn MSS, HCC, especially Folio 1, 211, where O'Flynn observes: "Mellen's character is well known to the unfortunate who *trust* him for *large* or small accounts." For the second petition drive led by O'Flynn, see Petitions of Walsh et al., O'Flynn et al., Duggan et al., and Creamer et al., June 23, 1884, Board of Ald. Petitions. The signers of these petitions were also overwhelmingly Irish and working class, based on listings checked in the *Worcester Directory*.
20. On Thayer, see unidentified clipping, Dec. 19, 1916, Clipping File, WHM; *WDT*, July 7, 1889 and Chapter 4, this volume. On Athy, see Franklin P. Rice, ed., *The Worcester of Eighteen Hundred and Ninety-Eight* (Worcester, 1899), 549–51, and Vincent E. Powers, "'Invisible Immigrants': The Pre-Famine Irish Community in Worcester, Massachusetts, From 1826–1860" (Ph.D. thesis, Clark Univ., 1977), 437–40.
21. "Report of Finance Committee," Dec. 17, 1883, and "Common Council Records," June 16, 18, 1884, both in Board of Aldermen MSS; *WDT*, July 1, 1884; *Boston Sunday Herald*, June 22, 1884. See similar analyses in *WS*, June 28, 1884; *Boston Sunday Herald*, June 29, 1884.
22. *WST*, Dec. 28, 1884.
23. *Boston Sunday Herald*, June 22, 1884.
24. Interestingly, both men were Democrats, as was Edward Winslow Lincoln. Davis and Lincoln, however, appear to have been part of the "aristocratic" faction of the party, which backed "Citizens" candidates for local office. (Their fathers had been law partners.) Bigelow, howev-

er, belonged to the pro-labor faction of the party. On local politics, see Chapter 4, this volume.

25. *Park Report, 1884,* 208; *Park Report, 1879,* 23. See Peterson, "Origins of the Comprehensive City Planning Ideal," 102–3, on parks as part of intercity competition.
26. Gilman Bigelow Howe, *Genealogy of the Bigelow Family* (Worcester, 1890), 412–13; *WEP,* Nov. 10, 1935; "Horace H. Bigelow," *Worcester Magazine* 14 (Sept. 1911):591; *WDT,* Sept. 4, 6, 10, 1879, Apr. 11, 1882; *WEG,* May 6, 1875, June 1, 1907. Bigelow's efforts to cultivate a mass audience for his amusement enterprises and his "populist" views may have also played a role in his gift. See Chapter 7, this volume.
27. *Park Report, 1879,* 22–3. On the rise of land values in other cities, see Peterson, "Origins of the Comprehensive City Planning Ideal," 103–5. See F. W. Beers, *Atlas of the City of Worcester* (New York, 1870), 11, and *Worcester House Directories* for Lincoln family holdings. (Timothy J. Meagher suggested this point to me.)
28. Unidentified clipping, July 28, 1901, Clipping File, WHM; *WT,* Nov. 16, 1886.
29. For continuing East Side pressure, see *WDT,* Mar. 31, Apr. 30, May 25, June 23, 30, July 13, 1885, May 1, 5, 7, June 8, 12, July 19, Nov. 30, 1886. On emergence of system-wide park planning: Peterson, "Origins of the Comprehensive City Planning Idea," 101; Boyer, *Urban Masses and Moral Order,* 236.
30. *WEG,* Sept. 25, 1886; *Park Report, 1886,* 24. Of course, working-class residents also argued for the health benefits of parks. See, for example, *WDT,* Jan. 6, 1885.
31. David Montgomery, "Trade Union Practice and Syndicalist Theory" (paper, 1969, copy in author's possession). J. F. Roche writes that the two East Side sites were "well adapted for playgrounds" and "bought primarily for playgrounds" in "Historical Sketch of the Parks and Playgrounds of Worcester" (M.A. thesis, Clark Univ., 1910), 12, 13.
32. Roche, "Historical Sketch of the Parks and Playgrounds," 9–30.
33. *WT,* June 15, 1899, July 12, 1899; unidentified clipping, Sept. 1904; *WEG,* undated clippings, Sept. 1904; *WT,* undated clippings, Sept. and Oct. 1904, 1905; *WT,* Dec. 19, 1904; all in Parks Commission Scrapbooks, Worcester City Hall; hereafter cited as PC Scrapbooks. Petition of R. H. Mooney et al., for a park in Quinsigamond Village, Sept. 12, 1898, Board of Ald. Petitions.
34. Petition of John G. Hagberg et al., July 1, 1901, Board of Ald. Petitions. See also *WT,* Dec. 24, 1901.
35. *LN,* June 22, 1907. See also unidentified clipping (1897) in PC Scrapbooks; *WT,* Dec. 8, 1894.
36. *WS,* undated clipping (probably 1897), unidentified clipping (1897), both in PC Scrapbooks.
37. *Park Report, 1904,* 14–15. See also *Park Report, 1908,* 1044.

38. "Our Common," *Light* 4 (Nov. 7, 1891):6; *WT*, July 16, 1895; *WEG*, Jan. 13, 1908; *WST*, July 3, 1910; *Park Report, 1894*, 5; *Park Report, 1914*, 835; *Park Report, 1902*, 7; *WST*, Aug. 5, 1893 (this last reference was found in the materials developed by CSP-AC); G. F. Hoar to City Council, June 22, 1887, Board of Ald. Petitions; *WDT*, July 5, 1887. See also *WT*, July 4, 1893; *WEG*, Mar. 26, 1910.
39. Olmsted, Jr., and Kimball, *Frederick Law Olmsted*, 2:171; Kasson, *Amusing the Million*, 15; *WDT*, June 22, 1880, May 13, 1886, July 2, 1887.
40. *WT*, undated clipping (c. 1947) on "Lake Quinsigamond's Great Days," Scrapbook on Lake, WHM; *WT*, Apr. 30, 1888, May 6, 1889. See also controversy about liquor at the lake in 1877, *WEG*, Apr. 30, May 1, 1877.
41. Unidentified clipping, Aug. 12, 1898, PC Scrapbooks; *WT*, Apr. 11, 1901. See also *WT*, May 2, 1901.
42. *WES*, Aug. 1, 1879; *LN*, July 8, 1916. On the same problem in other cities, see Edward Baker, "Some Abuses of Public Parks," *Sixth Report of the American Park and Outdoor Art Association* (Boston, 1902), 25; *WT*, July 1, 1893; Boyer, *Urban Masses and Moral Order*, 207.
43. PC Minutes, May 5, 1913; *Park Report, 1913*, 881; interview with Louis Lomatire, Worcester Bicentennial Oral History Project, Worcester, 1976 (typescript in possession of author). On Italian use of East Park, see also *Park Report, 1913*, 868; PC Minutes, May 5, 1913; *Park Report, 1916*, 921; PC Minutes, May 14, 1917; "Cosmopolitan Worcester," *Worcester Magazine* 18 (Aug. 1915):180.
44. *Park Report, 1914*, 829; *WT*, June 12, 1910. For comments on conflicts over park design and use in other cities, see Robert D. Lusiak, "From the Grand Plaza to the Electric City: A Review of the Planning Heritage of Buffalo, N.Y., 1804–1920" (M.S. thesis, State Univ. of New York at Buffalo, 1972), 18–35. Kasson, *Amusing the Million*, 11–17; Hardy, "'Parks for the People'"; Irving Howe, *World of Our Fathers* (New York, 1976), 212.
45. Henry Seidel Canby, *The Age of Confidence: Life in the Nineties* (New York, 1934), 28; Harold Frederic, *The Damnation of Theron Ware*, ed. Everett Carter (1896; rpt. Cambridge, Mass., 1960), 242, 244, 246.
46. "Editorial," *Light* 1 (July 19, 1890):3. On the growth of active sports and recreation in the 1890s, see John Higham, "The Reorientation of American Culture in the 1890's," in John Higham, *Writing American History: Essays on Modern Scholarship* (Bloomington, Ind., 1970), 78, 80; Foster Rhea Dulles, *America Leans to Play: A History of Popular Recreation*, 1607–1940 (1940; rpt. Gloucester, Mass., 1963), 198–9. On the midcentury roots of this change in attitude, see Daniel T. Rodgers, *The Work Ethic in Industrial America, 1850–1920* (Chicago, 1978), 102; Edward E. Hale, *Public Amusement for Poor and Rich* (Boston, 1857).
47. R. M. Washburn, *Smith's Barn: "A Child's History" of the West Side Worcester, 1880–1923* (Worcester, 1923), 33–4, 40–1; George H.

Haynes, *The Life of Charles B. Washburn* (Boston, 1931), 228; Charles A. Nutt, *History of Worcester and Its People,* 4 vols. (New York, 1919), 3:62–4. An important recent account of the shift in the leisure habits of the rich is Lewis A. Erenberg, *Steppin' Out: New York Nightlife and the Transformation of American Culture* (Westport, Conn., 1981).

48. Washburn, *Smith's Barn,* 88–96; *WEG,* Apr. 6, 1945, Dec. 8, 1954; Nutt, *History of Worcester,* 3:283–6. On Ichabod Washburn, see Chapters 2 and 4, this volume.

49. *WT,* Apr. 26, 1916. See also *WT,* Mar. 27, Apr. 20, 1916. On the commission Smith played an important role in fighting for Sunday baseball and was known as the "father of the Public Golf Links." The new name of the commission also reflected the combination of the Playground Commission and the Parks Commission.

50. Nutt, *History of Worcester,* 3:285; Higham, "Reorientation of American Culture," 78; Jean-Christophe Agnew, "The Struggle for Existence" (Lecture, Yale University, Oct. 13, 1980, copy in author's possession); Rodgers, *Work Ethic in Industrial America,* 109. See also James Gilbert, *Work Without Salvation* (Baltimore, 1977), 68.

51. For a Worcester reformer on the uses of leisure, see U. Waldo Cutler, "City and Citizen: Studies in Community Organization as Illustrated in a Typical American City" (typescript of lectures, c. 1917, available at WHM). The growing enthusiasm for these reform schemes in Worcester can be traced in the Board of Trade's *Worcester Magazine,* 1901–15. On the Vrooman incident, see Chapter 4, this volume.

52. Dorothy Ross, *G. Stanley Hall: The Psychologist as Prophet* (Chicago, 1972), 300. See also Dominick J. Cavallo, "The Child in American Reform: A Psychohistory of the Movement to Organize Children's Play, 1880–1930" (Ph.D. thesis, State Univ. of New York at Stony Brook, 1976), 179–97; Dominick J. Cavallo, "Social Reform and the Movement to Organize Children's Play During the Progressive Era," *History of Childhood Quarterly* 5 (Spring 1976):509–22 (Cavallo's work is now available in book form: *Muscles and Morals: Organized Playgrounds and Urban Reform, 1880–1920* [Philadelphia, 1981]); Bernard Mergen, "The Discovery of Children's Play," *American Quarterly* 27 (Oct. 1975):399–420; Kett, *Rites of Passage,* 217–21.

53. Finfer, in "Leisure as Social Work in the Urban Community," examines the playground movement from the perspective of its social-control intentions. Cavallo, in "Child in American Reform," focuses more on its personality models. Richard Knapp offers an institutional history of the Playground Association in "Play for America: The National Recreation Association, 1906–1950" (Ph.D. thesis, Duke Univ., 1971). A good recent overview is Boyer, *Urban Masses and Moral Order,* 242–51. Local studies include Goodman, *Choosing Sides;* Benjamin McArthur, "The Chicago Playground Movement: A Neglected Feature of Social Justice," *Social Service Review* 49 (Sept. 1975):376–95; Richard

Knapp, "Parks and Politics: The Rise of Municipal Responsibility for Playgrounds in New York City, 1887–1905" (M.A. thesis, Duke Univ., 1968); Gerald Marsden, "Philanthropy and the Boston Playground Movement, 1885–1907," *Social Service Review* 35 (Mar. 1961):48–58. Clarence Rainwater's *The Play Movement in the United States: The Study of Community Recreation* (Chicago, 1922) is an excellent overview by a partisan of the play movement.

54. Robert Sklar, *Movie-Made America: A Social History of American Movies* (New York, 1975), 124.
55. *WT*, June 22, 29, 1910; *WST*, July 12, 1908. Lithuanians did acquire a park in 1923. Elaine M. Kokernak, "The Lithuanian Immigrant in Worcester" (Sufficiency Paper, Worcester Polytechnic Institute, May 1980).
56. *Park Report, 1907*, 3; "An Interpreter of Nature," *Light* 2 (Sept. 13, 1890):6. The wealth of a fourth, long-term parks commissioner, Stephen Salisbury, was also in real estate, although he was also closely connected to the city's manufacturing families.
57. This is based on a collective biography of the city's parks commissioners developed from information in Nutt, *History of Worcester;* Rice, *Worcester of Eighteen Hundred and Ninety-Eight;* and the *Worcester Directory.*
58. "Inaugural Address of Mayor James Logan," Jan. 6, 1908, in *Worcester City Documents, 1907* (Worcester, 1908), 17–18; *WEP*, Dec. 9, 1908. The law required one playground for the first 10,000 inhabitants and one for each additional 20,000; Everett B. Mero, "Massachusetts Adopts Playground Law," *Playground* 2 (Dec. 1908):17–21; Everett B. Mero, "Playgrounds in Massachusetts," *Playground* 3 (Mar. 1909):19–22.
59. *Park Report, 1905*, 13; *Park Report, 1898*, 17; *Park Report, 1909*, 611. See further on equipment in *Park Report, 1903*, 12; *Park Report, 1899*, 17; *Park Report, 1908*, 1038.
60. *Park Report, 1903*, 7; *Park Report, 1911*, 571; Henry S. Curtis, quoted in Jean-Christophe Agnew, "American Intellectuals and the Drama of Social Control, 1870–1915" (paper presented at Mid-Atlantic Radical Historians Organization Conference, New York, N.Y., Apr. 1977).
61. *Park Report, 1907*, 6; John J. McCoy, *The Playground Movement* (New York, n.d., but probably 1911), 10–11. See also Board of Trade, Minutes, Oct. 10, 14, 1909, Feb. 10, 1910 (available at Worcester Chamber of Commerce); William Francis Hyde, "Who Shall Have Our Jacks and Jills – Satan or Society?" *Worcester Magazine* 12 (Aug. 1909):269–71.
62. The list of Playground Association directors is from the Parks Commission MSS. The biographical profile is based on Nutt, *History of Worcester*, and the *Worcester Directory.* See also Washburn, *Smith's Barn*, 95.
63. "Report of George Booth for 1910" (typescript in Parks Commission MSS); *WT*, May 20, 21, 23, 26–8, 30, 31, June 1–5, 8, 10–12, 14, 15, 22, 23, 30, 1910. In 1898 Curtis went from Clark University to the New

York schools, where he led that city's nascent playground movement. In 1906 he helped found the Playground Association of America and became its first secretary; Knapp, "Parks and Politics," 144–5.

64. W. F. Hyde, "Report on Playgrounds, 1910," May 8, 1911; Emmett Angell, "Report on Playgrounds, 1910," Dec. 4, 1910; both are letters to George F. Booth in Parks Commission MSS.
65. *WEG*, Feb. 15, 1913; *WT*, July 28, 1912; *WEG*, Jan. [?] 1914, in PC Scrapbooks.
66. Playground Association of America, Leaflet No. 2, Oct. 11, 1909, in Playground Association of America, *Miscellaneous Publications*, 1907–9, Gund Library, Harvard University; "Third Inaugural Address of Mayor James Logan," Jan. 1910, in *Worcester City Documents, 1909* (Worcester, 1910), 46.
67. McCoy, *Playground Movement*, 8; Ellen Murphy, "Report on Sewing," Parks Commission MSS; *WT*, Oct. 10, 1910.
68. Ada S. Glickman, "The Delinquent Girl in Worcester" (M.A. thesis, Clark Univ., 1932), 13–26; *WT*, Oct. 10, 1910; McCoy, *Playground Movement*, 7. See also Emmett Angell, *Play* (Boston, 1910), 26. On the assimilationist strand in the playground movement, see David Glassberg, "Restoring a 'Forgotten Childhood': American Play and the Progressive Era's Elizabethan Past," *American Quarterly* 32 (Fall 1980):359–61.
69. "Playground Census" (typed sheets in Parks Commission MSS). Since there is no way to know how the Playground Association determined ethnicity, it is possible that these figures may overstate the percentage of foreign-stock children using the playgrounds. For example, third-generation children may have been counted as foreign stock. Nevertheless, the playgrounds still received heavy immigrant use.
70. Interestingly, the English and the English Canadians – the largest ethnic groups to be underrepresented at playgrounds – were also the groups most likely to be undercounted (i.e., counted as "American") by the Playground Census. The overall patterns may also have been distorted because of the differences in the age structures of the different ethnic communities, but there is no systematic evidence on this point.
71. The names of the playground supervisors (and some background information) were found in the Parks Commission MSS.
72. Cavallo, "Child in American Reform," 135; Paul W. Shankweiler, "A Sociological Study of the Child Welfare Program of Worcester, Massachusetts" (Ph.D. thesis, Univ. of North Carolina, 1934), 555–6. Ultimately some parks and playgrounds became crime centers rather than crime preventers. See Jane Jacobs, *The Death and Life of Great American Cities* (New York, 1961), 89–111.
73. Mergen, "Discovery of Children's Play," 416.
74. Although the articles were politically motivated by the *Telegram*'s op-

position to the playgrounds, the comments seem authentic; *WST*, Aug. 4, 1912.

75. Quoted in *Park Report, 1890*, 40.

6. The struggle over the Fourth

1. "The Vacant Fourth," *Survey* 22 (July 3, 1909):482.
2. *WEG*, July 8, 1868, July 6, 1869, July 3, 1876; *WDT*, July 1, 1880, July 2, 1887; Board of Aldermen Minutes, June 23, 1897, Board of Aldermen MSS, Worcester City Hall; *WT*, July 3, 1893, July 5, 1897; *WDT*, July 5, 1890; *WT*, July 3, 4, 1892. See also *WDT*, July 5, 1887; *WT*, July 4, 1895.
3. *WDP*, July 5, 1875; *WST*, July 4, 1886; "The Day We Celebrate," *Light* 3 (July 4, 1891):431. See also *WT*, July 9, 10, 1890.
4. Julia Ward Howe, "How the Fourth of July Should Be Celebrated," *Forum* 15 (July 1893):572.
5. *WEG*, July 3, 1876; *WT*, July 5, 1899; *WT*, July 4, 1901; "What People Might Think," *Worcester Magazine* 5 (Aug. 1902):79; *WT*, July 4, 1903.
6. *WST*, July 5, 1903.
7. Ibid. For less sensational coverage, see *WEP*, July 6, 1903.
8. Jesse May Thornton, "Character, Composition, and Distribution of the Southeastern Europeans in Worcester" (M.A. thesis, Clark Univ., 1934), 30–1.
9. "What People Might Think," *Worcester Magazine* 6 (Aug. 1903):70; *WEP*, July 5, 1902; *WT*, July 4, 1907. For similar complaints nationally, see Mrs. Isaac L. Rice, "Our Barbarous Fourth," *Century Magazine* (June 1908), as reprinted in Robert H. Schauffler, ed., *Independence Day* (New York, 1934), 267.
10. "The Spectator," *Outlook* 77 (July 9, 1904):587.
11. "The Week," *Outlook* 86 (June 22, 1907):354; "Prevention of Our Annual Holocaust," *Independent* 55 (Nov. 26, 1903):2821–2; Raymond W. Smilor, "Creating a National Festival: The Campaign for a Safe and Sane Fourth, 1903–1916," *Journal of American Culture* 2 (Winter 1980):612, 614.
12. For this view, see Smilor, "Creating a National Festival," 611–22. For a different interpretation, see William H. Cohn, "A National Celebration: The Fourth of July in American History," *Cultures* 3 (1976):141–56, and William H. Cohn, "Popular Culture and Social History," *Journal of Popular Culture* 11 (Summer 1977):167–79.
13. Minutes, Apr. 23, 1904, Scrapbook, Twentieth Century Club of Worcester, Worcester Public Library; *WST*, Apr. 24, 1904; *WT*, July 4, 1904; "As It Should Be," *Worcester Magazine* 7 (Aug. 1904):150.
14. *WT*, July 5, 1905, July 4, 5, 1906, July 4, 1908, July 6, 1909.
15. The number of injuries dropped about 90% between 1909 and 1910; *WT*, July 5, 1910. The figures on injuries come from annual newspaper reports and thus are probably incomplete.

16. "The Vacant Fourth," 482; "Celebrating Liberty," *Outlook* 92 (June 5, 1909):312; David Glassberg, "Restoring a 'Forgotten Childhood': American Play and the Progressive Era's Elizabethan Past," *American Quarterly* 32 (Fall 1980):359. See also William Orr, "An American Holiday," *Atlantic Monthly* 103 (June 1909):782–9; August H. Brunner, "Suggestions for Celebrating Independence Day," *Playground* 4 (Apr. 1910):1–20.
17. Luther H. Gulick, "The New and More Glorious Fourth," *World's Work* 18 (July 1909):11784–7.
18. Lee F. Hammer, *How the "Fourth" Was Celebrated in 1911* (New York, 1911); *WT,* Apr. 4, June 11, 13, 14, 16, 29, July 5, 9, 1911; *WEG,* Apr. 4, July 1, 3, 1911; *WEP,* July 1, 1911. See also *WT,* July 4, 5, 1912; "The Practicability of an Experiment in Patriotism," *Worcester Magazine* 15 (Aug. 1912):222–4; *WT,* July 4, 5, 1913; "The Passing of Gunpowder and Rowdyism," *Worcester Magazine* 16 (Aug. 1913):251–2.
19. See *WT,* July 5, 1911, for list of committee members. I identified the occupations of the members in the *Worcester Directory.* On Tulloch, see *WEG,* June 20, 1938. On Stoddard, see Rae M. Spencer, *The Gift of Imaginative Leadership* (Worcester, 1972), 62.
20. *LN,* Apr. 1, 1911.
21. *WT,* July 4, 1914; *WST,* July 5, 1914, July 4, 1915; *WT,* July 5, 6, 1915. In 1915 *The Literary Digest* noted "a relapse from the Sane Fourth idea" in "A Fourth 'Sane and Nearly Safe,'" *Literary Digest* 51 (July 17, 1915):102.
22. "Americanization Day, A New Idea for July 4," *Survey* 34 (May 29, 1915):189; "Americanization Day," *Outlook* 110 (June 30, 1915):485; *WT,* July 6, 1915. On the national shift in the progressive movement, see John Higham, *Strangers in the Land: Patterns of American Nativism,* 2nd ed. (New York, 1970), 194–263.
23. *WT,* July 5, 1916; *WT,* July 2, 5, 1917; *WEG,* July 2, 5, 1917; "Ceremony of Citizenship," program, Pamphlet Collection, WHM.
24. *WT,* July 4, 5, 1916; *LN,* June 3, 1916. On Smith, see Chapter 5, this volume. *The Outlook* noted the participation of large "employers of emigrant labor" in the Americanization Day movement; "Americanization Day," 485.
25. *WT,* July 5, 1916. See also *Skandinavia,* July 5, 1916; *Norton Spirit,* July 1916 (from excerpts compiled by Kevin Hickey, CSP-AC). On the machinists' strike, see Chapter 1, this volume.
26. *LN,* June 3, July 8, 1916.
27. *LN,* May 3, June 28, July 5, 1917; *WT,* July 5, 1917; "Ceremony of Citizenship." The *Labor News* continued to charge the promoters of the Safe and Sane Fourth with a lack of patriotism and an excess of Anglophilia. See, for example, *LN,* Feb. 28, 1918. For the same paper's reluctant support of the war effort, see *LN,* March 1, 8, 22, April 5, 19, June 14, 1917.

28. *WT*, July 5, 1919; July 5, 1910; "The Practicability of an Experiment in Patriotism," 223–4; *WT*, July 5, 1913.
29. *WT*, July 5, 1919, *WST*, July 5, 1925. The number of fire alarms is based on annual newspaper reports.
30. On the size of the ethnic middle class in 1900, see Timothy J. Meagher, "'The Lord Is Not Dead': Cultural and Social Change Among the Irish in Worcester, Massachusetts" (Ph.D. thesis, Brown Univ., 1982), 161. On geographical dispersion, see Harold F. Creveling, "The Pattern of Cultural Groups in Worcester" (Ph.D. thesis, Clark Univ., 1951); William Harold Somers, "A Socio-Historical Study of the Jewish Community of Worcester, Massachusetts" (M.A. thesis, Clark Univ., 1933); Meagher, "'Lord Is Not Dead,'" 400–56; Vincent E. Powers, "The Irish in Worcester," in *Commemorating the 150th Anniversary of the Irish Community in Worcester* (Worcester, 1977).
31. See, for example, *WST*, July 5, 1908; *WEG*, July 1, 1911.
32. For participation of the ethnic middle class, see persons identified in *WT*, July 5, 1911, and masthead of form letter (dated June 21, 1917) from Harry Worcester Smith, Pamphlet Collection, WHM. On Mooney, see Charles A. Nutt, *History of Worcester and Its People*, 4 vols. (New York, 1919), 3:515–16 (emphasis added).
33. Meagher, "'Lord Is Not Dead,'" 573, 580–92, 652; "Editorial Comment," *Worcester Magazine* 12 (July 1909):249; *WT*, July 6, 1909, July 2, 1917. For the similar social composition of the K of C in Boston, see David Bixby, "The Knights of Columbus in Boston, 1892–1917" (Honors thesis, Harvard Univ., 1976).
34. *WT*, July 5, 1917.
35. Meagher, "'Lord Is Not Dead,'" 545–96.
36. S. N. Behrman, *The Worcester Account* (London, 1954), 144–53.
37. *WST*, July 4, 1915; *WT*, July 5, 1915, July 5, 1917; Nutt, *History of Worcester*, 2:451. For a fascinating exploration of class tensions within a Worcester ethnic community, see Somers, "A Socio-Historical Study of the Jewish Community."
38. Meagher, "'Lord Is Not Dead,'" 545–96.
39. *WT*, July 5, 1907; "Cosmopolitan Worcester," *Worcester Magazine* 18 (Aug. 1915):179–81; *WT*, July 2, 5, 1910. See also Leon T. Miscavage, "The Polish-American Experience in Worcester" (paper, 1976, available at WHM), which notes conflicts with the police (usually Irish) over Polish wedding celebrations.
40. Peter Roberts, *Anthracite Coal Communities* (New York, 1904), 55; also quoted in Herbert Gutman, "Work, Culture, and Society in Industrializing America, 1815–1919," *American Historical Review* 78 (June 1973):547–8; *WT*, July 5, 1915; quoted in Elaine M. Kokernak, "The Lithuanian Immigrant in Worcester" (Sufficiency Paper, Worcester Polytechnic Institute, May 1980), 17.

7. The commercialization of leisure

1. "The Practicability of an Experiment in Patriotism," *Worcester Magazine* 15 (Aug. 1912), 222–4; *WT*, July 5, 1912.
2. *WT*, July 4, 5, 1912, July 3, 1920.
3. *Mass Spy*, July 10, 1861, July 9, 1862; David E. Vincent, "Lake Quinsigamond: An Assessment of Past and Present Land Use" (M.A. thesis, Clark Univ., 1963), 14; unidentified clipping, Aug. 6, 1894, Clipping File, AAS; *WDP*, July 4, 1873; *WEG*, July 3, 6, 1875, July 3, 1876, May 4, 1878.
4. On Bigelow, see Charles A. Nutt, *History of Worcester and Its People*, 4 vols. (New York, 1919), 4:769–71; Franklin P. Rice, ed., *The Worcester of Eighteen Hundred and Ninety-Eight* (Worcester, 1899), 563–5; Gilman Bigelow Howe, *Genealogy of the Bigelow Family* (Worcester, 1890), 412–13; *WT*, July 4, 1911 (obituary); "Horace H. Bigelow," *Worcester Magazine* 14 (Sept. 1911):591; Patrick A. Dowd, "Horace H. Bigelow – A Great Personality of Old Worcester," *WST*, Feb. 3, 1935; "Horace H. Bigelow," *Light* 2 (Feb. 21, 1891):6–7; *WEP*, Nov. 10, 1935; Massachusetts volumes of R. G. Dun and Co. Collection, Baker Library, Harvard University Graduate School of Business Administration, 100:300, 450; hereafter cited as RGD.
5. *WST*, June 28, 1885; *WS*, July 6, 1885; *WDT*, June 24, 1885.
6. *WES*, Apr. 14, 1879.
7. *WDT*, Dec. 15, 1881, Apr. 11, 1882; Howe, *Genealogy of the Bigelow Family*, 413; *WS*, July 4, 1882; *WDT*, July 5, 1882; Letterhead stationery of J. F. Bigelow in James Drennan MSS, WHM.
8. *WDT*, Apr. 11, 1882; advertisement in *Worcester Directory, 1883* (Worcester, 1883), 670–1.
9. Vincent, "Lake Quinsigamond," ix; *A Day's Outing*, Summer 1887 (copy at AAS). On Quinsigamond Boat Club, see R. M. Washburn, *Smith's Barn: "A Child's History" of the West Side Worcester, 1880–1923* (Worcester, 1923), 86–8. On the Lakeside Boat Club, see unidentified clipping, c. 1895, Clipping File, AAS. On the Washington Social Club, see Chapter 3, this volume.
10. *WEG*, July 3, 1879; *WES*, July 5, 1879. The description of the crowd is based on my analysis of the occupations (identified in the *Worcester Directory*) and ethnic backgrounds of twenty-five accident victims and witnesses to an accident resulting from the overturning of a steamboat at the lake that day. The names were found in the newspapers and the James Drennan MSS.
11. *WS*, July 6, 1885; *WT*, July 5, 1890. See also *WST*, July 12, 1887.
12. *WT*, July 7, 1896; *WEG*, July 15, 1907. See also *WEG*, July 17, 20, 1907, and *WT*, Sept. 30, 1907 (for a defense). For discussions of the same problem in other years, see *WDT*, July 22, 23, 1879; Conrad Hobbs,

"The Ruin or the Redemption of Lake Quinsigamond," *Worcester Magazine* 16 (Feb. 1913):35–41; Fred Willis, "Worcester's Lake and Hills," *Worcester Magazine* 11 (Aug. 1908):192–3; "Editorial Comment," *Worcester Magazine* 11 (Aug. 1908):185; Chamber of Commerce Minutes, Feb. 10, June 9, July 14, 1910, available at Worcester Chamber of Commerce office.

13. *WEG*, Apr. 30, 1877.
14. *WEG*, May 1, 1877. On Sunday laws in Massachusetts, see Michael H. Bolotin, "The Lord's Day Act in the Commonwealth of Massachusetts: A Political History, 1629–1961" (M.A. thesis, Clark Univ., 1962).
15. Dowd, "Horace H. Bigelow"; unidentified clipping, Sept. 9, 1882, Clipping File, WHM. See also *WDT*, July 24, 31, Aug. 7, 14, 1882.
16. Only July Fourth outstripped Sundays as a summer business day for Bigelow's enterprises; see, for example, *WDT*, May 13, June 9, 1885, May 17, 1886; *WT*, May 2, 1887.
17. RGD, 100:300, 450; *WDT*, Dec. 2, 3, 6, 1879; *WT*, Nov. 27, 1886.
18. For a sense of changing attitudes toward Bigelow, see "Horace H. Bigelow," *Light*; "Horace H. Bigelow," *Worcester Magazine*. On changing elite attitudes toward active recreation, see Chapter 5, this volume.
19. U.S. Department of Commerce, *Historical Statistics of the United States*, 2 vols. (Washington, D.C., 1975), 1:164, 165, 168. Of course, there were wide variations in wages for blue-collar jobs. In 1907, for example, Worcester clothing workers had an average income of $362, boot and shoe workers earned $567, and workers in the machine-tool industry averaged $602; Walter S. Foley, "Heterogeneity of Population as Correlated with Diversity of Industries in Worcester and Other Massachusetts Cities" (M.A. thesis, Clark Univ., 1910), 11–12. For an excellent, recent discussion of working-class incomes in this period, see Peter R. Shergold, *Working-Class Life: The "American" Standard in Comparative Perspective, 1899–1913* (Pittsburgh, 1982).
20. Sebastian DeGrazia, *Of Time, Work and Leisure* (Garden City, N.Y., 1964), 419; Garth Jowett, *Film: The Democratic Art* (Boston, 1976), 18; *Worcester House Directory* (Worcester, 1920), 14. On hours, see also Joseph Zeisel, "The Workweek in American Industry, 1850–1976," in Eric Larrabbee and Rolf Meyersohn, eds., *Mass Leisure* (Glencoe, Ill., 1958), 145–53; *Historical Statistics of the United States*, 1:169–70.
21. *WT*, July 3, 5, 6, 1920.
22. *WT*, May 1, 8, 16, 22, July 5, 1905, July 4, 1906, July 5, 1918. John Kasson's provocative analysis of Coney Island in *Amusing the Million* (New York, 1978) has influenced my treatment of White City.
23. Irving Bernstein, *The Lean Years: A History of the American Worker 1920–1933* (1960; rpt. Baltimore, 1966), 63–5.
24. Robert Coit Chapin, *The Standard of Living Among Workingmen's Families in New York City* (New York, 1909), 210–13. (The expenditure average

was actually lower than $8.50, since this figure includes only families earning more than $600 per year.) See also Louise Boland More, *Wage-Earner's Budgets* (New York, 1907).

25. *WT*, July 5, 1894.
26. S. N. Behrman, *The Worcester Account* (London, 1954), 35–8. See also Chapter 6, this volume.
27. Kasson, *Amusing the Million*, 108. Intermarriage rates among Lithuanians in Worcester were quite low in the years 1910–15 but rose dramatically by the early 1930s; William Wolkovich-Valkavičius, "Lithuanians of Worcester, Massachusetts: A Socio-Historic Glimpse at Marriage Records" (paper, Boston College, 1978, copy available at WHM).
28. Property holdings calculated from *Worcester House Directory, 1900, 1918*, and U.S. Manuscript Census, Worcester, 1870. I computed the distance from home to saloon as a straight line rather than as actual walking distance.
29. *WT*, Dec. 14, 1909. In 1889 license fees for first-class common victuallers (the category of most saloonkeepers) went from $750 to $1,200 and the number of licenses awarded in this category dropped from forty to twenty-nine. By 1896 the fees had risen again to $1,500. As late as 1885 these licenses had cost only $300. See annual reports in newspapers and Minutes, Board of Aldermen, Worcester City Hall. For various charges and countercharges about the degree of brewery control of licenses, see *WT*, Mar. 16, 1901, Apr. 12, 1906, Dec. 9, 1908, Dec. 7, 11, 13, 1909, Apr. 19, 30, May 14, Dec. 12, 1910, Apr. 13, 14, 1911, Mar. 29, 1912, Dec. 4, 5, 1914; *WEP*, Dec. 11, 1907, Feb. 21, 1908; *WEG*, Dec. 11, 1907; *Catholic Messenger*, Dec. 4, 1908, Dec. 17, 1909; *WST*, Sept. 8, 1912.
30. "Second Inaugural Address of Mayor George M. Wright," Jan. 5, 1914, in *Worcester City Documents, 1913* (Worcester, 1914), 29.
31. *WEG*, Mar. 21, July 5, 1910; *WT*, Apr. 2, 3, 7, 14, May 10, 1910. On more rigorous police enforcement, see *WT*, May 2, 1910. A newly formed Liquor Dealers' Association also initiated self-policing of its members; *WT*, May 9, June 23, 1910.
32. *WEG*, Mar. 22, 1910; *WST*, Apr. 4, 1915; *LN*, Dec. 6, 1913; *WT*, Dec. 12, 1910. See also *WT*, June 12, 1910; *WST*, Apr. 4, Oct. 13, 1915.
33. *WT*, Mar. and Apr. 1918; Apr. 10, 12, 13, 1915, Mar. 28, 1916; *LN*, Sept. 6, 1914. Voting figures are from annual reports in *WT*.
34. *WT*, Dec. 11, 1895, Apr. 9, 1901.
35. Harry Gene Levine, "Notes on Work and Drink in Industrializing America" (paper presented at the National Institute on Alcohol Abuse and Alcoholism Research Conference on Alcohol Use and the Work Environment, Belmont, Md., Dec. 1978). *WT*, Feb. 18, 1914; Anti-Saloon League leaflet, Temperance Society Pamphlets, WHM. J. B. Moss, assistant manager of American Steel and Wire, belonged to the

Worcester Club; see *Worcester House Directory, 1920*, 354. For continuing opposition to specific licenses, see *WT*, May 19, 1910, Mar. 20, 29, 30, Apr. 4, 7, 12, 1912, Apr. 8, 1913.

36. *Catholic Messenger*, Nov. 26, Dec. 3, 10, 1909; Timothy J. Meagher, " 'The Lord Is Not Dead': Cultural and Social Change Among the Irish in Worcester, Massachusetts" (Ph.D. thesis, Brown Univ., 1982), 306–10.
37. *WST*, Sept. 8, 1912.
38. Roderick Duncan McKenzie, *The Neighborhood: A Study of Local Life in the City of Columbus, Ohio* (Chicago, 1923), 599–600; Lester P. White, "Elements Affecting Organized Labor in Its Relationship with the Worcester Branch National Metal Trades Association Since 1916" (M.A. thesis, Clark Univ., 1924), 16; *WST*, Apr. 4, 1915. Another important, related factor was the shifting structure of work. Many jobs that had particularly encouraged heavy drinking – strenuous outdoor labor, for example – were being replaced by semiskilled factory jobs.
39. *WST*, Apr. 4, 1915; John H. Meagher, "Why Worcester Should Vote for License," *Worcester Bulletin* 1 (Nov. 30, 1912):6; Jesse May Thornton, "Character, Composition, and Distribution of the Southeastern Europeans in Worcester" (M.A. thesis, Clark Univ., 1934), 44, 63; Harold F. Creveling, "The Pattern of Cultural Groups in Worcester" (Ph.D. thesis, Clark Univ., 1951), 108; Behrman, *Worcester Account*, 31. On the use of the saloon and drinking by "new" immigrants, see Peter Roberts, *Anthracite Coal Communities* (New York, 1904), 262, 269; Antonio Mangano, *Sons of Italy: A Social and Religious Study of the Italians in America* (New York, 1917), 108–9; Phyllis H. Williams, *South Italian Folkways in Europe and America* (New Haven, 1938), 117; Wolkovich-Valkavičius, "Lithuanians of Worcester," 20. Matt Babinski describes Worcester's 1930s East Side ethnic bars in *By Raz: 1937* (Worcester, 1978), 27–32.
40. This ethnic analysis is based on inference from the last names of saloonkeepers. About six of the saloonkeepers were from French-Canadian backgrounds. Most of the "new immigrant" saloonkeepers were Poles or Lithuanians (about seven total), two were Italian, and one was Jewish. In 1910 the Polish Naturalization and Registration Club complained that the only Polish license applicant had been rejected; *WT*, Apr. 18, 1910. On the problem of noncitizens getting liquor licenses, see interview with Isabel F. McGuire, Worcester Bicentennial Oral History Project, 1976 (typescript of interview in author's possession). In 1910, 58% of the license applicants were from Irish backgrounds; Meagher, " 'Lord Is Not Dead,' " 290.
41. G. Stanley Hall, *Morale: The Supreme Standard of Life and Conduct* (New York, 1920), 224–5, 228. The book was originally presented in weekly lectures at Clark University. (Reference courtesy of Jean-Christophe Agnew.) On Hall's political views after World War I, see Dorothy

Ross, *G. Stanley Hall: The Psychologist as Prophet* (Chicago, 1972), 421, 430.

8. From rum shop to Rialto

1. Vachel Lindsay, *The Art of the Moving Picture,* rev. ed. (1922; rpt. New York, 1970), 235, 242; Lucy France Pierce, "The Nickelodeon," *World Today* 15 (Oct. 1908):1052; *WT,* Oct. 26, 1915. For other discussions of the relation of the saloon and the movie theater, see Kathleen D. McCarthy, "Nickel Vice and Virtue: Movie Censorship in Chicago, 1907–1915," *Journal of Popular Film* 5, no. 1 (1976):37–55; William T. Foster, *Vaudeville and Motion Picture Shows: A Study of Theaters in Portland, Oregon* (Portland, Ore., 1914), 28–9; Charles Stelzle, "Movies Instead of Saloons," *Independent* 85 (Feb. 28, 1916):311; John Collier, "Cheap Amusements," *Charities and the Commons* 20 (Apr. 11, 1908):73–6; John J. Phelan, *Motion Pictures as a Phase of Commercialized Amusements in Toledo, Ohio* (Toledo, 1919), 22, 108–9; Barton W. Currie, "The Nickel Madness," *Harper's Weekly* 51 (Aug. 24, 1907):1245–6; Simon Patten, *Product and Climax* (New York, 1909), 45; Adele F. Woodward, "The Motion Picture as Saloon Substitute," in Raymond Calkins, ed., *Substitutes for the Saloon,* rev. ed. (Boston, 1919), 358–67.
2. Charles Stelzle, "How One Thousand Workingmen Spend Their Spare Time," *Outlook* 106 (Apr. 4, 1914):762; Garth Jowett, *Film: The Democratic Art* (Boston, 1976), 192.
3. *WST,* July 7, 1947; *Worcester Directory, 1907* (Worcester, 1907); *LN,* Sept. 22, 1906; *WEG,* Sept. 22, 1906. On the early development of movies in Worcester, see *WT,* Aug. 30, 31, 1897, Nov. 14, 1898; *WEG,* Aug.–Sept. 1898; Nov. 11, 1898; *Park Theatre Program,* Theater Pamphlet Collection, WHM. Showings of movies in these years can be traced in the advertisements in the local newspapers and in the records of the Worcester License Board, Worcester City Hall; hereafter cited as Lic. Bd.
4. *WEP,* Sept. 29, 1906; *WEG,* Apr. 4, 5, 1907; *WT,* Apr. 5, 1907; *WEP,* May 21, 1907; *WEG,* Apr. 8, May 11, 25, 18, 1907. For an excellent discussion of the relationship between early movies and vaudeville, see Robert C. Allen, "Vaudeville and Film, 1895–1915: A Study of Media Interaction" (Ph.D. thesis, Univ. of Iowa, 1977). On vaudeville in general, see John DiMeglio, *Vaudeville U.S.A.* (Bowling Green, Ohio, 1973); Albert McLean, *American Vaudeville as Ritual* (Lexington, Ky., 1965); Douglas Gilbert, *American Vaudeville: Its Life and Times* (New York, 1940); Gunther Barth, *City People: The Rise of Modern City Culture in Nineteenth-Century America* (New York, 1980), 192–228.
5. The Pastime charged five cents; the Bijou's pricing varied between a mix of five- and ten-cent charges (lower price during the day) and a flat five-cent charge; *WT,* Dec. 9, 1909; *WST,* Jan. 16, 1910; *LN,* Sept. 27, 1915. Since the cheap theaters did not regularly advertise, it is difficult

to follow their prices with precision. On the development of the nickelodeon, see Robert Sklar, *Movie-Made America: A Social History of American Movies* (New York, 1975), 14–19; Russell Merritt, "Nickelodeon Theaters, 1905–1914: Building an Audience for the Movies," in Tino Balio, ed., *The American Film Industry* (Madison, Wis., 1976), 59–79; Jowett, *Film*, 29–46; George Pratt, ed., *Spellbound in Darkness: A History of the Silent Film*, rev. ed. (Greenwich, Conn., 1973), 39–54; Daniel Joseph Czitrom, "Media and the American Mind: The Intellectual and Cultural Reception of Modern Communication" (Ph.D. thesis, Univ. of Wisconsin, 1980), 60–127; Robert C. Allen, "Motion Picture Exhibition in Manhattan 1906–1912: Beyond the Nickelodeon," *Cinema Journal* 17 (Spring 1979):2–15; Jeffrey Kmet, "Milwaukee's Nickelodeon Era: 1906–1915," and Douglas Gomery, "Movie Exhibition in Milwaukee, 1906–1947: A Short History," both in special issue of *Milwaukee History* 2 (Spring 1979):2–17. Gomery notes that Milwaukee's first nickelodeons, like Worcester's first movie houses, were located downtown.

6. *LN*, May 22, 1909; *WST*, Jan. 16, 1910. Information on proprietors is from *Worcester Directory, 1900–20*. The Pastime may have been originally known as the Star; *LN*, Mar. 13, 1909. Information on Graf is from *Worcester Directory* and on "Gaspard and Charlie" from James L. Gilrein, interview, Worcester, Mar. 1, 1978, and Lic. Bd., May 27, 1909.
7. Most of the data on numbers of seats was obtained from the *Worcester Directory*, but this listing is incomplete. The rest of the material is derived from newspaper reports and personal interviews. Thus, the figures here are only estimates, but they are probably quite close to the actual numbers.
8. Prentice G. Hoyt, "Conditions of Three of the Cheaper Theaters of Worcester," *Worcester Bulletin* 1 (Nov. 16, 1912):5; Michael Davis, *The Exploitation of Pleasure* (New York, 1911), 30–1; George Esdras Bevans, *How Workingmen Spend Their Spare Time* (New York, 1913); John Collier, "Moving Pictures: Their Function and Regulation," *Playground* 4 (Oct. 1910):232; Pierce, "The Nickelodeon," 1052; George E. Walsh, "Moving Picture Drama for the Multitude," *Independent* 64 (Feb. 6, 1908):306– 20; Jane E. Snow, "The Workingman's College," *Moving Picture World* 7 (Aug. 27, 1910):458; Collier, "Cheap Amusements," 75. Bevans did not even attempt to construct a random or representative sample of New York City workers; he took whatever questionnaires he could get filled out. However, there are probably not any egregious biases in the data, and it is the only information from this period giving such detailed data on the spare time of *any* workingmen.
9. Philip H. Cook, "History of the Drama in Worcester" (paper, 1947, copy available at AAS), 12; Charles A. Nutt, *History of Worcester and Its People*, 4 vols. (New York, 1919), 2:795; Elizabeth A. Johnson, *Worcester Illustrated, 1875–1885* (Worcester, 1978), 14–15. On Bristol's Dime Mu-

seum and other cheap amusements, see, for example, *WDT*, Dec. 13, 1883, Dec. 1, 17, 1884, Jan. 1, Feb. 21, June 17, 1885, Jan. 15, Apr. 29, June 25, 1886, June 24, 1889; *WST*, Dec. 21, 1884, Jan. 4, 1885, May 8, 1904; *Worcester Weekly Amusement Bulletin*, Jan.–May, Sept.–Oct. 1892 (copy available at WHM); Lic. Bd., 1902–10.

10. Cook, "History of the Drama in Worcester," 54. In the absence of regular advertisements and press coverage, these theaters are difficult to trace with precision, but see Lic. Bd., 1902–6, and *WST*, May 1, 8, 1904. Another factor in the shift from live entertainment to movies may have been an effort by theater managers to avoid problems with actors' unions and theatrical "trusts"; see *WT*, Dec. 13, 1904, Aug. 4, 6, 1906; *WEG*, Oct. 13, 1905.

11. *WST*, Aug. 8, 1912. According to a pamphlet published in 1927 by the Worcester Telegram and Gazette (*The Story of the Worcester Telegram and Gazette*), which was likely to exaggerate local prosperity, the average wage in Worcester was $650 in 1915, $1,080 in 1918, and $1,360 in 1927. The 1912 budget was for a family earning $896.15, an above average wage. The average recreational spending in a study of New York workers was about sixteen cents per week. For a family earning between $1,000 and $1,100 per year (the range of a skilled construction worker), the average recreational spending was about twenty-eight cents per week. On this basis, a family of five could go to a five-cent movie once each week. (The lowest priced seats at the Worcester Theatre, which presented live drama, were usually twenty-five cents.) See Robert Coit Chapin, *The Standard of Living Among Workingmen's Families in New York City* (New York, 1909), 210–13. See also National Industrial Conference Board, *The Cost of Living Among Wage Earners, Worcester, Mass., June, 1920* (New York, 1920), 8.

12. David Brody, *Steelworkers in America: The Nonunion Era* (1960; rpt. New York, 1969), 34–40, 279; Elizabeth Beardsley Butler, *Women and the Trades, Pittsburgh, 1907–1908* (1909; rpt. New York, 1969):333. See also Margaret F. Byington, *Homestead: the Households of a Mill Town* (1910; rpt. Pittsburgh, 1974), 111, and discussion of hours in Chapter 7, this volume. Gunnar Forslund recalls workers stopping at downtown movie theaters on their way home from work, but this was probably in the years around World War I and after; interview, Worcester, Mar. 29, 1978.

13. U.S. Bureau of the Census, *Thirteenth Census, 1910*, 11 vols. (Washington, D.C., 1913), 1:858–9; *WST*, Feb. 7, 1915; Rollin L. Hartt, *The People at Play* (1909; rpt. New York, 1975), 133. See also Frederick J. Haskin, "The Popular Nickelodeon," *Moving Picture World* 2 (Jan. 18, 1908):37.

14. Interview with Fred Fedeli, Shrewsbury, Mass., Feb. 23, 1978; Hoyt, "Condition of Three of the Cheaper Theaters," 5.

15. Thomas F. Power, comp., *Messages From Recent Pilgrims* (Worcester, 1921), 12.

16. Collier, "Cheap Amusements," 75; Haskin, "Popular Nickelodeon," 37; Jane Addams, *The Spirit of Youth and the City Streets* (New York, 1909), 91; John Collier, "The Motion Picture," in *Proceedings of the Child Conference for Research and Welfare,* 2 vols. (New York, 1910), 2:109; Davis, *Exploitation of Pleasure,* 29–35; Charles V. Tevis, "Censoring the Five-Cent Drama," *World Today,* 19 (Oct. 1910):1137.
17. Edward Chandler, "How Much Children Attend the Theater: The Quality of the Entertainment They Choose and Its Effect Upon Them," *Proceedings of the Child Conference,* 1:57; women quoted in Elizabeth Ewen, "City Lights: Immigrant Women and the Rise of the Movies," *Signs* 5, no. 3 (1980):58. On parent–child conflicts over movies, see also Herbert Blumer, *Movies and Conduct* (New York, 1933), 157–61.
18. Frederic C. Howe, "What to Do With the Motion-Picture Show: Shall It Be Censored?" *Outlook* 107 (June 20, 1914):413; Mary Heaton Vorse, "Some Picture Show Audiences," *Outlook* 98 (June 24, 1911):445; *WST,* Apr. 10, 1910; *LN,* Aug. 27, 1910.
19. *WEP,* Sept. 22, 25, 29, 1906. Russell Merritt finds that Boston movie houses also solicited female patronage; he sees this effort as part of a larger strategy to develop respectable, middle-class audiences; "Nickelodeon Theaters," 73–4.
20. U.S. Bureau of the Census, *Eleventh Census, 1890* (Washington, D.C., 1897), 2:742–3; *Thirteenth Census, 1910* (Washington, D.C., 1914), 4:194–207; Butler, *Women and the Trades,* 333. See also *LN,* July 18, 1908.
21. Joseph M. Patterson, "The Nickelodeon," *Moving Picture World* 2 (Jan. 4, 1908):21; this article originally appeared in *Saturday Evening Post* (Nov. 23, 1907):10–11, 38; Sklar, *Movie-Made America,* 16; "A Democratic Art," *Nation* 97 (Aug. 28, 1913):193. See similarly Allen, "Vaudeville and Film," 324.
22. Lewis Jacobs, *The Rise of the American Film: A Critical History* (1939; rpt. New York, 1968), 156. For an interesting discussion of the favorable depiction of immigrants in early films, see Thomas Cripps, "The Movie Jew as an Image of Assimilationism, 1903–1927," *Journal of Popular Film* 4, no. 3 (1975):193. For the debate over the influence of progressive reform on these early films, see Robert Sklar's review of Lary May's *Screening Out the Past: The Birth of Mass Culture and the Motion Picture Industry* (New York, 1980) in *American Historical Review* 86 (Oct. 1981):945, and May's response in the June 1982 issue of the same journal (pp. 913–14). The paper prints deposited at the Library of Congress and restored to film by Kemp Niver are a valuable resource for the pre-1912 years, but even these 3,000 films are not a full or representative sample of the films of those years; Kemp R. Niver, *Motion Pictures from the Library of Congress Paper Print Collection, 1894–1912* (Berkeley and Los Angeles, 1967). I viewed *The Fatal Hour* at the Library of Congress.
23. Richard Sennett, *The Fall of Public Man* (New York, 1977), 206–7, 73–81.
24. David Grimsted, *Melodrama Unveiled: American Theater and Culture,*

1800–1860 (Chicago, 1968), 53; Hartt, *People at Play,* 7–8. See similarly Robert C. Toll, *Blacking Up: The Minstrel Show in Nineteenth-Century America* (New York, 1974), 12.

25. John Corbin, "How the Other Half Laughs," *Harper's New Monthly Magazine* (Dec. 1898), reprinted in Neil Harris, ed., *The Land of Contrasts, 1880–1901* (New York, 1970):160–1, 162, 164; Irving Howe and Kenneth Libo, eds., *How We Lived: A Documentary History of Immigrant Jews in America, 1880–1930* (New York, 1979), 246. See also A. Richard Sogliuzzo, "Notes for a History of the Italian-American Theatre of New York," *Theatre Survey,* 14 (Nov. 1973):59–75; Irving Howe, *World of Our Fathers* (New York, 1976), 484.
26. Cook, "History of the Drama in Worcester," 19; *WST,* Apr. 4, May 1, 1904. For appearances of Yiddish companies in Worcester, see *LN,* Nov. 17, 1906, Apr. 6, 1912.
27. Walter Prichard Eaton, "Class Consciousness and the 'Movies,'" *Atlantic Monthly* 115 (Jan. 1915):51; *WEP,* Oct. 6, 1906.
28. "The Nickelodeon," *Moving Picture World* 1 (Apr. 27, 1908):140; *WST,* June 20, 1915; *LN,* Dec. 28, 1907; Hoyt, "Condition of Three of the Cheaper Theatres," 5; Addams, *Spirit of Youth,* 86; *WST,* Jan. 8, Nov. 8, 1914, Apr. 4, 1915. Drinking was not limited to the movie audience, apparently. In 1910 the projectionist at the Pastime Theatre was arrested in the theater for drunkenness; *WT,* Feb. 25, 1910. For national concern about sex and movie theaters, see the Vice Commission of Chicago, *The Social Evil in Chicago* (Chicago, 1911), 217–18.
29. Hoyt, "Condition of Three of the Cheaper Threaters," 5; *WST,* Nov. 21, 1915; Ewen, "City Lights," 52; Addams, *Spirit of Youth,* 85–6.
30. *WT,* Feb. 28, 1916; John W. Ripley, "All Join in the Chorus," *American Heritage* 10 (June 1959):50–9; *WEP,* Jan. 9, 1908; interview with Frank Nagle, Worcester, Mar. 1, 1978; interview with Fedeli; *WEP,* May 7, 14, 1910; *LN,* Aug. 6, 1910, Jan. 28, 1911. Exactly how bike races fit on a small theater stage is not clear.
31. Interview with Leo LaJoie, Worcester, Feb. 28, 1978; interview with Fedeli; interview with Robert Werme, Worcester, Mar. 1, 1978.
32. *WST,* Apr. 10, 1910; Hoyt, "Condition of Three of the Cheaper Theaters," 5. See also *Catholic Messenger,* Jan. 17, 1908.
33. *WST,* Sept. 6, 13, Apr. 26, 1914, Feb. 13, 1916; Hartt, *People at Play,* 90–1. See also *WST,* May 16, 1915. There is some evidence that Worcester movie theater managers took this criticism to heart. The poet Stanley Kunitz, who grew up in Worcester's Jewish community in the early twentieth century, writes in a poem entitled "The Magic Curtain" that between shows at the Front Street movie houses: "ushers with atomizers ranged the aisles, emitting lilac spray"; *The Testing Tree* (Boston, 1971), 33.
34. *WT,* Jan. 24, 25, 27, Feb. 1, 5, 7, 14, 1910. See also Thomas C. Carrigan, "Juvenile Delinquency in Worcester" (M.A. thesis, Clark Univ., 1910),

227–31; *Catholic Messenger*, Feb. 11, 18, 25, 1910; on Hill, see *WT*, Aug. 7, 1912.

35. *WT*, Jan. 25, Feb. 28, Mar. 7, 14, 21, 1910. See also the controversy over the showing of the film of the Johnson–Jeffries heavyweight fight in *WT*, July 4, 7, 1910; *LN*, July 9, 1910.
36. *LN*, Mar. 26, 1910; *WEG*, Mar. 30, July 6, 1910.
37. *Catholic Messenger*, May 10, 17, 24, 31, 1907, May 20, 1910. See also Feb. 11, 18, 25, Mar. 4, 1910. (References courtesy of Timothy J. Meagher.)
38. *WT*, Jan. 20, 1910; *WDT*, Dec. 15, 1884.
39. Interview with Ms. Forslund, Mar. 29, 1978; interview with Chester Olson, Mar. 1, 1978; interview with Ted Bergsten, Feb. 23, 1978, all in Worcester. Further insight on Swedes and moviegoing in Worcester came from interviews with Mr. and Mrs. Algot Eckstrom, Mar. 1, 1978, and Ethel Nelson Bigelow, Aug. 5, 1980, both in Worcester.
40. Quote in John Bodnar, "Materialism and Morality: Slavic-American Immigrants and Education, 1890–1940," *Journal of Ethnic Studies* 3 (Winter 1976):9 (emphasis added). For movies and the challenge to middle-class culture, see Sklar, *Movie-Made America*, 88–90; May, *Screening Out the Past*, xi–xv.
41. There is a vast literature on movie censorhip. Two good starting places on this subject are Jowett, *Film*, 108–82, and Arthur McClure, "Censor the Movies! Early Attempts to Regulate the Content of Motion Pictures in America, 1907–1936," in Arthur McClure, ed., *The Movies: An American Idiom* (Rutherford, N.J., 1971), 117–52. Also see McCarthy, "Nickel Vice and Virtue"; Robert Fisher, "Film Censorship and Progressive Reform: the National Board of Censorship of Motion Pictures, 1909–1922," *Journal of Popular Film* 4, no. 2 (1975):143–56; Richard Corliss, "The Legion of Decency," *Film Comment* 4 (Summer 1968):24–61; Paul W. Facey, *The Legion of Decency: A Sociological Analysis of the Emergence and Development of a Social Pressure Group* (1945; rpt. New York, 1974). Some interesting contemporary comment can be found in Tevis, "Censoring the Five-Cent Drama"; William Inglis, "Morals and Moving Pictures," *Harper's Weekly* 54 (July 30, 1910):12–13; Howe, "What To Do With the Motion-Picture Show"; John Collier, "Censorship and the National Board," *Survey* 35 (Oct. 2, 1915):9–14; Orrin G. Cocks, "Applying Standards to Motion Picture Films," *Survey* 32 (June 27, 1914):337–8; Boyd Fisher, "The Regulation of Motion Picture Theaters," *American City* 7 (Sept. 1912):520–2; John Collier, "Should the Government Censor Motion Pictures?" *Playground* 6 (July 1912):129–32.
42. Tevis, "Censoring the Five-Cent Drama," 1138; "The Film Manufacturer and the Public," *Moving Picture World* 1 (May 25, 1907):179.
43. *WT*, Mar. 21, 1910; *WST*, Apr. 17, 1910; interview with Fedeli. Kmet, "Milwaukee's Nickelodeon Era," 5, discusses self-regulation by exhibitors.

44. Hoyt, "Condition of Three of the Cheaper Theaters," 3; Public Education Association of Worcester, Mass., *Seventh Annual Report, May, 1912* (Worcester, 1912), 15 (emphasis added). For similar complaints elsewhere, see Vice Commission, *Social Evil in Chicago,* 247; Phelan, *Motion Pictures,* 23.
45. *WT,* Feb. 5, 1914. For further discussion of the sabbath movie question, see *WT,* Jan. 26, 30, 31, Feb. 1–3, 4, 7–10, 12, 14–17, 22, Mar. 6, 8, June 4, 1914; "Report of Sunday Recreation Commission," *Worcester Magazine* 17 (July 1914):201; *LN,* Feb. 7, 1914.
46. *WT,* Feb. 9, 3, 1914.
47. *WST,* Dec. 21, 1913, Feb. 1, 1914, Apr. 18, 1915. See also Cook, "History of the Drama in Worcester," 54. Allen, "Vaudeville and Film" provides an extensive discussion of the relationships between the two forms.
48. *WEG,* Jan. 18, 1919. Data on seats from *Worcester Directory,* newspaper reports, and interviews. Merritt, "Nickelodeon Theaters," 75, estimates that movie attendance probably doubled between 1908 and 1914.
49. *WT,* Nov. 19, 1917.
50. My argument here follows that of Russell Merritt, "Nickelodeon Theaters," 65, 67.
51. *WT,* Mar. 9, 1913, Sept. 11, 18, 25, Dec. 29, 1916, Feb. 19, 1917. For other examples of the upgrading of conditions in Worcester movie theaters, see *WST,* Jan. 17, Feb. 14, 21, Apr. 18, Sept. 26, Nov. 14, 1915; "New England Column," *Moving Picture World* 23 (Feb. 20, Mar. 6, 1915):1168, 1483; 24 (Apr. 17, 1915):429; 25 (July 24, 1915):693; *WT,* Aug. 21, 1916.
52. See, for example, *WST,* Feb. 7, Sept. 5, 19, Nov. 7, 1915, Jan. 2, 23, 1916; *WT,* Aug. 21, 1916, June 25, Aug. 1, 13, 1917.
53. Samuel Katz, "Theatrical Management," in Joseph P. Kennedy, ed., *The Story of Films* (Chicago, 1927), 266–7; interview with Fedeli; *WST,* July 8, 1915, Nov. 18, 1928; May, *Screening Out the Past,* 148. See also Harold B. Franklin, *Motion Picture Management* (New York, 1927).
54. Sklar, *Movie-Made America,* 42; Tino Balio, "Struggles for Control: 1908–1930," in Balio, *American Film Industry,* 109–10; *WST,* Mar. 21, 1915; *WT,* Sept. 29, 1915.
55. *WT,* May 15, 16, 22, 29, June 7, 8, 14, 15, 19, 1916.
56. May, *Screening Out the Past,* 147–66.
57. Katz, "Theatrical Management," 269; A. J. Balaban (as told to Carrie Balaban), *Continuous Performance* (New York, 1942):69–71; May, *Screening Out the Past,* 166.
58. Interview with Gunnar Forslund; interview with Fedeli; *WT,* Aug. 7, 1916.
59. Interview with Fedeli; *LN,* May 7, 1920. There were about 4,050 seats

in neighborhood theaters and about 10,050 seats in "first-class theaters."

60. *LN*, Mar. 15, 1917; *WST*, Mar. 8, Feb. 20, 1914; Apr. 14, 1915; Sister Joan Bland, *Hibernian Crusade: The Story of the Catholic Total Abstinence Union of America* (Washington, D.C., 1951), 238; *Worcester Directory, 1914*. For a memoir of an Irish-Catholic childhood in Worcester (c. 1920–50), which mentions giving up movies for Lent, see Ellen Horgan Biddle, "The American Catholic Irish Family," in C. Mindel and R. W. Habenstein, eds., *Ethnic Families in America: Patterns and Variations* (New York, 1976), 105. The movies also had an impact on the Swedish Good Templars. "The automobile, the radio, and talking moving pictures," notes a history of the IOGT, "were the things that made . . . the lodge meetings gird themselves for some stiff competition or go out of business"; *Fifty Years: The Eastern Grand Lodge* (n.p., 1946), 39. For the lingering suspicion of the movies by Worcester Catholics, see Timothy J. Meagher, "'The Lord Is Not Dead': Cultural and Social Change Among the Irish in Worcester, Massachusetts" (Ph.D. thesis, Brown Univ., 1982), 286, 632; *Catholic Messenger*, July 12, 1918.
61. *WT*, Feb. 7, 1915; *WST*, Apr. 4, 1915.
62. *WST*, Apr. 4, 1915; *Skandinavia*, Feb. 24, 1915. See also Mar. 3, 10, June 16, 1915.
63. Marguerite Prevy to Eugene V. Debs, 1921 in Debs MSS, Cunningham Library, Indiana State University, Terre Haute. (Reference courtesy of Nick Salvatore.)
64. Seventy-seven percent of the voters opposed state censorship; *WEG*, Nov. 8, 1922. See also *WEG*, Nov. 1–4, 7–9, 1922; *WT*, Oct. 30, Nov. 1, 3, 1922. For a general discussion of the Massachusetts referendum, see Jowett, *Film*, 167–9; U.S. Congress, House, Committee of Education, *Proposed Federal Motion Picture Commission, Hearings*, 69th Cong., 1st sess. (1926), 398–404.
65. *WT*, July 2, 1922; *WST*, Nov. 25, 1928. Interestingly, the film featured in the 1922 advertisement was *Divorce Coupons*: "a tale of society with romance, fashions, and thrills."
66. For a discussion of some of the forces of change in this era, see Harry Braverman, *Labor and Monopoly Capital: The Degradation of Work in the Twentieth Century* (New York, 1974); Stuart Ewen, *Captains of Consciousness: Advertising and the Social Roots of the Consumer Culture* (New York, 1976); Paul Baran and Paul Sweezy, *Monopoly Capital* (New York, 1966). Three doctoral theses treat the issues of consumption and leisure in twentieth-century working-class life: John Darrell Alt, "Leisure, Labor, and Consumption: A Critical Sociology of Reification" (Ph.D. thesis, Washington Univ., 1977); Garth Massey, "'Embourgeoisement' and the Working Class: A Critique" (Ph.D. thesis, Indiana Univ., 1975); Charles Francis Owen, "Consumerism and Neocapitalism: The

Politics of Producing Consumption" (Ph.D. thesis, Univ. of Minnesota, 1976).

67. Phyllis Williams, *South Italian Folkways in Europe and America* (1938; rpt. New York, 1969), 118–19; Ella L. Vinal, "The Status of the Worcester Negro" (M.A. thesis, Clark Univ., 1929), 116. See also Roderick Duncan McKenzie, *The Neighborhood: A Study of Local Life in the City of Columbus, Ohio* (Chicago, 1923), 599–600. In Muncie, Indiana, in the 1920s, of 122 working-class families surveyed by the Lynds, 38 reported that no member "goes at all" to the movies; Robert S. Lynd and Helen Merrell Lynd, *Middletown* (1929; rpt. New York, 1956), 264.
68. *WT*, May 1, 1916; information in Rialto Theatre Record Book, copy in possession of Fred Fedeli, who kindly allowed me to consult it.
69. *WT*, Jan. 15, 1917; *WST*, Jan. 29, Feb. 5, Apr. 9, May 21, 1922.
70. David Robinson, *Hollywood in the Twenties* (New York, 1968), 34–5; Jacobs, *Rise of the American Film*, 395; Sklar, *Movie-Made America*, 110–17. Sklar discusses the problems of incomplete sources on page 88.
71. This film showed at the Rialto on Mar. 15, 1928. Description is from Kenneth W. Munden, ed., *American Film Institute Catalog, Feature Films, 1921–1930*, 2 vols. (New York, 1971), 1:759; hereafter cited as *AFI Catalog*.
72. *AFI Catalog*, 1:31. *Babe Comes Home* showed at the Rialto Mar. 10, 1928. *Rough House Rosie*, which showed at the Rialto Feb. 29, 1928, has a similar plot: A boxer tries to abandon his working-class habits to win a woman but, ultimately, wins her without changing and is also successful as a boxer. Ibid., 1:667–8. For a similar analysis, see Herbert Gans, "Hollywood Films on British Screens: An Analysis of the Functions of American Popular Culture Abroad," *Social Problems* 9 (Spring 1962):325– 6.
73. May, *Screening Out the Past*, 147–66; Sklar, *Movie-Made America*, 153; *WST*, Jan. 25, 1925. Obviously the *Telegram* failed to consider that many of the working-class movie customers who had not yet learned the new time discipline of moviegoing did not have telephones.
74. Marietta Knight, "The Worcester Board of Motion Picture and Theatre Review, Nov., 1916–Dec., 1929," typescript, available at the Worcester Public Library.
75. Alice V. Emerson, "The Failure of Organized Labor in Worcester (1880–1940)" (M.A. thesis, Clark Univ., 1966), 29–35; Charles Francis Johnson, "The Organized Labor Movement as a Social Force in Worcester, 1888–1913" (M.A. thesis, Clark Univ., 1935), 13.
76. *WST*, May 1, 1904.
77. See "Ku Klux Klan in Worcester, 1923–1924," articles from the *WST* and *WEP*, selected and compiled by Kevin Hickey, Jamie Giguere, and Cheryl Richardson for CSP-AC.

78. Lindsay, *The Art of the Moving Picture*, 236; Ewen, "City Lights," 65.
79. Mary P. Ryan, "The Projection of a New Womanhood: The Movie Moderns in the 1920's," in Jean E. Friedman and William G. Shade, eds., *Our American Sisters* (Boston, 1975), 373. Blumer, *Movies and Conduct*, 221, 159. See also May, *Screening Out the Past;* Jacobs, *Rise of the American Film;* Ewen, "City Lights."
80. S. N. Behrman, *The Worcester Account* (London, 1954), 43.
81. Blumer, *Movies and Conduct*, 159, 158.

Conclusion

1. Henry Ford, *My Life and Work* (Garden City, N.Y., 1922), 113. (Reference courtesy of Jean-Christophe Agnew.) On Washburn's house, see the beginning of Chapter 2, this volume. On Institute Park, see the end of Chapter 5, this volume.
2. Raymond Williams, "Base and Superstructure in Marxist Cultural Theory," *New Left Review*, no. 82 (Dec. 1973):11.
3. Lester P. White, "Elements Affecting Organized Labor in Its Relationship with the Worcester Branch National Metal Trades Association Since 1916" (M.A. thesis, Clark Univ., 1924), 16.
4. On possible links between labor militancy in the 1930s and "Americanism," see Gary Gerstle, "The Pursuit of Legitimacy: Labor Militancy and 'The Spirit of Americanism,' 1930–1948" (paper presented at the Annual Meeting of the Organization of American Historians, Detroit, Mich., Apr. 4, 1981), and Gary Gerstle, "Founding Fathers and Powerful Proletarians: Illustrations of an American Labor Movement" (paper presented at the Conference on New Deal Culture, Washington, D.C., Oct. 15, 1981); Roy Rosenzweig, "*United Action Means Victory:* Militant Americanism on Film," *Labor History* 24 (Summer 1983). Peter Friedlander's *Emergence of a UAW Local, 1936–1939: A Study in Class and Culture* (Pittsburgh, 1975) provides some important insights into the role of younger workers from different ethnic backgrounds in the birth of the CIO. The most revealing portrait of the cultural and political awakening of second- and third-generation ethnic industrial workers in the 1930s is found in Thomas Bell's brilliant novel *Out of This Furnace* (1941; rpt. Pittsburgh, 1976).

A note on sources

"The most significant bibliographic feature of this enquiry," Robert Malcolmson writes in the introduction to *Popular Recreations in English Society, 1700–1850* "is the lack of a well-defined body of essential sources." This study of American working-class recreation has similarly drawn on a scattered and heterogeneous body of sources in an effort to uncover and present the social lives of the workingmen and -women who populated late nineteenth and early twentieth century Worcester. The intention of this note is not to provide a comprehensive guide to those sources – most of which are included in the notes – but to suggest some of the major types of sources that are useful in studying popular recreation on the local level.

Newspapers

In the early days of the "new social history," newspapers were often dismissed as sources for understanding the history of the common people. But whereas Worcester newspapers did not regularly mention the names of the so-called common people, they did contain an enormous amount of information about their lives and culture. For this reason, they were the most important single source used in this study.

Drinking, temperance, and the saloon were not only central to late nineteenth and early twentieth century working-class culture, they were also central topics for newspaper coverage in this period. Each December when Worcesterites voted on whether to allow liquor licensing in their city, the newspapers were filled with reports and commentary on drinking and drink places. Similarly, the annual spring ritual of issuing new liquor licenses usually provoked another flood of stories on the drink trade. The local press was more apt to provide detailed coverage of a July Fourth lawn party of a local industrialist than a get-together of French-Canadian carpenters and their families. Nevertheless, the newspapers did usually report on the more organized and formal working-class gatherings – the picnics of the Ancient Order of Hibernians and the Swedish churches, for example. If only because Worcester newspapers in this period were often embroiled in fierce circulation battles, they provided fairly comprehensive coverage of social events occurring in all the city's ethnic communities.

Nevertheless, Worcester newspapers were generally biased toward the native middle and upper classes. Most of the daily English-language papers, for example, supported the Republican party during this period. This bias was not an insurmountable problem for two reasons. First, it is possible, albeit difficult, to follow E. P. Thompson's injunction that "everything transmitted to us through the polite culture has to be scrutinized upside down" (Eighteenth-Century English Society: Class Struggle Without Class?" *Social History* 3 (1978):157). Second, Worcester in this period had such an enormous range of newspapers that it is possible to read one against another. In the course of this study, I examined around twenty different local newspapers. Thus, the Irish and pro-labor *Worcester Daily Times* offered a sharp contrast to the more elite and Republican *Worcester Evening Gazette* and *Worcester Spy*. Other alternative and more popular perspectives came from the Democratic *Worcester Evening Star* and *Worcester Evening Post* as well as from the city's foreign-language papers, which I was able to examine: *Worcester Veckoblad*, *Scandinavia* (later spelled *Skandinavia*), *L'Etendard National*, *Le Foyer Canadien*, *Le Travailleur*, *Le Courrier de Worcester*, and *L'Opinion Publique*. The *Messenger* (called the *Catholic Messenger* after 1906) spoke for local Irish Catholics, but which group within the Irish-Catholic community it spoke for changed over time. After 1906, the *Labor News* was the official voice of organized labor in Worcester. Various special-interest publications offered insight into specific groups within the city: the *American* (nativists), *Light* (a "society" magazine), the *Worcester Argus* (a short-lived voice of the Knights of Labor), the *British-American* (British immigrants), the *No-License Advocate* (temperance), *Worcester Magazine* (published by the Board of Trade but quite broad in its coverage). The *Worcester Telegram* and the *Worcester Sunday Telegram* are the papers most frequently cited here. Although the *Telegram* was editorially hostile to both labor and immigrants, its search for the largest possible readership and a streak of anti-elitism in its editor led it to cover closely developments within the city's ethnic working-class communities.

Manuscript sources

The manuscript sources for this study were limited, but particular collections did provide crucial insights into specific subjects. Fascinating biographical information on Worcester's saloonkeepers can be found in the R. G. Dun and Company credit reports (available at Baker Library, Harvard University Graduate School of Business Administration) and in the sketches of "Rumsellers of Worcester," compiled by Irish antiquarian Richard O'Flynn, whose papers (available at the College of the Holy Cross in Worcester) are essential sources for understanding Worcester's Irish community. To understand the shadier side of the local drink trade I consulted the fascinating papers of City Marshal James Drennan (available at the Worcester Historical Museum – WHM) and the records of the Worcester Central District Court (located at the Central District Courthouse and made available to me through the Massachusetts Criminal History Systems Board). The court records also list the names of the thousands of Worcesterites arrested for drunkenness.

Petitions to the Board of Aldermen (located in the basement of Worcester City Hall) over liquor-licensing questions illuminate the social composition of the pro- and anti-liquor forces. Further information on the temperance movement in Worcester can be gleaned from: the temperance broadsides available at the WHM and the American Antiquarian Society (AAS); the Temperance Pamphlet collections at the same two repositories; the records of the Worcester Reform Club (available at the AAS); the O'Flynn papers; and the records of the St. John's Temperance and Literary Guild (located at St. John's Church but made available to me through the courtesy of Timothy J. Meagher).

Diaries would be an excellent source for reconstructing how people spent July Fourth, but only a few exist that reflect the working-class or ethnic communities in Worcester – for example, Stephen Littleton (AAS) and John F. Nourse (WHM). The more abundant diaries of the middle class and the elite – for example, Stephen Salisbury II and Stephen Salisbury III, Charles S. Hale, Nathaniel Paine, Catherine White Forbes (all at the AAS) – are useful, however, in specifying changing elite and middle-class patterns of July Fourth celebrations. The court records enable us to see the important role drinking played on the nation's birthday. And the O'Flynn papers are extremely valuable on the Irish organizations, which sponsored many Independence Day parades and picnics. Finally, the Scrapbooks of the Twentieth Century Club (at the Worcester Public Library) give a sense of the reform milieu that gave birth to the Safe and Sane July Fourth movement.

I was fortunate to locate (with the help of the Parks and Recreation Commission) the nineteenth and early twentieth century records of the Parks Commission and the Playground Commission in a tool shed at Green Hill Park. These important records contain the minutes of Parks Commission meetings as well as correspondence and reports on the early playground movement. The Parks Commission Scrapbooks (located at their City Hall offices) contain a wealth of clippings from the turn of the century. Finally, the Board of Aldermen petitions include park petitions, which enabled me to reconstruct the crucial role that Worcester's ethnic working class played in the parks movement.

Government documents

Given the concern of local government for public morality in this period, government documents are a major source for any study of popular recreation. The published annual *City Documents* are of particular use, since they include the Parks Commission Reports (a particularly revealing source in the late nineteenth century when they were written by Edward Winslow Lincoln), the City Marshal Reports (which included not only arrest statistics but commentary on the enforcement of the liquor law), and the annual addresses of the mayors. The annual reports of the Massachusetts Bureau of Statistics of Labor are among the most important available sources for understanding late nineteenth and early twentieth century working-class life. In this study they proved particularly useful for information on hours and wages, housing, working-class social life, strikes and unionization, working-class budgets, and drunkenness and other liquor law violations. The Massachusetts State Census reports are an important supplement to the published U.S. Census volumes; together, these enable one to construct a general portrait of population, ethnicity, jobs, and manufacturing in Worcester in this period. Other important government documents I consulted were: the *Hearings* of the U.S. Senate Committee on Relations Between Labor and Capital; the Reports of the 1867 Massachusetts investigation of the workings of the liquor laws; and published volumes of cases brought before the Massachusetts Supreme Judicial Court (which contain descriptive information on local drink sellers).

City directories and manuscript censuses

Taken by themselves, city directories and manuscript censuses tell us relatively little about working-class recreation. However, when used in conjunction with other sources, they are a powerful tool for illuminating the class and ethnic context of the recreational world of the Worcester worker. In the course of this study, I traced more than 5,000 individuals to the annual volumes of the *Worcester Directory*, the biannual volumes of the *Worcester House Directory* (which contain information on real estate holdings), and the 1870, 1880, and 1900 U.S. Manuscript Censuses for Worcester. The lists of people traced (which came from newspapers, pamphlets, petitions, court records, and other sources) were quite diverse: They included saloonkeepers, temperance society members, liquor license petitioners, people arrested for drunkenness and other liquor law violations, members of ethnic societies, members of such reform bodies as the Safe and Sane Committee and the Playground Committee, July Fourth celebrants, people injured in July Fourth accidents, guests of the Worcester Continentals, members of the Centennial Committee, parks petitioners, and movie theater managers and owners. Although all this tracing can become burdensome, it is a prerequisite to any precise judgments about the social context of working-class recreation and the conflicts over that recreation. To understand the spatial context of working-class recreation with a similar preciseness, I mapped the locations of saloons, the homes of saloonkeepers, and movie theaters over time.

Studies of Worcester

There are no published scholarly histories on any aspects of Worcester's past. However, some recent unpublished doctoral dissertations – for example, Timothy J. Meagher on the Irish, Vincent E. Powers on the early Irish migration, Joshua Chasan on Worcester elites, Charles Buell on social mobility, Bryan Thompson on Worcester Italians, and Edwin Weiss on elite residences – have uncovered and presented important dimensions of the city's past. Robert Roberge's master's thesis on Worcester's three-deckers is another valuable recent study. (See Notes for Chapter 1 for complete citations of these works.) In addition to these very helpful studies, anyone interested in the history of Worcester should consult the master's and doctoral theses written by earlier generations of graduate students at Clark University. These works, which date back to the beginning of the twentieth century and which are particularly strong in geography and sociology, often include firsthand observations about life in Worcester.

The compendious histories of Worcester by Charles A. Nutt, *History of Worcester and Its People,* 4 vols. (New York, 1919), and Franklin P. Rice, ed., *The Worcester of Eighteen Hundred and Ninety-Eight* (Worcester, 1899), are valuable not only for the information they provide on industries, organizations, and politics but even more for the hundreds of biographical sketches of prominent Worcesterites. Another invaluable local source is Charles Washburn's detailed study of *Industrial Worcester* (Worcester, 1917). Two excellent memoirs – Robert Washburn's *Smith's Barn: "A Child's History" of the West Side Worcester, 1880–1923* (Worcester, 1923) and S. N. Behrman's *The Worcester Account* (London, 1954) – offer colorful portraits of growing up in the very different worlds of the WASP West Side and the Jewish East Side.

Other sources

The local recreational practices and institutions described here need to be placed in their national context. For the saloon, the writings of reformers provide important firsthand data on the culture of the barroom, albeit from a particular viewpoint. I followed the Playground and the Safe and Sane July Fourth movements in the national periodicals of progressive reform. The early movie house received considerable coverage in the trade press and in national periodicals, which I also consulted. These sources are listed in the notes to the appropriate chapters.

Finally, oral history interviews can provide important insights into unrecorded aspects of popular recreation, particularly for the early twentieth century. Considerations of time prevented me from making as extensive use of oral history as I would have liked. Nevertheless, I consulted the transcripts of about a half dozen people interviewed during the course of the Worcester Bicentennial Oral History Project, 1976 (available at the Worcester Public Library). In addition, about thirty people generously shared their recollections of life in early twentieth century Worcester with me.

Index

movies — lower price
democratic seating
novelty + excitement
location
family went together
censorship

Diversified occupation
" ethnic groups
" religious groups

No labor unions organization
Low labor unrest
Blacklists
Family + kinship network – basic unit of social life for all ethnic groups. p. 31

p. 40 – Uses of increased leisure time

More $ more leisure = saloons.
(commercial enterprise) ↑

Celebrations – release from discipline
showed hostility towards "betters"
affirmed solidarity of ethnic commun
reassure ethnic ties
raised money for relief organization

Playgrounds – structured
Guide + assimilate immigrants

4th Move to get rid of ethnic celebration

Increase in wages, more leisure time

Movie theater – challenged localism

Workers didn't challenge elite